Manchester Medieval Sources Series

series advisers Rosemary Horrox and Janet L. Nelson

This series aims to meet a growing need among students and teachers of medieval history for translations of key sources that are directly usable in students' own work. It provides texts central to medieval studies courses and focuses upon the diverse cultural and social as well as political conditions that affected the functioning of all levels of medieval society. The basic premise of the series is that translations must be accompanied by sufficient introductory and explanatory material, and each volume, therefore, includes a comprehensive guide to the sources' interpretation, including discussion of critical linguistic problems and an assessment of the most recent research on the topics being covered.

also available in the series

Mark Bailey *The English manor c.1200–c. 1500*

Malcom Barber and Keith Bate *The Templars*

Simon Barton and Richard Fletcher *The world of El Cid: Chronicles of the Spanish Reconquest*

Andrew Brown and Graeme Small *Court and civic society in the Burgundian Low Countries c.1420–1530*

Samuel K. Cohn, Jr. *Popular protest in late-medieval Europe: Italy, France and Flanders*

Trevor Dean *The towns of Italy in the later Middle Ages*

P. J. P. Goldberg *Women in England, c.1275–1525*

Rosemary Horrox *The Black Death*

I. S. Robinson *Eleventh-century Germany: The Swabian Chronicles*

I. S. Robinson *The papal reform of the eleventh century: Lives of Pope Leo IX and Pope Gregory VII*

Michael Staunton *The lives of Thomas Becket*

Craig Taylor *Joan of Arc: La Pucelle*

Elisabeth van Houts *The Normans in Europe*

David Warner *Ottonian Germany*

CRIME, LAW AND SOCIETY IN THE LATER MIDDLE AGES

Manchester University Press

D1555009

MedievalSources*online*

Complementing the printed editions of the Medieval Sources series, Manchester University Press has developed a web-based learning resource which is now available on a yearly subscription basis.

MedievalSources*online* brings quality history source material to the desktops of students and teachers and allows them open and unrestricted access throughout the entire college or university campus. Designed to be fully integrated with academic courses, this is a one-stop answer for many medieval history students, academics and researchers keeping thousands of pages of source material 'in print' over the Internet for research and teaching.

titles available now at MedievalSources*online include*

Trevor Dean *The towns of Italy in the later Middle Ages*

John Edwards *The Jews in Western Europe, 1400–1600*

Paul Fouracre and Richard A. Gerberding *Late Merovingian France: History and hagiography 640–720*

Chris Given-Wilson *Chronicles of the Revolution 1397–1400: The reign of Richard II*

P. J. P. Goldberg *Women in England, c. 1275–1525*

Janet Hamilton and Bernard Hamilton *Christian dualist heresies in the Byzantine world, c. 650–c. 1450*

Rosemary Horrox *The Black Death*

Graham A. Loud and Thomas Wiedemann *The history of the tyrants of Sicily by 'Hugo Falcandus', 1153–69*

Janet L. Nelson *The Annals of St-Bertin: Ninth-century histories, volume I*

Timothy Reuter *The Annals of Fulda: Ninth-century histories, volume II*

R. N. Swanson *Catholic England: Faith, religion and observance before the Reformation*

Elisabeth van Houts *The Normans in Europe*

Jennifer Ward *Women of the English nobility and gentry 1066–1500*

Visit the site at *www.medievalsources.co.uk* for further information and subscription prices.

CRIME, LAW AND SOCIETY IN THE LATER MIDDLE AGES

selected sources translated and annotated
by Anthony Musson with Edward Powell

Manchester University Press
Manchester and New York

distributed exclusively in the USA by Palgrave Macmillan

Copyright © Anthony Musson and Edward Powell 2009

The right of Anthony Musson and Edward Powell to be identified as the authors of this
work has been asserted by them in accordance with the Copyright, Designs and Patents
Act 1988.

Published by Manchester University Press
Oxford Road, Manchester M13 9NR, UK
and Room 400, 175 Fifth Avenue, New York, NY 10010, USA
www.manchesteruniversitypress.co.uk

Distributed exclusively in the USA by
Palgrave Macmillan, 175 Fifth Avenue, New York, NY 10010, USA

Distributed exclusively in Canada by
UBC Press, University of British Columbia, 2029 West Mall,
Vancouver, BC, Canada V6T 1Z2

British Library Cataloguing-in-Publication Data
A catalogue record for this book is available from the British Library

Library of Congress Cataloging-in-Publication Data applied for

ISBN 978 0 7190 3801 3 *hardback*
        978 0 7190 3802 0 *paperback*

First published 2009

18 17 16 15 14 13 12 11 10 09   10 9 8 7 6 5 4 3 2 1

Typeset in Monotype Bell
by Koinonia, Manchester
Printed in Great Britain
by the MPG Books Group

In memoriam David Topliss

CONTENTS

PREFACE

This book was the brainchild of Ted Powell, conceived in the early 1990s when he was a don in Cambridge and coincidentally supervising my PhD thesis. Much water has flowed under the bridge since those days and both of us subsequently left academia to gain professional qualification in the law. Ted now has a flourishing practice as a solicitor and the pressure of such commitments meant that although he had planned the scope of the volume and collected together a number of the sources he was unable to devote the necessary time to seeing the project through in its entirety. Having returned to university life to lecture in law I was approached to take on the mantle and make his initial vision a reality. Although in my hands the volume has been customised and personalised to a certain extent I am indebted to Ted not only for his initial work, but also for his encouragement and advice during the book's gestation. I would like to thank Rosemary Horrox for her support and for entrusting me with the task of assuming responsibility for the volume and to Alison Welsby for her patience in awaiting its completion. I am grateful to certain colleagues for suggestions and references, comments and criticisms, particularly Mark Ormrod, Eddie Jones, Henry Summerson, David Crook, Jonathan Rose, Andrew Ayton and the anonymous referees. I would equally like to thank my legal history students upon whom I have foisted some of the examples and aired some of the ideas. Finally, I am extremely grateful to Natasha Goldsworth for her help in preparing the typescript.

AJM
Exeter

ABBREVIATIONS

AHR   *American Historical Review*

AJLH   *American Journal of Legal History*

Bellamy, *Criminal Trial*   J. G. Bellamy, *The Criminal Trial in Later Medieval England* (Stroud, Sutton Publishing, 1998)

Bellamy, *Treason*   J. G. Bellamy, *The Law of Treason in the Later Middle Ages* (Cambridge, Cambridge University Press, 1970).

BIHR   Bulletin of the Institute of Historical Research

BJRL   Bulletin of the John Rylands Library

Boundaries, ed. Musson   *Boundaries of the Law: Geography, Gender and Jurisdiction in Medieval and Early Modern Europe*, ed. A. Musson (Aldershot, Ashgate Publishing, 2005)

Cam, *Hundred Rolls*   H. M. Cam, *The Hundred and the Hundred Rolls* (London, Merlin Press, 1963)

Castor, *Duchy*   H. Castor, *The King, the Crown, and the Duchy of Lancaster: Public Authority and Private Power, 1399-1461* (Oxford, Oxford University Press, 2000)

Clanchy, 'Highway robbery'   M. T. Clanchy, 'Highway robbery and trial by battle in the Hampshire eyre of 1249', in *Medieval Legal Records*

Clanchy, *Memory*   M. T. Clanchy, *From Memory to Written Record: England 1066-1307* 2nd edn (Oxford, Blackwells, 1993)

CPR   *Calendar of Patent Rolls*

EETS   Early English Text Society

EHR   *English Historical Review*

Expectations, ed. Musson   *Expectations of the Law in the Middle Ages*, ed. A. Musson (Woodbridge, Boydell Press, 2001)

Fifteenth-Century Attitudes, ed. Horrox   *Fifteenth-Century Attitudes: Perceptions of Society in Late Medieval England*, ed. R. Horrox (Cambridge, Cambridge University Press, 1994)

HMC   Historical Manuscripts Commission

HR   *Historical Research*

Hunnisett, *Coroner*   R. F. Hunnisett, *The Medieval Coroner* (Cambridge, Cambridge University Press, 1961)

JBS   *Journal of British Studies*

JLH   *Journal of Legal History*

JMH   *Journal of Medieval History*

JSA   *Journal of the Society of Archivists*

LHR   *Law and History Review*

LQR   *Law Quarterly Review*

Maddern, *Violence*   P. C. Maddern, *Violence and Social Order: East Anglia, 1422–1442* (Oxford, Clarendon Press, 1992)

Maddicott, *Law and Lordship*   J. R. Maddicott, *Law and Lordship: Royal Justices as Retainers in Thirteenth and Fourteenth Century England, P&P* supplement, 4 (Oxford, 1978)

Medieval Ecclesiastical Studies   Medieval Ecclesiastical Studies in Honour of Dorothy M. Owen, ed. M. J. Franklin and C. Harper-Bill, Studies in the History of Medieval Religion, 7 (Woodbridge, Boydell Press, 1995)

Medieval Legal Records   Medieval Legal Records Edited in Memory of C. A. F. Meekings, ed. J. B. Post and R. F. Hunnisett (London, HMSO, 1978)

Musson, *Medieval Law*   A. Musson, *Medieval Law in Context: the Growth of Legal Consciousness from Magna Carta to the Peasants' Revolt* (Manchester, Manchester University Press, 2001)

Musson, *Public Order*   A. Musson, *Public Order and Law Enforcement: the Local Administration of Criminal Justice, 1294–1350* (Woodbridge, Boydell Press, 1996)

Musson and Ormrod, *Evolution*   A. Musson and W. M. Ormrod, *The Evolution of English Justice: Law, Politics and Society in the Fourteenth Century* (Basingstoke, Macmillan Press, 1998)

NMS   *Nottingham Medieval Studies*

ODNB   *Oxford Dictionary of National Biography*

OJLS   *Oxford Journal of Legal Studies*

Ormrod, *Political Life*   W. M. Ormrod, *Political Life in Medieval England, 1300–1450* (Basingstoke, Macmillan, 1995)

P&P   *Past and Present*

PBA   *Proceedings of the British Academy*

PJP   *Proceedings before the Justices of the Peace in the Fourteenth and Fifteenth Centuries*, ed. B. H. Putnam (London, Ames Foundation, 1938)

PL   *Paston Letters and Papers of the Fifteenth Century*, ed. N. Davis, 2 vols (Oxford, Clarendon Press, 1971-6)

Powell, *Kingship*   E. Powell, *Kingship, Law and Society: Criminal Justice in the Reign of Henry V* (Oxford, Clarendon Press, 1987)

Powell, 'Law and justice'   E. Powell, 'Law and justice', in *Fifteenth-Century Attitudes*, ed. Horrox

PPC   *Proceedings and Ordinances of the Privy Council of England*, ed. N. H. Nicolas, 7 vols (London, 1834–37)

RP   *Rotuli Parliamentorum,* 7 vols (London, 1767–1823)

RPHI   *Rotuli Parliamentorum Anglie Hactenus Inediti,* ed. H. G. Richardson and
   G. Sayles, Camden Society 3rd series, 51 (1935)

RS   Rolls Series

SCCKB   *Select Cases in the Court of King's Bench,* ed. G. O. Sayles, Selden Society,
   55, 57, 58, 74, 76, 82, 88 (London, 1936–71)

SR   *Statutes of the Realm,* 11 vols (London, Record Commission, 1810-28)

SS   Selden Society

Stones, 'Folvilles'   E. L. G. Stones, 'The Folvilles of Ashby Folville, Leicestershire and their Associates in Crime', *TRHS* 5th series, 7 (1957).

Summerson, 'Capital punishment'   H. Summerson, 'Attitudes to capital
   punishment in England, 1200-1350', in *Thirteenth Century England VIII,* ed.
   M. Prestwich, R. Britnell and R. Frame (Woodbridge, Boydell Press, 2001)

TCWAAS   *Transactions of the Cumberland and Westmorland Archaeological and
   Antiquarian Society*

TNA   The National Archives, Kew

   C   Chancery

   CP   Court of Common Pleas

   E   Exchequer

   JUST   Justices Itinerant

   KB   Court of King's Bench

   SC   Special Collections

TDA   *Transactions of the Devonshire Association*

TRHS   *Transactions of the Royal Historical Society*

GLOSSARY

Note: words marked with an asterisk in the text denote an entry in this glossary.

Abjure the realm   Leave the king's jurisdiction. Offenders who had obtained sanctuary and duly confessed their guilt to the coroner were assigned a port and were not allowed to leave the road or deviate from the direction on pain of rearrest until they had crossed the sea and left the jurisdiction.

Advowson   The right to nominate the incumbent of a church or benefice.

Alienation   Transference of ownership (of anything, though usually land) to another.

Amercement   A fine (literally 'at the mercy' of the king).

Arches, court of   The appeal court of the province of Canterbury, which met in London at the church of St Mary le Bow.

Assumpsit   An action to recover damages for the breach of an undertaking or non-performance of a contract.

Attach   Seize person or property by legal authority to compel attendance at court (see Distraint).

Attaint   A legal action by a defeated litigant against the jury trying the previous case.

Aumbry   A cupboard or closed recess in the wall (especially in a church).

Avowry   Acceptance by the litigant of the form pleaded by counsel in court.

Barrator   A quarrelsome person or hired bully. One who makes unfounded charges, maintains lawsuits, foments disputes between neighbours for gain, or buys and sells ecclesiastical preferment.

Beadles   Officials responsible for summoning tenants to the manor court.

Bedesman/woman   Humble petitioner. Literally someone who will pray for the person granting the petition.

Borsholder   The chief of a tithing or frank-pledge (in Kent). Also known as 'headborough'.

Capias   A writ ordering arrest and appearance in court.

Capital pledges   Leader of a tithing group responsible for securing the good behaviour of its members.

Certiorari   A writ calling the records of a case into king's bench upon complaint of a party that he or she has not received justice in a lesser court.

Coram Rege   The term given to proceedings in the court of king's bench.

Corpus cum causa   A writ from chancery to remove to the court of king's bench a person's 'body and record' (*habeas corpus cum causa*). The person was currently imprisoned. This writ was also regularly used to remove cases into chancery.

Corviser   A shoemaker.

Counters   Prisons and offices of the sheriffs of London and Middlesex which contained both temporary and long-term prisoners of various classes (except traitors and felons).

Country, placing on the   Choosing to be tried before jury.

Day (go without)   Able to leave court without the need for further appearance at a later date.

Day (have/keep a)   Day appointed for court appearance or for payment of a debt.

Decies tantum   A remedy for embracery, bribery or corruption of the jury by other means giving recovery of ten times the amount in damages.

Demesne, ancient   Land that formed part of the royal estate at the time of Edward the Confessor or William the Conqueror (and could be proved by Domesday Book).

Diem clausit extremum   A writ directed to the escheator to ascertain the extent and value of all the lands held by a tenant in chief on his or her death and who was his or her closest heir.

Distraint   Property, goods or chattels taken by the sheriff to ensure attendance at court or performance of an obligation.

Easterling   Native of eastern Germany or the Baltic coast, especially of the Hanse towns.

Enfeoffment   Investing a person with or putting them in possession of lands and tenements.

Error (writ of)   A writ removing a case from a lower court to the court of king's bench.

Escheat   Reversion by default of heirs (or upon forfeiture) of lands or goods to the king or lord.

Estovers   Essentials (such as wood) which a tenant is allowed to take from an estate in order to make necessary repairs to his house, hedges or implements.

Exaction   The calling of the defendant (and his non-appearance) at successive county courts.

Exigent   Legal process leading to outlawry.

Falchion   A broad, slightly curved sword with the cutting edge on the convex side.

Feoffment to use   Grant of freehold ownership of property to feoffees who are obliged by conscience to hold it on trust for the feoffor for the benefit or advantage (use) of the designated beneficiary.

Fine   Final concord (as distinct from amercement). A written agreement concerning landholding, a copy of which was retained by the royal court.

Forestalling   Selling goods before they have reached the appropriate market.

For good and ill   Jury trial at gaol delivery enabled by presentation of a writ *de bono et malo.*

Free alms   An ecclesiastical tenure by services of a spiritual nature or performance of a religious duty.

Free tenement   Freehold proprietorship of real property, estate or office.

Free warren   A royal franchise granted to a manorial lord allowing the holder to hunt small game (such as rabbit and pheasant) within a designated manor.

Gisarme   A battle-axe or halberd with a long blade in line with the shaft that was sharpened on both sides and ended in a point.

Haketon   A leather jacket plated with (or worn under) mail.

Hamsoken   Forcible breaking of the peace within a homestead.

Hauberk   A full-length coat of mail.

Languedebœuf   A pike or halberd with a head shaped like an ox tongue.

Launcegay   A type of lance.

Litster   A dyer of cloth.

Mainour (taken with)   (In possession of) stolen goods.

Mainpernor   One who acts as a pledge or surety for appearance in court or future good behaviour.

Mainprise (let to)   Vouched for by sureties and given bail.

Mazer   A drinking cup.

Messuage   A dwelling house with outbuildings and adjacent land.

Misprision   Concealment of felony.

Mort d'ancestor   One of the possessory assizes. It protected the inheritance of land from parents, siblings, uncles and aunts.

Mortmain   Lands or tenements held by the church that could not be alienated or transferred from its ownership (literally 'dead hand').

Neve   Derived from 'naïf', someone unfree from birth.

Nisi Prius   An additional clause inserted in the writ summoning a jury to appear at Westminster allowing the jury trial stage of a case to be held in the locality before specific royal justices whilst on assize rather than at

Westminster (if they came to the county before the next term set for the appearance of the jury at Westminster).

Novel disseisin One of the possessory assizes. It gave remedy to the free tenant ejected improperly from his property.

Ordinary The bishop of the diocese. He normally appointed a representative to receive convicted clerks for ecclesiastical punishment.

Pele A fortified tower.

Pricking-pallet A riding head-piece or helmet.

Prises Goods taken by royal officials for supplying troops or provisioning garrisons.

Puisne A judge of one of the central courts, other than the chief justice.

Purpresture An illegal enclosure or encroachment on land or property of another.

Quo Warranto Inquiry into the basis for a person's claim to hold franchises (literally 'by what warrant').

Recognizance A bond entered into before a court by which a person undertakes to perform an act on pain of financial penalty.

Regrating Buying up market commodities in order to sell them again at a profit in the same or a neighbouring market.

Replevin The restoration to, or recovery by, a person of goods or chattels distrained or taken from him on the provision of sureties. Also an action arising out of a case in which goods have been distrained or taken and replevied.

Rerebrace Plated armour for lower arm.

Sallet An armoured headpiece without visor or crest.

Scutage A tax levied on knight's fees (which could be paid in lieu of military service).

Seisin Possession of land as a freehold.

Seisin (livery of) A symbolical act where an object is handed over as a token of possession.

Strip and waste Destruction of a tenement and spoliation of land.

Suit of prison Surrendering to prison in anticipation of outlawry or before the processes had run their course.

Supersedeas A writ directing a court to stay proceedings on good cause shown.

Surety An assurance or payment to guarantee behaviour or attendance; a person who takes responsibility for another's undertaking (see Mainpernor).

Tronager A customs official who weighed merchandise at the 'tron' or 'beam'.

Turbary   The right to cut turf or peat for fuel on a common or on another person's land.

Vambrace   Plated armour for upper arm.

Venire Facias   A writ ordering that a person be summoned to appear in court, commonly used to secure the appearance of jurors.

INTRODUCTION

Legal history is very much a 'Cinderella' subject within the realm of historical interpretation and university course options. Traditionally it has been encountered in a dry and sterile atmosphere with little reference beyond its own immediate bounds. Its concentration predominantly on the historical developments in substantive law have meant that it is perceived as intractable and obscure, especially by students. For many years it perched on the edge of the degree programmes delivered by law schools and, where available, sat gawkily amongst the specialist modules offered by history departments. Recent decades have altered this to some extent with a move towards an interdisciplinary appreciation of historical themes and with the encouragement of research in many areas hitherto unexplored by 'traditional' legal historians.[1]

The subject is now increasingly being recognised as vitally important to the wider understanding of politics and society. This is not the extent of its reach, however, for as this volume demonstrates, legal history has a role in other 'histories', among them political thought, 'popular' culture, and gender relations. Moreover, its thought-processes are themselves being considerably influenced by research methods and perspectives derived from the social sciences, including sociology, anthropology and psychology. A burgeoning interest in literary works, not as an unmediated source for historical detail, but as a way of gauging (through engagement with literary theory and criticism) attitudes and perceptions, has also developed.[2] Attention, too, is turning now towards the visual arts and the study of ritual and symbolism as a means of recovering non-literate views and expressions.[3] Indeed, the interdisciplinary

---

1 K. J. M. Smith and J. P. S. McLaren, 'History's living legacy: an outline of "modern" historiography of the common law', *Legal Studies*, 21 (2001), 251-324; J. Rose, 'English legal history and interdisciplinary legal studies', in *Boundaries*, ed. Musson, pp. 169-86.

2 See for example: J. Coleman, *English Literature in History, 1350-1400: Medieval Readers and Writers* (London, Hutchinson, 1981); P. Strohm, *Hochon's Arrow: the Social Imagination of Fourteenth-Century Texts* (Princeton, NJ, Princeton University Press, 1992); *The Letter of the Law: Legal Practice and Literary Production in Medieval England*, ed. E. Steiner and C. Barrington (Ithaca, NY, Cornell University Press, 2002).

3 M. James, 'Ritual drama and the social body in the late medieval English town', *P&P*, 98 (1983), 3-29; M. Camille, *Mirror in Parchment: the Luttrell Psalter and the Making*

mode of thinking has led historians to talk not so much in terms of discreet categories or disciplines as the more embracing notions of 'cultures' and 'communities'.[4] In this volume, the overlap between political and legal cultures is especially significant.

In spite of the growing attraction of law in history, one of the major problems confronting students of the medieval period and the interested lay person is the nature of the sources. Much of the essential material is in legal manuscripts written in Latin or Anglo-Norman French. Some relevant material is available in print either transcribed from the original document or offered in translation, but a lot remains in the original format and language.[5] The vast majority of source material is not in print at all: this is particularly true of original proceedings before the royal courts, which survive in great bulk in the National Archives held at Kew. The proceedings of manorial and borough courts and of ecclesiastical tribunals can usually be located in county record offices or private collections and are idiosyncratic in their language, layout and written script. A number of such records has been published,[6] but

---

of Medieval England (London, Reaktion, 1998); P. Binski, 'Hierarchies and orders in English images of power', in *Orders and Hierarchies in Late Medieval and Renaissance Europe*, ed. J. Denton (Manchester, Manchester University Press, 1999), pp. 74–93; *Heraldry, Pageantry and Social Display*, ed. P. Coss and M. Keen (Woodbridge, Boydell Press, 2002).

4 This can be seen in the titles of various books and papers, for example: *Communities and Courts in Britain, 1150-1900*, ed. C. W. Brooks and M. Lobban (London, Hambledon Press, 1997); M. Hicks, *English Political Culture in the Fifteenth Century* (London and New York, Routledge, 2002); A. Musson, 'Legal culture: medieval lawyers' aspirations and pretensions', in *Fourteenth Century England III*, ed. W. M. Ormrod (Woodbridge, Boydell Press, 2004), pp. 17–30. The idea of 'community' as a meaningful description or entity, however, has been debated in the work of historians such as R. Virgoe in his collected essays: *East Anglian Society and the Political Community of Late Medieval England*, ed. C. M. Barron, C. Rawcliffe and J. T. Rosenthal (Norwich, University of East Anglia, 1997); C. Carpenter, 'Gentry and community', *JBS*, 33 (1994), 340-80; S. Walker, 'Communities of the county in later medieval England', in his collected essays: *Political Culture in Late Medieval England*, ed. M. J. Braddick (Manchester, Manchester University Press, 2006), pp. 68-80; G. Dodd, 'Parliament, petitioning and community in the fourteenth century', unpublished paper given at the International Congress of Medieval Studies, University of Western Michigan, Kalamazoo, 2001.

5 The volumes of records published by the Selden Society provide a transcription of the original material with a translation.

6 For example: *Manorial Records of Cuxham, Oxfordshire, 1200-1359*, ed. P. D. A. Harvey, Oxfordshire Record Society, 1 (Oxford, 1976); *Calendar of Plea and Memoranda Rolls of the City of London*, ed. A. H. Thomas and P. E. Jones, 6 vols (Cambridge, 1926-54); *The Records of the City of Norwich*, ed. W. Hudson and J. C. Tingey, 2 vols (Norwich, 1906-10); F. S. Pearson (trans. and ed.), 'Records of a ruridecanal court of 1300', in *Collecteana*, ed. S. G. Hamilton, Worcestershire Historical Society, 28 (1912).

the proportion is again very small in comparison with the extant documents. An up-to-date and accessible collection of translated sources
that can provide an appreciation of the wealth of legal material and
point the way towards further avenues is thus long overdue.[7]

This book provides an introduction to the English legal system and
its development during the period c 1215-1485. The opening section
considers the theoretical and ideological aspects of medieval law and
justice, examining (in Chapters 1 and 2 respectively) the concepts and
discourses to be found in official and non-official circles. The next section
concentrates on manifestations of crime and disorder (Chapter 3) and
the royal response to this in the form of the development of judicial
institutions (Chapter 4). The third section looks at the dispensation of
justice both inside and outside the courtroom. Chapter 5 is pivotal to the
book and examines in detail the machinery and functioning of criminal
justice both in the royal courts and in those autonomous areas exercising
delegated powers. The use of extra-judicial methods, such as arbitration
and 'self-help', are then considered (Chapter 6) in order to illustrate the
interaction of formal and informal methods of dispute settlement. The
examples reveal a spectrum of methods for achieving remedy. Chapter 7
focuses on the personnel of justice, the justices of the central courts and
the local officials who carried out the day-to-day administrative tasks.
The crown's ethical stances and ideals (harking back to the first chapter)
are highlighted, as too is the flipside, the ways in which the system
was undermined. In the final chapter the limitations and failures of the
system are assessed, particularly through the imaginative literature of
the period and real cases coming before the courts.

Historians' views of the late medieval period have altered considerably
over the past twenty-five years or so, in the wake of new insights and
compelling research concerning the diverse activities of all levels of
society. There has been increasing interest in the relationship between
law and society and particularly women's experience of the law.[8] In

---

7 For some earlier published collections containing medieval legal material see *English
   Constitutional Documents, 1307-1485*, ed. E. C. Lodge and G. A. Thornton (Cambridge,
   Cambridge University Press, 1935); L. O. Pike, *A Source Book of English Law* (London,
   Sweet & Maxwell, 1957); *Select Documents of English Constitutional History, 1307-1485*,
   ed. S. B. Chrimes and A. L. Brown (London, A. & C. Black, 1961); *English Historical
   Documents, 1327-1485*, ed. A. R. Myers (London, Eyre & Spottiswode, 1969); A. Hard-
   ing, *The Law Courts of Medieval England* (George Allen & Unwin, 1973); *English
   Historical Documents, 1189-1327*, ed. H. Rothwell (London, Eyre & Spottiswode, 1975).
   Not all the documents included are provided in translation.

8 M. M. Sheehan, *Marriage, Family and Law in Medieval Europe* (Toronto, University
   of Toronto Press, 1996); S. S. Walker, *Wife and Widow in Medieval England* (Ann

spite of the new directions taken, attitudes towards the law and legal institutions have (at least in some quarters) remained entrenched in the old orthodoxy of conflicts between the centre and the localities, competition between judicial agencies, corruption at all levels with patronage oiling the system.[9] Together with perceptions of the extent of crime and disorder in medieval England such views have been hard to shift. The introductions to each chapter not only provide an overview of the documents and themes illustrated, but also highlight the existing literature and historiographical trends. It should be stressed that these references are offered as guidelines and are by no means a comprehensive survey of the field. Equally the interpretations placed upon the various sources and historical events, while frequently taking into account differing readings and historical commentaries, are essentially personal ones.

The volume has a broad chronology, its examples cover developments in criminal justice essentially from the early thirteenth to the late fifteenth century. While it offers some sense of judicial evolution and 'progress', the unfolding story should not be read naively in terms of justice getting better over the centuries. Regard should be had also to the appropriateness of the judicial machinery for contemporary legal problems and expectations. The book more realistically affords vignettes at specific points in time and sets them within both the specific and the wider legal, social and political context accordingly. A balance between examples drawn from different centuries has been attempted, though a number of examples derive from the fifteenth century because it is better documented. It is important, however, not to read back into the earlier centuries the history of the fifteenth century merely because it has been studied by historians in greater detail. The danger is to view the examples outside their particular era, and without regard to competing influences, prevailing ideologies and conflicting historiography. By the mid-fifteenth century, for example, the situation and the debate on law and justice had altered as it became apparent that the violence and corruption sponsored by the upper classes, which in turn fuelled the Wars of the Roses, were a reflection of the lack of impartiality and

---

Arbor, University of Michigan Press, 1993); *The Welsh Law of Women*, ed. D. Jenkins and M. E. Owen (Cardiff, University of Wales Press, 1980); *Medieval Women and the Law*, ed. N. J. Menuge (Woodbridge, Boydell Press, 2000); L. J. Wilkinson, *Women in Thirteenth-Century Lincolnshire* (London, Royal Historical Society, 2007).

9 E. Powell, 'After "After McFarlane": the poverty of patronage and the case for constitutional history', in *Trade, Devotion and Governance*, ed. D. J. Clayton, R. G. Davies and P. McNiven (Stroud, Alan Sutton, 1994), pp. 1-16; Musson and Ormrod, *Evolution*, pp. 2-10, 175-6.

clear direction from the king.[10] The ideal of the monarch as upholder of public authority in partnership with his nobility and local society was then but a shallow reflection in reality. As an ideal it persisted and was insistently evoked, but the context was markedly different.

The book's focus on crime, public order and the administration of justice reflects the significance in the medieval period of the concept of order. In the modern age we no longer think of criminal behaviour in cosmic terms, of an individual's behaviour upsetting the equilibrium of the universe, and now regard 'breaches of the peace' as petty crimes. In the Middle Ages order was equated with divine order and breaches of the king's peace were in effect violations of God's peace. The development of the royal courts and their jurisdiction over crime can be seen therefore as a response to the king's responsibilities as God's representative on earth. Criminal law, however, was only one facet of the law actually experienced by contemporaries. To do justice to the civil side of litigation (which includes actions involving disputed title to land and a host of personal actions) would not be possible given the size of the present work, though ideally it should not be neglected in a rounded view of legal history.[11] Some elements of civil litigation will therefore be discussed when aspects of the disputing process are examined since it is here (and in certain other areas) that there is an overlap between the two.

Looking at 'law' in a wider context it is apparent that there were three main legal traditions operating concurrently in the country: common law, canon law and customary law. Justice was dispensed therefore not just in the royal courts, but in the ecclesiastical and local (customary) courts as well. The manorial and county courts generally dealt with minor transgressions, putting forward for royal examination more serious offences. The church courts normally concerned themselves with morality and personal conduct and in this respect their work overlapped conceptually with areas of criminal law. In its abhorrence and avoidance of the shedding of blood the church arguably attenuated the work of the criminal justice system. This occurred as a result of the administrative process known as 'benefit of clergy', which enabled clerical criminals convicted in the royal courts to avoid the death penalty and transfer to the ecclesiastical jurisdiction for corporal punishment. It can also be

10 A. J. Pollard, *The Wars of the Roses* (Basingstoke, Macmillan, 1988); C. Carpenter, *The Wars of the Roses* (Cambridge, Cambridge University Press, 1995).

11 J. H. Baker and S. F. C. Milsom, *Sources of English Legal History: Private Law before 1750* (London, Butterworths, 1986).

seen in the way the church offered criminals who reached its sanctuary the opportunity to confess their crimes and leave the realm, thereby escaping judgment of death. In addition to the three main systems of law operating in the country, there existed separate systems of laws relating to the royal forests and the border regions, and to mercantile, maritime and martial law. Rather than relying solely on strict legal rules, there was also recourse to natural law (or equitable) principles of conscience, reason and good faith. These were utilised informally in arbitration and by baronial councils, but during the fourteenth and fifteenth centuries operated increasingly within the institutional framework in the court of Chancery and regionally in the Mayors' courts.[12] The diversity of the English judicial scene, with its overlapping and sometimes competing jurisdictions, should therefore be appreciated. They were not all insular creations: some laws were trans-national in application, and some had procedural and substantive links with Roman civil law, which operated primarily in continental Europe.[13]

While this book focuses on criminal law, it attempts to go beyond the purely sensational aspect of medieval crime and justice. Study of the legal records offers not simply colourful illustrations of medieval crime and the various responses to it, but provides an insight into the character of medieval society and its governance as well as contemporary expectations of the law and legal institutions. Indeed, the sources included in this volume betray something of the tensions emerging between the theoretical framework and the practical realities of medieval political society. They also highlight the interplay between contemporary perceptions of order and disorder and give pointers towards an understanding of notions of law and justice and of the complex nexus of interests, attitudes and relationships (at times changing and redefining) prevailing in the later Middle Ages.[14]

The limitations of the medieval sources should be in the forefront of the reader's mind. Records should be judged on their own terms and with regard to their specific function as documents – the drawbacks are therefore usually directly related to their main function and the inten-

12 J. B. Post, 'Equitable resorts before 1450', in *Law, Litigants and the Legal Profession*, ed.
    E. W. Ives and A. H. Manchester (London, Royal Historical Society, 1983), pp. 68–79;
    T. Haskett, 'The medieval English court of chancery', *LHR*, 14 (1996), 245–313; P.
    Tucker, 'The early history of the court of chancery: a comparative study', *EHR*, 115
    (2000), 701–811.

13 Musson, *Medieval Law*, pp. 9–13; R. H. Helmholz, *The* Ius Commune *in England: Four
    Studies* (Oxford, Oxford University Press, 2001).

14 Maddicott, *Law and Lordship*, p. 33.

tion behind their creation. The majority of examples included in this volume come from the crown's plea rolls concerned with recording in proper form the decisions of the court and the amount of money (and goods or chattels) owed to the king. The technicalities of the law and intricacies of pleading were rarely of interest (hence the birth of law reporting – see below) and even though following the correct procedure was significant in legal terms, since it was habitual and well known to the clerks the actual procedural format followed was not necessarily recorded, merely glossed with an 'etc.'. There is much that the historian and the lawyer would like to glean from these voluminous records, but their narrow focus ostensibly robs them of both detail and context. As Clanchy observed, 'The routines of legal process, however carefully recorded, were neither the substance of the law, nor its political and social reality.'[15] It is necessary to combine the court records with law reports to get a fuller picture of the trial process and combine these with other documentation (such as royal instructions, chronicles or personal letters) to provide background to the appearance in court. That is not to say that examples of the types of cases appearing in the courts are not of legal or social significance in themselves. Some researchers have concentrated on the details recorded in the records and have duly employed the methodologies of the social sciences to analyse trends and global changes in litigation and in the administration of justice. These methodologies generally have limited application and value for the legal historian as the series of rolls are often incomplete and, where they do survive, do not necessarily provide enough information on which to base a reliable study. They may reveal more about methods of administration and record-making than the dynamics of criminal justice. A qualitative case study demonstrating the application of legal principles and highlighting the operation of legal procedure within a particular political and social context is sometimes supportable from the records, but often remains an ideal.

The records of parliament and enrolments of statutes provide important documentary evidence for legislative intentions and notions of justice. The parliament rolls in particular contain records of trials held before the assembled parliament and occasionally the king's council.[16] Petitions presented to the king in parliament seeking redress of various types of grievance were habitually included in the proceedings of parlia-

15 Clanchy, 'Highway robbery', p. 47.

16 *RP*; *The Parliament Rolls of Medieval England*, ed. C. Given Wilson et al. (Leicester, Scholarly Editions, 2005); *Parchment and People: Parliament in the Middle Ages*, ed. L. Clark, *Parliamentary History*, 23 (2004).

ment up to 1332. While only sporadically enrolled thereafter and in small numbers recourse can nevertheless be had to nearly 18,000 of the original documents (probably a small proportion of those submitted) filed in the National Archives which are now available in digital format on-line.[17] The vast collection of writs, letters patent and close and other administrative miscellanea generated by the royal chancery and exchequer (a significant amount of which has been collected together and printed in calendared form) offers a significant insight into the operation of royal government and a useful resource when seeking a context for judicial business.

For the principles of the law and its administrative procedures we must also turn to legal treatises. They purport to be accurate and up-to-date statements of the law in action, but the nature of the undertaking means they probably reflect practices prevalent at an earlier date or provide only a picture of a legal system frozen in time. Their importance to the legal historian in shedding light on the law in action is enhanced by the knowledge that practitioners used these texts. Handwritten annotations in surviving manuscript copies are useful for a study of subsequent changes in legal thought and practice. As in political treatises, however, the authors have their own agendas and are flush with ideals, sometimes tempered with pragmatism. An insight into the construction of legal argument in the medieval period and the reasoning behind judicial decisions can be obtained from the collections of cases made by students and practitioners which form the early law reports. These appear to flesh out the blandness of the plea rolls by giving the dialogue of the pleaders and judges (and occasionally the parties and witnesses). Modern editors have assiduously searched for the formal enrolment of such cases on the plea rolls and married together separate reports made of the same case. Sometimes these reports will focus on differing points of legal interest or reveal a variance in factual detail or in understanding of the progress of the trial. Often the decision will not be recorded, the main focus being the legal arguments employed. Brand has pointed to the use of reports for teaching purposes and highlighted the collation of real and fictional cases to provide study texts.[18] While their historical accuracy as supposedly verbatim accounts of trials is clearly questionable, they can

---

17 P. Brand, 'Petitions and parliament in the reign of Edward I', in *Parchment and People*, ed. Clark, pp. 14–38; G. Dodd, 'The hidden presence: parliament and the private petition in the fourteenth century', in *Expectations*, ed. Musson, pp. 135–49. See 'Catalogue' and 'Documents On-line' at www.tna.gov.uk.

18 P. Brand, 'The beginnings of English law reporting', in *Law Reporting in England*, ed. C. Stebbings (London, Hambledon Press, 1995), pp. 1–14.

be used to supplement the sparse accounts of the plea rolls to provide an understanding of the complexity and dynamics of trials.[19] Comparatively rarely, however, is the reporter's attention afforded to criminal trials,[20] partly owing to the disappearance of the eyres (which dispensed both civil and criminal justice), but also because the prime focus of legal education was on the civil side (as evidenced by the special construction of a 'crib' for law students in the court of common pleas).[21]

The accounts of chroniclers, by contrast, often provide a political and social context for the substantive law and the administrative processes of justice. Certain chroniclers provide us with narratives that illuminate constitutional and judicial events and sometimes they offer details and insights that are not available in the formal legal or parliamentary records.[22] Chronicles can be repositories of statutes or other legal documents (and testify to the perceived importance of that legislation or record), but more significantly, the reasons for a piece of legislation may be discussed and the appropriate political setting conveyed by the author. Moreover, where the chronicler observed or had information concerning a case, the processes of the law and the dynamics of a trial can be vividly brought to life, either supplementing the legal records or providing a view of proceedings that has otherwise been lost. Naturally problems of reliability arise and once again regard should be had to the purposes of the accounts. Chroniclers were sometimes writing contemporaneously and knowledgeably, sometimes they were writing about events in the distant past and were using models and exemplars that may or may not have been entirely accurate and trustworthy sources. Many accounts betray political bias, while the social position and ecclesiastical sympathies of certain writers shine through. As the examples in Chapter 2 demonstrate, chroniclers may provide a dynamic picture of involvement in the Peasants' Revolt, but the language and phraseology of the texts (as with the opinions of those sitting on post-rebellion juries) are themselves coloured to an extent by the desire to couch rebel actions in terms of the usurpation of royal authority.

19 J. H. Baker, *The Common Law Tradition: Lawyers, Books and the Law* (London, Hambledon Press, 2000), pp. 133-65.

20 For some examples see D. Seipp, 'Crime in the Year Books', in *Law Reporting in England*, ed. Stebbings, pp. 15-34.

21 P. Brand, 'Legal education in England before the Inns of Court', in *Learning the Law: Teaching and the Transmission of Law, 1150-1900*, ed. J. A. Bush and A. Wijfells (London, Hambledon, 1999), pp. 62-4.

22 C. Given-Wilson, *Chronicles and the Writing of History in Medieval England* (London, Hambledon & London, 2004).

Personal correspondence (exemplified here mainly by letters from the Paston and Plumpton collections) offers a view of law and justice that is removed from the national stage and the public arena. It is the local world with its legal realities and immediate pressures that is of interest. Poems and literary works similarly offer an insight into the personal world, though one where imagination and reflection have free reign, rather than firm reality. Although there may be real-world historicist correspondences, such sources should be read with an eye to the literary influences and conventions of the period as well as to the prevailing social mores. The satire and criticism that pervade many of the literary examples should not be divorced from their intention to entertain and educate, yet they remain valuable ways of approaching attitudes and expectations of law and justice.

This volume, therefore, in employing texts drawn from a wide range of sources, reflects something of the nature of the documents which lawyers and historians have at their disposal when constructing a picture of medieval society and exemplifies a number of the different genres with which medieval culture was familiar. Although the extracts are presented in an easily readable format, translating the Latin and Anglo-Norman French and using a modernised version of the Middle English where appropriate, attention is nevertheless drawn specifically to the languages of the originals. The languages of law and government were predominantly Latin and Anglo-Norman French, though the technical vocabulary and discourse deployed in the law courts gave rise to a discernible branch of the latter known as 'law French'. Some of the documents included, however, reflect changes in the use of language in bureaucratic and legal circles and in particular the adoption of English not just in chronicles and the imaginative literature, but in quasi-legal documents such as petitions and as a language of record in the rolls of parliament.[23] It is possible to view the influence of the other languages on the use of English: for example the very Latinate constructions of some of the English examples (such as the Paston letters) and the literal borrowings of words used in a legal context straight from the equivalent in Latin or French.

Where printed versions of the documents exist (in translation) the original manuscripts have been consulted in rendering it afresh and are cited accordingly. In some instances where there has not been any significant reinterpretation, the translation given is a modernised

---

23 W. M. Ormrod, 'The use of English: law, language and political culture in late medieval England', *Speculum*, 78 (2003), 750-87.

version or one based upon the edited text cited.[24] Whilst the translations are not entirely literal, they at least aim to convey a sense of the
prosaic nature of legal documents. We have therefore tried to retain
some flavour of the legal language, in particular the length, involvement and complexity of the sentence structure, reflecting the clerks'
apparent verbosity as they attempted to avoid ambiguity and pin down
a comprehensive version of the facts. The sign [...] denotes places
where words have been lost as a result of the physical state of the manuscript.[25] In instances where there is damage or erasure of the original
text but the sense is intelligible, accordingly the gist is given. While
an attempt has been made to retain the rhyming pattern in some of the
poetic examples, the need to provide an intelligible reading has over-
ridden this at times. Place names have been modernised where possible;
those unidentified have been italicised.

24 For example: 4.3, 5.5, 6.5.
25 For example: 3.4, 7.6, 8.7.

I: CONCEPTS OF LAW AND JUSTICE

In the later Middle Ages a broad intellectual background for concepts of law and justice existed based on a composite of the Bible and the tenets of Christianity, the corpus of Roman law and canon law, and (amongst others) the writings of Aristotle and St Thomas Aquinas.[1] The general principles of law, government and kingship were set out and elaborated by philosophers, theologians and jurists in influential treatises reaching throughout western Christendom bringing a diversity of languages, doctrines and opinions to the discourse on law and justice.[2]

It was a medieval commonplace that all law derived ultimately from God. The Old and New Testaments were repositories of the divine law, notably the Ten Commandments (set out in the Book of Exodus) and the teachings of Christ (contained in the Gospels). The so-called 'Golden Rule' - do unto others as you would have them do to you - appears in St Matthew's Gospel and was presented by Gratian in his influential *Decretum*, a synthesis of the rules and procedures of the church, as a timeless principle that formed the basis of all law. [1.1] The applied Christian doctrine was interwoven with the science of things divine and human that constituted Roman law jurisprudence, which placed emphasis on the universal quality of reason (*ratio*) and equated it with natural law (*ius naturale*). Law and reason therefore became inextricably intertwined and routinely invoked. Divine reason was considered by monarchs and subjects alike to be reflected in a constant standard of equity and justice, which was in turn defined as the judicial requirement 'to give to each his due'.[3] [1.2]

Aquinas was especially influential on medieval political thought, reconciling the teachings of Christ with Aristotelian logic to achieve a distinctive philosophy of law and the state. Mankind, he argued, could not apprehend the eternal law of God directly, but by applying reason (the divine spark which set man apart from and above the animals) he might deduce a body of principles based upon it, that is, the law of nature. Eternal law, therefore, was the application of divine reason to the universe and natural law was the means by which humans, as rational creatures, participated in the eternal law. The positive law which governed human societies derived from natural law and was unjust and invalid

---

1 J. Coleman, *A History of Political Thought: From the Middle Ages to the Renaissance* (Oxford, Blackwell, 2000), pp. 9–11.

2 A. Black, *Political Thought in Europe 1250–1450* (Cambridge, Cambridge University Press, 1992), pp. 34–41.

3 B. Tierney, *Religion, Law and the Growth of Constitutional Thought, 1150–1650* (Cambridge, Cambridge University Press, 1982), pp. 12–13; Coleman, *Political Thought*, pp. 35–6, 105–6; Powell, 'Law and justice', pp. 30–31.

unless it accorded with natural law and, by implication, eternal law.[4]

Custom was important for Aquinas since the repeated observance over time of the practices and procedures that embodied custom (he believed) helped inculcate respect for the law and, if custom accorded with reason, could take on the mantle and coercive force of substantive law. On the other hand, legislation which overrode customary rules and process hallowed through its long usage arguably undermined the habit of observance and thus weakened law's effectiveness and power. Magna Carta is England's prime example of custom achieving the status of law. Converting royal convenience into an individual's customary right, fashioning substantive law from routine practices and procedures, and emphasising custom, fairness and proportion, Magna Carta came to represent legal ideals for both ruler and the ruled and was placed symbolically at the head of the statute book.[5] ⌈**1.6**⌉

The relationship of the king to the law and the obligations of kingship were crucial themes addressed by jurists and political commentators.[6] The revival of interest in Roman civil law at the beginning of the twelfth century infused jurisprudential writing with ideas of strong centralist government under a divine emperor. Emphasis was especially placed on his legislative authority.[7] The king was supreme within his realm, his personal will was paramount, but he ruled under God and was morally obliged to govern in accordance with the laws of the land as far as they were applicable to him. As the custodian and guardian of the laws of his people he could temper their rigour with mercy and fairness or even set them aside if special necessity dictated.[8] ⌈**1.5**⌉

The English monarch's constitutional proprieties as far as law and justice were concerned were set out in his coronation oath. ⌈**1.4**⌉ The coronation ceremony embodied a form of double contract: one between the sovereign and his people (the royal oath) and one between the sovereign and the great men of the realm (their renewal of the bond of homage). While the oath was a straightforward statement of the sovereign's duties it was also regarded as a symbol of his own personal obligations to the realm.[9] Kings were expected to observe to the best of their ability the laws and customs of their predecessors (especially the laws

4 Coleman, *Political Thought*, pp. 81–109; Powell, *Kingship*, pp. 25–6.

5 J. C. Holt, *Magna Carta*, 2nd edn (Cambridge, Cambridge University Press, 1992), pp. 112–13; Powell, *Kingship*, pp. 27–8; F. Thompson, *Magna Carta: Its Role in the Making of the Constitution, 1300–1629* (New York, Octagon Books, 1978). It may also have been accorded priority in statute collections because it pre-dated other legislation included in the volume (even though Magna Carta itself was sometimes given in its later versions of 1225 or 1297).

6 E. H. Kantorowicz, *The King's Two Bodies: a Study in Medieval Political Theology* repr. (Princeton, NJ, Princeton University Press, 1981); J. Watts, *Henry VI and the Politics of Kingship* (Cambridge, Cambridge University Press, 1996), pp. 21–31.

7 Black, *Political Thought in Europe*, pp. 8, 139, 152; Tierney, *Constitutional Thought*, pp. 13–14, 24–5, 30–32.

8 Watts, *Politics of Kingship*, pp. 16–19.

9 H. G. Richardson, 'The English coronation oath', *Speculum* 24 (1949), 44–75.

of St Edward the Confessor), to maintain peace for the church and people, and do justice. The form of the oath was not set in stone. Henry III and Edward I additionally swore to maintain and recover the rights of the crown. From Edward II's coronation the oath included an obligation to uphold 'the laws and rightful customs which the community of your realm shall have chosen'.[10]

Writers analysing the nature of English law and the responsibilities of kingship absorbed aspects of this inherited tradition, but approached the subject from many different angles and with varying sources and agendas in mind. *Bracton* writing in the thirteenth century explicitly addressed the problem of what happened when the king ignored his obligations and was considered to be over-riding the law unjustly. He argued that since a king's authority derives from the law ('law makes the king') he undermines himself if he rules according to his own whims and private interests ('for there is no *rex* where will rules rather than *lex*').[11] Tyranny was thus characterised by the ruler's wilfulness and his failure to observe the law as he had sworn to uphold in his coronation oath.[12] ⎡**1.8**⎤

The conventions of administrative kingship meant that the king delegated his power and did not normally become personally involved in judicial matters. While the vast majority of disputes were adjudicated in his name, the king nevertheless remained the fount of justice and occasionally intervened in a case or sat in court in person. ⎡**1.7**⎤ The Arcadian setting and quality given by Joinville to his account of Louis IX not only associates the king's actions with the ideals of governance, but also depicts his special interest in justice and an ability to see a way through the complexities of law. St Louis' apparent correction of pleadings should be contrasted with Fortescue's forthright advice to his royal master. The latter says that it is not necessary for the prince to master all the technicalities or mysteries of the law, merely to apprehend and promote the qualities of justice. 'In fact you will render judgments better through others than by yourself, for none of the kings of England is seen to give judgment by his own lips.'[13]

In fact historical record does not bear this out as most, if not all, English monarchs acted in a judicial capacity at some point in their reigns.[14] This

10 M. Prestwich, *Plantagenet England, 1225–1360* (Oxford, Clarendon Press, 2005), pp. 28–9, 179.

11 Henri de Bracton, *De Legibus et Consuetudinibus Regni Angliae*, ed. G. G. Woodbine (4 vols; Cambridge, MA, 1968–77), vol. 2, p. 33.

12 The absolutist style of kingship adopted by Richard II is noted by Nigel Saul in 'The kingship of Richard II', in *Richard II: The Art of Kingship*, ed. A. Goodman and J. L. Gillespie (Oxford, Oxford University Press, 1999), pp. 37–57.

13 Sir John Fortescue, *De Laudibus Legum Anglie*, part 1, ch. 8.

14 For example: M. Clanchy, 'Did Henry III have a policy?', *History*, 53 (1968), 207–9; M. Prestwich, *Edward I* (London, Methuen, 1988), pp. 294–6; A. Musson, 'Edward II: the public and private faces of the law', in *The Reign of Edward II: New Perspectives*, ed. G. Dodd and A. Musson (Woodbridge, York Medieval Press, 2006), pp. 140–64; W. M. Ormrod, *The Reign of Edward III* (London and New Haven, Yale University Press, 1990), pp. 53–5; Powell, *Kingship*, pp. 132–3; C. D. Ross, *Edward IV* (London, Methuen, 1974), pp. 398, 401–2. Contrast this with the inactivity of Henry VI: Watts posits that

suggests that in late medieval England the king's personal involvement in justice was still a reality, even if it had become a matter of contention for a member of the judiciary such as Fortescue.[15] Indeed, the desire on the part of the rebels participating in Jack Cade's uprising in 1450 to have free access to the king in order to seek justice suggests the perception of the king as the fount of justice persisted.[16] This perception was probably assisted by the fact that the vicinity of the king's person (a twelve-mile radius) was accorded special treatment and gave rise to a special jurisdiction (and his personal protection).[17] The king's personal authority and his particular geographical location thus continued to be a significant focus for the exercise of justice.

When it came to legislation, the law-codes attributed to the Anglo-Saxon and Anglo-Norman kings offered an example of the king's apparent lead in promulgating laws for the good of his subjects.[18] Even though Edward I has been hailed as the 'English Justinian' and important and lasting legislation passed during Edward III's reign, over the course of the fourteenth and fifteenth centuries much of the initiative for the legislative process came from parliament (especially the commons) rather than the crown.[19] Indeed, it is observable that there was an internal logic and momentum to legislative enactments irrespective of the king's professed attitudes to justice.[20] Statements by Richard II to the effect that legislation derived from his breast coupled with the king's ability to ignore or repeal statutes that were abhorrent to the crown (also demonstrated by his three predecessors) were regarded with suspicion. Repudiation of the laws of the land where they were compatible with common law principles were felt to be an affront to the natural law and God's will. The apparent malleability of the laws and disregard for both Magna Carta and

the king may have sat in silence during arbitration proceedings in the king's council between Lord Bonville and the earl of Devon (Watts, *Politics of Kingship*, pp. 146–7).

15 It is remarkable that Fortescue's treatise 'On the Governance of England' was presented to Edward IV even though his model and ideas clearly did not chime with Edward's own ideology and active rule (Watts, *Politics of Kingship*, pp. 49–50).

16 See Chapter 2.

17 W. R. Jones, 'The court of the verge: the jurisdiction of the steward and marshal of the household in later medieval England', *JBS*, 10 (1970), 1–29.

18 *Ancient Laws and Institutes of England*, ed. B. Thorpe, 3 vols (London, 1840); *Leges Henrici Primi*, ed. and trans. L. J. Downer (Oxford, 1972); P. Wormald, *The Making of English Law: King Alfred to the Twelfth Century* (Oxford, Blackwell, 1999); B. O'Brien, *God's Peace, King's Peace: The Laws of Edward the Confessor* (Philadelphia, University of Pennsylvania Press, 1999).

19 A. Musson, 'Second 'English Justinian' or pragmatic opportunist? A re-examination of the legal legislation of Edward III's reign', in *The Age of Edward III*, ed. J. Bothwell (Woodbridge, York Medieval Press, 2001), pp. 69–88; D. L Rayner, 'The forms and machinery of the "commune petition" in the fourteenth century', *EHR*, 56 (1941), 198–233, 549–70; J. R. Maddicott, 'The county community and the making of public opinion in fourteenth century England', *TRHS* 5th series, 28 (1978), 27–43.

20 Musson and Ormrod, *Evolution*, pp. 146–57; Ross, *Edward IV*, pp. 341–50, 359–61; H. G. Hanbury 'The legislation of Richard III', *AJLH*, 6 (1962), 95–113.

immemorial custom in turn bred fear and uncertainty in the realm.[21]

Disregard for the law was the mark of a tyrant and the political community felt justified in attempting to limit the power of a king who had become tyrannical or unjust. [1.13] Practical attempts during the thirteenth and fourteenth centuries to restrain the king's prerogative power and achieve reform can be seen in the Provisions of Oxford of 1258, the Ordinances of 1311 and the Continual Council of 1386, where the government administration was entrusted to a body of magnates and officials responsible to parliament.[22] The national experience of the depositions of Edward II (1327) and Richard II (1399) and Henry VI (1461) undoubtedly coloured successive political and legal writers' contributions and (although deposition of a reigning monarch was not a practice peculiar to England)[23] in turn fostered a sense of the distinctiveness of English law and its governance. In the absence of clear scholastic arguments for forcible removal of an anointed king, the depositions themselves, however, were very much couched in terms of the inadequacies of the particular kings occupying the throne and did not in themselves develop new constitutional principles.[24] Their successors' positions were pragmatically confirmed and the new regime acknowledged so as to cause the minimum of administrative and political hiatus. Indeed, Edward II and Richard II's depositions were publicly presented as abdications.[25]

The emergence of parliament as a political institution is a phenomenon that is inextricably linked with the development of concepts of law, justice and kingship. The king was simply the head of the larger body politic: he was obliged to seek the assent of his subjects (through parliament) in matters of law and taxation. Moreover, as Bishop Stillington expounded in 1468, justice was equated with 'every person doing his office that he is put in according to his estate and degree'. [1.3] The expectations and responsibilities of the king in parliament and of the different estates within parliament formed a dynamic equation. 'In this speech alone, therefore, many of the key elements of the monarchical ideology … are to be found: the common weal arises out of a socially responsive justice

21 N. Saul, *Richard II* (New Haven, Yale University Press, 1997), pp. 366–404; A. Harding, *Medieval Law and the Foundations of the State* (Oxford, Oxford University Press, 2002), pp. 263–71.

22 J. R. Maddicott, *Simon de Montfort* (Cambridge, Cambridge University Press, 1994), pp. 152–60, 285–9; M. C. Prestwich, 'The Ordinances of 1311 and the politics of the early fourteenth century', in *Politics and Crisis in Fourteenth Century England*, ed. J. Taylor and W. Childs (Gloucester, Alan Sutton, 1990), pp. 1–18; J. R. Maddicott, *Thomas of Lancaster* (Oxford, Clarendon Press, 1970), pp. 106–20; W. M. Ormrod, 'Government by commission: the Continual Council of 1386 and English royal administration', *Peritia*, 10 (1996), 303–21; Saul, *Richard II*, pp. 157–75.

23 E. Peters, *The Shadow King*: Rex Inutilis *in Medieval Law and Literature* (New Haven, Yale University Press, 1970).

24 Saul, *Richard II*, pp. 418–34.

25 Ormrod, *Political Life*, pp. 78–82; P. Strohm, *England's Empty Throne: Usurpation and the Language of Legitimation, 1399–1422* (New Haven and London, Yale University Press, 1998); C. Valente, *The Theory and Practice of Revolt in Medieval England* (Aldershot, Ashgate Publishing, 2003).

which is administered by a pre-eminent king, in association with a counsel of his greatest subjects.'[26] In the wake of deposition and usurpation parliament played a role in legitimising the hand-over of power, though not in any formal constitutional sense. In 1483 Richard, duke of Gloucester, was reputedly petitioned to take the crown 'on the behalf and in the name of the three estates of the realm of England', but parliament itself was not directly involved and only ratified the title. The petition of 1483 (recorded on the rolls of parliament for 1484) invokes the tradition of law and custom as the Englishman's birthright (a national inheritance) and tries to rally support behind the idea that Richard's taking the crown is all for the benefit of the true Englishman. [1.11] As with the hand-over of power to Henry IV, the whole event was carried out in a very stage-managed fashion. We should bear in mind that the reality of a palace coup was usually less edifying than the high-sounding constitutional phrases of the records and a good deal more bloody: the in-coming monarch's authority and credibility were almost always bolstered by accusations of previous widespread official corruption and any opposition neutralised by physical attacks on the supporters of the previous regime.[27]

One of the most obvious manifestations of royal justice and exercise of the rule of law came through the trying of prisoners for criminal offences. The king had an unprecedented control over justice, including jurisdiction over all serious crimes (felonies), but usually delegated its administration to a group of legal experts. Specially authorised royal justices, therefore, presided over criminal trials, which were usually held at royal gaols. Possession of the correct legal authority to exercise the delegated power – provided by means of an appropriately worded royal commission - was essential in order to hear the case and carry out judgment. [1.12] Exceptions arose where a lord had been granted a franchise of *infangthief* and was permitted to have his own gallows and execute thieves who had been caught red-handed.[28] Beheading was reserved for traitors and outlaws, those whose behaviour had undermined royal authority and the rule of law or who deliberately failed to answer for crimes and stood outside the law.[29] By virtue of their renunciation of being under the king's peace, outlaws were traditionally regarded as having a 'wolf's head' and could be beheaded if apprehended. Their heads would then be taken to the king's chief representative of law and order in the shire, the sheriff. The penalty for felony was to be publicly hanged: a clear signal to all of royal authority and his justice in operation. Arguably hanging and beheading were not simply punishments, but also intended as a visual deterrent to others, especially as the heads (and quartered

---

26 Watts, *Politics of Kingship*, pp. 56–7 (quotation at p. 57).

27 For example: R. Horrox, *Richard III: A Study in Service* (Cambridge, Cambridge University Press, 1989), pp. 178–82; A. J. Pollard, *Late Medieval England, 1399–1509* (London, Longman, 2000), pp. 328–41; C. Shenton, 'Edward III and the coup of 1330', in *Age of Edward III*, ed. Bothwell, pp. 13–34.

28 J. B. Post, 'Local jurisdictions and judgment of death in later medieval England', *Criminal Justice History*, 4 (1983), 1–21; Summerson, 'Capital punishment', pp. 123–33.

29 See Chapters 3 and 5.

body parts) of notorious traitors were usually put on display.[30]

The king may have enjoyed a virtual monopoly of judgment, and indeed over the course of the thirteenth and fourteenth centuries the scope of royal juris-diction expanded considerably, but there were practical limitations on the power he could exercise over justice. [1.14] First, collective forms of judg-ment endured with extensive use made of juries for fact-finding and rendering verdicts. Jurors were subject to bribery, intimidation, prejudice, bias and perversity when reaching decisions and could thus at times obstruct the higher aims and ideals of royal justice.[31] Equally, the king was reliant not only on a corps of experienced royal judges and lawyers, but also on his landed subjects, especially a cadre of professional administrators and 'men of law' amongst the gentry in the localities who staffed judicial offices.[32] The relationship was a reciprocal one. While the king undertook to uphold the rights of his subjects under the law, his authority was underwritten by the mutual self-interest and local power structures of the landed elite. When (and where) there was lack of effective direction and management from the centre, the local administration of justice was jeopardised and law and order became difficult to maintain. The underpinnings of royal authority and good governance were in turn eroded or even collapsed. 'At every level, the functioning of the complex combination of law and office, obligation and influence, as a viable and co-ordinated social structure depended ultimately on the public authority of the crown.'[33] Law and justice were closely connected therefore not only with good kingship, but also with the stability of the body politic.

There is no single 'official' (in the sense of government-sponsored) text outlining the concepts of law and justice pertaining in late medieval England. The extracts included here are therefore drawn from a variety of sources, both the formal 'public' records of parliamentary and judicial proceedings and 'private' texts (such as treatises and chronicles) produced for, or dissemi-nated by, persons intimately connected with royal government and legal institutions.

In addition to being cornucopia of substantive law and procedure, the legal treatises of the period provide a window on to contemporary ideological stances. The body of rules and principles known as *Glanvill*, attributed to Ranulf de Glanvill (justiciar to Henry II), but probably composed by a clerk associated with his office, was an important manual for justices and legal practitioners from the late twelfth century. Standardising the administration of justice, most of the treatise concerns land law with criminal pleas forming only a brief part. Its prologue, highly influenced by Roman law and probably written with Henry II in mind, offers an ideal picture of law and justice, promoting the king's role as upholder of order and impartial arbiter. The author broadens his view to

30 P. Spierenburg, *The Spectacle of Suffering* (Cambridge, Cambridge University Press, 1984), p. 55.

31 See Chapter 8.

32 See Chapter 7.

33 Castor, *Duchy*, pp. 6–7.

include the operation of the royal courts, extolling their impartiality and the actions of the royal justices in dealing with cases which came before them in the king's name.[34]

Bracton, attributed to Henry de Bracton, was more likely the unfinished work of royal justice William Raleigh, later bishop of Winchester. It has been persuasively argued that Bracton, his clerk and later a royal justice, was in fact the continuator of the treatise, synthesising and setting out in a logical format the tenets of English law.[35] Given his agenda and the context in which he wrote, *Bracton*'s comments on royal authority may well have been inspired by personal contact with Henry III and written with his royal example in mind. Unfortunately the statements on kingship and the law are 'scattered and muddled' and so do not provide a coherent platform.[36]

Kings or rulers in waiting usually received advice from ministers or counsellors, but there was also a flourishing tradition of 'mirror-for-princes' literature directed specifically at the ruler and intended to help him recognise his responsibility to govern well and uphold justice.[37] Edward II is known to have possessed a copy of Giles of Rome's *De Regimine Principum*,[38] while Edward III received a treatise entitled *The Nobility, Wisdom and Prudence of Kings* from Walter de Milemete.[39] Richard II's tutor owned a copy of Giles of Rome and John Thorpe's tract *De Quadripartita Regis Specie*.[40] Thomas Hoccleve's *Regiment of Princes* may take us close to, or at least offers a useful pointer towards, the concerns and priorities of Henry V shortly before his accession to the throne. It is significant therefore that the work should concentrate predominantly on the importance of the coronation oath, the observance of justice, the keeping of the laws and the exercise of the royal prerogative of mercy. Henry's own emphasis on justice and order during his reign and his treatment of the coronation oath almost as a 'manifesto' may well have been influenced not only by this treatise, but also by his father's usurpation and the need for dynastic legitimacy.[41] [**1.9**]

34 J. Hudson, *The Formation of the English Common Law* (London and New York, Longman, 1996), pp. 150, 152–5.

35 P. Brand, 'The age of Bracton', in *The History of English Law: Centenary Essays on 'Pollock and Maitland'*, ed. J. Hudson (Oxford, Oxford University Press, 1996), pp. 66–89.

36 Clanchy, 'Did Henry III have a policy?', 208–9.

37 G. L. Harriss, 'Introduction: the exemplar of kingship', in *Henry V: The Practice of Kingship*, ed. G. L. Harriss (Oxford, Oxford University Press, 1985), pp. 1–29.

38 Clanchy, *Memory*, p. 162.

39 M. Michael, 'The iconography of kingship in the Walter of Milemete treatise', *Journal of the Courtauld and Warburg Institutes*, 57 (1978), 35–47; Ormrod, *Political Life*, pp. 64–5.

40 Saul, 'Kingship of Richard II', pp. 44–5, 51–4; R. H. Jones, *The Royal Policy of Richard II: Absolutism in the Later Middle Ages* (Oxford, Blackwells, 1968).

41 N. Perkins, *Hoccleve's* Regiment of Princes: *Counsel and Constraint* (Woodbridge, Boydell Press, 2001), pp. 50–84; Powell, *Kingship*, pp. 126–34.

Sir John Fortescue (c 1395–c 1477), sometime chief justice of the king's bench, chancellor to Henry VI and a member of Edward IV's council, perhaps comes closest to embodying the concepts of law and justice as they existed in the late fifteenth century. He wrote the major treatises 'On the Nature of the Law of Nature', 'The Governance of England' and 'In Praise of the Laws of England'. The latter was written for Prince Edward, son of Henry VI. His work, however, includes no references to the two great treatises of an earlier age, *Glanvill* and *Bracton*, nor does Fortescue cite specifically from parliamentary or judicial records. His text nevertheless embodies the general principles expounded by the great philosophers and theologians, Aristotle, St Augustine, St Thomas Aquinas and Giles of Rome, underpinned with frequent reference to the Bible, Roman law and canon law, placing him clearly within the mainstream of contemporary European political and legal thought.[42] ⌈**1.10**⌉

This chapter aims not simply to provide an overview of official concepts as discernible in the medieval records, but to offer a sense of the way in which these documents enshrine the concerns of the period and were very much informed by their context. As such it is possible to detect and chart aspects of consolidation, progression and divergence in English legal and political thought.

---

42 Powell, *Kingship*, pp. 23–4.

1.1 Definitions of justice: the Golden Rule

Fortescue, writing in the fifteenth century, sees justice as synonymous with the law of nature. He articulates in his treatise (through a series of *Distinctiones* or tracts) concepts long familiar through St Matthew's Gospel and canon law, though in fact he derives much of his argument from St Thomas Aquinas' *Summa Theologica*. It was from the law of nature that the positive laws of human societies proceeded, including the laws of England.

Sir John Fortescue, *De Natura Legis Naturae*, ed. Lord Clermont (London, 1864), part 1, ch. 4 [Latin]

The human race was subject to the law of nature from the time of the expulsion from Paradise until the people of Israel received the written law from God through Moses on Mount Sinai. This was a period of some three thousand six hundred and forty-four years, according to the writings of Augustine (*De Civitate Dei*, Books 15 and 16) and Josephus in his book *De Antiquitatum Historiis*. For that reason the whole of that era is called the age of the law of nature; and the next era until the birth of Christ is called the age of given law, and the era from then until the present day is called the age of grace.

The Law of Nature was not, however, supplanted in the later eras, but remained in full force and strength and so remains today. Moreover Our Lord has confirmed it and ordered it to be observed saying, 'All things therefore whatsoever you would that men should do to you, do you also to them. For this is the law and the prophets' (Matthew 7: 12). And the law which Our Lord thus declared and ordered to be kept is expressly declared to be the Law of Nature by Canon Law which states (Gratian *Decretum* Distinctio 1, ch. 1) that the natural law is as contained in the Gospel, where each man is ordered to do to others as he would like to be done by, and not to do as he would not like to be done by.

1.2 Definitions of justice: 'ius suum cuique tribuere' – to give each man his right

The notions of fair dealing and reciprocity are emphasised in this passage. Again, there is strong evocation of the role of the divine, not only in initiating and underlying all things, but as providing a constant and unfailing point of comparison by which human endeavours can be measured. In setting out the basic principles of the common law, it is significant that *Bracton*, writing in the thirteenth century, relies heavily on a maxim already familiar in Roman (civil) law. Indeed, the author's indebtedness to Roman law is apparent throughout the treatise.

Henry de Bracton, *De Legibus et Consuetudinibus Regni Angliae*, ed. G. E. Woodbine (4 vols; Cambridge, MA, 1968–77), vol. 2, pp. 22–3 [Latin]

What is Justice?

Since all human laws flow from justice as water flows from a spring, and follow the dictates of justice, let us see what justice is and why it is so called. Let us see also what *ius* (right) is, why it is so called and what its precepts are; also what law and custom are, without which no one can be just, nor justice done or just judgements given between man and man.

Justice is the constant and everlasting will to give each man his right. This definition may be understood in two ways, first as regards God the Creator and secondly as regards mankind, God's creatures. As regards God the Creator, the meaning of the definition is quite clear, since justice is that divine disposition to order all things rightly and justly. For God gives to each man according to his works. God is not variable or transitory in His will and dispositions; rather His will is constant and everlasting. For He has no beginning and will have no end. The definition of justice is to be understood in another way as regards God's creatures, that is the just man. The just man has the will to give each man his right, and so that will is called justice.

1.3 Definitions of justice: the three estates under the king

Bishop Robert Stillington was chancellor to Edward IV and this extract is taken from a report of his speech to the 1467 parliament on its resumption of business in May 1468 at a time when peace both internally and externally was a matter of considerable concern. In his discourse he underlines the hierarchy of laws within the universe: the law of God, the law of nature and positive law (the law and customs of the realm of England). This, as outlined above, would have been familiar to his audience. Stillington, however, echoing the rhetorical style of the treatise writer, links law and justice to observance of the constitutional proprieties of the realm and the discharge by each of the three estates of its incumbent responsibilities. The strong desirability of public order is associated with a sense of social hierarchy. The three complementary and mutually supportive estates – the Lords Spiritual, Lords Temporal and Commons – are understood to carry out their political functions under the guiding hand and watchful eye of the king, whose own duties and designs are equally made clear. The striking part of this definition is its particularity to the English context and its emphasis on hierarchy and peace.

RP, vol. 5, pp. 622–3: the speech of the chancellor Robert Stillington, bishop of Bath and Wells (1468) [English]

It was shown by the king's command and in his name, by the mouth of the right reverend father in God the bishop of Bath and Wells, chancellor of England, to the said Lords and Commons, that justice was the foundation, source and root of all prosperity, peace and politic rule of every realm, upon which all the laws of the world have been established and based, which depends on three forms of law: that is to say, the law of God, the law of nature and positive law; and according to the sayings of all the philosophers felicity and peace in every realm are always the result of justice, as is demonstrably shown by the reasoning of the philosophers. Wherefore first he asked, what is justice? Justice is every person doing his office that he is put in according to his estate or degree, and as for this land it is understood that it stands by three estates, and above that one ruler: that is Lords Spiritual, Lords Temporal and Commons, and over that the Royal Estate above, that is our Sovereign Lord the King, who had commanded him to say to them that it was his ultimate intention to administer law and justice, and to plant, fix and set peace throughout his realm, with the advice of his Lords Spiritual and Temporal, and also to provide an outward peace for the defence and security of the realm.

1.4 Kingship and the rule of law: the coronation oath of Richard II (1377)

Despite its obviously public nature, the oath-taking ceremony itself would probably not have been heard by the assembled grandees, as it was conducted privately in the chapel of St Edward the Confessor by the archbishop of Canterbury. The version contained in *Bracton* (comprising three undertakings) was recast for Edward II's coronation, significantly with the addition of a precept designed to secure the king's observance of the charters and laws that the community of the realm would determine in the future. The corporate existence and welfare of the kingdom (as founded in the concept of the crown) was thus considered to be of wider import than the king's personal rights. By implication the king was part of the community of the realm and answerable to it. The oath sworn by Richard II was recorded in the parliament rolls as part of the Record and Process which formally and publicly (in parliament) set out the reasons for his deposition as a means of contrasting his original undertakings with the reality of his reign.

RP, vol. 3, p. 417 [Latin]

There follows the customary form of oath taken by the kings of England at their coronation, which the archbishop of Canterbury is accustomed to demand and receive from them, as is recorded in the service-books of the archbishops and bishops. This oath was taken by Richard the second, king of England at his coronation and received by the archbishop of Canterbury.

Will you, for God's Church, the clergy and the people, preserve entirely peace and concord in God, to the best of your ability?

He shall answer: I will.

Will you, in all your judgments, see that right and impartial justice is done, in mercy and truth, to the best of your ability?

He shall answer: I will.

Do you grant that the just laws and customs which the people shall have chosen shall be maintained, and do you promise to defend and uphold them to the honour of God, and to the best of your ability?

He shall answer: I grant and promise.

1.5 Kingship and the rule of law: the king as guarantor of justice

The Prologue to the treatise *Glanvill* sets out the writer's ideological stance before embarking on the practical text. The identification of the concepts of reasonableness and longstanding as necessary elements of the laws and customs of the realm highlights the notions of fairness, proportion and custom which permeated legal theory and practice from the twelfth century onwards. Justice is also seen to incorporate discretion and involve maintenance of the difficult balance between apparent harshness and mercy. This picture of a perfectly functioning system appears very much as a template for a regime, or could be read as an encouragement to (or even, more cynically, an inverse criticism of) the prevailing regime. As we will see in Chapters 2, 7 and 8 the high ideals professed as existing in the twelfth century were somewhat different from the perceived reality in the fourteenth and fifteenth centuries.

Glanvill, ed. G. D. G. Hall (Oxford, 1965), Prologue, pp. 1–2 [Latin]

There can be no doubt how justly, how mercifully and how wisely the king (who is the author and lover of peace) has treated his subjects in time of peace. For the standards of equity in the royal court are so high that no judge there is so shameless or rash as to dare to deviate in the least from the path of justice, nor stray at all from the way of truth. Indeed, in the royal court a poor man cannot be crushed by the power of his opponent, nor can anyone be denied a hearing through fee or favour. The king respects those laws and customs of the realm which are reasonable and of long standing. More praiseworthy still, he heeds the advice of those of his subjects most learned in the laws and customs of the realm whom he knows surpass other men in authority, wisdom and eloquence, and whom he has found to be most able to decide cases and settle disputes reasonably and justly, acting now with severity, now with clemency as seems to them most appropriate.

1.6 Kingship and the rule of law: the king as guarantor of justice

The principles laid down in the Great Charter in 1215 were attempts at solutions to problems of law and justice that had emerged from the increasing impositions of royal justice and exercise of the royal prerogative during King John's reign. Clause 17 aimed at enabling litigants with cases invoking the king's common (or general) jurisdiction to know the precise location for pleading their case, either the common bench at Westminster or wherever the general eyre was visiting.[1] Increasingly over the later medieval period, especially with regard to clauses 39 and 40, Magna Carta (in its frequent reissues and confirmations) took on mythical qualities and became the touchstone for constitutional propriety, the king's good faith, and guarantees of justice.[2]

Magna Carta cc. 17, 39, 40 in J. C. Holt, *Magna Carta* 2nd edn (Cambridge, Cambridge University Press, 1992), pp. 454, 460 [Latin]

[17] Common pleas shall not follow our court but shall be held in some fixed place.

[39] No free man shall be taken or imprisoned or disseised or outlawed or exiled or in any way ruined, nor will we go or send against him, except by the lawful judgment of his peers or by the law of the land.

---

1 M. T. Clanchy, 'Magna Carta and the common pleas', in *Studies in Medieval History presented to R. H. C. Davis*, ed. H. Mayr-Harting and R. I. Moore (London, 1985), pp. 220–24.

2 See also 1.8 and Chapter 2.

[40] To no one will we sell, to no one will we deny or delay right or justice.

1.7 Kingship and the rule of law: the king as the fount of justice

If the previous extracts highlighted the ideals and the expectations of the king with regard to justice, the following examples offer a glimpse of how these were well-accepted assumptions about the duties of a ruler. Even though royal judges normally stood in the place of the king in the courts dispensation of justice was still perceived to be focused on the person and office of the king. Joinville's description is highly symbolic (harking back to an even older tradition) and underlines the desirable quality of convenient access to royal justice. St Louis IX (1226–70) of France, like St Edward the Confessor (for the English), provided an iconic model king. The 'hands-on' approach was adopted by English kings when the circumstances dictated, usually when there had been some wrong-doing when they were in the immediate vicinity or had personally been made aware of the case. The sovereign occasionally presided over sessions of his court in person, as exemplified by Edward III and Edward IV. Moreover, petitions directed to the king by private individuals (especially persons of high status) were often heard by him personally and justice dispensed accordingly where matters of royal grace were concerned. The apparent assiduousness of Edward II in this respect (in 1320) contrasts with the traditional view of this monarch.

(a) King Louis IX of France at Vincennes

Jean, Sire de Joinville, *Histoire de Saint Louis*, ed. N. de Wailly (Paris, 1874), Book 1, chs 11–12, pp. 20–22 [French]

A friar came to King Louis at the castle of Hyeres, where we had landed from the sea. He preached a sermon to instruct the king, in which he said that he had read the Bible and books which told of pagan princes, and that there never was a kingdom lost, either among believers or unbelievers, nor changed lordship but for default of justice. 'Now', he said, 'the king who is on his way to France should take care to do good and speedy justice to his people, so that Our Lord will allow his kingdom to remain in peace throughout his life.' ...

... The king did not forget this advice, but ruled his kingdom loyally according to the law of God, as you will hear. He so ordered things that the lord Nesle and the good count of Soissons, and others of us who were at court, would go after mass to hear pleas of the gate, which are now called Requests.

When he came out of church he would summon us and sit at the foot of his bed, seating us around him, and ask if there were any pleas which could not be settled without him. We would tell him and he would summon the parties and ask them, 'Why do you not accept what our men are offering you?' They would reply, 'My lord, they are offering us too little.' Then he would answer, 'You should take what they are prepared to give you.' Thus the holy king would do his best to set them on the path of right and reason.

Many times in summer he used to go and sit in the wood of Vincennes after mass and lean against an oak tree and make us sit round him. And everyone who had business would come to speak to him directly without being hindered by ushers or anyone else. Then the king would himself ask, 'Is there anyone here who has a suit?' Those who had a suit would stand up and the king would say, 'Be silent all of you, and your suits will be settled in turn.' Then would summon Pierre de Fontaine and Geoffrey de Villette and say to one of them, 'Settle this suit for me.' If he noticed anything to correct in the pleadings of those who spoke for him or for someone else, he would correct it himself out of his own mouth.

(b) King Edward I of England

TNA KB 27/124 m. 74 [Latin][3]

Afterwards Ralph de Hengham came into the bench and into the presence of Gilbert de Thornton and Roger Brabazon and recorded that the aforesaid Agnes approached the queen at Clarendon and complained concerning a certain William of Patney that he tricked her out of her land in that he took enfeoffment from the aforesaid Agnes, namely, of two carucates of land with appurtenances in Uphill and Crediton by reason of a marriage to be contracted between them, and this marriage could not be duly performed because of a legal impediment contracted on the part of the said William.

And on this there came the lord king himself who clearly understood that deed, and immediately ordered swift justice to be done to the aforesaid Agnes. And the aforesaid William, who was present in court, was immediately attached* and came before him and Walter of Wimborne, and having been questioned about the aforesaid deed said that he ought

---

3 For the actual case see TNA KB 27/56 m. 6 (Trinity 1280); *SCCKB*, vol. 1, pp. 65–6. For the record and process see *SCCKB*, vol. 2, pp. 20–23.

not to reply concerning his free tenement without the king's writ. And this same matter was shown to the lord king who said that in such a case he ought to reply without any writ, especially since he was found in his court ...

Afterwards the lord king ordered Gilbert de Thornton and his associates to hear and determine the said plea.

(c) King Edward II of England

Register of Thomas de Cobham, Bishop of Worcester, 1317–27, ed. E. H. Pearce, Worcestershire Historical Society, 39 (1930), pp. 97–8 [Latin]

Our lord the king, in the parliament summoned to London bore himself splendidly, with prudence and discretion ... Present almost every day in person, he arranged what business was to be dealt with, discussed and determined.

All those wishing to speak with reasonableness he listened to patiently, assigning prelates and lords for the hearing and implementation of petitions, and in many instances supplying ingeniously of his own discernment what he felt to be lacking.

(d) King Edward III of England

RP, vol. 2, p. 267 [French]

Blanche of Liddell [Lady Wake] ... humbly requests our lord the king and all his good council that on this matter [concerning the bishop of Ely][4] they will arrange that she and her own people can live in peace because they are greatly threatened from one day to another. Wherefore I pray my lord the king that if he cannot deliberate properly at this time, that he will take the dispute entirely into his very gracious hands until he has leisure to try it and that it ought not to be tried outside his presence. It is wished this may be done, most honoured lord, for the love of God, at the request of the said Blanche.

Which petition, once it had been heard, our lord the king granted the last clause of her petition, and openly said, 'I take the dispute into my hands.'

---

4 The dispute centred on the overlordship of a manor at Colne in Huntingdonshire. The bishop of Ely was allegedly implicated in the murder of one of Lady Wake's supporters and the arson of buildings at Colne: see J. Aberth, 'Crime and justice under Edward III: the case of Thomas de Lisle', *EHR*, 107 (1992), 283–301.

(e) King Henry V of England

Gesta Henrici Quinti, ed. F. Taylor and J. S. Roskell (Oxford, 1975), p. 68 [Latin]

And a certain robber was brought to the king in that field,[5] an Englishman, who against God and the royal edict,[6] had snatched from a church and hidden in his sleeve a pyx of gilded copper, which perhaps he believed to be gold, and in which our Lord's body [the Host] had been reserved. And in the next village where we passed the night, by the king's decree, punishing in the creature the affront to the creator, just as Phinehas did with Zimri,[7] when sentence had been passed, he perished by hanging.

1.8 Kingship and the rule of law: the tyrannical ruler

The deposition articles of Richard II were enrolled retrospectively on the parliament rolls as a matter of record, rather than according a formal parliamentary role in the deposition, in what amounts to a carefully sanitised and justificatory account of events: the king did not renounce the throne willingly nor publicly. The rule of law was the distinguishing feature of medieval kingship and this principle was emphasised at the deposition. He was accused of misgovernance, including providing no justification for his levies, accusing those working for the common good of the most heinous crime possible (treason) and using coercion and political influence on the judiciary, the guardians of the laws. The notion that he maintained that laws emanated from him alone was one of the most serious allegations against him because it repudiated the practice that the laws were created by the king and his subjects together. The Roman law maxim 'the prince has all the laws in the shrine of his breast', which Richard's alleged statement appears to follow, was inimical to English law and its invocation indicative of a lack of discipline on the part of the king. The justification for his removal from the throne, crystallised in the deposition articles, is couched in terms of Richard II's perjury: his breaking of his legal obligations as contained in the royal oath and thus his contract with the kingdom. The royal prerogative could not cloak his flouting of the law.[8]

---

5 A field next to the walled town of Corbie in France.

6 On landing in France Henry had specifically decreed that stealing from a church would be punishable by death.

7 This is a reference to the Book of Numbers 25: 6–9, 14.

8 See M. Bennett, *Richard II and the Revolution of 1399* (Stroud, Sutton Publishing, 1999) and C. M. Barron, 'The deposition of Richard II', in *Politics and Crisis in Fourteenth Century England*, ed. J. Taylor and W. Childs (Gloucester, Alan Sutton, 1990); C. Given-Wilson, *Chronicles of the Revolution, 1307–1400: The Reign of Richard II* (Manchester, Manchester University Press, 1993), pp. 172–3, 175–8, 180–81.

RP, vol. 3, pp. 418–19: deposition articles of Richard II (1399) (nos 1, 9, 16, 26, 27) [French]

[1] The first charge against the king is of misgovernment. That is to say he gave away the goods and possessions belonging to the crown to unworthy persons, and unwisely squandered them in other ways; and in consequence he imposed taxes and other heavy and insupportable burdens on the people without good cause. Also, whereas certain spiritual and temporal lords were appointed by parliament, with his consent and approval, to govern the kingdom, and faithfully laboured with all their strength and at their own expense to promote the just government of the kingdom; nevertheless the king conspired with his adherents and planned to accuse those lords, who were acting for the welfare of the kingdom, of high treason. And in order to carry out his evil plan he violently drove the judges of the kingdom, by threats of death and torture, to destroy those lords.[9]

[9] Also, notwithstanding that the king swore at his coronation that in all his judgments he would see that right and impartial justice was done, in mercy and truth, to the best of his ability,[10] despite his oath the king harshly and without mercy ordered on pain of severe penalties, that no one should ask for any favour or intercede with the king on behalf of the banished duke of Lancaster. In so doing the king acted against his obligation to show mercy, and heedlessly broke his coronation oath.

[16] Also the king did not wish to preserve and uphold the just laws and customs of his realm, but rather according to the prompting of his own will (*voluntas*) he did whatever he desired. Sometimes, especially when the laws of his realm had been declared and expounded to him by the judges and other members of his council, and he should have done justice to petitioners according to those laws; he actually said, with a determined and severe expression, that his laws were in his mouth, several times he said they were in his breast. He also said that he alone could change and establish the laws of the realm. And misled by this belief he would not permit justice to be done to many of his liege men, but through threats and intimidation forced many men from pursuing common justice.

9 This is a reference to the Continual Council of 1386 and Richard's 'Questions to the Judges' issued secretly in 1387 (see S. B. Chrimes, 'Richard II's questions to the judges, 1387', *LQR*, 72 (1956), 365–90). In a reassertion of royal authority in 1397 Richard wreaked revenge upon the Lords Appellant (who had presented the Appeal of Treason at the Merciless Parliament of 1388).

10 See 1.4 above for Richard II's coronation oath.

[26] Also whereas the lands and tenements, goods and chattels of each free man may not be seized unless duly forfeited according to the laws of the realm, which had been in use since time out of mind; nevertheless the king, with the intention of weakening those laws, frequently asserted in the presence of many lords and other members of the community of the realm that the life of each one of his liege men and his lands, tenements, goods and chattels were subject to his will (*voluntas*), without any forfeiture: which is altogether contrary to the laws and customs of the realm.

[27] Also, although it has been enacted and ordained and hitherto confirmed, 'that no free man should be arrested, etc., nor in any way destroyed, and that the king shall not proceed against him or send anyone against him except by a lawful judgment of his peers or by the law of the land' (c. 39 Magna Carta). Nevertheless, by the will and command and order of the king, many of the king's subjects were maliciously accused of allegedly speaking words publicly or in secret which were insulting, scandalous or disrespectful to the person of the king. They were arrested and imprisoned and brought before the constable and marshal of England in the court of Chivalry. And when they stood accused in that court those subjects were only permitted to plead not guilty to all charges and that they would justify and defend themselves by their own bodies;[11] notwithstanding that their accusers were strong and healthy young men, and they themselves were often old and weak, maimed or infirm. From this there would have followed the destruction not only of the lords and magnates of the realm but also of every member of the commons of the realm. Therefore since the king wilfully breached a law of his own realm, he undoubtedly committed perjury.

1.9 Kingship and the rule of law: advice to princes

With the example of Richard II probably still fresh in the mind, Hoccleve emphasises the binding contractual nature of kingship in the strongest terms, warning that for a king to depart from his coronation vows not only violates the codes of chivalry representing a personal breach of faith, but also in legal terms constitutes a breach of covenant. Using the imagery of a good harvest, the author underlines the beneficial effects for the king's subjects of his adherence to the rule of law and more generally notes its contribution to political stability.

11 The implication is that they would undergo trial by battle – see Chapter 5.

Thomas Hoccleve, *Regiment of Princes* from *Hoccleve's Works*, ed. F. J. Furnivall, vol. 3, EETS, extra series 72 (London, 1897), pp. 80, 91, 100 (stanzas 314, 360–61, 397) [English]

On a King's Keeping his Coronation Oaths; And on Truth and Cautious Speech

The oaths that at your creation
Shall be spoken with your tongue, observe them well;
Let no pretended justification
Make you slip aside or swerve from them;
Keep them alive, let them not die in you;
It is not knightly to deviate from an oath;
A true king ought to be a good example.

On Justice

            ... a king is by covenant
Of the oath made at his coronation,
Bound to preserve justice.

And a king, in fulfilling that, is
Likened to God, which is true righteousness;
And men of India say and hold this –
'A king's justice is a great richness
To his people, as plenty or largesse
Of earthly good, and better than rain
Falling at eve from heaven,' so they say.

On Observing the Laws

Prince excellent, hold your laws dear
Observe them, and offend them in no way!
By oath to keep it, bound is the power
Of kings; and by it are kings nobly
Sustained; law is both lock and key
Of safety; while law is kept in the land,
A prince in his estate may safely stand.

1.10 Kingship and the rule of law: advice to princes (England contrasted with France)

The central theme of Fortescue's treatise is the need for safeguards against the poverty of the king (arising from a combination of debts and excessive gifts) and the potential for royal tyranny stemming from this. The crisis of governance of the 1440s and 1450s clearly provided impetus and a context for his work.[12] Addressed initially to Henry VI and then revised and presented to Edward IV it can be taken to represent both a warning and prudent advice. When considering good governance and the qualities of kingship, the example of Louis IX keeping 'justice between subject and subject' is not denied by Fortescue, but he is at pains to contrast the benefits for their subjects derived from the rule of English kings as opposed to their French counterparts. The point of comparison here then is the behaviour of the monarchs and their willingness to act within or under the law rather than above it. He sets out the twin duties of promoting peace and doing justice, but warns against arbitrary rule, invoking the Roman law maxim '*quod principi placuit legis habet vigorem*' (what pleases the prince has the force of law),[13] which was applicable to royal governance in France. Tyranny is associated directly with the manner in which revenue is raised: a king's lack of money (or desire for more) is equated with abuse of his judicial powers in the pursuit of finance. The state of the royal coffers is seen as a yardstick for good governance. There is also emphasis on the public rather than the private good and the reciprocity of interests between ruler and the ruled.

Sir John Fortescue, *On the Governance of England*, ed. C. Plummer (Oxford, 1885), ch. 4, pp. 116–18 [English]

Since our king reigns over us by laws more favourable and good to us than the laws by which the French king rules his people, it is reasonable that we should be more good and profitable to him than the subjects of the French king are to him; which it would seem that we are not, considering that his subjects yield to him more in a year than we do to our sovereign lord in two years, although they do so against their wills. Nevertheless when it is considered how a king's office stands in two things, one to defend his realm against their external enemies by the sword, the other that he defend his people internally against wrongdoers by justice, as appears in the first book of Kings,[14] which the French king does not do, though he may keep justice between subject and subject; since he oppresses them more himself than all the wrongdoers of the realm would have done were there were no king. And since

12 Watts, *Politics of Kingship*, pp. 46–50.

13 Justinian, *Institutes*, 1.1.4.

14 1 Samuel 8: 20.

it is a sin to give no food, drink, clothing or other alms to them that have need, as shall be declared on the Day of Judgment, how much greater a sin it is to take from the poor man his food, his drink, his clothing, and all that he has need of, which truly the French king does to many a thousand of his subjects, as has before been openly declared. Which thing, though it may now be coloured *per ius regale*, that is 'by royal law', yet it is tyranny. For, as St Thomas Aquinas says, when a king rules his realm only for his own profit and not to the good of his subjects, he is a tyrant. King Herod reigned over the Jews *dominio regali*, that is 'by royal lordship'; yet when he slew the children of Israel, he was in that a tyrant, even though the laws say, *quod principi placuit legis habet vigorem*, that is, 'what pleases the prince has the force of law' ... For these words said to the prophet, 'show them the law of the king'[15] mean no more than 'show them the power of the king'.

Wherefore as often as such a king does anything against the law of God, or against the law of nature, he does wrong, notwithstanding the said law declared by the prophet. And it is so, that the law of nature wills in this case that the king should do to his subjects as he would be done to himself, if he were a subject; which would not be that he should be almost destroyed as are the commons of France. Wherefore, albeit that the French king's revenues are by such means much greater than the revenues which the king our sovereign lord has from us, yet they are not well taken, and the might of his realm is almost destroyed thereby. Considering this I do not want the king's revenues from this realm to be made great by any such means. And yet of necessity they must be greater than they are at present. And truly it is very necessary that they should always be great, and that the king have abundantly wherewith his estate may be honourably kept for many reasons ...

1.11 Kingship and the rule of law: good kingship and political stability

The original of this petition does not survive, but it was recited in the parliament of January 1484 at which Richard, duke of Gloucester's title to the throne was ratified. It invokes the trinity of laws (divine, natural, human) and the concept of reason, integral to medieval thinking on justice, and denounces Edward IV's rule as tyrannical. It complains that he has brought about a deterioration in the state of public order and permitted the proliferation of disputes and private feuds. These failings, it is maintained (employing the language of legal proof),

15 1 Samuel 8: 9.

are common knowledge and obvious to the whole kingdom. As a propagandist and legitimising instrument, the petition presents Richard III as offering not simply an alternative but, by implication, a return to kingship under the rule of law. The new regime is envisaged as benefiting both the lowest members of society, the poor and powerless, and those at its apex, who, it is said, have suffered during the recent battles of Edward IV's reign. The high-flown language and lofty ideals mask the background to Richard III's accession: arbitrary arrests, executions and murders and a usurpation of kingly power.

RP, vol. 6, pp. 240–41: the petition at the accession of Richard III (1483) [English]

In addition to this, amongst other things more especially we consider how, during the time of the reign of King Edward IV late deceased (after the ungracious pretended marriage, as all England has cause to say, made between King Edward and Elizabeth,[16] sometime wife of Sir John Grey, for many years naming herself Queen of England) the order of all politic rule was perverted, the laws of God and God's church, and also the laws of nature and of England, and also the laudable customs and liberties of the same to which every Englishman is heir, broken, subverted and despised against all reason and justice; so that this land was ruled by self-will and pleasure, fear and dread, all manner of equity and laws laid apart and despised; whereof ensued many misfortunes and mischiefs, such as murders, extortions and oppressions, especially of poor and powerless people; so that no man was sure of his life, land, nor livelihood, nor of his wife, daughter or servant, and every good maiden and woman stood in dread of being ravished and defiled. And besides this, what discords, civil war, effusion of Christian men's blood were done and committed within the same, especially by the destruction of the noble blood of this land, is evident and notorious through all this realm, to the great sorrow and sadness of all true Englishmen.

1.12 Kingship and the rule of law: the royal monopoly of justice

To assume judicial power by acting without the requisite authority or reasonably appropriate justification was not simply to usurp the mantle of royal justice, but also to undermine the whole system by providing an alternative jurisdiction.[17] Although accused of usurping royal powers and judicial murder, the offenders in

---

16 Elizabeth Woodville, whom Edward IV married secretly in 1464. Richard's title rested largely on his claim (in canon law) that as a result of Edward IV's pre-contract of marriage with Eleanor Butler prior to his marriage to Elizabeth Woodville, Edward V was illegitimate.

17 See Chapter 2 which contains various examples of occasions when royal powers were aped and appropriated.

this passage may in fact have been exercising summary jurisdiction (by decapitation) on outlaws.[18] Such conduct was traditionally accepted, but by the fifteenth century required an appearance in court and public exoneration. This may account for the fact that when they appeared in court they all presented royal pardons.[19] An important corollary to the power of judgment was exercise of the royal prerogative of mercy.

TNA JUST 3/188 m. 49 [Latin]

DELIVERY OF THE KING'S GAOL AT LEICESTER BEFORE WILLIAM THIRNING AND ROBERT TIRWHIT, JUSTICES COMMISSIONED TO DELIVER THE SAID GAOL, ON THE MONDAY AFTER THE FEAST OF ST MARGARET IN THE NINTH YEAR OF THE REIGN OF KING HENRY IV [23 July 1408]

Nicholas Holt, William Bate of Saxby, Richard Barsby, John Dalby, chaplain, William Cook of Thorpe Satchville and John Green of the same were arrested on the grounds that:

Whereas on Monday after the feast of the Translation of St Thomas the Martyr in the eighth year of the reign of King Henry IV [11 July 1407], Richard Bradford and Robert Webster came to visit Nicholas Holt at his house at Thorpe Satchville [Leics.] because of the sincere love and affection which they had towards the said Nicholas, and asked him for food and drink as they had done many times before, the said Richard Barsby and others, servants of Nicholas Holt, on the day and at the place aforesaid, seized the said Richard Bradford and Robert Webster, assaulted them and placed them in chains, and held them prisoner until the arrival of the said Nicholas, William Bate, William Cook and John Green.

The accused then falsely and feloniously discussed and planned amongst themselves how they might kill the said Richard Bradford and Robert Webster, and chose the said Nicholas Holt and William Bate as judges to condemn them to death; then the said Nicholas and William, together with the other accused, falsely and feloniously usurping and taking upon themselves the royal power and without any legal authority, condemned the said Richard Bradford and Robert Webster to be beheaded. Afterwards, on the following Wednesday [13 July 1407] in the same place ... the said Nicholas Holt and William Bate forced a certain John Brace, servant of Nicholas, against his will and in fear of his life, to behead the

---

18 For a murder passed off as a legitimate exercise of summary justice see 7.15.

19 For further discussion of pardons and examples of the pardoning of offences see Chapter 5.

said Richard Bradford and Robert Webster in the presence of the said Nicholas and all the felons named above. After they had beheaded the two men, the said Nicholas and the other felons named above buried the bodies of the said Richard Bradford and Robert Webster in a field and sent their heads to Leicester, against the crown and dignity of the lord king and to the manifest weakening and detriment of his laws.

[Nicholas Holt, Richard Barsby, John Dalby, William Cook and John Green subsequently appeared in court and presented royal pardons.]

1.13 Kingship and the rule of law: the limits of royal power

These recommendations occur in what has been regarded by some to be an addition to (or interpolation in) the text of *Bracton* and reflect the heated debate during the first half of the thirteenth century as to whether the king had peers and could be legitimately constrained. It closely follows real-life events during the reign of Henry III, namely judgment in the Upavon case in 1234, regarding exercise of the royal will.[20] This passage seems to refute an earlier section of the treatise that maintained that the king had no earthly peer and submitted voluntarily to the law.

Bracton, *De Legibus*, ed. Woodbine, vol. 2, p. 110 [Latin]

The king has a superior, namely God. Also the law by which he is made king. Also his *curia*, namely the earls and barons, because if he is without bridle, that is without law, they ought to put the bridle on him. That is why the earls are called the partners of the king; he who has a partner (*socium*) has a master.

1.14 Kingship and the rule of law: the limits of royal power

This episode dramatised by the chronicler Matthew Paris concerns the robbery of foreign merchants in the pass of Alton, near Winchester in 1248, which was tried in the Hampshire eyre of 1249.[21] It illustrates the king's personal concern for justice and underlines the serious attitude adopted towards law breaking committed in the presence of the king. This is dramatic licence on the part of the chronicler as in fact Henry III was at Winchester during the sessions of the eyre rather than at the time of the robbery. The passage also underlines the

20 Upavon manor (Wilts.) was taken from Peter de Maulay by Henry III in 1228 and granted in hereditary right by royal charter to Gilbert Basset. In 1232 Henry arbitrarily disseised Basset of the manor and returned it to Maulay: see D. Carpenter, *The Reign of Henry III* (London, Hambledon Press, 1996), pp. 37–43.
21 Clanchy, 'Highway robbery', pp. 25–61.

limits of royal power. The monarch may have had a monopoly of justice and the theoretic underpinnings for his exercising of power, but in reality he was reliant on the co-operation of his subjects in the upholding of law and order. The refusal of jurors to come forward with indictments and the participation of members of the gentry in the robbery highlights some of the problems faced. Henry's personal appeal therefore appears very much a last resort, though his desire to call upon the whole kingdom to locate the malefactors and their accomplices reflects the perceived reach of the agencies carrying out royal inquiries. This was also reflected in the use of approvers[22] to try and gain information about the crime and its perpetrators. The apparent frankness and sense of exasperation portrayed in the passage was supposedly characteristic of Henry III and offers a glimpse of the man behind the crown.

Matthew Paris, *Chronica Majora*, ed. H. R. Luard (7 vols; RS, 1872–84), vol. 5, pp. 57–8. Henry III's speech at Winchester in 1249 to the men of Hampshire after the Alton Pass robbery [Latin]

The lord king therefore called a gathering of the bailiffs and free men of the same county, namely Hampshire. And said to them with a scowling look: 'What is it that I hear concerning you? The complaint of the despoiled has reached me. Out of necessity I have to come to investigate. There is no county or neighbourhood in the whole breadth of England so infamous or disgraced by such crimes. For when I am present, in the same city or suburbs or in adjoining places there have been robberies and homicides. Nor are these bad things all. Even my own wine exposed both to plunder and pillage is carried off by these malefactors, laughing and getting drunk as they go. Can such things can be tolerated further? To eradicate this and like crimes, I have commissioned wise men to rule and guard my kingdom together with me. I am but one man; I do not want, nor am I able, to carry alone the burden of the whole kingdom without co-operation. I am ashamed and weary of the stench of this city and the adjacent area. I was born in this city, and never was such disgrace inflicted on me as here. It is probable, however, and believable and now fairly well apparent, that you citizens and compatriots are infamous accomplices and confederates. I will call together all the counties of England, so that they might detect your crimes, judging you as traitors to me, nor will guileful arguments profit you further.'

22 Criminals turning king's evidence – see Chapter 5.

II: 'POPULAR' CONCEPTS OF LAW AND JUSTICE

Having examined the formal definitions and theoretical notions of law and justice it is important to survey some of the alternative and more 'popular' perceptions of them.[1] Just as there was no single authoritative or comprehensive text outlining concepts of law and justice prevailing in late medieval England so there cannot be said to have been a unified or authentic 'popular' attitude towards them. Indeed the term 'popular' itself is far from straightforward and unproblematic. We should not assume that as 'a system of shared meanings, attitudes and values, and the symbolic forms in which they are expressed or embodied',[2] 'popular' culture represented a coherent or integrated belief system, irrespective of gender, geography and social environment.[3] Indeed, challenges to the practical application of the official notions of justice came from a broad range of persons touched by the increasing scope of royal justice and other forms of royal intrusion in the shires.[4]

If, however, we are looking for evidence of the attitudes of the peasantry and lower echelons of urban society it is now acknowledged that members of these groups were actively engaged in debate on the local and national stages (whether exhibited physically in terms of violent confrontations or more peacefully, but no less forcefully, within the legal arena).[5] The behaviour and actions of peasant and urban communities have been analysed in the context of complex rituals

1 Powell, *Kingship*, pp. 38–44; M. Hicks, *English Political Culture in the Fifteenth Century* (London and New York, Routledge, 2002), pp. 116–40.

2 Definition of culture from A. L. Kroeber and C. Kluckhohn, *Culture: a Critical Review of Concepts and Definitions* new edn (New York, 1963) cited in Prologue to P. Burke, *Popular Culture in Early Modern Europe*, revised and repr. (Aldershot, Ashgate, 1994) p. x.

3 T. Harris, 'Problematising popular culture', in *Popular Culture in England, c.1500–1850*, ed. T. Harris (Basingstoke, Macmillan, 1995), pp. 1–27; see also R. Scribner, 'Is a history of popular culture possible?' *History of European Ideas*, 10 (1989), 175–91.

4 J. R. Maddicott, 'The English peasantry and the demands of the crown, 1294–1341', in *Landlords, Peasants and Politics in Medieval England* , ed. T. H. Aston (Cambridge, Cambridge University Press, 1987), pp. 285–359; C. Dyer, 'The social and economic background to the rural revolt of 1381', in *The English Rising of 1381*, ed. R. H. Hilton and T. H. Ashton (Cambridge, Cambridge University Press, 1984), pp. 9–42; C. Carpenter, 'Law, justice and landowners in late medieval England', *LHR*, 1 (1983), 225–31.

5 R. H. Hilton, *Bond Men Made Free: Medieval Peasant Movements and the English Rising of 1381* (London, Methuen, 1977); R. B. Goheen, 'Peasant politics? Village communities and the crown in fifteenth-century England', *AHR*, 96 (1991), 42–62; D. A. Carpenter, 'English peasants in politics, 1258–1267', *P&P*, 136 (1992), 3–42; A. Harding, 'The revolt against the justices', in *The English Rising of 1381*, ed. Hilton and Ashton pp. 165–93; C. Liddy, 'Urban conflict in late fourteenth-century England: the case of York in 1380–81', *EHR*, 118 (2003), 1–32.

and festive drama, for which the law or its administration provided a setting or point of contact in many instances.[6] The examples provided here had a variety of catalysts: discontent at food shortages and royal exactions; heightened expectations and disappointments; perceptions of misbehaviour on the part of officials as well as the abusive exercise of lordship. The responses (opinions, ideas, actions and gestures) occur against a backdrop of civic struggles, uncertain local conditions and turbulent periods in national politics. In particular definite agendas emerged in connection with large-scale movements for reform such as the so-called Peasants' Revolt (1381) and Cade's Rebellion (1450).[7]

Since the views of the majority of the peasantry and urban artisans, especially the non-literate and disaffected, were not recorded or remained unformulated, it is difficult to reconstruct their perceptions. 'Popular' concepts of law and justice can nevertheless be filtered from the records of public encounters or gleaned from details contained by chance in other documentary sources or in literary works.[8] [**2.12**] To aid recovery of such elements, attention can also be paid to the expression of 'popular' opinion as revealed through gesture and action. Delivering prisoners from gaols and affixing rabbits to the pillory had symbolic resonance with regard to the exercise of jurisdiction and the rights of lordship. [**2.6, 2.7**] Analysis of these attitudes points towards a distinct awareness of the workings of justice and employment of legal concepts. It highlights an understanding of the power of legal documents among the lower echelons of society, and betrays their particular perceptions of the role of the king.

Modern commentators have pointed to the level of legal awareness displayed at certain 'flashpoints' and the apparent sophistication of the lower social classes' responses to royal government.[9] The sources accordingly reveal an underlying grasp of natural law concepts of fairness and justice, right and *ius*, often underpinned by reference to custom, reason and a symbolic body of law or quasi-law (such as Magna Carta, Domesday Book or the 'law of Winchester').[10] [**2.9–11**,

6 C. Phythian Adams, 'Rituals of personal confrontation in late medieval England', *BJRL*, 73 (1991), 76–89; C. Humphrey, *The Politics of Carnival: Festive Misrule in Medieval England* (Manchester, Manchester University Press, 2001).

7 *The Peasants' Revolt of 1381*, ed. R. B. Dobson 2nd edn (London, Macmillan, 1983); I. M. W. Harvey, *Jack Cade's Rebellion of 1450* (Oxford, Clarendon Press, 1991).

8 A. J. Prescott, 'Judicial records of the rising of 1381', unpublished PhD thesis, University of London, 1984; R. F. Green, *A Crisis of Truth: Law and Literature in Ricardian England* (Philadelphia, University of Pennsylvania Press, 1999); S. Justice, *Writing and Rebellion: England in 1381* (Berkeley and Los Angeles, CA, and London, University of California Press, 1994).

9 N. Brooks, 'The organization and achievements of the peasants of Kent and Essex in 1381' in *Studies in Medieval History Presented to R. H. C. Davies*, ed. H. Mayr-Harting and R. I. Moore (London, Hambledon Press, 1985), pp. 247–70; W. M. Ormrod, 'The peasants' revolt and the government of England', *JBS*, 29 (1990), 2–19.

10 Powell, *Kingship*, pp. 43–4; A. Musson, 'Appealing to the past: perceptions of law in late medieval England', in *Expectations*, ed. Musson, pp. 165–79; *Select Cases in Manorial Courts*, ed. L. Poos and L. Bonfield, SS, 114 (1997), pp. xxx–xxxi; J. R. Maddicott, 'Poems of social protest in early fourteenth-century England', in *England in the Fourteenth Century*, ed. W. M. Ormrod (Woodbridge, Boydell Press, 1986), pp. 138–41.

2.13⌉ The 'alternative' platforms offered by the lower echelons of society, and indeed the court actions initiated by them, betray some understanding of legal forms and administrative procedure from which their access to legal advice or a basic understanding of the workings of the law can be inferred.[11] Unfree tenants who invoked 'ancient demesne'* status did so because they knew that this gave them an advantage over other villeins in allowing them access to the common law.[12]

Actions at times of political upheaval or during isolated manifestations of discontent demonstrate an appropriation of royal forms and procedure (by way of either simple parody or close imitation). In a sense, we should not be surprised that royal forms (such as the language and style of proclamation) were employed since they were a familiar part of everyday life and easily understood. Proclamation of statutes, decrees and royal instructions in public places within the county was a common occurrence. Since they were delivered in English (translated from the French or Latin), the stock phrases would be well known and easily repeatable, thereby creating a sense of quasi-royal authority.[13]

As was noted in the previous chapter, a formal royal commission was required for carrying out judicial functions. This did not stop the disaffected or legally minded from holding 'mock' trials (as occurred in 1344 in Ipswich following sessions of the court of king's bench) ⌈**2.3**⌉ or sitting in actual judgment on prisoners (as happened in 1381 to some of those released from gaols).[14] Literary precedents for alternative or 'rough' justice as illustrated in Langland's *Piers Plowman* and the anonymous *Tale of Gamelyn* were thus played out in reality. ⌈**2.5**⌉ As Strohm points out, literary works inhabit 'the ill-defined zone between imagination and social practice … in which texts stand the best chance of changing the way people actually behave'.[15]

11 P. Hyams, 'What did Edwardian villagers understand by law?', in *Medieval Society and the Manor Court*, ed. Z. Razi and R. M. Smith (Oxford, Clarendon Press, 1996), pp. 69–102; R. Faith, 'The "great rumour" of 1377 and peasant ideology', in *English Rising of 1381*, ed. Hilton and Aston, pp. 43–73; P. R. Schofield, 'Peasants and the manor court: gossip and litigation in a Suffolk village at the close of the thirteenth century', *P&P*, 159 (1998), 3–48; R. M. Smith, 'Some thoughts on "hereditary" and "proprietary" rights in land under customary law in thirteenth and early fourteenth century England', *LHR*, 1 (1983), 95–128.

12 R. S. Hoyt, *The Royal Demesne in English Constitutional History, 1066–1272* (Ithaca, NY, 1950), pp. 192–207; M. J. McIntosh, *Autonomy and Community: The Royal Manor of Havering, 1200–1500* (Cambridge, Cambridge University Press, 1986), pp. 42–9.

13 Clanchy, *Memory*, p. 266; J. A. Doig, 'Political propaganda and royal proclamations in late medieval England', *HR*, 71 (1998), 258–60; Justice, *Writing and Rebellion*, pp. 13–14, 66–8.

14 Note also the forcible abduction of Robert Baldock in 1326 when imprisoned in Bishop Orleton's London home (having been sentenced to perpetual internment) so that the London mob could 'try' him in the rightful gaol of the city, Newgate: *Annales Paulini* in *Chronicles of the Reigns of Edward I and Edward II*, ed. W. Stubbs (2 vols; RS, 1882–83), vol. 1, pp. 320–21.

15 P. Strohm, *Hochon's Arrow: The Social Imagination of Fourteenth-Century Texts* Princeton, NJ, Princeton University Press, 1992), p. 99.

In the absence of a special royal commission it is apparent that justification for murderous actions by 'the crowd' could be sought simply by using the word 'traitor'. Treason as an offence received precise definition in the Statute of Treasons of 1352.[16] However, the non-institutional understanding of the scope of the crime and the process of 'trying' offenders did not necessarily coincide with the official one. In practice, therefore, 'treason' carried a range of meanings and there was potential ambiguity, particularly when it was employed as a watchword.[17] [2.1] The emotive term acquired (at least in 1381) a 'popular' currency to include anyone in a position of authority who was deemed to be acting against the interests of the realm. The beheading of those officials and lawyers informally adjudged to be 'traitors' was probably justified psychologically by the widespread practice of exercising summary judgment on notorious outlaws and traitors, which, although no longer legally acceptable, retained its customary force, particularly in the border regions.[18]

The legal system was increasingly dependent upon the use of the written word in matters of legal proof and judicial administration. Documents and charters, the products of a literate culture, were required to be produced in court and at all levels of the judicial system records of the proceedings were enrolled. Record-keeping and a familiarity with writs, charters and written agreements filtered down the social scale during the thirteenth and early fourteenth centuries with the consequence that the majority of the peasantry and lower echelons of urban society gained confidence in a literate culture and consequently raised their expectations.[19] There is evidence that letters 'as if in royal style' (*quasi sub stilo regio*) were written by men who came not from the lower classes, but gentry families.[20] In their identification with those standing outside the law and in opposition to royal government we may observe in this context a narrowing of ostensible class distinctions.

An awareness of the significance of legal documents and public records as well as tacit acknowledgement of their power can be observed in the behaviour exhibited towards them. A desire to prevent alterations to customary services and maintain traditional rents led groups of peasants from the thirteenth century onwards to claim their land had 'ancient desmesne' status (that the land was part of the royal estate at the time of Edward the Confessor or William the Conqueror) and seek to have it (and thus the advantages such status brought)

16 25 Edward III st. 5 (*SR*, vol. 1, pp. 319–20).

17 Bellamy, *Treason*. For an examination of these concepts from a literary point of view see Green, *Law and Literature*, pp. 208–37.

18 C. J. Neville, 'The law of treason in the English border counties in the later Middle Ages', *LHR*, 9 (1991), 1–30.

19 M. Prestwich, 'English government records', in *Pragmatic Literacy, East and West, 1200–1330*, ed. R. Britnell (Woodbridge, Boydell Press, 1997), pp. 95–106; Clanchy, *Memory*, pp. 76–8; W. M. Ormrod, 'Robin Hood and public record: the authority of writing in the medieval outlaw tradition', in *Medieval Cultural Studies: Essays in Honour of Stephen Knight*, ed. R. Evans, H. Fulton and David Mathews (Cardiff, University of Wales Press, 2006), pp. 57–74.

20 Stones, 'Folvilles', 117–36; J. G. Bellamy, 'The Coterel gang: an anatomy of a band of fourteenth-century criminals', *EHR*, 79 (1964), 698–717.

proved in court through the judgment of Domesday Book.[21] Their actions were fuelled by reliance upon the symbolic book and on their confidence in the legal system's ability to uphold their claims. The ambivalent nature of their appreciation of the significance of record-keeping was demonstrated during the 1381 rebellion when both reverent and destructive attitudes towards legal records were witnessed.

The reverential attitude can be seen, for example, in a desire to cloak actions in the legitimacy conferred by royal authority. A number of rebels in 1381 claimed to possess royal commissions giving them authority to deal with traitors. Even Wat Tyler (it was said) sought a commission for his desired extermination of all men of law. The symbolic power of a royal document when in someone's personal possession could be employed to specific effect. It could be used to induce awe (perhaps in ignorance of its text) and to justify (either in advance or retrospectively) 'popular' actions.[22] A more destructive attitude can be observed in the deliberate searches for charters and other muniments and demands from officials for their plea rolls or rolls of the manor court, which were then symbolically burnt in public. Even this behaviour, however, was not simply mindless destruction by an illiterate peasantry, but betrayed an element of premeditation and purpose in its challenge to seignorial jurisdiction.[23]

The pivotal position of the king in relation to 'popular' concepts and activities is equally noteworthy and suggests an acceptance of the quasi-divine royal characteristics that were displayed on coins, seals and other royal images and were part and parcel of official ideology and propaganda. The disaffected and the outlaw, as with the urban and peasant rebels, wished to uphold royal rule, even if they somewhat naively expected the king to champion their cause.[24] As the periodic pursuit of 'traitors' and the sentiments of the letter ascribed to 'Lionel, king of the rout of raveners' [2.2] demonstrate, 'popular' action was taken to remedy situations and provide a supplement to royal justice when and where it was considered not to be working effectively. Generally, the movements against royal authority were highly politicised, with reasoned objections to government policies put forward. However, it was royal ministers and legal officials, the exponents of the law and the king's advisers, who were targeted rather than specifically the king himself. The intention appears to have been to cleanse the system rather than overthrow it completely.[25]

21 P. R. Schofield, *Peasant and Community in Medieval England, 1200–1500* (Basingstoke, Palgrave Macmillan, 2003), pp. 16–17; Faith, 'Great rumour', pp. 43–73.

22 Prescott, 'Judicial records', p. 103; Ormrod, 'Peasants' revolt', 15.

23 Musson, *Medieval Law*, pp. 244–6.

24 Ormrod, *Political Life*, p. 63; R. W. Kaeuper, *Chivalry and Violence in Medieval Europe* (Oxford, Oxford University Press, 1999), pp. 113–18; W. M. Ormrod, 'Law in the landscape: criminality, outlawry and regional identity', in *Boundaries*, ed. Musson, pp. 7–20; A. J. Pollard, *Imagining Robin Hood: the Late Medieval Stories in Historical Context* (London and New York, Routledge, 2004).

25 Ormrod, 'Peasants' revolt', 13–14, 17, 25–6; M. Bush, 'The risings of the commons in England, 1381–1549', in *Orders and Hierarchies in Medieval and Renaissance Europe*, ed. J. Denton (Toronto, University of Toronto Press, 1999), pp. 109–16.

2.1 The murder of Walter Stapeldon, bishop of Exeter, for treason (1326)

This event occurred during the politically troubled final year of Edward II's reign. In the wake of Queen Isabella's invasion many Londoners were determined to put to death anyone who opposed her or endangered their liberties.[1] The mob's beheading of the bishop of Exeter (to whom the king had entrusted the keepership of the city of London) followed the popular and emotive rallying cry of 'traitor'. According to one chronicler, Queen Isabella thanked the mayor of the city 'for his late bloody act, which was styled an excellent piece of justice'.[2] In this context treason is not given its strict legal definition, but can be shown in popular usage to have embraced wider concepts such as breach of trust or oath of office. The Londoners apparently believed that the king, on the bishop's advice, had ensured that few criminals were punished in the city courts. Moreover, according to one chronicler, Stapeldon had demanded the keys to the city gates from the mayor of London. Worried about their liberties and the lack of obvious signs of justice they reacted accordingly with their own style of retribution. The bishop's body was later reburied in Exeter Cathedral and an inquiry launched into the circumstances of the murder, but not until three years after the event.[3]

Croniques de London, ed. G. J. Aungier, Camden Society, original series, 28 (1844), p. 52 [French]

Proclamation was made in Cheapside that the enemies of the king and the queen and their son ought to leave the city immediately on peril of what might happen ... The same day at the same hour [noon] a certain Sir Walter de Stapeldon that was bishop of Exeter, and the year before treasurer to the king, came riding towards his house in Old Deans Lane to his dinner and there was proclaimed a traitor. And he hearing the cry rode in flight towards St Paul's and was there encountered and unhorsed and taken to Cheapside and there he was robbed and his head cut off. And one of his squires, who was a robust man, who went by the name of William Walle, fled and was stopped at London Bridge and taken to Cheapside and beheaded. And another squire, John of Paddington, keeper of the aforesaid bishop's manor outside Temple, who was believed to have done wrong, was beheaded the same day in Cheapside. The same day close to evening the monks of St Paul's came and took the body of the said bishop without its head and carried

1 R. M. Haines, *King Edward II: Edward of Caernarfon, His Life, His Reign and Its Aftermath, 1284–1330* (Montreal and Kingston, McGill-Queen's University Press, 2003), pp. 178–80, 182–3.

2 *Croniques de London*, ed. Aungier, p. 53.

3 M. C. Buck, 'Stapeldon, Walter (b. in or before 1265, d. 1326)', *ODNB*.

it to St Paul's. They had been given to understand that he had died excommunicate because of which the body was carried to the church of St Clement outside Temple Bar [St Clement Danes] and those of the church put the body outside. And it is said that women and poor persons took the naked body, but a woman gave an old sheet to cover his belly and they laid him in waste ground without digging a grave. And his squires naked too were placed near to him without the offices of a priest or clerk and the place is called the Lawless Church.

2.2 A threatening letter from 'Lionel, king of the rout of raveners' (1336)

The survival of this text derives from its enrolment in the king's bench plea rolls after the recipient brought it to the attention of the king's council. We know from the records that a number of threatening letters demanding ransom were issued to their targets by criminal gangs operating in the early 1330s.[4] The sophistication of this letter suggests that it was not the product of common criminals or members of a low social class. It is written in French and employs the language of the romances. It equally demonstrates an understanding of legal terminology and procedure, not only employing the form of address and formulae of a royal writ,[5] but making subtle alterations, such as reversing the usual word order of the address clause. The letter is addressed to Richard de Snowshill, who was rector of Huntington in Yorkshire and the archbishop of York's administrator, and operates on several levels. Its tone is threatening and is clearly meant as a warning. Snowshill was sufficiently intimidated (perhaps fearing he would suffer the fate of the bishop of Exeter) to take it to the king immediately. On another level Lionel's rule is set up as an alternative form of justice, one that is to be taken seriously, although he does not actually claim precedence over God or the king of England. On another level still it functions as a petition to the archbishop of York (through his emissary) concerning rival candidates (unnamed) seeking ecclesiastical preferment through presentation to the benefice of Burton Agnes by rival patrons.[6] The reference to 'the Greenwood' evokes the habitat of the outlaw and provides a powerful symbol of that fictional alternative world.[7]

TNA KB 27/306 *Rex* m. 27 [French]

4 HMC, *Reports on the Manuscripts of Lord Middleton* (London, 1911), pp. 278–9; Stones, 'Folvilles', 134–5.

5 J. Watts, 'Looking for the state in later medieval England', in *Heraldry, Pageantry and Social Display in Medieval England*, ed. P. Coss and M. Keen (Woodbridge, Boydell Press, 2002), pp. 243–4.

6 A. Musson, 'Attitudes to justice in fourteenth-century Yorkshire', *Northern History*, 39 (2002), 173–85.

7 See Chapter 8.

Lionel, king of the rout of raveners, to our false and disloyal Richard de Snowshill, greeting without love. We command you on pain of whatever you may forfeit to us and to our laws that you, on seeing these our letters, should utterly abandon the maintenance of your candidate for the vicarage of Burton Agnes [Yorks.] and allow the abbot of our lady of Bootham[8] to have his right; so that his choice may take effect in favour of the man to whom he has granted the vicarage, who is more fit for advancement than you or any of your family. And if you do not do this we swear, first by the king of Heaven then by the king of England and our crown, that you will have such orders from us as the bishop of Exeter had in Cheapside,[9] and that you will be found, even in Coney Street [York].

Show this letter to your lord, and tell him to leave aside his treacherous schemes and confederacies, and to allow that right be done to the man whom the abbot has presented, or by the aforesaid oaths he will suffer one thousand pounds' worth of damage at the hands of us and our men. And if you will not obey our commands we shall command our sheriff of the North to make great distraint* upon you as abovesaid.

Given at our castle of the North Wind in the Tower of the Greenwood in the first year of our reign.

2.3 Mock judicial sessions at Ipswich (1344)

The imitation of legal forms and procedures (including the *sub poena* writ)[10] is manifested in an incident that occurred in Ipswich, Suffolk, probably in August 1344 during judicial sessions held in the borough. The justices who were targeted (and whose appearance was demanded), Shareshull and Notton, had sat in the county earlier in the year under the unpopular 'new inquiries' commissions issued in 1343 (which included a detailed list of articles concerning illicit export of wool and coin and aid given to the king's enemies).[11] The heavy penalties exacted by such commissions gave rise to serious complaints of 'outrageous fines and ransoms' in the 1344 parliament.[12] The murder of John Holtby (for his role in supporting the king's interests) and the mock sessions involving the summoning of the justices (detailed below) may have been a local reaction to this.

8 St Mary's Abbey, York.

9 See 2.1 above.

10 A writ requiring the presence of a named individual under a stated penalty for non-attendance: see W. M. Ormrod, 'The origins of the *sub poena* writ', *HR*, 61 (1988), 11–20.

11 *CPR 1343–45*, p. 98 (1 December 1343).

12 *RP*, vol. 2, p. 238.

TNA KB 27/338 m. 162d [Latin]

Memorandum that in Michaelmas term in the eighteenth year of the reign of King Edward III [1344] when the king's bench was sitting at Ipswich and many evildoers were there indicted before the lord king concerning the death of John of Holtby feloniously killed there because the same John was going about the king's business there in front of William Shareshull and his colleagues, justices of the present king assigned to hear and determine sundry felonies and trespasses in the county of Suffolk, the lord king was then and there given to understand that, immediately after the aforesaid felony was committed, many of the same town, both from the greater and the middling and lesser sorts of people, in encouragement, consolation and comfort of the aforesaid evildoers and others who have behaved themselves badly against the peace of the lord king and causing alarm to everybody else who willingly accepted the lord king's peace, brought to the aforesaid felons, in subversion of the peace of the crown and the dignity of the lord king, presents in the form of food and drink and gold and silver and sang to them there so many sublimely joyous songs that it was as if God had come down from Heaven.

The king was also given to understand that after the aforesaid William Shareshull and his aforesaid colleagues had completed their session in the same town according to the terms of the lord king's commission held by them and had departed from the same town, the aforesaid evildoers and many other accomplices of theirs from the same town came to the hall of pleas in the same town and sitting on the steps of the same hall there, caused proclamation to be made that the aforesaid William Shareshull was to appear before them under penalty of a hundred pounds and William Notton under penalty of forty pounds and similarly they summoned many others who appeared on behalf of the lord king in the session of the aforesaid justices, some under penalty of twenty pounds and others under penalty of ten pounds and some at more and others at less, in contempt of the king and in mockery of the aforesaid justices and ministers of the lord king in his devoted service.

2.4 Quasi-royal initiatives during social unrest in Boston, Lincolnshire (1347)

The capacity of ordinary people to appropriate and use for their own purposes the modes of organisation and standard administrative procedures favoured by royal (and civic) government is demonstrated here. The rebels are specifically accused of lacking the requisite authorisation for their actions and operating outside the proper jurisdiction of the law. Interestingly the king and his people are invoked as a joint entity of governance. In a fusion of military and civic duties the rebels have elected a 'captain and mayor' and it is claimed that they threaten and have carried out various 'misdeeds', possibly instances of their own 'rough justice'.

TNA C 66/221 m. 22d [Latin]

The king to his beloved and faithful Gilbert de Umfraville, earl of Angus, Nicholas Cantilupe, John Willoughby, Hugh Hastings, John Kirkton, William Thorp, Richard Willoughby and William Skipwith, greeting. Because we are given to understand that certain evildoers and disturbers of the peace, having associated themselves with many other evildoers and disturbers of our peace mutually confederate in countless numbers in the town of Boston [Lincs.] and neighbouring districts, and drawing to themselves royal power have risen up in manner of war against us, our crown, dignity and rule and against the honest men and merchants of the aforesaid town and others living in the same town, and have chosen between them a certain Thomas of Holkham, cordwainer, an evildoer of similar kind, as captain and mayor, and have boarded hostilely and in warlike fashion various ships of various merchants and others of our faithful subjects carrying corn and various foodstuffs, goods and merchandise to a limitless value with our licence in the port of the said town, and have notoriously plundered the said merchants and the masters of ships and their mariners of the aforesaid corn, goods and merchandise, and many others of our faithful people in the town of their goods and merchandise, and with force and arms they have arrested men coming to the aforesaid town and other honest men of the said town who were unwilling to allow their wrongdoings and by fear of death have compelled them to swear to maintain their misprisions and plaints promoted by them for their part treacherously against us and our aforesaid royal power and our people, the which same felons and evildoers, so they could make swifter preparation for such felonies and wrongdoing have ordained among themselves for a certain common bell to be rung for the purpose of summoning them frequently before this time to prepare themselves for felonies and wrongdoing and they have committed felonies, treacheries and wrongdoings and perjuries and have also made quasi-royal proclamations and prohibitions that each and every person who has withdrawn from the town on the occasion of this aforesaid dissension shall return to the said town within a certain time to maintain the misprisions and plaints aforesaid or they will cause their houses within the aforesaid town to be pulled to the ground and the timber thereof and all their goods and chattels in the said town to be burned, and have committed and daily commit many other crimes, felonies and misdeeds within the said town and outside and have made and daily make other proclamations, under grave penalties to be inflicted by them both on their own authority and without process of law in contempt and betrayal of us and breach of our peace and against the form of the statute promulgated concerning not carrying arms against our peace[13] and our proclamations and prohibitions made often thereon, and also in terror of our people and open disruption, we assign you to inquire, hear and determine[14] the aforesaid treachery, felonies and misdeeds that have been so perpetrated as we are unwilling to leave them unpunished.

2.5 Concepts of 'rough justice' in literature

(a) Langland's *Piers Plowman*

The poet discusses here types of labour and the apportioned talents for occupations, notably the art of persuasion practised by lawyers. Towards the end the tone alters as he claims that some people specialise in the recovery (and perhaps redistribution) of unjust gains. The importance of a strong hand is highlighted and it is implied that recovery against 'false men' will be through the kind of restorative justice practised by outlaws. These lines (probably written in the late 1370s) immortalise the real-life band of brothers, the Folvilles, who were from the gentry class, but were outlawed following the murder of royal judge Roger Bellers in 1326.[15] The phrase 'Folvilles laws' suggests that in the popular mind there existed certain concepts of justice equated with the righting of wrongs and the overturning of established judicial machinery when it was considered to be operating unreasonably. The implication is that these so-called rules would take effect against all deceit and unfairness practised in the courts. The text is ambiguous, however, on whether 'Folvilles laws' are beneficial. It could be read that men are false because they use 'Folvilles laws'.

13 Statute of Northampton (1328) c. 3.

14 The phrase 'hear and determine' is used to indicate trial of the matter: see Chapter 4.

15 Stones, 'Folvilles', pp. 117–36; see also 3.2.

William Langland, *Piers Plowman*, ed. D. Pearsall (Exeter, University of Exeter Press, 1994), pp. 350–52 (C text XXI, ll. 229–51) [English]

To some men he gave wit with words to declare,
To win with truth what the world asks,
As priests and preachers and apprentices of law:
They to live honestly by labour of the tongue
And by wit to instruct others as Grace would teach them.
And some he instructed in crafts and cunning of sight,
With selling and buying their living to win.
And some he taught to labour on land and on water
And live by that labour an honest life and true.
And some he taught to plough, to thatch and to cook,
As their wit would when the time comes.
And some to divine and to divide numbers,
And to take measurements skilfully and colours to make.
And some to see and to say what should befall
Both of joy and of woe and be aware before it occurred,
As astronomers through astronomy and philosophers wise.
And some to ride and some to recover what unrightfully was won;
He instructed men to win it back again through strength of hands
And to fetch it from false men with Folvilles laws.
And some he taught to live in longing to be hence,[16]
In poverty and penitence to pray for all Christians.
And all he taught to be honest and each craft to love the others
So there should be neither boasting nor quarrelling among them all.

(b) *The Tale of Gamelyn*

The mid-fourteenth-century song of Gamelyn shares some similarities of style and content with the Robin Hood ballads and other examples of outlaw literature such as *Adam Bell*. It is included here as there is a lengthy courtroom scene the details of which demonstrate an understanding of the legal processes. In common with other texts in this genre it emphasises reversals. Gamelyn is forced to act because of the treatment (false indictment) his brother has suffered. He takes the place of the judge and rather than act arbitrarily orders a jury (albeit comprising his own men) to try the new line-up of prisoners (the judge, sheriff and original twelve-man jury) before him. All are convicted and hanged. Gamelyn goes on to be appointed to high judicial office by the king.[17] The audience of the tale may have relished the brutality of the passage

16 Seeking salvation as ascetics.

17 Chief justice of the forest; Sir Ote is also made a justice (ll. 889–92).

(even if it made some officials slightly uncomfortable), though they would
have noted how the hero is reconciled to the authority of the king and
comes to be an accepted part of the legal establishment.[18]

Middle English Verse Romances, ed. D. B. Sands (Exeter, University of Exeter
Press, 1986) (ll. 805–82) [English]

'I see well', said Gamelyn 'the Justice is sitting;
Go ahead, Adam, and see how things are proceeding.'
Adam went into the hall and looked all around,
He saw standing there lords both great and proud,
And Sir Ote his brother very securely fettered;
Then Adam went out of the hall as if he were afraid.
Adam said to Gamelyn and to all his fellows,
'Sir Ote stands fettered in the moot hall.'
'Young men', said Gamelyn 'hear this all of you;
'Sir Ote stands fettered in the moot hall.'
If God gives us grace to succeed,
Whoever brought matters to such a head shall pay for it.'
Then said Adam who had grey locks,
'Christ's curse shall he have who bound him so tight!
If you will, Gamelyn, act according to my plan,
There is none in the hall shall bear away his head.'
'Adam', said Gamelyn 'we will let no one do so,
We will slay the guilty and let the others go.
I will go into the hall and speak with the Justice;
On those that are guilty I will be avenged.
Let none escape by the door; take heed, young men.
For I will be the Justice making judgments today.
God speed me this day at my new work!
Adam, come along with me, for you shall be my clerk.'
. . .
Right where the Justice sat in the hall,
In went Gamelyn amongst them all.
Gamelyn had his brother unfettered from his bonds,
Then said Sir Ote his brother who was courteous,
'You had almost, Gamelyn, waited too long,
For the inquest is out on me[19] that I should hang.'

---

18 R. W. Kaeuper, 'An historian's reading of the tale of Gamelyn', *Medium Aevum*, 52
   (1983), 51–62.

19 The jury has already delivered its verdict.

'Brother,' said Gamelyn 'if God give me good rest! [20]
This day shall be hanged those that have been on your inquest;
And the Justice too that is the Judge,
And the sheriff also through whom it began.'[21]
Then said Gamelyn to the Justice,
'Now your power is ended you must arise;
You have given judgments that are unjustly decided,
I will sit in your seat and rearrange them properly.'
The Justice sat still and did not rise at once,
And Gamelyn split open his cheek bone;
Gamelyn took him by the arm and said no more,
But threw him over the bar and broke his arm.
No one durst say to Gamelyn anything but good,
Terrified of the company that outside stood.
Gamelyn sat himself down in the Justice's seat,
And Sir Ote his brother by him and Adam at his feet.
When Gamelyn was sat in the Justice's stead,
Listen to the joke that Gamelyn played.
He caused to be fettered the Justice and his false brother,
And had them come to the bar, the one with the other,
When Gamelyn had done this he had no rest
Till he had discovered who was on the inquest,
That condemned his brother Sir Ote to hang;
It seemed to him a very long time before he found out who they were.
But as soon as Gamelyn knew where they were,
He had every one of them fettered together,
And brought them to the bar and set them in a row;
'By my faith!' said the Justice, 'the sheriff is a wicked man!'
Then said Gamelyn to the Justice,
'You have given dooms worthy of the worst assize;[22]
And the twelve jurymen that were on the inquest,
They shall be hanged this day, if ever I have rest.'
Then the sheriff said to young Gamelyn,
'Lord, I appeal to you for mercy, you are my brother.'
'For this reason', said Gamelyn 'you shall have Christ's curse,
For if you were master I should indeed have worse.'
So to cut the tale short and not remain long,

20 An oath used several times in the passage.

21 For the process of outlawry see Chapter 5.

22 Judgments appropriate to the worst court or in a most illegal manner.

He established an inquest comprising his own men.
The Justice and the sheriff were both hanged high,
To swing about on the ropes and in the wind dry;
And the twelve jurymen (sorrow may they have that reck)[23]
They were all hanged fast by the neck.

2.6 Symbolic gesture: peasants delivering gaols (1381)

During the rural and urban uprisings of 1381 it is noticeable that gaols (both
royal and privately owned gaols) were targeted by the rebels. The widespread
release of prisoners was not only intended to free specific prisoners (such as
John Ball), but also operated as a symbol of their new order and the erosion of
the authority of the previous one. While it is the natural instinct during any
uprising to free prisoners, the chroniclers' choice of language and the apparent
co-ordination indicate the rebels had (or were perceived to have) a deliberate
plan. The rebels again appropriate royal administrative methods: pledges were
sought for loyalty and good behaviour from prisoners at St Albans (similar
to the royal system of mainprise*). There they also accorded to themselves
judicial powers. Beheading a man who 'deserved death' suggests the playing
out of local squabbles and that they considered him an outlaw or traitor to
their regime.

The Anonimalle Chronicle, 1333–1381, ed. V. H. Galbraith (Manchester, 1927),
pp. 136–7, 140–42 [French]

On the Friday next following [7 June 1381] they arrived at Rochester
and there encountered a great number of the commons of Essex ...
and they laid strong siege to the castle and the constable defended it
vigorously for half a day, but at last for the fear that he had of such a
multitude of people who had irrationally come from Essex and Kent he
delivered the castle to them and they entered it and let out of prison
their companion[24] and all the other prisoners ...

On the Wednesday [12 June 1381] and before the hour of vespers the
commons of Kent, to the grand total of sixty thousand, arrived in Southwark where the Marshalsea prison was, and they broke up and threw to
the ground all the houses of the Marshalsea and removed from prison
all the prisoners that were imprisoned there for debt or for felony ...
And in Fleet Street the said commons of Kent broke open the Fleet

---

23 Show any interest or care.

24 John Ball, a popular preacher, had been imprisoned for attacking the church. On the
basis of his seditious letters and populist sermons he was acknowledged as one of the
leaders of the rebellion and was later put on trial and hanged at St Albans.

prison, removed all the prisoners and let them go where they would ...
And then one party of rebels went towards Westminster ... and broke
open Westminster prison, and let out all the prisoners condemned by
the law.

The St Albans Chronicle: The Chronica maiora *of Thomas Walsingham*, ed. J.
Taylor, W. R. Childs and L. Watkiss (Oxford, Clarendon Press, 2003), vol. 1,
p. 450 [Latin]

Then with considerable arrogance they hastened to the monastery
gates to demonstrate how much power had been gained from the aforesaid Wat Tyler. When they arrived at the gates, which were opened
for them, with unspeakable arrogance they ordered the porter to open
the prison to them ... [The villeins] entered and brought out all the
prisoners, and ordered them to go free on condition that they would in
future be loyal and favourable to the community and wholeheartedly
support them. A certain man, however, whom they adjudged worthy of
death, brought out of prison along with the others, they themselves, as
judges and executioners, beheaded on the large piece of land in front
of the abbey gates; and with the diabolical cry which they had adopted
during the beheading of the archbishop[25] they carried the head and fixed
it to the top of the pillory, so that it might be obvious to everyone that
they were able to bring into action the new laws and were protected by
the new privileges.

2.7 Symbolic gesture: the temporary overthrow of the rights of lordship of St Albans Abbey (1381)

The scenes at St Albans reveal an understanding amongst the townsfolk of the
ceremony of livery of seisin* (and the rights entailed in taking possession) and
demonstrate the use of transgressive symbolic gesture in a political context.
The rabbit embodies the lord's rights of free warren* and it is carried on a spear
as a form of hunting trophy or as if it were a banner or cross in some civic or
religious procession. The pillory, usually situated in the market square, was a
place of public humiliation and punishment and has been appropriated by the
rebels.

Gesta Abbatum Monasterii Sancti Albani, ed. H. T. Riley (3 vols; London, 1867–
69) vol. 3, p. 303 [Latin]

And when they had seen the crowd which came together at their orders,
thinking themselves great men, they were not a little cheered and their

25 Simon Sudbury, archbishop of Canterbury.

spirits were raised; and soon joining together their right hands they took a pledge from each other and ceremonially using the branches of trees they accorded themselves seisin of the warren, of the common woods, of the open spaces in the woods and of the field of free alms* of Sopwell Bury. They took a certain live rabbit, taken by force among them in the open field by the crowd of people and declared that it should be carried before them on a spear and fixed it upon the pillory in the town of St Albans as a symbol of the freedom and of the warren thus gained.

2.8 Symbolic gesture: 'rough music' against the archbishop's official (1303)

The tradition of 'ridings', placing a person backwards on an animal, belonged to a universal repertoire of symbolic punishment and usually signalled public disapprobation, either for offences committed and otherwise unpunished, or for conduct that offended against popular mores.[26] The term 'rough music' is given to the often cacophonous music (whether instrumental or vocal) and dancing accompanying the 'riding', but is also given general application to the whole phenomenon of the ritual itself.[27] It is not clear what Richard Christian had done to offend local opinion, but he may have cited people before the church court.

TNA C 66/123 m. 9d [Latin][28]

The king to his beloved and faithful Roger de Hegham, William Haward and Ralph de Sandwich, greeting. We assign you to hear and determine [the following] complaint of the most venerable father, Robert, archbishop of Canterbury, concerning the persons who, notwithstanding our ordinance for the preservation of our peace during our absence in Scotland, by night invaded the archbishop's dwelling at Canterbury while he was in it, cut to pieces and broke the gates, assaulted the servants and ministers of the said archbishop, carried away his goods and took Richard Christian, the archbishop's dean of Ospringe, sent by the same archbishop to Selling in the county of Kent to make certain

26 R. Mellinkoff, 'Riding backwards: theme of humiliation and symbol of evil', *Viator*, 4 (1973), 153–86.

27 M. Ingram, 'Juridical folklore in England illustrated by rough music', in *Courts and Communities in England, 1100–1900*, ed. C. Brooks and M. Lobban (London, Hambledon Press, 1997), pp. 61–82.

28 The original text of the manuscript roll is now very difficult to discern even under ultraviolet light and so the translated extract draws on the calendared entry (*CPR 1301–7*, pp. 197–8) where necessary.

citations and do other things that were incumbent upon him by reason of his spiritual office, and with his face turned to the horse's rump, holding the tail in his hand instead of the bridle, led him with songs and dances through the middle of the town of Selling, and afterwards cut off the tail, ears and lips of his horse and threw the same Richard into filthy mud and prevented him from exercising the office committed to him by the said archbishop.

2.9 The power of legal documents: a petition from the tenants of Bocking to their manorial lord (early fourteenth century)

This petition from the customary tenants (tenants holding unfree land from a manorial lord according to the custom of the manor) concerns perceived abuses in the holding of the manor court and the extent of their services owed to the manorial lord, in this case the prior of Christ Church, Canterbury, prompted by the arrival of a new steward, who is identified as John le Doo. The petition mentions the holding of the lord's 'leet', which for liberties or hundreds in private hands was the equivalent to the sheriff's tourn or court of the hundred.[29] The language of the petition with its legal and conciliar formulae suggests the originators had access to legal advice. The replies are equally couched in terms similar to those of parliamentary petitions. The petitioners articulate clearly the basis for their complaints: the steward has offended against existing customary practice, the guiding principle of reason and Magna Carta. The lack of consultation regarding customs and practices as well as the novelty and personal intervention on the part of the steward is emphasised by 'of his own conceit'. The passage underlines the importance of the local community in the remembrance of custom and the holding of inquests to adjudicate on manorial issues. The financial implications of the steward's changes are clearly understood. The petitioners focus on the steward's behaviour as they cannot allege wrongs against the prior himself as it is his own court. How far the grievances were remedied is unknown. The petition and reply survive because they were copied into a new rental in the later fourteenth century and this may suggest that some importance was attached either to the issues themselves or to the fact that the petition had been initiated by the tenants.

J. F. Nichols, 'An early fourteenth-century petition from the tenants of Bocking to their manorial lord', *Economic History Review*, 2 (1929–30), 300–7 (Clauses 1, 3 and 8) [French]

[1] To their very dear, honourable and rightful lord, the poor tenants of Bocking pray to your lordship for grace and remedy, that, whereas you have your leet in your manor of Bocking aforesaid on the feast of St

29 Cam, *Hundred Rolls*, pp. 125–7, 186–7.

Matthew [21 September] and the custom of the said manor is such that the tenants for the time being ought to make full presentment through thirty-six 'capital pledges',* duly sworn, on that same day, of matters touching the crown, as of indictments and of purprestures* which may be redressed on that day, and for other matters of which they may be in doubt, they ought to have, and always have had, an opportunity of adjourning for further consideration until the next meeting of the court three weeks later to make full presentment, now comes John le Doo, your bailiff, and, on the first day of the leet on his own understanding, without making inquest, proceeds against the presenting jurors and against reason amerces them on a charge of concealment before present-ment has been made, and for such amercement* has caused them to be heavily distrained,* on which account they pray for remedy.

Reply was made that the deed had not been done by him nor by his wish, and that in future he would not allow such bad things to occur to any tenant of the vill but that they should be maintained in their customs in all matters.

[3] Furthermore, sire, that whereas the aforesaid tenants who were liable to be amerced in your court ought, when so amerced, to be assessed by their peers according to the extent of their trespass, then came the said John le Doo and refused to accept such level of assessment, but has of his own volition, increased their burdens by two or even three times more and by such means has harassed the tenants and brought them to destruction, against all reason and the Great Charter that Holy Church ought to uphold. And for this they pray remedy.

(Reply as above)

[8] Moreover, whereas they ought by reason of their tenure to mow your meadows in your manor aforesaid, and spread the grass and turn and load the hay, and afterwards carry it to your granges, by which service they ought to be and have been accustomed since time imme-morial to be quit of suit of court and of all other services from the day that they commence to mow for the three whole weeks next following, your bailiff John le Doo comes and demands that they shall do suit at your court during the aforesaid three weeks, which demand is evidently against reason and contrary to their customs, and by this pretext he has grievously amerced them and caused them to be distrained, and for this they pray remedy.

(Reply as above)

2.10 The power of legal documents: peasant faith in Domesday Book (1377)

The petition tells us about the concerns and legal activities of groups of peasants as well as the fears of its composers. On one level it suggests that peasants could be organised (both administratively and financially) and (as the indictment (b) below reveals) had gone to the trouble of obtaining legal advice in pursuit of their endeavours. Access to justice is not a problem: they have sought redress legitimately through the mechanisms of the courts and are clearly aware that a transcription of the relevant passage from Domesday Book may provide the necessary legal proof in an action concerning labour services or decide whether the land pertaining to their manor possesses ancient demesne* status. This faith in Domesday Book, occasionally misplaced but often upheld, provided the driving force for a series of peasant claims against tenurial services and implies the Book (as quasi-law) had considerable symbolic as well as practical value.

The petition represents the interests of the manorial lords from whom the peasants hold their land. In its composition, the petition employs the language common to charges of conspiracy and in doing so may be deliberately portraying the peasants as an organised and threatening force. Their precociousness in using the legal system against their lords is highlighted and both they and their legal advisers are portrayed as troublemakers. Interestingly there is a warning of rebellion (a premonition of the Peasants' Revolt) coupled with fear that the peasants would ally with the French (who had recently attacked the English coast). The composers of the petition are thus evoking a threat to the external and internal order of the realm, the defence of which and the maintenance of public order was (as we have seen in Chapter 1) regarded as a priority for the king as ruler.

The indictment demonstrates the desire of the government to identify and prosecute for conspiracy and maintenance (see Chapter 8) those considered to be behind the peasant actions. It also encapsulates the perception that invoking Domesday Book offered the pathway to freedom.

(a)

RP, vol. 3, pp. 21–2 [French]

To our lord the king and to the council of parliament, the commons of the realm show that in many parts of the kingdom the villeins and those holding land in villeinage, who owe services and customs to the lords for whatever reasons within divers lordships both of Holy Church and of lay lords, have through the advice, procurement, maintenance and abetting of certain persons, for money taken from the abovesaid villeins and tenants, purchased in the royal court exemplifications of Domesday

Book concerning manors and vills within which the said villeins and those holding land are living; by colour of which exemplifications, through their evil intention and through wicked interpretation placed on them by the said advisers, procurers, maintainers and abettors, they have withdrawn and are withdrawing their customs and services owed to their lords, maintaining that they are completely discharged of all manner of servitude owed both from their bodies and from their above-said tenures.

And they have refused to let the officials of the said lords distrain* them for the abovesaid customs and services and are confederate and allied to stand against their said lords and their officials by force, and that each will help the other at such a time as they are distrained for that reason; and they threaten to kill the officials of the said lords if they distrain them for the abovesaid customs and services, so that the lords and their officials do not distrain them for their customs and services, out of fear for the death of any man that could easily happen through their rebellion and resistance.

And therefore the said lords are losing and have lost much profit from their lordships to the very great disherison and diminishing of their estate, and the corn of many people in the kingdom remains unharvested and perished forever for the reason abovesaid to the great damage of the whole commonalty; so that there is a fear that unless a remedy is put into action swiftly war could easily break out within the same kingdom because of their abovesaid rebellion, or that they might join with foreign enemies to be avenged on their lords if a sudden invasion of the said enemies occurs. And to sustain these errors and rebellions they have collected between them great sums of money to meet costs and expenses. And many of them have now come to court[30] to obtain encouragement in their abovesaid plans.

Wherefore may it please our said lord the king and the council to ordain due and swift remedy both towards the advisers, procurers, maintainers and abettors and towards the said villeins and tenants and especially towards those who have come now, as has been said, so that those staying in the royal household may have jurisdiction for their punishment and avoid such peril as occurred recently in the kingdom of France[31] by such rebellion and alliance between villeins against their lords.

---

30 Bringing actions in the court of king's bench. Some also petitioned parliament itself.

31 In 1358 there had been a rising in France known as the Jacquerie.

(b)

TNA JUST 3/221 m. 4 [Latin]

INDICTMENTS OF FELONY BEFORE WILLIAM MONTAGUE AND HIS ASSOCIATES, KEEPERS OF THE PEACE OF THE LORD KING IN THE AFORESAID COUNTY [WILTSHIRE] TAKEN IN DIVERS OF THEIR SESSIONS AND UNDETERMINED.

The twelve jurors [named] said ... that John Godfray in the first and second years of the reign of King Richard the Second [1377–78] was consulted by divers villeins from the county of Wiltshire ... who wished action to be taken to procure exemplifications through the record of Domesday Book to prove that they ought to be free, to the grave damage of the lords and great men of the county.[32]

2.11 Wat Tyler's demands: the 'law of Winchester' (1381)

The portrayal of Wat Tyler by the chroniclers, perhaps keen to exaggerate the threat posed to the king and established government, is that of a man confident in his own beliefs and clear in his intended extermination of lawyers and the overthrow of the existing legal order. In desiring a commission and wishing to legislate by decree, he nevertheless is prepared to utilise the administrative methods of royal government. The chronicler evokes the familiar picture of a tyrannical ruler, relying on his own arbitrary judgment and dictating the laws himself. His reputed declaration that the laws 'would emanate from his mouth and lips' foreshadows one of the accusations made against Richard II at his deposition.[33] In the second extract, Tyler reveals to the king a remarkable platform of reform, ranging from the abolition of villeinage and outlawry to the removal of lordship and redistribution of ecclesiastical possessions. The 'law of Winchester' remains enigmatic, but could be understood to refer to the articles of local policing in the Statute of Winchester (1285), to Domesday Book, or an undefined body of principles analogous to Magna Carta that were strongly held in peasant circles.[34] The king's answer is legalistic in the sense that he tempers his acceptance of the demands with a concern for what is just or fair, whilst maintaining his own status.

---

32 The rest of this presentment is fairly illegible and isolated phrases make little sense out of context.

33 See 1.8.

34 A. Harding, 'The revolt against the justices', in *English Rising of 1381*, ed. Hilton and Aston, p. 166; Musson, 'Appealing to the past', in *Expectations*, ed. Musson, pp. 175–8.

(a)

St Albans Chronicle, ed. Taylor, Childs and Watkiss, vol. 1, p. 434 [Latin]

Now [Wat Tyler] wished above all to obtain a commission for himself and his men to behead all lawyers, escheators and everyone that either had been trained in the law or by virtue of their office participated in it. He believed that once all those learned in the law had been killed everything would be ordained according to the decrees of the common people; in future there would be no law at all, or, if there were to be, it would be decreed by his own opinion. Indeed he is said to have declared with great arrogance on the day before these events, having placed his hand to his lips, that within four days all the laws of England would emanate from his own mouth and lips.

(b)

Anonimalle Chronicle, ed. Galbraith, p. 147 [French]

And the king asked [Wat Tyler] what points he wanted to have and he should have them willingly and without contradiction, written out and sealed. And thereupon the said Wat recited the points which were to be demanded; and he asked that there should be no law except the law of Winchester and that in future there should be no outlawry in any process of law, and that no lord should have lordship, save only if it were divided amongst everyone, except for the king's own lordship; and that the goods of Holy Church should not remain in the hands of the religious, nor of parsons and vicars, nor others belonging to Holy Church; but the beneficed clergy should have adequate sustenance and the rest of their goods should be divided among their parishioners; and there should be only one bishop in England and only one prelate, and all the lands and tenements of the possessioners[35] should be taken from them and divided up among the commons, reserving only for them their reasonable sustenance; and that there should be no more villeins in England, and no serfdom or villeinage but that all should be free and of one status. And the king responded to this tolerantly, and said that Wat should have all that he could properly grant, reserving only for himself the regality of his crown.

---

35 An ecclesiastic enjoying endowments.

2.12 An historical 'Friar Tuck' (1417)

This extract from a commission offers an example of someone assuming the mantle of one of the celebrated outlaws familiar from the Robin Hood ballads. The real name of the leader of this gang of marauders was Robert Stafford, who was chaplain of Lindfield in Sussex. He was eventually pardoned for his misdeeds in 1429.

TNA C 66/400 m. 27d [Latin]

To our beloved and faithful William Lasingby and Robert Hull greeting. We are given to understand that a certain person assuming the unusual name of 'Frere Tuk' and other evildoers and breakers of the peace armed and arrayed in manner of war have entered with force and arms parks, warrens and chaces of various of our lieges in the counties of Surrey and Sussex at various times without licence and of their own free will, hunted therein and carried off deer, hares, rabbits, pheasants and partridges and burned the houses and lodges for the keeping of the parks, warrens and chaces and threatened the keepers with death or bodily mutilation ...

Since we are unwilling for the aforesaid wrongs and other aforesaid bad deeds to go unpunished if such are being committed we assign you together or separately to inquire on the oath of lawful men of the said counties both within liberties and outside them as to whatsoever person and status, degree or condition the aforesaid 'Frere Tuk' formerly was and concerning his real name and the names of each and every of the aforesaid evildoers who together with the aforesaid 'Frere Tuk' carried out the aforesaid wrongs and obtain the full truth concerning the wrongs and all other articles, circumstances and matters whatsoever.

2.13 The demands of the Kentish rebels during Cade's Rebellion (1450)

The demands of the Kentish rebels made during the popular uprising of 1450 take us full circle.[36] The clauses below show a clear awareness of the tenets underpinning law and justice as espoused by *Bracton* and Fortescue and underline the pervasive belief in concepts such as the 'golden rule' and in the importance of reason. There is recognition that the king should be subject to

36 The manuscript text of this extract (now Oxford, Magdalen College MS Misc. 306) could be a copy brought to Blackheath by John Payn for Sir John Fastolf (I. M. W. Harvey, *Jack Cade's Rebellion of 1450* (Oxford, Clarendon Press, 1991), p. 188). Harvey reprints (pp. 188–90) the manuscript text exactly as it appears in HMC 8th Report.

the law and that he is bound by his coronation oath. There are echoes of the claims underlying the Peasants' Revolt seventy years earlier that the rebels should be identified as the true servants and friends of the king, while it is his advisers (especially at this time William de la Pole) who have been the cause of the king's misfortunes. Indeed, they highlight how the king's fortunes (both financially and metaphorically) are at a low ebb and how his susceptibility to influence stems partly from his lack of resources. Absorbing contemporary political thought, properly functioning justice at home is seen as the cure: it will enable the king to keep peace at home and regain his territory abroad.

The main thrust of the demands centres on the alleged problems with the judicial system. While there is faith in the system to the extent that a specific inquiry into those regarded as undermining it (traitors and bribers) is desired and its outcome welcomed, there is a worry that justice is being harmed through the power of money, fear and undue favour. In particular the expectation of fair dealing engendered by the court of Chancery ('court of conscience') is felt to have been eroded or lost. Access to the king to seek justice is therefore a central plank in the rebel platform. Again, as with the Peasants' Revolt, although it may be a rhetorical stance, the rebels are happy to go home if the faults are put right. Their awareness of the process by which laws and royal commands are disseminated and of the value of documents as evidence is manifest in the demands.

HMC 8th Report, appendix, pp. 266–7 [English]

These are the accusations, problems and causes of the gathering and assembly of us your true liegemen of Kent, the which we trust to God to remedy with help of him our king our sovereign lord and all the commons of England and to die therefore:

1. First, we considering that the king our sovereign lord raised dishonestly and wickedly by the insatiable, covetous, malicious and arrogant men daily and nightly about his highness, the same daily and nightly is informed that good is evil and evil is good contrary to Scripture, *Ve vobis qui facitis de bono malum* [Woe to you who make evil out of good].

2. Also, they say that our sovereign lord is above his law and that the law is made to his pleasure and that he may breach it as often as he likes without any discussion: the contrary is true or otherwise he should not have been sworn in his coronation oath to keep it, the which we conceive to be the highest point of treason that any subject may commit against his prince to make him reign in perjury.

3. Also, they say the king should live upon his commons and that their bodies and goods are his; the contrary is true, for then he would never need to summon parliament and to ask aid from them.

4. Also, they inform the king that the commons would first destroy the king's friends and afterwards himself, and then bring in the duke of York to be king, so that by their dishonesty and lies they make him hate and destroy his true friends and to favour the false traitors that call themselves his friends. And if there were no better reason to know such a friend by, he may be known by his covetousness.

5. Also, they say it would be a great reproof to the king to resume what he has given of his livelihood, so they will allow him neither to have his own nor to keep forfeited lands or tenements or any other goods but that they ask it from him, or else they take money from others to get it for them.

6. Also, it is to be remembered that these false traitors will allow no man to come into the king's presence for any cause without a bribe, whereas there ought to be no bribery but that every man might have his due by coming in due time to [the king] to ask justice or grace as the cause requires.

7. Also, it is a heavy thing that the good duke of Gloucester, impeached of treason by one false traitor alone, was so soon murdered and never might come to answer.[37] And the false traitor Pole impeached by all the commonwealth of England, which number exceeded an inquest of twenty-four thousand, might not be allowed to die as law would require,[38] but instead those said traitors who supported Pole, who were as false as Forteger,[39] desire that the king our sovereign lord should fight his own subjects to the destruction of all his people and of himself thereto.

8. Also, they say whom the king wills shall be traitors, and whom he wills as not traitors, none shall be; and that has been very evident hitherto. For if any of the traitors about him feel ill will towards any man high or low they will find false arguments to ensure that they die as a traitor, in order to have his lands and goods, but they will not in such a case allow the king to have them [forfeited lands and goods] to pay either his debts or for his provisions therewith, nor to be the richer by one penny.

37 On arrival for parliament at Bury St Edmunds in February 1447 Gloucester was arrested and thrown into prison with accusations of treason made against him. He died, believed murdered, three days later.

38 The king stopped the trial and sent Suffolk into exile: R. Virgoe, 'The death of William de la Pole, duke of Suffolk', *BJRL*, 47 (1964–65), 489–502.

39 This may be a reference to Sir John Fortescue described as 'false to believe' by the Kent rebels: *Three Fifteenth Century Chronicles*, ed. J. Gairdner, Camden Society, new series 28 (1880), p. 98.

9. Also, the law is used for nothing else these days except to do wrong, for almost nothing is advanced except dishonest matters by reason of law because of meed,[40] respect, or favour, and no remedy is had in the court of conscience or otherwise.

10. Also, we say that our sovereign lord may well understand that he has had false counsel, for his lords are lost, his merchandise is lost, his commons destroyed, the sea is lost, France is lost, and himself so poor that he may not pay for his food or drink; he owes more than ever did a king in England, and yet daily his traitors that are about him wait for whatever thing should come to him by [operation of] his law and then ask it from him.

11. Also, they ask for gentlemen's lands and goods in Kent and call us rebels and traitors and the king's enemies, but we shall be found his true liege men and his best friends with the help of Jesu, to whom we cry daily and nightly, with many thousand more, that God in his righteousness shall take vengeance on the false traitors of this royal realm that have brought us into this poverty and misery.

12. Also, we will that all men know that we will neither rob nor steal, but with these faults amended, we shall go home, wherefore we exhort all the king's true liege men to help us, for whosoever he is that wishes not that these faults were amended, he is falser than Jew or Saracen, and we shall with a good will fight him as we would a Jew or Saracen; whoso is against this, we will mark him, for he is not the king's true liege man.

13. Also, we want it be known that we do not blame all the lords, nor all that are about the king's person, nor all gentlemen, nor all men of law, nor all bishops, nor all priests, but such as may be found guilty by a just and true inquiry by the law, whereto we move and desire that some true judge with certain true lords and knights may be sent into Kent to inquire into all such traitors and bribers, and that justice may be done upon them whoever they are; and that our sovereign lord direct his letters patent to all his people there openly to be read and proclaimed that it is our sovereign lord's will and he desires all his people truly to inquire into every man's behaviour and the deficiencies that reign, not setting any impediment for love, for respect or for hate and that justice be done immediately; and thereupon the king to keep in his own hands their lands and goods and not give them to any man unless to keep them for his

40 See Chapter 8 for such allegations.

own wealth or else to make his invasion into France, or else to pay therewith his debts. By our writings you may grasp whether we are the king's friends or his enemies. Those aforesaid problems thus duly remedied, that from henceforth upon pain of death no man who is about the king's person should take any bribe for any bill of supplication or repetition, or for advancing or impeding any cause, our sovereign lord shall reign with such great worship, love of God and his people, that he shall be able with God's help to conquer where he will; and as for us we shall be ready to defend our country from all nations and will go with our sovereign lord wherever he will command us.

14. Also, he that is guilty will squirm against this but he shall be humbled and shall be ashamed to speak against reason; such people will perhaps go to the king and say that if they are removed from his presence, they will then depose the king, for that way the thieves would live longer; but if we were disposed against our sovereign lord, as God forbid, how then might his traitors help him?

> 'God be our guide and then shall we prosper,
> Whosoever says nay, is false for their money rules.
> Truth for his tales talks.
> God send us a fair day! Away, traitors, away!"

III: CRIME AND DISORDER

Crime has a perennial fascination for historians of all periods and the Middle Ages has an unenviable reputation amongst amateur and professional researchers alike for yielding detailed and explicit accounts of violence and criminal activity. This chapter concentrates on recorded instances of crime and disorder and so does much to confirm the reputation of the late medieval period for unparalleled violence and lawlessness. It should be remembered of course that these are especially selected examples of serious offences and of the breakdown of law and order and should not be taken as a commentary on the effectiveness of royal justice in the later Middle Ages.

Descriptions of crime and disorder can nevertheless afford a valuable perspective on reality and although the cases recorded here are telescoped chronologically and provide only a brief snapshot, they do reveal something of the nature of criminal activity amongst different classes of society. In the medieval period the Latin word *crimen* (from which is derived the English word 'crime') had broad connotations and was employed for behaviour that was considered to be sinful as well as an offence against the public interest. As we shall see in Chapter 5, crime was not purely an infringement of the king's authority and interests, but could constitute a private wrong as well. It was possible therefore for the king and a private individual (as victim or wronged party) both to have an interest in the same case, blurring the distinction made in modern times between criminal law (where the state undertakes prosecution) and civil law (where the wronged party brings the case).[1]

The thirteenth and fourteenth centuries witnessed an expansion in the king's criminal jurisdiction. The most serious crimes comprised high and petty treason, and the category of offences known as felonies. High treason (first defined by statute in 1352)[2] covered 'compassing and imagining' (devising and plotting) the death of the king, his consort, or eldest son;[3] violating his consort, eldest unmarried daughter or his eldest son's wife; levying war against the king in his realm or adhering to the king's enemies; counterfeiting the great seal or the coinage of the realm; killing the chancellor, treasurer or judges in open court. [**3.15, 3.16**] The political intrigues that dogged English kings, particularly Edward II, Richard II and Henry IV, focused attention on what constituted treasonous behaviour. In many cases during these periods it was

---

1 Powell, *Kingship*, pp. 47–50.

2 25 Edward III st. 5, c. 2.

3 For the offence to be made out the king did not actually have to be killed, nor was an attempt on his life necessary. As can be seen from 3.15 the offence was construed very widely, though preparatory acts were usually required as evidence.

constitutional attitudes that dictated the elements of treason. Moreover, in some cases the common law was not followed, either because the treasonous behaviour came prior to or fell outside the statutory definition, or it occurred during a period of civil war when the law of arms (influenced by Roman civil law) was relevant. In such cases civil law notions of *lèse-majesté* were invoked giving rise to a conceptual overlap between the law of arms and the law of treason.[4] By the fifteenth century the definition of treason was extended to include inciting subjects against their sovereign and in the 1420s even prison breach by persons indicted or suspected of treason became treasonable.[5] Subversion of the natural and divinely instituted social hierarchy, implicit in the killing of a master by his servant and of a husband by his wife, constituted a lesser variety of treason (petty treason).[6] [**3.9, 3.10**]

Felony as a group of crimes included homicide, robbery, larceny, rape, arson and prison breach (though the last ceased to be a separate felony in 1295).[7] Of these, homicide and rape were the two viewed with the most seriousness in that (along with treason) they were exempted from general pardons in 1390.[8] [**3.11**] Although the term 'murder' came to be used as a technical term in the late fourteenth century to denote premeditated killings, fine distinctions between the different types of culpable homicide were generally not drawn even in the fifteenth century.[9] Similarly, whilst rape was regarded as an emotive and serious crime, there was a good deal of ambiguity about the charge during the late medieval period with frequent blurring of the legal distinction between rape (forcible sexual intercourse) and ravishment (forcible seizure and carrying away).[10] [**3.12**]

A lesser group of criminal offences came under the heading of trespasses. In practice the dividing line between what constituted a felony and what amounted to trespass was blurred. Moreover, until the mid-thirteenth century, trespasses, minor wrongs or misdemeanours were not deemed to warrant royal judicial attention and were tried in the county and hundred courts or in courts leet. After 1250, however, an allegation that an act had been carried out with

---

4 Bellamy, *Treason*; M. Keen, 'Treason trials under the law of arms', *TRHS* 5th series, 12 (1962), 85–103; M. Strickland, 'A law of arms or a law of treason? Conduct in war in Edward I's campaigns in Scotland, 1296–1307', in *Violence in Medieval Society*, ed. R. W. Kaeuper (Woodbridge, Boydell Press, 2000), pp. 39–77.

5 Powell, *Kingship*, pp. 50, 252–60.

6 Maddern, *Violence*, pp. 104, 119.

7 Bellamy, *Criminal Trial*, pp. 57–92.

8 13 Richard II, st. 2, c. 1. See Chapter 5.

9 J. M. Kaye, 'The early history of murder and manslaughter', *LQR*, 83 (1967), 365–95; Powell, *Kingship*, pp. 179–80; Maddern, *Violence*, pp. 89–90.

10 J. B. Post, 'Ravishment of women and the statutes of Westminster', in *Legal Records and the Historian*, ed. J. H. Baker (London, Royal Historical Society, 1978), pp. 150–60; S. S. Walker, 'Convicted ravishers: statutory strictures and actual practice in thirteenth and fourteenth century England', *JMH*, 13 (1987), 237–50; A. Musson, 'Crossing boundaries: attitudes to rape in late medieval England', in *Boundaries*, ed. Musson, pp. 87–104.

violence and in breach of the king's peace (*vi et armis et contra pacem*) could bring the matter within the purview of the royal courts. Although trespass was never presented as a 'plea of the crown' in the eyre and thus remained conceptually distinct from felony, it gradually acquired status as a crime and should be contrasted with an action of civil trespass brought by a wronged party. [**3.9**]

The examples included in this chapter provide illustrations of all the serious crimes and also, in various contexts, the lesser offence of trespass. In addition to the narrative of events provided by criminal indictments, the detailed confessions of professional thieves, counterfeiters and confidence tricksters give an insight into the criminal milieu, including the character and exploits of some of the perpetrators and their often daring schemes.[11] [**3.7, 3.8, 3.13, 3.16**]

To arrive at an idea of the prevalence of crime in late medieval England some historians have applied the techniques of the social sciences to the court records in an attempt to provide patterns of crime and its prosecution.[12] While such methods can provide useful pointers towards trends in limited geographical areas and within short time periods, the dangers and drawbacks of using the medieval sources in such undertakings should be kept in mind.[13] Their idiosyncrasies and incompleteness mean they are unsuited to rigorous data analysis, unless enhanced by the very latest statistical methods.[14] In more qualitative attempts at analysis, other historians have tried to look behind the accusations of criminal behaviour to the motives of those bringing the prosecutions.[15]

Inevitably many of the examples focus on high-profile crimes of violence amongst the upper strata of society. Attention has been drawn to the criminal gangs led by members of the gentry, notably the Folvilles and the Coterels of

11 H. Summerson, 'The criminal underworld of medieval England', *JLH*, 17 (1996), 197–224; J. B. Post, 'The evidential value of approvers' appeals: the case of William Rose, 1389', *LHR*, 3 (1985), 91–100; H. Röhrkasten, 'Some problems of the evidence of fourteenth-century approvers', *JLH*, 5 (1984), 14–22; H. Summerson, 'Counterfeiters, forgers and felons in English courts, 1200–1400', in *Expectations*, ed. Musson, pp. 105–16.

12 J. B. Given, *Society and Homicide in Thirteenth-Century England* (Stanford, CA, Stanford University Press, 1977); C. I. Hammer, 'Patterns of homicide in a medieval university town: fourteenth-century Oxford', *P&P*, 78 (1978), 3–23; B. A. Hanawalt, *Crime and Conflict in English Communities, 1300–1348* (Cambridge, MA, Harvard University Press, 1979); H. Summerson, 'Crime and society in medieval Cumberland', *TCWAAS*, 82 (1982), 111–24; R. C. E. Hayes, 'Ancient indictments for the North of England, 1461–1509', in *The north of England in the Age of Richard III*, ed. A. J. Pollard (Stroud, Alan Sutton, 1996), pp. 19–45.

13 R. B. Pugh, 'Some reflections of a medieval criminologist', *PBA*, 59 (1973), 83–103; J. B. Post, 'Some limitations of the medieval peace rolls', *JSA*, 4 (1973), 633–9; E. Powell, 'Social research and the use of medieval criminal records', *Michigan Law Review*, 79 (1981), 967–78.

14 See for example: D. Klerman, 'Settlement and the decline of private prosecutions in thirteenth-century England', *LHR*, 19 (2001), 1–65.

15 R. L. Storey, 'Malicious indictments of clergy in the fifteenth century', in *Medieval Ecclesiastical Studies*, pp. 221–40; Musson, *Public Order*, pp. 218–20.

the fourteenth century.[16] [**3.2**] The kidnap and holding to ransom of one of the leading royal judges of the day, Richard Willoughby, six years after their implication in the murder of another royal judge, Roger Bellers, highlights the audacity of the Folville brothers and their associates.[17] Such exploits helped gain them the literary immortality accorded them by the poet Langland and chroniclers of the day.[18] As we saw in Chapter 2, legendary figures could shape attitudes and imaginations and provide a context for criminal exploits and violent encounters.[19]

Members of the upper classes who engaged in criminal behaviour or blatant thuggery may have been treated differently from the lower echelons of society, but they did not necessarily escape royal attention. Edward III made examples of several magnates (notably Thomas de Lisle, bishop of Ely[20] and John, Lord FitzWalter), whose violent conduct and flagrant flouting of his laws affronted him. The king's bench sessions of 1351 heard accusations of a spree of crimes committed by FitzWalter and his men over the past decade. [**3.3**] The allegations against him covered extortion, illegal distraints and putting the people of Essex in fear of their lives and livelihoods. According to the charges he cheated people out of their lands and territories and withheld payments owing to his victims, intimidating them to such an extent that they dared not sue him. FitzWalter's henchmen appear to have been acquitted by the local juries, but he himself was committed to the Tower of London for his misdeeds. Although FitzWalter was later pardoned by Edward III, he was punished through the confiscation of his estates, which he spent the next ten years trying to regain (by substantial payments).[21]

It is important, however, not to view the evidence for crime and disorder (especially amongst the gentry classes) in an undifferentiated and impressionistic fashion, but with regard to the context in which any such lawlessness and criminal activity occurred and the various influences giving rise to it.[22] The circumstances and setting for crime and disorderly violence often stemmed from a variety (or a combination) of factors such as war (both domestic and

16 B. A. Hanawalt, 'Fur-collar crime: the pattern of crime among the fourteenth-century English nobility', *JMH*, 8 (1974–75), 1–17; N. M. Fryde, 'A medieval robber baron: Sir John Moleyns of Stoke Poges, Buckinghamshire', in *Medieval Legal Records*, pp. 197–222.

17 Stones, 'Folvilles', 117–36; J. G. Bellamy, 'The Coterel gang: an anatomy of a band of fourteenth-century criminals', *EHR*, 79 (1964), 698–717.

18 See 2.5 and *Chronicon Henrici Knighton*, ed. J. R. Lumby, vol. 1 (RS, 1889), pp. 460–61.

19 R. F. Green, *A Crisis of Truth: Literature and Law in Ricardian England* (Philadelphia, University of Pennsylvania Press, 1999), pp. 165–205.

20 J. S. Aberth, *Criminal Churchmen in the Age of Edward III: The Case of Thomas de Lisle* (University Park, PA, Pennsylvania State University Press, 1996).

21 *Essex Sessions of the Peace, 1351, 1377–1379*, ed. E. C. Furber, Essex Archaeological Society, 3 (1953), pp. 61–5.

22 For example: P. Booth, 'Men behaving badly? The west march towards Scotland and the Percy-Neville feud', in *The Fifteenth Century III: Authority and Subversion*, ed. L. Clark (Woodbridge, Boydell Press, 2003), pp. 96–116.

foreign), political faction, cross-border relations, legal disputes, gender relations, economic hardship and social dislocation.[23]

The kidnap and robbery of Lewis Beaumont, bishop-elect of Durham and two cardinals should be seen in the context of professional and personal rivalries and viewed against the backdrop of war with Scotland and the unsettled political climate of Edward II's reign.[24] [**3.1**] The attack occurred in 1317 on the main road north between Darlington and Durham. The cardinals were papal legates who had come to England to settle various ecclesiastical disputes and broker an Anglo-Scots truce. They were on the way to Scotland when they were caught up in the attack on Beaumont, waylaid and robbed by a force led by Sir Gilbert Middleton. Lewis Beaumont was felt by many churchman and leading laymen to be an unsuitable candidate for the episcopacy and the 'community of the bishopric of Durham' (notably the priory) in particular was keen to prevent his installation. The ransom sought from the diocese of Durham, therefore, was not necessarily a one-sided piece of extortion. The Durham community employed *schavaldores*, local bandits, to protect their interests,[25] spending 20% of their yearly expenditure in payments to them during the temporary vacancy in the see. Thomas of Lancaster may in fact have been the mastermind behind Middleton's attack, though he evidently felt unable to intervene in the aftermath to save Middleton from a traitor's fate. The situation, however, may have been even more complex: the *schavaldores* or bandits may equally have been hired by the Scots since Robert Bruce was apparently anxious to avoid the unpalatable terms of the truce.[26]

Serious violence usually had political overtones and when perpetrated by members of the gentry was either engineered by or targeted against whoever was in the ascendancy within the community. The violence exemplified in the Mynors brothers' vendetta (1408–12) erupted as a result of a struggle for power in Staffordshire, in part a reaction against the domination of local administration in the county by a narrow group of retainers of the duchy of Lancaster.[27]

23 R. A. Griffiths, 'Local rivalries and national policies: the Percies, the Nevilles and the Duke of Exeter, 1452–1455', *Speculum*, 43 (1968), 589–632; B. McLane, 'A case study of violence and litigation in the early fourteenth century: the disputes of Robert Godsfield of Sutton-le-Marsh', *NMS*, 23 (1984), 22–44; S. J. Payling, 'The Ampthill dispute: a study of aristocratic lawlessness and the breakdown of Lancastrian government', *EHR*, 104 (1989), 881–907; C. J. Neville, *Violence, Custom and Law: The Anglo-Scottish Border Lands in the Later Middle Ages* (Edinburgh, Edinburgh University Press); S. M. Butler, *The Language of Abuse: Marital Violence in Later Medieval England* (Leiden, Brill, 2007).

24 R. M. Haines, *King Edward II: Edward of Caernarfon, His Life, His Reign and Its Aftermath, 1284–1330* (Toronto and Kingston, McGill-Queen's University Press, 2003), pp. 106–7, 263–4.

25 A. King, 'Bandits, robbers and *schavaldours*: war and disorder in Northumberland in the reign of Edward II', in *Thirteenth Century England IX*, ed. M. Prestwich, R. Britnell and R. Frame (Woodbridge, Boydell Press, 2003), pp. 115–30.

26 C. McNamee, *The Wars of the Bruces: Scotland, England and Ireland, 1306–1328* (East Linton, Tuckwell, 1997), pp. 84–5.

27 Castor, *Duchy*, pp. 208–13.

[**3.4**] The Mynors were an old Lancastrian family, but they had fallen into obscurity by the fifteenth century and were unable to profit in any way from Henry IV's accession. They were closely allied to Hugh Erdswick of Sandon and took part in various raids in the first decade of the century for which they were indicted.[28] Some members of the group obtained pardons but William and John Mynors were unreconciled. Although the brothers were eventually called to account for their lawless behaviour before the new king, Henry V, they clearly had no real difficulty obtaining a pardon in 1412 despite their violent wrecking of mills and a virtual siege of Wolverhampton. It should be noted as an example of Henry V's astute political management and concern for a more balanced regional administration, that once Erdswick and William and John Mynors had come to the king's attention (following involvement at Agincourt) they became trusted servants of the crown in both military and local government affairs.[29]

Exploring gentry ('fur collar') crime has its social fascination, though it should be noted that its manifestation frequently coincided with periods of social and political unrest, particularly during bouts of civil war and times when there was a lack of definite royal leadership. Weak kingship created political vacuums, which encouraged warring gentry factions and in turn provided opportunities for unscrupulous landowners to take advantage of the turmoil. This was evident during the 1320s,[30] but was equally an acute problem in the mid-fifteenth century during the troubled reign of Henry VI. The plan hatched in 1450 by the Staffords to avenge the death of Richard Stafford coincided with the banishment and murder of the duke of Suffolk and may have acted as a challenge to those then brought into the centre of power.[31] [**3.5**] The murder of Nicholas Radford in 1455 was the prelude to violent disturbances in Devon and stemmed from the longstanding dispute between the earl of Devon and William, Lord Bonville, which was exacerbated by Henry VI's political ineptitude in granting to the two men the same honorial office in 1440. The dispute tilted in Bonville's favour in 1452 when the earl of Devon was disgraced for his part in Richard of York's attempted coup. Bonville's ascendancy was aided by new political, social and familial contacts. Devon's increasing isolation encouraged him in causing maximum disruption to law and order in the south-west in an attempt to destroy his erstwhile enemy.[32] [**3.6**]

28 *RP*, vol. 3, pp. 630–32.

29 Powell, *Kingship*, pp. 209–11, 213–14, 216, 231, 234–5; Castor, *Duchy*, pp. 213–15, 218–20.

30 S. L. Waugh, 'The profits of violence: the minor gentry in the rebellion of 1321–1322 in Gloucestershire and Herefordshire', *Speculum*, 52 (1977), 843–69.

31 R. L. Storey, *The End of the House of Lancaster* 2nd edn (Stroud, Alan Sutton, 1986), pp. 57–8.

32 *Ibid.*, pp. 85–103, 165–71; M. Cherry, 'The struggle for power in mid fifteenth-century Devonshire', in *Patronage, the Crown and the Provinces in Later Medieval England*, ed. R. A. Griffiths (Gloucester, Alan Sutton, 1981), pp. 123–44; H. Kleineke, 'Why the West was wild: law and disorder in fifteenth-century Devon and Cornwall', in *Fifteenth Century III*, ed. Clark, pp. 77–8, 89, 92–3.

The violence exhibited in medieval society should not simply be dismissed as 'lawless' or aberrant behaviour, but assessed more critically in terms of contemporary cultural definitions and understood within the prevailing discourses on chivalry.[33] The armed retinues and martial displays of force frequently described in the indictments should be regarded as forming part of the chivalric ethos of glory and might. They find resonance in the importance given to visual demonstrations of worship and power. Chivalric literature stressed prowess and defence of honour, but also (in its reformist messages) highlights the ambiguous and contradictory elements of the ideal, particularly in ambivalent attitudes towards women and issues of public order.[34]

We make no excuse for presenting here some of this rich vein of material since it is a potent reminder of the value of the legal records as sources for social history. Indeed, as the noted historian K. B. McFarlane once remarked, 'it is the very richness of the sources which has given the later Middle Ages a bad name'.[35] Not surprisingly the majority of extracts in this section are drawn from the legal records themselves: coroners' and gaol delivery rolls as well as proceedings from king's bench, oyer and terminer and peace sessions and from visitations of the general eyre. The institutions themselves will be examined in the following chapter, but here it is necessary to focus on the content and language of the documents as they show the law in action and reveal something of its strengths and limitations. Accusations demanded words of felonious intent and disputants (or their lawyers) were concerned to push home the level of outrage and any advantage to be gained by portraying events in the most graphic terms possible or using legal terminology and evocative language to blacken an opponent's name.[36] Consequently it should be remarked that the indictments (like chroniclers' accounts) whilst maintaining a certain level of truth are not impartial statements of events. As a counterbalance to the possible distortion of reality afforded by these documents it is important to examine the full context of the accusation and consider also trial verdicts and jury explanations where available.[37]

33 Maddern, *Violence*; R. W. Kaeuper, *Chivalry and Violence in Medieval Europe* (Oxford, Oxford University Press, 1999). See also essays in *Violence in Medieval Society*, ed. Kaeuper.

34 M. Keen, *Chivalry* (New Haven, Yale University Press, 1984), pp. 224–37; Kaeuper, *Chivalry and Violence*, pp. 29, 39, 215–30, 278–9; Maddern, *Violence*, pp. 13–14, 75–9, 205.

35 K. B. McFarlane, *The Nobility of Medieval England* (Oxford, Oxford University Press, 1973), p. 114.

36 Maddern, *Violence*, pp. 90–92.

37 See also Chapter 5.

3.1 Magnate and gentry violence: the kidnapping of Lewis Beaumont, bishop of Durham, by Gilbert Middleton (1317)

An attack on Lewis Beaumont, bishop of Durham elect and two cardinals occurred in 1317 on the road north between Darlington and Durham and was carried out by a force (which may have included the earl of Lancaster's men and some Yorkshiremen) commanded by Sir Gilbert Middleton.[1] Various contemporary chronicles include the event in their accounts.[2] Middleton had been in the king's service, but in the frontier conditions existing in the north of England made his living from banditry, specialising in kidnapping and holding people to ransom. His actions were not only denounced in terms of felony (especially his part in the robbery), but also as treason (one of the indicators being to ride in warlike fashion with flag unfurled). Middleton was arrested and taken to London where he was imprisoned in the Tower and brought to Westminster for trial on 26 January 1318.[3]

Historiae Dunelmensis Scriptores Tres, Gaufridus de Coldingham, Robertus de Gray-stanes et Willielmus de Chambre, ed. J. Raine, Surtees Society, 9 (1839), pp. 100–1 [Latin]

In 1317 two cardinals came to England, namely Gaucelin d'Euse and Luca dei Fieschi, to make peace or impose a truce between the English and the Scots. Also Lewis Beaumont received a papal letter concerning his election as bishop of Durham but was not yet able to be consecrated where he wanted and by whom he wanted. He thought, therefore, in order to glorify the saint's name he would undergo the service of consecration on the feast of St Cuthbert in September of the abovesaid year [4 September][4] and in the presence of the cardinals heading to Scotland be enthroned on the same day. But when the cardinals and Lewis came to the ford between Ferryhill and Woodham Gilbert de Middleton met them with a large force of armed men; who although they initially spared Lewis and the cardinals, for they did not intend to kill them, and released many members of the cardinals' household, and they neither kidnapped the cardinals nor the others, but robbed them all instead. Lewis and his brother Henry, however, they led captive with them to Mitford Castle, of which the aforesaid Gilbert was keeper

1 M. Prestwich, 'Gilbert de Middleton and the attack on the cardinals, 1317', in *Warriors and Churchmen in the High Middle Ages: Essays Presented to Karl Leyser*, ed. T. Reuter (London, Hambledon Press, 1992), pp. 179–94.

2 For example: *Vita Edwardi Secundi: The Life of Edward II*, ed. W. R. Childs (Oxford, Clarendon Press, 2005), pp. 142–5; *Johannis de Trockelowe Annales*, ed. H. T. Riley (RS, 1866), pp. 98–101.

3 TNA KB 27/231 m. 112d; printed in *SCCKB*, vol. 4, p. 78.

4 Translation of St Cuthbert.

rather than lord. They released, however, two horses belonging to the two cardinals and allowed the cardinals to journey freely to Durham. This event occurred on the feast of St Giles, namely 1 September in the year abovesaid. The cardinals, therefore, robbed of all their possessions, arrived thus in Durham, without servants and nothing more than the clothes they were wearing ... Lewis and his brother, however, were later speedily released from their imprisonment once a sum of money and hostages had been handed over.

3.2 Magnate and gentry violence: the kidnapping of a royal justice by the Folville gang (1332)

The kidnapping of royal justice Sir Richard Willoughby was a daring and very high-profile event in the early years of Edward III's reign. The trail of the Folvilles' misdeeds stretched across several counties in the Midlands according to jurors summoned to report before newly appointed peace commissioners and the findings of a commission of oyer and terminer with a wide jurisdiction (covering the counties of Oxfordshire, Leicestershire, Nottinghamshire, Derbyshire, Lincolnshire, Cambridgeshire, Huntingdonshire, Essex and Hertfordshire) issued in March 1332. The seriousness with which their wrongdoing was viewed is demonstrated both by the language in the commission (of threats to the kingdom and usurpation of royal authority) and by Edward III's personal presence at the sessions in Lincolnshire. The Folville gang were joined in this enterprise by another gentry-led gang, the Coterel brothers.[5] Eustace Foville is clearly identified as the ringleader. It is also noticeable that there was a network of receivers and people bringing them food or information to aid their nefarious enterprises. The bands of brothers did not appear to answer the charges and were outlawed. Some were later pardoned in return for military service.[6]

(a)

TNA JUST 1/1411b mm. 1, 2, 4d, 7 [Latin]

PLEAS OF THE CROWN HELD AT STAMFORD BEFORE RALPH NEVILLE, GEOFFREY SCROPE, WILLIAM HERLE, JOHN STONOR AND JOHN STURMY, JUSTICES OF THE LORD KING ASSIGNED TO INQUIRE INTO DIVERS FELONIES, TRESPASSES AND WRONGS COMMITTED IN LINCOLNSHIRE ON THE MONDAY

---

5 Stones, 'Folvilles', 117–36; J. G. Bellamy, 'The Coterel gang: an anatomy of a band of fourteenth-century criminals', *EHR*, 79 (1964), 698–717.

6 For examples of this phenomenon see 5.17.

AFTER PALM SUNDAY IN THE SIXTH YEAR OF THE REIGN OF
KING EDWARD THE THIRD [13 April 1332]

Lincolnshire [Stamford day and date as above]

The jurors present that Eustace Folville feloniously killed John de
Makesey at Stamford in the first year of the reign of King Edward III
[1327].

And that the said Eustace, Richard Folville, parson of the church of
Teigh [Rutland], Robert Folville, Walter Folville and Laurence
Folville, brothers of the said Eustace together with others unknown
in the wood of *Freshrib* in Uffington in the first year of the reign of
King Edward III [1327] at dawn of a certain day robbed Hugh Crake
of Ryhale of four horses worth £4. And that the said Eustace Folville,
Richard Folville, Robert Folville, Walter Folville and Laurence Folville
in the same year robbed Walran de Baston of a cask of wine worth 50s
in the fields of Uffington.

[Kesteven] The jurors of the wapentake of Kesteven present that
Robert Folville, parson of Teigh, William Folville, Nicholas de Botheby
and Nicholas de Eton together with others unknown on the Tuesday
after St Hilary in the fifth year of the reign of King Edward III [14
January 1332] feloniously took Richard Willoughby from *Suesternemor*
to *Moorhaugh* in Lincolnshire and held him there for one night until
he made fine with them of 1300 marks and thus held him there in their
keeping until the said sum was paid.

And that Eustace Folville, Robert Folville, Thomas Folville, Sir William
Marmion, Robert Lovet, parson of the church of Ashwell, John Lovet,
William Peshoun of Berugby, William Langham of Wymondham,
William le Long of Oakham, Roger chaplain of the parson of Ashwell
... James Coterel, John Bradbourne, Roger Bradbourne ... and many
others unknown were accessory to the said Richard Folville and others
in committing the said felony and had a share of the ransom.

And that the same Eustace, Robert, Walter, Laurence, Richard and
Thomas Folville with Henry chaplain of Bytham, John Lovel and
others unknown on the Sunday after St Faith, virgin, in the twentieth
year of the reign of King Edward II [12 October 1326] robbed brother
Robert Cort at Stainby of two horses and harness belonging to him
worth £20.

And that the said Eustace and his brothers are common thieves,
robbers and slayers of men on the king's highway between Stamford

and Grantham and in the woods of *Moorhaugh* and *Horsehead* and other places in the said county.

And that Alan de Baston canon of Sempringham and brother John de Irnham canon of the same house received the said Eustace and his brothers in Sempringham Priory at the grange called Lestenholm in the Marsh after the said felonies knowing them to be felons.

Northamptonshire [session at Stamford date as above]

Jurors of the geldable[7] of Northamptonshire present that James Coterel, Laurence Folville, Walter his brother and Richard Folville, parson of Teigh, and Nicholas Botheby took Richard Willoughby and abducted him to a certain place in Northamptonshire called Sevenoaks and held him there until he voluntarily made fine with them.

And that Eustace Folville was chief of their organisation and their maintainer in all things and had his share of the ransom.

Leicestershire [sessions at Melton Mowbray on Thursday in Easter week 6 Edward III – 23 April 1332]

[Goscote] The jurors of the hundred of Goscote present that ... Eustace Folville, Richard, Walter, Robert and Laurence his brothers came to Shenton to the manor of the warden of Kirkby and there feloniously seized, drove off and carried away three oxen, a bull, capons and hens and other goods and chattels worth £6 in the first year of the reign of King Edward III [1327]

And that the same Eustace and his brothers in the same year came to Wymondham to the manor of John Hamelyn and there seized and drove off 29 sheep and other goods worth £30.

And that the same Eustace and his brothers ... with others unknown feloniously seized a mare and colts at Leicester worth £100 from the earl of Lancaster.

And that they feloniously seized goods worth £200 from the burgesses of Leicester in the third year of the reign of King Edward III [1329].

And that Robert Folville, Laurence his brother (and others named) entered the church of Kirkby and took the half a year's profits of the said church and similarly entered the manor of the warden of the church and

---

7 Land outside of the franchise and so subject to normal taxation and administration. Originally the term referred to those liable to pay 'geld' (the tax paid to the crown by English landholders before the Norman Conquest and continued under Norman kings), but long survived actual 'geld'.

feloniously broke the doors and windows and took and carried away 100s worth (£5) of the goods and chattels.

[Framland] The jurors of the hundred of Framland present that Richard Folville, parson of Teigh, Robert Lovet, parson of Ashwell, John his brother, Robert Folville and Laurence his brother, Richard Corbet of Burton and William Folour of Melton together with others unknown seized Richard Willoughby at Eastwell[8] and led him from wood to wood until he made fine with them. And this was through the command, help and plan of Eustace Folville who had his share of the said fine.

(b)

HMC *Report on the Manuscripts of Lord Middleton* (London, 1911), pp. 276–7 [Latin] (Presentments from sessions held by keepers/justices of the peace in Nottinghamshire and Derbyshire, 1332–33)

The jurors of the first inquest of the county of Derby present that Eustace Folville, Laurence Folville, Walter Folville, Robert Folville, and Richard Folville, parson of the church of Teigh, received and had as their share in the park of Markeaton about the Purification in the sixth year of the reign of King Edward III [c 2 February 1332], by the hands of evildoers unknown, 300 marks from the ransom of Richard Willoughby, knowing of and consenting to the robbery thereof. And that James Coterel, Nicholas Coterel, John Coterel, John de Bradbourne and William de Bradbourne had 40 marks for their part in the robbery. And that Robert Tuchet, lord of Markeaton, Edmund Tuchet, parson of the church of Mackworth, Robert Bernard and Hugh de Gunston, proctors of the church of Bakewell, received and maintained James Coterel and Eustace Folville, outlaws, at Bakewell, Mackworth, and Markeaton about the feast of St Valentine in the sixth year of the reign of King Edward III [c 14 February 1332]. And that James Coterel, Nicholas and John, his brothers, Roger Sauvage, Stephen de Edensor [Derby.], Walter and Adam, servants of James, Eustace Folville, Laurence, Walter and Robert, his brothers, Robert Griseleve, Edmund and Roger his brothers. William Corbet of Tasley [Salop], Nicholas de Eton, John de Dinston of Walton [Derby.], William de la Warde, the younger, Robert son of Richard Foljambe, Nicholas de la Firde, Robert son of Matthew de Vylers, Nicholas de Sparham and Walter Comyn ride with

---

8 There is a discrepancy as to the exact place as Gartree hundred jury says Eaton, the next village.

armed force secretly and openly, and are maintainers and receivers of
Ralph son of Geoffrey of Repton, Roger le Megre and Reginald de la
More, notorious thieves, outlawed in that county, and that they received
them at Dean Hollow in the second week of Lent, in the sixth year of
the reign of King Edward III [c 15 March 1332]. And that Geoffrey
le Woodward of Markeaton is a maintainer and receiver of Eustace
Folville and other outlawed evildoers, carrying to them food in the park
of Markeaton for the use of Eustace, James Coterel and others, and that
he had a share of the money stolen from Richard Willoughby, namely
100s [£5].

3.3 Magnate and gentry violence: John, Lord FitzWalter and the siege of Colchester (1343)

These passages highlight a spree of crimes committed by John, Lord Fitz-
Walter and his men over a period of about nine years.[9] It is unusual to find
a man of FitzWalter's stature facing charges in this fashion. Significantly
many of the presentments (as here) were couched in terms of treasonous
behaviour (drawing to himself royal power) through his extortion tactics.
The indictments are also phrased so as to emphasise FitzWalter's actions
as beyond the restraint of the laws of the land and in contempt of the
king's protection. Intimidating jurors and interfering with the work of the
coroner were serious offences, while substituting one of the county coroners for a coroner of the liberty went against the rights and privileges of
the franchise. The alleged siege of the town of Colchester and ambushing
of its inhabitants (forcing them to pay for the redemption of the town)
clearly united the community against him. The dispute with the burgesses
concerning jurisdiction there followed a complaint by FitzWalter in 1343
that his park had been invaded and his steward, John Osekyn, wounded.
Osekyn was killed later that year.[10]

TNA KB 27/366, *Rex*, mm. 30 (i, iiid, iv) [Latin]

Jurors of various hundreds in the county of Essex presented to the
court of king's bench sitting at Chelmsford in Michaelmas term in the
twenty-fifth year of the reign of King Edward III [1351].

Also they presented that on the Monday after St Ambrose in the fourteenth year of the reign of King Edward III [10 April 1340] the said
John FitzWalter and others of his household laid siege to the town of

---

9 For an examination of FitzWalter's career see W. R. Powell, 'Lionel de Bradenham
and his siege of Colchester in 1350', *Essex Archaeology and History*, 22 (1991), 68–9.

10 *Essex Sessions of the Peace*, ed. Furber, p. 88.

Colchester and placed ambushes for the men of the said town on each side of the town and assaulted those whom they were able to intercept namely Robert Besse going to Manningtree, Robert Tanner going to Maldon and many others; so that no one of the said town dared to leave the town to go to any market or fair whatsoever from the said Monday until Pentecost following [10 April to 4 June] until John Waryn, Matthew FitzRobert, William Hadleigh and many others from the town of Colchester had bound themselves to the aforesaid John FitzWalter for £40 each and paid him the money for the ransom of the community of the town. And the aforesaid John made such extortions and hardships to the oppression of the people, drawing to himself royal power against the law of the land by taking such ransoms.

Also they presented that the said John FitzWalter commanded all his men, namely on Monday next after Pentecost in the sixteenth year of the reign of King Edward III [20 May 1342], that they and each of them keep an eye on all the men of the town of Colchester lest they go out of the said town or elsewhere towards any market around about to carry out their business because a certain John Osekyn of Lexden had been killed at Mile End within the liberty of Colchester. And after the aforesaid John had been found dead the coroners of the liberty of the town of Colchester approached the body of the same John Osekyn to carry out that which was incumbent upon their office and held an inquest concerning the aforesaid death. Because it did not please the same John FitzWalter that the jury did not unjustly indict many men of the town of Colchester before the aforesaid coroners of the death of the aforesaid John, or of consenting to it, because the same John Fitz-Walter had hatred for the said men of the town of Colchester, the same John procured a foreign coroner[11] from the county of Essex against the freedom conceded to the said burgesses by the lord king and after the burial of the said John Osekyn caused an inquiry to be made concerning the said death by foreign inquest[12] in the presence of the same John FitzWalter. And because the members of the aforesaid foreign inquest refused to indict of the death of the aforesaid John Osekyn certain persons of the said town whom he hated unjustly and arbitrarily and which he handed over by bill to the same inquest, the same John Fitz-Walter commanded his men, namely John Scace and others, to threaten those of the said foreign inquest and beat them where they could be found. So certain men on the command of the same John FitzWalter

11 ie a coroner from outside the town (one of the county coroners)
12 ie a jury from outside the town

came to the house of Henry Neuard of Great Birch one of the aforesaid foreign inquest and entered the close of the same Henry against
his wish and broke the door and windows of his house there namely
on the Wednesday after Trinity in the sixteenth year of the reign of
King Edward III [29 May 1342] and beat the same Henry there and
wounded him seriously and left him there for dead.

Also they presented that from the Monday next after Pentecost in the
sixteenth year of the reign of King Edward III to the feast of St Mary
Magdalene following [20 May to 22 July 1342] the majority of the men
of the town of Colchester for fear of the same John FitzWalter and his
men, who were surrounding the said town on all sides, kept themselves
within the town of Colchester itself, withdrawing their trade and business without transacting anything they shut the gates of the said town
nightly. Having been armed the men of the same town defended in the
manner of war the same town day and night for eight weeks and more
as if men and town were besieged by their enemies. He caused their
ploughs to be taken unjustly by two of his said household together with
the animals of the said burgesses from their fields within the liberty
of Colchester and caused the same animals to be abducted and each
plough with all its gear taken and driven towards his manor of Lexden,
within which time the said John sent certain of his followers to certain
men of the same town asking whether the same men, to have love[13] and
peace with the same John, had agreed to make fine with him or not. So
certain men of the said town by fear and coercion of the same John and
terrified of his men, just as those who are without a leader are, made
fine with the same John FitzWalter for £40 in silver and for security of
their £40 a certain bond of 100 marks was created by certain persons
at the nomination and personal command of the same John and through
coercion and tearfully was sealed by certain persons of the said town
with their seals. Which certain £40 by reason of the said fine the same
John commanded the bailiffs and men of the town of Colchester to raise
from the community of the same to pay the same John. So certain of the
bailiffs and men aforesaid paid £40 namely the said fine unwillingly to
certain attorneys of the same John.

13 ie a payment for his goodwill

3.4 Magnate and gentry violence: the murder of two of the Mynors brothers at Wolverhampton church and the remaining brothers' vendetta (1411–12)

The indictment here couches the Mynors brothers' actions in terms of an act of rebellion and maintains that they held the locality in a grip of fear, threatening both life and limb and the livelihood of individuals within the community. A long string of offences committed in Staffordshire and Derbyshire during the years 1408–9 led to parliamentary complaint against them and an order to surrender themselves before the justices of king's bench.[14] As the examples show, they nevertheless continued their campaign of intimidation and depredation, especially in the area around Wolverhampton. The rather extreme reaction of the community against two of the brothers, Thomas and Robert Mynors, suggests a 'popular' act of vengeance presumably justified by the violation of the sanctity of the church.

TNA JUST 2/162 m. 2d [Latin]

Inquest held at Wolverhampton on the Wednesday after the Purification of the Blessed Virgin Mary in the twelfth year of the reign of King Henry IV [4 February 1411] before the said coroner [William Forster] on the view of the bodies of Thomas Mynors, Robert Mynors, Haukin Wolley, Robert Holyns and John Holyns on the oath of [twelve named jurors] who said on oath that the said Thomas Mynors, Robert Mynors, Haukin Wolley, Robert Holyns and John Holyns on the Wednesday last before the feast of the Purification in the abovementioned year came with force and arms to the church of Wolverhampton and in the same church without reason maliciously assaulted Richard [...] parson of Wolverhampton and mutilated and injured him in the same church and [...] the said church. And on this the constables of the same town came to arrest the parties and restore peace just as the law demanded.[15] And the said Thomas Mynors, Robert Mynors, Haukin Wolley, Robert Holyns and John Holyns were unwilling to submit to the arrest of the said constables but stood against them to defend themselves. And then seeing the malice and destruction of the church and also the mutilation of the same Richard the local populace fell on them and mutilated and killed the said Thomas Mynors, Robert Mynors, Haukin Wolley, Robert Holyns and John Holyns.

14 *RP*, vol. 3, p. 632.

15 This is the gist of the sentence rather than an exact translation as the edge of the roll has been damaged and the last word in the sentence lost.

TNA JUST 1/815 m. 6d [Latin]

The jury [twelve names] said … that John Mynors (who has a pardon), William Mynors (who has a pardon), John Hardhead (who was remanded to the custody of the marshal of the king's bench and then obtained a pardon), Thomas Lynhales, Thomas Duffield, John Wygynton, Henry Crapper and Richard Mirthamong together with others on the Saturday before the feast of the Conception of the Blessed Virgin Mary in the thirteenth year of the reign of King Henry IV [5 December 1411] at Sedgley feloniously killed and murdered Roger Ring of Wolverhampton; and that the said John Mynors, William, John Hardhead, Thomas, Thomas, John Wygynton, Henry and Richard are notorious thieves and robbers, ambushers of highways and despoilers of fields.

And that John Warynges received them at Penn on the following Tuesday in the above said year [8 December 1411] knowing that they had carried out the said felony. And that Adam Deykyn received them at Tetenhale on the Thursday after the feast of the Conception of the Blessed Virgin Mary in the above said year [10 December 1411] and so regularly from then onwards knowing that they had carried out the said felony. And that Ralph Chernok received them at Wrottesley on the following Sunday [13 December] knowing that they had carried out the said felony. And that Richard Parkhouse received them at Sedgley on the Tuesday after the feast of St Lucy, virgin in the said year [15 December] and so regularly from then onwards knowing that they had carried out the said felony. And that Richard Duddeley prior of Sandwall received them at Sandwall on the Thursday after the said feast of St Lucy in the abovesaid year [17 December] knowing that they had carried out the said felony. And that William Bordhewer, Thomas Benettes, Robert Colfox and William Crapper received them at Sedgley knowing that they had carried out the said felony namely on the Saturday before the feast of St Thomas Apostle in the abovesaid year [19 December] and so regularly from then onwards. And that Thomas Chilterne and Henry Hancokes received them at Wednesbury on the Monday before the said feast of St Thomas [14 December] and so regularly from then onwards knowing that they had carried out the said felony. And that Thomas Kemp of Bramshall received them at Bramshall on the Monday after Christmas Day in the abovesaid year [28 December] and so regularly from then onwards knowing that they had carried out the said felony. And that John Clerk of Stramshall received them at Stramshall on the following Wednesday in the abovesaid year [30 December] and so regularly from then onwards. And that John Chapman of Hednesford received them at

Hednesford on the Monday after Christmas Day in the abovesaid year [28 December] and so regularly from then onwards knowing that they had carried out the said felony.

Also John Mynors, William Mynors, John Hardhead, John Wygynton, Thomas Lynhales and Richard Mirthamong on the Sunday after the feast of the Circumcision of our Lord in the thirteenth year of the reign of King Henry IV [2 January 1412] came armed and arrayed as if for war together with others unknown against the peace as if rebels to the manor of Tunstall, near Wolverhampton, and there broke the water mill of William Bushbury and the millstones of the same mill by night and threw down *le forpount* and the floodgates of the same so that the water held in the pool there to sustain the same mill was totally drained, and a certain iron rind of the said mill (worth 5s) and twelve iron pikes (worth 4s) were feloniously stolen from the goods and chattels of William Bushbury there; and after the said felony and trespass thus committed they came the same night to a certain mill of Robert Wolden dean of Wolverhampton called *le Dommulne* and broke the said mill and threw down *le forpount* and the floodgates and feloniously stole from the goods and chattels of the said dean there one mill-rind (worth 20d) and eight pikes (worth 20d); and the same night they broke the mill of Gosbroke and the mill of Seisdon and *Heyclyf* Mill against the peace of the lord king; and that they commanded everyone and every village around the town of Wolverhampton and threatened them on pain of their lives and mutilation of their limbs that they should not transport any food to the town of Wolverhampton by which the faithful liegemen of the lord king might live, in destruction of the said liegemen so that for loss of the mills and food stuffs they almost perish for hunger.

3.5 Magnate and gentry violence: the Stafford–Harcourt feud (1448–50)

The following skirmish arose as a result of frustration with the tardiness of the legal processes and (in the opinion of the Stafford camp) the continued evasion of justice by Robert Harcourt. The background to this dramatic and seemingly large-scale encounter (boasting 200 men and 1000 arrows fired) was the killing of Richard Stafford in May 1448. A non-fatal blow to the head by Harcourt himself was followed up by a mortal wound in the back from one of Harcourt's men in response to a lunge from Stafford with his dagger. Sir Humphrey Stafford was also struck and fell from his horse. In the ensuing mêlée there were deaths on both sides as the parties clashed. Although Harcourt was indicted, arrested and kept in Chester Castle for a while, he successfully obtained a stay in proceedings. Humphrey Stafford was forced to petition for the law to proceed. Although his request was granted, Harcourt remained unpunished nearly a year after the event, possibly through the endeavour of William de la Pole, duke of Suffolk. Whilst the plan to avenge the death of Richard Stafford failed in the short term (resulting in the siege of the church in Stanton Harcourt) and Harcourt received a pardon, he was eventually killed by Humphrey Stafford's bastard son in 1469.

TNA KB 9/266 m. 51 [Latin]

Inquest held at Oxford before Richard Bingham, Dru Barentyn and William Marmion, justices of the lord king together with Sir William Lovell, Robert Hungerford, Lord Moleyns, John Fortescue, William Yelverton, Sir Robert Shottesbroke, John Norys, Thomas Danyell and Richard Quatermayns assigned by letters patent to inquire into whatsoever trespasses and riots of whatsoever kind committed or perpetrated within Oxfordshire by Humphrey Stafford lately of Grafton in Worcestershire esquire, son and heir of Humphrey de Stafford lately of Grafton in Worcestershire knight and others named in the same letters and to hear and determine the same trespasses and riots on Wednesday after St Faith in the twenty-ninth year of the reign of King Henry VI [7 October 1450] on the oath of [twelve named jurors] who said on oath that whereas Humphrey de Stafford lately of Grafton in Worcestershire, knight, now dead, and Thomas Burdet lately of Arrow, Worcestershire, esquire planned for a long time to kill and murder Robert Harcourt, knight, and finally set out to destroy him, a certain Humphrey Stafford lately of Grafton in the county of Worcestershire son and heir of the said Sir Humphrey Stafford, John Trussell of Billesley, Warwickshire, esquire, Richard Beauchamp lately of Grafton, Worcestershire gentleman, Thomas Bayle lately of Oseley, Warwickshire, yeoman [and forty-four others named] and many other evildoers and disturbers of the peace of the lord king amounting to 200 men armed and arrayed rebelliously in the manner of war and insurrection on the Friday next before the Invention of the Cross in the twenty-eighth year of the reign of King Henry VI [1 May 1450] at Field within the forest of Wychwood in Oxfordshire rose up through the abetment, rousing and procurement of the said Thomas Burdet and gathered themselves together to carry out the plan; and then while it was almost still night, warlike in the manner of insurrection, they rode up to the manor of the said Robert Harcourt at Stanton Harcourt and assaulted there with force and arms the same Robert and William Harcourt and also Thomas Ruggely [and several other named servants of Robert Harcourt] at dawn on the

Saturday following [2 May]. And they wished to have killed the same then and there with lances, pollaxes, languedebœufs,* gisarmes,* bows and arrows and also other various sorts of weapons they had brought. Pursuing as if in battle, they drove them towards a certain bell tower at Stanton Harcourt; and also beat, wounded, injured and maltreated then and there Matthew Sawyer, William Dyly, Richard Stokeman so that their lives were despaired of.

And the same Humphrey Stafford, esquire and all the other aforesaid evildoers along with him perceiving that they were not able to get the same Robert Harcourt out of the said tower to kill him on account of the strength of the same tower, besieged the said church and the whole village of Stanton Harcourt there and behaved in warlike fashion there towards the said Robert and those on his side disposed to resist and anyone else resisting the same evildoers and they raised all manner of war and siege against the dignity of the king and the allegiance owed by those evildoers continuing there for six hours of the same Saturday and shot a thousand arrows at the same Robert Harcourt, William Harcourt and servants of the same abovesaid Robert saying and proclaiming that unless the said Robert Harcourt came out of the said tower and surrendered himself to them voluntarily they would burn the said church and the same Robert within it. And because the same Robert refused to do this they started a fire there within the said church under the upper chamber of the same bell tower so as to compel the said Robert Harcourt and the servants remaining with him, with this happening and smoke from the aforesaid fire rising, to leave the said tower. And when the said Humphrey Stafford esquire and all those abovesaid evildoers remaining with him perceived that they were not able to kill the said Robert Harcourt they took seven of his horses (worth £14) seven saddles with equipment, seven bridles (worth 10 marks) eight coverlets, eight pairs of blankets and twelve pairs of sheets (worth £10) of that same Robert and also divers other goods and chattels of the same Robert (worth £10).

3.6 Magnate and gentry violence: the murder of Nicholas Radford by the earl of Devon's men (1455)

Radford was a local lawyer of some distinction ('apprentice of the law' was the term for someone who had studied at the Inns of Court but either had not been called or had refused to obey a call to the order of serjeants-at-law) serving as justice of the peace and recorder of the city of Exeter. He was also Bonville's legal adviser. The outrageous treatment he suffered has made this crime notorious since unlike many of the other examples of violence in this volume it was premeditated. It preceded the formation of a large private army, a spate of pillaging, the siege of Powderham Castle and the takeover of Exeter by the Courtenays. A year later, however, they had been pardoned and there is no further evidence of conflict.[16]

There are three contemporary accounts of this murder: a petition to parliament by Radford's cousin and executor (given here), the indictment of his murderers at sessions held at Exeter in August 1456 (before James, earl of Wiltshire, John Fortescue, Peter Arden, Richard Bingham and Thomas Croxton) and a letter dated 28 October 1455 written to John Paston by the lawyer James Gresham upon hearing the news.[17] The text describes the encounter vividly, complete with conversational exchanges, as if it were an eyewitness account. The petitioner makes a point of highlighting Radford's virtues and the violation of God's peace and the king's. It is clear from Sir Thomas Courtenay's behaviour and the conduct of his henchmen that the chivalric ethos or the code of conduct befitting Radford's status as a gentleman has been breached. Courtenay's promise as a 'true knight and gentleman' is shown to be hollow, while the desecration of the body, regarded as distasteful, is compared to the treatment that could have been expected from Jews or Saracens. Note the alleged parody of the coroner's inquest, in which charade Radford was indicted for suicide. The subsequent treatment of the body, its removal from the coffin and lack of proper burial, was probably part of an attempt to treat it in a manner appropriate to the finding.

TNA SC 8/138/6864 [English]

To the king our sovereign Lord.

Please it your highness tenderly to consider that whereas Nicholas Radford late of Devonshire, gentleman, one of the most notable and renowned apprentices of your law in this your realm of England, being by your commission one of the justices of the peace in the said Devonshire thirty years and more, having all his days a great zeal to do justice and true execution of your laws, and namely upon felons, murderers, and robbers of your people, and other misdoers and rebels against your laws and your peace, to the great comfort and rest of your people of the same shire, on Thursday the twenty-third day of October in the thirty-fourth year of your noble reign [1455], he was in God's peace and yours in his own property called Uppecote in the town of Cadley in the same shire. There came the same day and year, Thomas Courtenay late of Tiverton in the said shire, knight, son to Thomas, earl of Devon, Nicholas Philip otherwise called Nicholas Gye late of the same town

16 G. H. Radford, 'Nicholas Radford, c.1385–1455', *TDA*, 35 (1903), 252–4, 256–7, 264; *eadem*, 'The fight at Clyst in 1455', *TDA*, 44 (1912), 252–65.

17 TNA KB 9/16; *PL*, vol. 1, no. 257.

and shire, yeoman, John at More otherwise called John Penyale, late of
Exilond [Exe Island] in the same shire, tailor, John Briggham late of
Tiverton in the same shire, yeoman, William Layn, late of the same town
and shire, yeoman, Thomas Overy otherwise called Thomas Amory,
late of Exeter in the same shire, tailor [and ninety-four others named]
with other riotous persons whose names are yet unknown arrayed
in manner of war, that is to say with jacks, sallettes,* bows, arrows,
swords, bucklers, languedebœufs,* long daggers, and other defensive
weapons, greatly against your peace, sovereign lord, at midnight of the
same Thursday, and made an assault on the said property and hostilely
surrounded it. The said Nicholas, his wife and all his household at the
time were there in their beds. The which misdoers as soon as they had
surrounded the said property made there a great shout and set on fire
the gates of the said property. And the said Nicholas Radford woke,
and hearing a great noise and tumult about his said property, arose and
opened the window of his chamber. And seeing the said gates on fire,
he asked who they were that were there and whether there were any
gentlemen among them. And the said Nicholas Philip answered and
said, 'There is Sir Thomas Courtenay.'

And then the said Sir Thomas Courtenay hearing the said Nicholas
Radford speak, called to him, saying in this manner, 'Come down Radford
and speak with me.' And then the said Nicholas Radford knowing the
voice of the said Sir Thomas Courtenay, knight answered saying to him
these words: 'Sir, if you will promise me on your faith and truth, and as
you are a true knight and gentleman, that I shall have no bodily harm,
nor hurt of my goods, I will come down to you.' And then the said Sir
Thomas Courtenay, knight answered the said Nicholas Radford again,
and said to him in this manner, 'Radford come you to me, and I promise
you as I am a true knight and gentleman you shall be safe both of your
body and of your goods.' Whereupon the said Nicholas Radford trusting
faithfully upon that promise, came out of his chamber with torch light,
and did set open the gates and let him in and then the said unruly
people crowded in with him. And the said Nicholas Radford seeing so
many people within his said property, was sore afraid, and said to Sir
Thomas Courtenay, 'Sir, what are all these people doing here?' and he
answered again and said 'Radford, you shall have no home,' and thereupon the said Sir Thomas Courtenay had the said Nicholas Radford
take him to the chamber which he lay in, and he did so, and there the
said Sir Thomas Courtenay both ate and drank, and from there came
out into the hall, and the said Nicholas Radford with him, and there
they stood together at the sideboard, and drank of his wine. And there

the said Sir Thomas Courtenay cleverly held the said Nicholas Radford with tales, while the said Sir Thomas Courtenay's men broke open the chamber doors and coffers of the said Nicholas Radford, and then and there the said misdoers abovenamed and others feloniously robbed the said Nicholas Radford of £300 and more in cash lying in his trussing coffers, and other goods and jewels, bedding, gowns, furs, books, and ornaments of his chapel, to the value of 1000 marks and more, and the goods they trussed together and, with the said Nicholas Radford's own horse,[18] carried them away.

And among other rifling then and there, they found the said Nicholas Radford's wife in her bed, painfully sick as she had been these two years and more, and rolled her out of her bed, and took away the sheets that she lay in, and trussed them with the rest of the said goods.

And then after, the said Sir Thomas Courtenay left his talking with the said Nicholas Radford at the sideboard and said to the said Nicholas Radford, 'Have done with it, Radford, for you must go with me to my lord, my father,' and Radford said he would go with him readily, and made himself ready to ride, and bade his servant make a horse ready for him, and his servant answered him, 'Sir your horse has been taken away and loaded with your goods' and the said Nicholas Radford hearing that said to the said Sir Thomas Courtenay, 'Sir, I am aged, and may not suitably go upon my feet, and therefore I pray you that I may ride'; and the said Sir Thomas Courtenay answered again in this manner, 'Do not worry, Radford, you shall ride well enough soon, and therefore come with me.' And he went forth with him a stone's throw and more from his said place within Cadley aforesaid, and there the said Sir Thomas Courtenay, knight, spoke secretly with the said Nicholas Philip, Thomas Philip and John Amory and forthwith spurred his horse and rode away and said 'Farewell Radford.' And the said Nicholas Philip, Thomas Philip and John Amory and other forthwith turned upon the said Nicholas Radford, and then and there the said Nicholas Philip with a small dagger smote the said Nicholas Radford a tremendous deadly stroke across the face, and felled him to the ground, and then the said Nicholas Philip gave him another stroke upon his head from behind so that the brain fell out of his head. And the said Thomas Philip that time and then with a knife feloniously cut the throat of the said Nicholas Radford, and the said John Amory that time and there with a long dagger smote the said Nicholas Radford from behind on his back through to the heart. And so the said Nicholas Philip, Thomas Philip and John Amory thus each gave the said

18 Six horses (indictment).

Nicholas Radford deadly wounds, and then and there feloniously and horribly slew and murdered him. And the said Sir Thomas Courtenay knight, Nicholas Philip, Thomas Philip and John Amory and the other misdoers abovenamed, with the rest of the said misdoers at that time and there feloniously procured, encouraged, planned and abetted the others to do the said horrible murder and felony in the form abovesaid. And forthwith after the said horrible murder and felony thus done, the said Sir Thomas Courtenay with all the said misdoers rode to Tiverton in the said shire of Devon where the said earl the Friday next after the said Thursday feloniously received, comforted and harboured the said Sir Thomas Courtenay, Nicholas Philip, Thomas Philip, and John Amory and other misdoers abovenamed, with the said rest of the misdoers with the said goods, knowing them to have done the said murder, robbery and felony in the form aforesaid.

And the Monday next after the said Thursday, Henry Courtenay late of Tiverton in the shire of Devon, esquire, brother to the said Sir Thomas Courtenay, knight, and godson to the said Nicholas Radford, with various of the said misdoers and others, came to the said place at which the body of the said Nicholas Radford lay, in his chapel of his said property in Cadley, and there and then the said Henry Courtenay and those misdoers took upon them the office of coroner without authority, and made one of them sit down, and called before him an inquest of the persons who murdered the said Nicholas Radford, by such strange names as no man might know them by, nor never men heard tell of such dwelling in that country. These misdoers, scornfully appearing by such names as they were called, made such a presentment as pleased them, and such as is reported that they should indict the said Nicholas Radford of his own death, in great contempt and derision of your laws. And soon after that, the said Henry and various of the said misdoers, with other misdoers to a great number, constrained certain persons there that were servants to the said Nicholas Radford to bear his body to the church [of Cheriton Fitzpaine][19] ... and there the said misdoers took the body of the said Nicholas Radford out of his coffin that he was laid in, and rolled him out of his gravesheet in which he was wound; and there and then cast the body completely naked into the pit, and with such stuff of stones as the said Nicholas Radford had recently purveyed for his tomb to be made there, threw them upon his body and head, and horribly broke and crushed it, having no more compassion nor pity than as if it had been a Jew or a Saracen; one of the most heinous examples that has been seen or heard in this your realm before now.

19 From indictment.

3.7 Burglary of the royal treasury (1303)

Commissions of oyer and terminer (dated approximately 6 June and 10 October 1303 - the second containing leading royal judges) were issued pursuant to the burglary of the treasury of the king's wardrobe situated in the precincts of Westminster Abbey.[20] The crime occurred on 24 April 1303 while the main organs of government were relocated in York near the Scottish war zone. The perpetrator was probably Richard of Pudlicott, a clerk who had renounced his calling and sometime merchant, who bore a grudge against Edward I since he had been arrested and imprisoned as a surety for Edward's debts in the Low Countries and lost his lands in the process. As a result of the furore arising from the crime Pudlicott was arrested and found guilty and at this point may have made his lengthy confession. Strangely he implicated no one else, although many people were charged and at least half a dozen laymen hanged. It is likely, however, that he did have inside help, probably from Adam de Warfield and some of the monks supposedly guarding the crypt where the treasure was stored. The monks were released, but Richard of Pudlicott, despite pleading his clergy,[21] was hanged in October 1305. The confession itself should not be taken as wholly reliable evidence of what happened, though some of the jurors accepted or corroborated evidence in it. The chronicle accounts are equally suspect as they appear to have been intent on minimising the scandal to religious orders inherent in the Westminster monks' negligence.[22]

TNA E 101/332/8 m. 4d [French]

Richard de Pudlicote ... said that ... he had noticed a ladder standing against a house, which was in the process of being roofed, close to the gate of the palace towards the abbey, and put this ladder against a window of the chapter house that was opened and closed by a rope, and entered there swinging himself down by the same rope and from there went to the door of the refectory and found it locked shut and with his knife opened it and went inside and found six silver goblets in an aumbry* behind the doors, and thirty or more silver dishes in another aumbry and under a bench wicker baskets containing drinking bowls arranged next to each other and all these he carried off and closed the doors after him without locking them shut. Then he sold the drinking bowls and the silver dishes and goblets and spent such gains before Christmas next following. And consequently his financial resources were used up, so he thought how he could try and break into the king's treasury.

20 *CPR 1301-7*, pp. 192, 194–5.

21 See Chapter 5.

22 T. F. Tout, *A Medieval Burglary* (Manchester, Manchester University Press, 1915).

And in order to carry this out he got to know the premises of the abbey and where the treasury was and how he might be able to get into it; so eight days before Christmas he began to enter by breaking in there with tools which he had to accomplish this; that is to say, two vessels for the earth, one large, one small and knives and many other iron implements. And from then onwards he was engaged in breaking in under cover of night whenever he could work on this and saw an opportunity from eight days before Christmas to the fortnight after Easter following [17 December 1302 to 21 April 1303]. The which then for the first time he entered on a Wednesday night the vigil of St Mark, and the whole of St Mark's day [24–25 April 1303] he remained inside and organised that which he wished to carry away. And that which he carried away he carried outside the following night and of this he left part outside the breach till the next night following and the rest he carried with him as far as the gate behind St Margaret's church and put it under the wall beyond the gate covered with a mound of earth – about twelve pitchers and in each pitcher he put some jewels and standing and covered cups.[23] Besides this, he put a large pitcher with precious stones and a cup in a wooden coffer. Besides this he put three pouches full of jewels and vessels, one of which was full of cups, whole as well as broken. In the other was a large crucifix and jewels, a case of silver with gold dishes. In the third, nine cups, plates and saucers and an image of Our Lady of silver-gilt and two little silver pitchers. Besides this, he carried to a ditch outside the gate a pot and a silver cup. Besides this he carried away with him silver dishes, saucers, plates for spices, a cup, rings, clasps, precious stones, crowns, belts and other jewels, the lion's share of which were later found in his possession. And this same Richard says that when he took these out of the treasury, he carried them at the same time out of the gate, close to St Margaret's church, in the cemetery of St Margaret's church without leaving anything behind him within that gate.

3.8 Highway robberies at Notting Hill and Tottenham (1400–2)

This extract provides an example of the formulaic and repetitious nature of many jury presentments. The requisite evidential details such as when (day and year) and where (place and county) had to be included and the seals of the jurors appended in order for an indictment to be valid.[24] It was clearly possible

23 i.e. cups with stems and lids
24 See Chapter 5.

to offer notoriety as a reason for an accusation without providing specific details of victims and crimes. The presentments here are couched in terms of the affront to the dignity of the king as well as the destruction of the king's people and the law of England that the wrongdoing represents. It is noticeable that a number of the defendants have aliases and that some of their names crop up in both the 1400 and 1402 presentments.

TNA KB 9/185/1 m. 12, /190 m. 39 [Latin]

Inquisition held in the court of king's bench at Westminster in the Michaelmas term in the second year of the reign of King Henry IV [1400]

The jury present that William Faunt, John Samme of Norwich, John Fythyan, Hugo Hosier alias Corby, John Palmer, William Crompe, John Baxter alias York, William Pyrie, Thomas Pyrie, John Jay tailor, Thomas Andrew alias Kelsay or Kelshull, lately staying at Wycombe alias Andrew Kelsey, John Riche of Kent, Thomas Draper, William Stretton lately staying at Campden [Glos.], John Sopere, Thomas Mordon, Thomas Amesbury and Henry Thornton dyer on the Monday after the feast of Pentecost in the first year of the reign of King Henry IV [7 June 1400] at Notting Hill [Middx.] associating with many felons unknown as rebels, plunderers, ambushers of highways against the dignity of the lord king and the common law of England planned to destroy many lieges of the lord king travelling by road. And thus on the day and year abovesaid the aforesaid John Samme and others carrying out ambushes on the highway of the lord king and of his people travelling between the city of London and the village of Acton feloniously and traitorously robbed there Simon Gay chapman of £50 in money and feloniously and traitorously killed and murdered there the same Simon by various ambushes of the highway.

And they present that the said John Samme and the others are common and notorious thieves, robbers, despoilers of fields and ambushers of highways feloniously and traitorously robbing, killing, murdering and destroying the common people of the lord king on the roads to various markets within the aforesaid county and tillers of fields working about their fields to the greatest destruction of the people of the lord king and the destruction of the law of England. And the jurors say that the robbers rebelled for the said causes the abovesaid day, year, place and said county. And that they are common robbers.

Inquisition held in the court of king's bench in the Trinity term in the third year of the reign of King Henry IV [1402]

The jurors present that Robert Berkworth alias Bekworth alias Edward the Hermit,[25] Thomas Andrew alias Andrew Kelsey, Thomas Draper, thief, William Faunt, John Russell of Somerset, Richard Hauteyn and Agnes Leche on Sunday after Easter in the third year of the reign of King Henry IV [2 April 1402] at Stamford Hill in the aforesaid county [Middx.] together with other felons unknown as common ambushers of highways and despoilers of fields on the highway between the town of Tottenham and London lay in ambush to rob the common people of the realm of the king of England and the lieges of the same king coming along the said highway and with all their will and works feloniously and traitorously murdering, killing and destroying and principally the men of law of England so that no law will be able to be used in the said kingdom. And thus through the various ambushes feloniously and traitorously as common felons and robbers of the lord king and of his kingdom intending to destroy and plunder whatsoever lieges of the lord king were passing along the highways of England the day, year, place and county aforesaid, they feloniously and traitorously robbed two unknown men of ten pounds of silver in money.

And they present that the aforesaid Robert Berkworth, Thomas Andrew, Thomas Draper, William Faunt and John Russell are common robbers and notorious thieves, despoilers of fields and ambushers of highways, feloniously and traitorously robbing, killing, murdering and destroying the common people of the lord king on the roads towards various markets within the aforesaid county, and tillers of fields labouring about their fields in the greatest destruction of the people of the lord king and destruction of the law of England. And as robbers rebelled for the said causes the abovesaid day, year, place and said county. And that they are common robbers.

3.9 Domestic violence: the murder of Thomas Beeston JP by his wife (1420)

There is nothing in the court roll that might shed further light on this case. We are left pondering various questions. What had Beeston done wrong? Was his wife in love with her accomplice? It must have been an unusual experience for the justices of the peace before whom the case was presented to try the

25 Interlineated – placed himself (on the jury) and (let him be) hanged.

murderers of one of their own colleagues. It is probably for this reason that the case was referred to the king's bench.

TNA KB 9/216/2 m. 21 [Latin]

PLEAS OF THE CROWN HELD AT ROTHWELL BEFORE SIR JOHN BEAUFO, WILLIAM PALMER AND JOHN CATESBY, JUSTICES OF THE PEACE IN NORTHAMPTONSHIRE, ON THE MONDAY AFTER THE NATIVITY OF THE BLESSED VIRGIN MARY IN THE EIGHTH YEAR OF THE REIGN OF KING HENRY V [9 September 1420]

An inquisition was held at Rothwell before the said justices on the aforesaid day by the oath of John Lenton of Woodford [and eleven other named jurors]: who said under oath that Katherine Beeston who was the wife of Thomas Beeston of Sywell [Northants], gentlewoman, and John Colle senior of Sywell, husbandmen, on Saturday the eve of Trinity Sunday in the eighth year of the reign of King Henry V [8 June 1420] did feloniously slay and murder Thomas Beeston, late justice of the peace in Northamptonshire and husband of the said Katherine at Sywell.

3.10 Domestic violence: a woman killed by her servant (c 1338)

The Year Books comprise cases or notes on points of law recorded by lawyers for future practical or educative use. The entries were usually compiled from cases in the court of common pleas and so rarely concern criminal matters. The killing of a mistress by her servant amounted to petty treason. Under the common law a girl of thirteen had not yet reached the age of discretion and so could not suffer death or mutilation since it was felt that she was too young to realise that what she was doing was wrong. This 'old law' is contrasted, however, with more recently decided case law attributed to judge Henry Spigurnel (d. 1328), which suggests that if the child acts deliberately or there is evidence to show he or she acted with premeditation (the law uses 'malice' to denote intention) then the child should not be protected by the presumption that they do not know the difference between right and wrong.

Year Books of Edward III: 11 & 12 Edward III, ed. A. J. Horwood (RS, 1883), p. 627 [French]

Also a girl of thirteen years of age was burnt because while she was servant to a woman she killed her mistress: and it was found to be so and adjudged treason. And it was said that by the old law no one under age was hanged or suffered judgment of life or limb. But SPIGURNEL found that an infant of ten years of age killed his companion and concealed him: and he caused him to be hanged, because by the concealment he showed that he knew how to distinguish evil from good. And so malice makes up for age.

3.11 Rape: violent assault on Margaret Perman (1438)

This example concentrates on the attempted rape of Margaret Perman by Thomas Elam, which (as the indictment shows) led to her unfortunate death. Although the attacker was unable to commit the full offence, clearly a violent struggle took place during which Margaret was severely injured. At his trial (not included here) Elam protested his innocence, but the gruesome details of the encounter and the victim's death from her injuries, for which he was blamed, probably swayed the jury and he was duly convicted.

TNA JUST 3/210 m. 7d [Latin]

Thomas Ylom otherwise called Elam, lately of Rougham in the county of Norfolk, labourer, being in the prison of the castle of the lord king at Norwich was taken for this that he is indicted before the justices of the peace of the lord king in the aforesaid county of this that he on the Thursday next after Passion Sunday in the sixteenth year of the reign of the present lord king [Henry VI] [3 April 1438] feloniously entered the close and house of Margaret Perman at Rougham and being then there attempted to rape her feloniously and feloniously bit the said Margaret with his teeth so that he ripped off the nose of the said Margaret with that bite and broke three of her ribs there from which the same Margaret eventually died on the Saturday next following [5 April] because of the poison and infection of the same bite.

3.12 Rape: the trial of Ralph Taylor, chaplain (1427)

Although the requisite words of felony were employed in the indictment, it would appear that the sexual intercourse was consensual, so rape as such was not the real issue, hence the eventual acquittal. The indictment was probably brought as a result of his continued fornication (despite receiving ecclesiastical censure), which was offending the community. The wording of the indictment links church and state in condemnation of his behaviour. At a time when the morality of the clergy was being called into question community action was being taken against his recidivist behaviour.[26] While there was probably never any danger of conviction, Taylor's appearance in the royal courts may have brought the message home.

26 Storey, 'Malicious indictments', in *Medieval Ecclesiastical Studies*, pp. 221–40.

TNA JUST 3/203 m. 49 [Latin]

DELIVERY OF THE KING'S GAOL AT WARWICK BEFORE JOHN COCKAYNE AND JAMES STRANGWAYS, JUSTICES COMMIS-SIONED TO DELIVER THE SAID GAOL, ON SATURDAY THE FEAST OF ST PETER'S CHAIR IN THE FIFTH YEAR OF THE REIGN OF KING HENRY VI [22 February 1427]

Ralph Taylor of Moreton Daubeney [Moreton Morrell] in Warwick-shire, chaplain, was arrested on the grounds that:

[1] On the Monday next after the feast of St Lawrence the Martyr in the third year of the reign of King Henry VI [13 August 1425] at Moreton aforesaid he did feloniously rape Alice Begger and did carnally lie with her. Later the said Ralph was summoned to appear on this charge at Halford [War.] before his venerable father in Christ Philip, bishop of Worcester, and was ordered by the bishop, by way of ecclesiastical censure and on pain of excommunication, that he should henceforth send the said Alice away from his house and withdraw himself from any contact with her.

[2] On the Monday next after the feast of All Saints in the fourth year of the reign of King Henry VI [5 November 1425] at Moreton aforesaid he did again feloniously rape the said Alice and did carnally lie with her and has kept her in his own house, from day to day and night to night from the Monday next after St Lawrence aforesaid until the date of this indictment; and thus the said Ralph continues to indulge publicly in the shameful and abominable sin of debauchery and sacrilege, in utter contempt of the bishop's command and the aforesaid threat of excom-munication, and against the catholic faith of Holy Church and against the peace, crown and power of the king; and the said Ralph Taylor was indicted of these offences before Richard Clodesdale, sometime sheriff of the said county, in his tourn held at Kineton on the Tuesday next before the feast of St Alphege in the fourth year of the reign of King Henry VI [16 April 1426].

The jurors came and having been chosen, tried and sworn said upon their oath that the said Ralph Taylor was not guilty of the felonies of which he had been charged and did not take flight because of this prosecution. Therefore it is considered that he is acquitted and free to go.

3.13 A medieval con-man: 'Edward the Hermit' (1402)

The activities of Edward the Hermit offer an unusual insight into the world of the medieval criminal. Although he is referred to here only by what we can assume to be his professional alias, we have already come across him in an earlier example [**3.8**] where as Robert Berkworth he was the ringleader in the Tottenham highway robbery of 1402. His scam is clearly to dupe widows into believing that he can save them from an impending catastrophe and cast out evil spirits as long as their valuables are in front of him. Unfortunately we do not know the outcome of the trial of which this presentment is the initial piece.

TNA KB 9/190 m. 51 [Latin]

Inquisition held before Thomas Camoys, knight, Henry Huse, knight, John Tremayn, John Tauke, John Preston and Robert Oxenbridge justices of the peace of the lord king in the county of Sussex at East-bourne on Wednesday in the week of Pentecost in the third year of the reign of King Henry IV [17 May 1402] on the oath of [twelve named jurors].

Who said on oath that Edward the Hermit plotting how he could rob Johanna lately wife of John Coggere by pretending to be a prophet on Friday the feast of St Matthias in the third year of the reign of King Henry IV [24 February 1402] feloniously broke and entered the close and house of the same Johanna at Mayfield speaking to the same Johanna these words: 'Unless divine grace and my intervention help you the whole house and all your goods and chattels will be consumed by fire and you will be blind before the third day of this coming May.' The said Johanna fearing the said words asked him to help her in this matter. And the said Edward told the same Johanna, 'Collect all your goods and chattels before me as I am able to conjure away all malign spirits.' So Johanna by his command collected all her goods and chattels and thus by the said false machinations the said Johanna the day, year and place aforesaid was feloniously robbed of a bowl (worth 20s), six silver spoons (worth 12s), six gold rings (worth 20s), three pairs of beads of jet and amber with a silver gilt crucifix (worth 12s), two gowns with silver fastenings (worth 10s) and 6s in cash of the same Johanna found there and he is a common thief.

3.14 Sorcery: plotting the death of the king and his uncles (1427)

This highly detailed confession sheds light on the way that gangs of criminals formed and operated.[27] The defendant, suspected of counterfeiting coin, has turned king's evidence in the hope of saving himself from the gallows. This is another example of belief in the magic arts, but the intended victims, the king and his uncles, provide a more serious political context. The details of the confederacy, the secrecy, the swearing of oaths and the careful chain of involvement appear to offer an insider's view. It was important procedurally for the coroner to show that the confession was not made under duress. The sheer amount of information and the special precautions taken suggests that it was more or less a true reflection of the gang's relations rather than a clever attempt by the approver to couch the story in terms of involvement and alliance.

TNA KB 9/224 m. 258 [Latin]

Approver's appeal: be it remembered that on the Wednesday after St Martin in the sixth year of the reign of King Henry VI [12 November 1427] before Thomas Greswald coroner of the king's bench at Westminster John Parker of St Neots [Hunts.] in the custody of the marshal of king's bench on suspicion of counterfeiting coin, spontaneously of his own free will said, confessed and affirmed that he and William Billington of Canterbury, Kent, mercer and jeweller on 18 July 1426 at Canterbury in the house of William Billington had spoken concerning various matters in secret thus that among other things the said William Billington assured the same John Parker that it would be charitable and advantageous for the whole kingdom to destroy the said king and his uncles, namely Bedford and Gloucester, at which the said John replying to the same William said that he had heard of a clerk who through sorcery could drain the life out of whomsoever he wished to kill, so that no one would ever work out how the death had occurred. So it was agreed by the same John and William that the said John would inquire concerning the said clerk and give him notice as soon as he could and later, namely 14 November following, the said William unexpectedly met John in the parish of St Mary Woolnoth in Lombard Street ward in London and asked him why he had given William no answer on the said matter touching the king as he had promised. And the said John said that he had been unable to come and because he understood that the said William was unwilling to concern himself with the same matter further. At which they went to a tavern together and drank there sweet wine, discussing between them the matter touching the said king; and the

27 See 3.17 and Chapter 5.

said William told John that he knew and had certain persons in London of his knowledge and company strongly supporting his said proposition. Then William and John thus associated went to Bucklersbury and there joined up with Elias Davy of London, mercer, and William Felton of London, attorney, and went to a tavern in the parish of St Pancras in Cheap ward in London and there on [14 November] drank wine. Then William Billington said that he would go out on business and at once returned and said to John Parker that he with Elias Davy and William Felton would communicate concerning the matter of the said king just as they communicated together previously and withdrew from them. And on this the said Elias Davy and William Felton said to John Parker that if he swore to them on the Bible[28] that he would keep secret their deliberation and that of others of their company concerning the undertaking they would disclose to him their secret plan, otherwise they were unwilling to communicate further with him concerning the said matter. With this the aforesaid William Felton drew a Bible out from his sleeve and offered it to John Parker to swear upon. And the said John Parker swore on the Bible to each and every aspect of the aforegoing matter proving his assent and agreement to the plan of the said Elias Davy and William Felton and others of their company, as was determined by them. Having done so Elias Davy and William Felton said that it would be charitable and advantageous for the whole realm to destroy the king and his uncles if they could do so and that the majority of the people would stand with them in their opinion; and whatever they desired they would possess in a short time; and they said to John Parker if he would work effectively in this respect he would have 100 marks under the contract and be self-sufficient for the rest of his life. At which John Parker said to Elias Davy and William Felton that he knew a clerk who by his magic art could drain the life from anyone so subtly that no trace would be left once he had died. And the said Elias Davy and William Felton said to John Parker that there was another of their company with much influence in this respect and that they believed he was in St Paul's London in Farringdon ward. Then they all went to the said church to confer with him and when they arrived they did not find him. And then they agreed that they would meet there on the morrow. And John Kirkeby, lately of Huntingdon, until recently a draper and now a corvisor,* met them and the said William Felton said to John Parker concerning John Kirkeby that this was the exceedingly powerful man they had in mind. The said John Kirkeby asked them 'Are

---

28 Literally 'book' but must mean Bible or book of Gospels.

we are all sworn together?' to which they said 'Yes'. And then they all discussed and agreed to carry out the death of the king and his uncles so that John Parker would ask after the said clerk who through the art of magic could destroy anyone thus as said before and would give notice of him to the said Elias Davy and William Felton and others of their company; and he came the Christmas following to the house of Elias Davy in Harrow to discuss the said matters – whence he appeals.

3.15 Political sedition: the trial of John Whitelock, supporter of Richard II (1413)

In political terms, the spectre of Richard II still dogged the Lancastrian dynasty even after fourteen years.[29] On the death of Henry IV in 1413 rumours were circulated in London by Ricardian sympathisers that Richard II was still alive in Scotland. John Whitelock was captured with two other conspirators and sent to the Tower of London. He appeared before the court of king's bench charged with plotting rebellion, planning the death of Henry V and his father, adhering to the king's enemies in Scotland and honouring Thomas Ward, the pseudo-Richard II, as the true king of England. Among other things it was alleged that during parliaments of both Henry IV and Henry V's reigns Whitelock had broadcast his claim by posting bills on church doors in London, Westminster and Bermondsey. One of Whitelock's original bills (found to have been written by one of his accomplices, Thomas Clerk) survives attached to the king's bench indictment. The extract included here is the bill as recorded (in English) in the trial proceedings. Note that he adopts the language of royal charters ('make you all to know that') as had occurred in 1381.[30] Whilst awaiting jury verdict he managed to escape and was never recaptured. It was suspected that he was also associated with Lollard sympathisers. Although Whitelock's conspiracy was at first blush a fairly trivial affair, the swiftness of Henry V's actions in attempting to curb rumours (Whitelock was speedily brought to trial and Richard II ceremonially reburied) and his anger at the lapse in security suggests he was wary of threats to the new regime.[31]

TNA KB 27/609 *Rex* m. 14 [English]

To all you reverend and worshipful knights of the shires of England and burgesses of the boroughs, commons and all other true liege men of the crown of England, and to all others who hear or see this bill, in default of a better man I, John Whitelock, groom and afterwards

---

29 See P. Morgan, 'Henry IV in the shadow of Richard II', in *Crown, Government and People in the Fifteenth Century*, ed. R. E. Archer (Stroud, Alan Sutton, 1995), pp. 9–11.

30 See Chapter 2.

31 Powell, *Kingship*, pp. 137–8.

yeoman with King Richard during the time of thirty winters: I make you all to know that I have been in Scotland these nine years and more to do such service to one who was sometime your liege lord and mine, as lay in my power, for I was sworn upon a book[32] to be a true servant to the aforesaid King Richard for the term of my life if he lived so long. Wherefore, forasmuch as you are in doubt about his still living, I, the aforesaid John Whitelock, make you all to know that that same person, King Richard, who occupied the crown of England twenty-two winters and more, and that person who married Queen Anne and, after her decease, the French king's daughter, Isabel, is in the ward and keeping of the duke of Albany in Scotland. To prove this so, I, the aforesaid John Whitelock, will swear before you all upon a Bible and if you believe it not, I will swear it on God's sacred body and use it to show that it is King Richard in person. If you believe it, I shall bind myself to whatever honest person you will in England under ward and keeping of certain true lords, spiritual and temporal, knights, esquires, burgesses of substance, with protestations that that person in Scotland be brought into England among his true people, without any harming of his person and of his friends; also to ordain for him all that should be ordained for such a lord, to the pleasure of God and the salvation of the worship of England, having regard to the great wrong that is done to him, which is proclaimed in all Christendom; also that I, John Whitelock, may have sufficient to live on so that I die not in prison for hunger, thirst or cold, and be neither murdered nor poisoned nor through duress of prison be in any way impaired until the time when it is known whether my report is found true or false with the lords, spiritual and temporal, and commons. And if it is found true, I ask for free pass out of prison and my name to be taken as that of a true man; and if it be found false, then take me out of prison and lead me to King Harry and his sons, and the vilest death that may be ordained for me, let me have it. For one thing I tell you: say not another day that you have not been warned of things that may befall, for I tell you, for as much as God bought me with his flesh and his blood on the cross, body and soul, and my father and my mother have begotten and given birth to me into this world, I commit myself to the devil, ever to lie in hell, body and soul, without departing, and never to have mercy of God nor partake in any prayer in Holy Church from this day until the day of doom,[33] if that person that was sometime King Richard is not alive in Scotland, as I have said before.

32 A Bible or Book of gospels.
33 ie Judgment Day

3.16 The criminal underworld: the appeal of William Rose (1389)

The approver William Rose was something of a medieval 'supergrass'.[34] Incarcerated in Winchester Castle from at least early February 1389, he confessed to a series of crimes initially before the sheriff and the city coroner and then before the county coroner over a period of three days (the time usually allowed for making appeals). Rose reeled off the names of as many as fifty-four of his former associates in crime and the roll appears to be the original draft of his accusations. Although there was no standard number of successful appeals that an approver was expected to make in order to win his freedom (some commentators have put it at five), few ever achieved their freedom. Rose said he was prepared to fight to prove the veracity of his charges (certainly against his first three appellees), but we do not know whether trial by battle was ordered in their cases.[35] His accusations in this passage predominantly concern robberies and thefts, but there is also information about a homicide and counterfeiters of coin. Rose's activities were geographically widespread as his confession here draws on events occurring in no fewer than four different counties. His associates themselves come from even further afield and if genuine suggest he enjoyed an extensive network of contacts and accomplices. Rose himself survived a further seven years until he was ordered to be hanged in October 1396.

TNA JUST 1/797 mm. 2–4 [Latin]

The appeal of William Rose of Loughborough made on 16 February in the twelfth year of the reign of King Richard II [1389] in the presence of Henry Popham sheriff of Hampshire and Henry Jordan a royal coroner in Winchester.

He appeals John Brasyer of Woburn Chapel near Dunstable [Beds.] in that the said John feloniously stole a bay horse (worth 16s) in the company of the said William Rose in the field at Towcester on the Monday before the feast of the Assumption of the Blessed Virgin Mary in the twelfth year of the reign of King Richard II [10 August 1388].

... Also he appeals John Saddler of Oxford dwelling at Carfax in that he is the maker of false coin. Also he appeals John Daniel of Ashwell by Woburn Chapel and William Courser of Braintree that on the Monday before the feast of All Saints in the said year [26 October 1388] he feloniously stole six oxen (worth 8 marks) in the field of Dunmow [Essex] together with the said William Rose. Also he appeals John Goldsmith of Mitcheldean in the forest of Dean in that he is a maker of false gold coin.

34 This appeal is discussed in detail in Post, 'Evidential value of approvers' appeals, 91–100.

35 For approvers' appeals and trial by battle see Chapter 5 (especially 5.11).

... Also he appeals Simon Fisher of Wycombe in that he together with the said William in the field of Tring in the vale of Aylesbury on the Thursday before the feast of the Invention of the Cross in the eleventh year of the reign of King Richard II [30 April 1388] feloniously stole three horses (worth £4) from a certain grange of the prior of Bicester [Oxon.].

The appeal of William Rose of Loughborough, Leicestershire, king's approver, made on oath at Winchester in the king's prison before Thomas Cauteshanger coroner of Hampshire on Thursday, Friday and Saturday after the feast of St Matthias in the twelfth year of the reign of King Richard II [25–27 February 1389].

On which Thursday the said William confessed himself before the said Thomas the coroner to be a thief in that he with John Gilling, Nicholas Dancaster of Hartford staying at Royston at the house of Thomas Taverner, and John Somerville staying at Conington in Leicestershire came into the hundred of Crondall in Hampshire on Grateley heath on the king's highway which leads from Bagshot to Hartford Bridge on Monday on the feast of the Exaltation of the Cross in the twelfth year of the reign of King Richard II [14 September 1388] at a place called *Dynhaghe* and feloniously killed John Byncombe of Taunton in the said place and robbed the said John of two horses (worth 40 shillings) of packs with cloth, linen and wool (worth £16) of which the said William had his share (6s 8d worth) and he is prepared to prove the same against the said John, Nicholas and John with his body.

The same William approver says that he together with John Brasyer, Andrew Coursor of Haseley in Oxfordshire, John Chishine of Haseley in Oxfordshire, and George Middleton staying at Abingdon in Ock Street came to Hartford Bridge in Oxfordshire on the highway which leads from Oxford to Tetsworth on Thursday after the feast of St Peter's Chains in the twelfth year of the reign of King Richard II [6 August 1388] and there robbed William Mercer of Dadlington of a brown horse (worth £1 6s 8d), bowls of gold and of silver, beads of amber and took handkerchiefs and silk and linen cloth worth £20. And he says that the aforesaid are common thieves involved in many robberies.

IV: THE DEVELOPMENT OF CRIMINAL JUSTICE

The period covering the late thirteenth to the early fifteenth century was a crucial one in terms of the evolution of a practical and lasting system of criminal justice.[1] At its outset the general eyre was still in operation. This was an omnicompetent travelling court, which had periodically administered justice in the localities since the days of Henry II. Initiated on a countrywide scale as a means of enforcing the assize of Clarendon (1166), during the thirteenth century it became the principal agency carrying out and supervising the exercise of royal justice in the provinces.

The teams of justices in eyre named in the commission operated throughout the country on defined county circuits. Empowered to hear all civil pleas (mainly land litigation) as well as pleas of the crown, the justices in eyre were responsible for the administration of both civil and criminal justice.[2] Until the mid-thirteenth century the articles of the eyre (the list of questions put to juries), which embodied its jurisdiction, betrayed an overriding concern for the king's own rights, especially the feudal and proprietary rights of the crown. Although the criminal side was apparently subsidiary and limited to felony, particularly homicide, the amount of space devoted to criminal matters in the eyre rolls suggests otherwise.[3] In the second half of the thirteenth century (after 1254 and again after 1278) new articles extended the eyre's scope in the criminal field. [**4.1**] Many of the new articles, however, were not specifically criminal. They concerned the usurpation of royal rights (the *quo warranto** inquiries) and the conduct of royal and seigneurial officials, though in fact much of the *quo warranto* business was not conducted under the articles of the eyre, but in response to the claims to franchises made at the beginning of the eyre.[4] The elaboration of the articles in any event brought new business in the form of trespass litigation.

Recognition of trespass as a matter of interest to the crown considerably enlarged the scope of royal criminal jurisdiction as many matters previously

---

1 For arguments favouring evolutionary over revolutionary change see Musson and Ormrod, *Evolution*, pp. 1–7.

2 W. L. Warren, *Henry II* (London, Methuen, 1973), pp. 281–4, 286; W. T. Reedy, 'The origins of the general eyre', *Speculum*, 41 (1996), 717–23; J. Hudson, *The Formation of the English Common Law* (London and New York, Longman, 1996), pp. 123–59, 184.

3 *Crown Pleas of the Wiltshire Eyre, 1249*, ed. C. A. F. Meekings, Wiltshire Record Society, 16 (1960), pp. 37–69.

4 D. W. Sutherland, *Quo Warranto Proceedings in the Reign of Edward I* (Cambridge, Cambridge University Press, 1963); Cam, *Hundred Rolls*, pp. 22–41.

remedied in the local courts could now come before the eyre justices.[5] Although minor offences and wrongs continued to be remedied in local courts, such an expansion in the business undertaken by the eyre, especially cases involving the usurpation of franchises, began to overwhelm the agency and the duration of its sessions lengthened accordingly.[6] Following its suspension in 1294 (owing to war with France) it was not recalled to the national stage until a brief experiment under chief justice Geoffrey le Scrope in 1329–31.[7] The revival of the eyre at that time was itself highly symbolic and an attempt to turn the clock back to the style of law enforcement witnessed during Edward I's reign.[8] [**4.3**]

The eyre's useful life was already over by 1300, therefore, but its influence continued to be felt both at governmental level, where some tribunals such as the trailbastons were fashioned in its image, and at the local level, where the memory of its visitations with their searching inquiries and punishing financial exactions died hard. The next century saw a series of expedients and experiments to replace it, many of which had already emerged during the thirteenth century as supplements to the eyre's lengthening and increasingly supervisory visitations.[9]

An attempt to achieve an immediate impact on law enforcement came towards the end of Edward I's reign through the countrywide imposition of general commissions of oyer and terminer. From the late thirteenth century commissions in general and special forms to hear (oyer) and determine (terminer) cases of alleged wrongdoing were a device increasingly employed in the provinces and for a while they became a standard part of the judicial machinery. [**4.6**] General oyer and terminer commissions were usually issued for a group of counties and contained broad powers to punish an entire class of offenders, as in the case of the powerful 'trailbaston' commissions. [**4.2**] With a reduced number of highly focused articles of inquiry the 'trailbaston' commissions of 1305–7 (so named after criminal gangs armed with sticks or 'bastons') were intended to provide swifter and more efficient judicial sessions than the eyre, coupled with exactions that were less swingeing and unpopular. The rationale behind their launch stemmed partly from political motives: a reassertion of royal authority and a desire to exploit the improving domestic situation following successful foreign wars; partly from the backlog of cases resulting from the suspension of the general eyre ten years previously; and partly from a perceived increase in lawlessness in the country: a side effect of the troops returning from Edward

---

5 A. Harding, 'Plaints and bills in the history of English law', in *Legal History Studies 1972*, ed. D. Jenkins (Cardiff, University of Wales, 1975), pp. 65–70.

6 D. Crook, *Records of the General Eyre* (London, HMSO, 1982); C. Burt, 'The demise of the general eyre in the reign of Edward I', *EHR*, 120 (2005), 1–10.

7 D. Crook, 'The later eyres', *EHR*, 97 (1982), 241–68.

8 *The Eyre of Northamptonshire, 3–4 Edward III, AD 1329–1330*, ed. D. W. Sutherland, vol. 1, pp. 5–6; A. Musson, 'Appealing to the past: perceptions of law in late medieval England', in *Expectations*, ed. Musson, p. 174.

9 Crook, 'Later eyres', pp. 241–43; Musson, *Medieval Law*, pp. 137–45.

I's campaigns in France and Scotland.[10] The commissions heralded a clean-up operation prior to a relaunch of the general eyre. Indeed it was envisaged that the 'trailbaston' commissions would be, as Edward I put it, 'like a drink before the medicine'.[11]

For a while general oyer and terminer commissions in this mould became an established part of the judicial machinery and were often initiated as a result of law-enforcement drives and serious investigations into wrongdoing. While they had the power to hear felonies, the numerous trespasses coming before the justices were put to the crown's financial advantage with the imposition of fines in remission of imprisonment. Increasingly during the fourteenth century general oyer and terminer commissions were used as a vehicle to investigate not just general disorder, but the conduct of royal officials.[12] [**4.6b**]

The 'trailbaston' commissions (and the 'new inquiries' of the 1340s in particular) gained unpopularity themselves from the heavy fines meted out and the detailed inquiries they undertook. Indeed the terms 'eyre' and 'trailbaston' became synonymous as the latter was equated in the 'popular' and parliamentary mind with the penalties of the eyre, with the result that the mere threat of imposition was used to the crown's fiscal advantage in the second half of the fourteenth century.[13] In the later fourteenth and fifteenth centuries general oyer and terminer commissions were employed less frequently as the assize justices and court of king's bench took over much of the investigation of the behaviour of officialdom. Rather than being nationwide vehicles, instead they targeted major disturbances in particular counties (or small groups of counties).[14]

Special commissions could be obtained from chancery (usually through a petition to the crown) by private individuals (upon payment of a fee) for inquiry into specific incidents or as a means of settling disputes within a given area. [**4.6a**] Although felony lay within their scope, they were primarily utilised for cases involving trespass. The flexibility inherent in the special commissions, the swiftness of their proceedings and their capacity to focus on particular wrongs in specific areas made them popular with litigants and important tools in the disputants' armoury. The ease with which commissions could be obtained and the plaintiff's ability to nominate justices (usually a mixture of royal justices

10 A. Harding, 'Early trailbaston proceedings from the Lincoln roll of 1305', in *Medieval Legal Records*, pp. 143–68; A. Phelan, 'Trailbaston and attempts to control violence in the reign of Edward I', in *Violence in Medieval Society*, ed. R. W. Kaeuper (Woodbridge, Boydell Press, 2000), pp. 129–40.

11 *SCCKB*, vol. 2, p. cl.

12 *The 1341 Royal Inquest in Lincolnshire*, ed. B. W. McLane, Lincoln Record Society, 78 (1988).

13 G. L. Harriss, *King, Parliament and Public Finance in Medieval England to 1369* (Oxford, Clarendon Press, 1975), pp. 405–10; W. N. Bryant, 'The financial dealings of Edward III with the county communities', *EHR*, 83 (1968), 762–4; W. R. Jones, 'Keeping the peace: English society, local government and the commissions of 1341–44', *AJLH*, 18 (1974), 307–20.

14 Musson and Ormrod, *Evolution*, p. 49; Powell, *Kingship*, pp. 139, 201–5; C. D. Ross, *Edward IV* (London, Methuen, 1974), pp. 397–8.

and local men) made them useful retributive devices or vehicles for putting pressure on an opponent. As such they were prone to misuse. Rather than physical punishment, the plaintiff urged the payment of a sum in damages, which was decided upon by the justices.[15]

The court of king's bench had traditionally followed the itinerary of the king, but the king hearing cases personally was largely a fiction.[16] In the fourteenth century the king's bench came to have special jurisdiction over criminal cases of treason and felony, and accordingly a separate section in its plea rolls was set aside for criminal proceedings (denoted by *Rex* at the top of the membrane). Although the king's bench was frequently domiciled at Westminster, from the 1320s the court was increasingly sent into the provinces and appears to have been responding to problems of law enforcement there.[17] [**4.4**] This policy was expressed explicitly in the parliament of 1352 in response to a petition on the matter: 'The king will send his bench where there is need.'[18]

In the provinces the king's bench took cases according to articles of inquiry sent out to jurors, but it could also act as a court of first instance, hearing plaints and bills as had been the case under the eyre. Apart from the 1320s the court was probably at its most active regionally in the late 1330s and during the 1350s, the latter period being when Sir William Shareshull was chief justice (1350–61).[19] [**4.5**] Over the years it had become established practice for the court to assume jurisdiction over all pleas of the crown in the county where it sat and to undertake to deliver the gaols of prisoners awaiting trial, though arguably the court did not fully constitute itself at every venue and so the extent of its mobility may to some extent be illusory. As the fourteenth century progressed it was also increasingly common for undetermined cases before the justices of the peace or oyer and terminer commissioners (as well as those before justices of assize) to be transferred to the king's bench.[20]

There were limitations in the use of the court of king's bench as a 'superior eyre' in terms of any nationwide policy on law and order. Although its ability to review proceedings of lower courts meant the geographical range of its purview was wide, its physical presence in particular counties and its regional coverage were uneven and restricted in practice. Aside from being harnessed for itinerant visitations during Henry V's reign and a brief removal to York in 1392, the court remained static at Westminster from 1362 and for much of the fifteenth century.[21] There it became increasingly the focus for disputes between

---

15 R. W. Kaeuper, 'Law and order in fourteenth century England: the evidence of special commissions of oyer and terminer', *Speculum*, 54 (1979), 734–84.

16 See Chapter 1 for examples of the monarch's personal involvement in justice.

17 *SCCKB*, vol. 4, pp. xix, lix–lxv; vol. 6, pp. ix–xii.

18 *RP*, vol. 2, p. 238.

19 B. H. Putnam, *The Place in Legal History of Sir William Shareshull* (Cambridge, Cambridge University Press, 1950), pp. 109–10.

20 Musson and Ormrod, *Evolution*, pp. 17–20, 53–4.

21 Powell, *Kingship*, pp. 14, 63, 173–94.

the landed gentry who frequently sued (on the plea side) writs of trespass *vi et armis* (with force and arms) alleging violence to the person or damage to property, or initiated writs of *certiorari** (on the *Rex* side) removing a case from the lower courts to king's bench (with all the added nuisance value).[22]

A more permanent solution to the problems of local justice was found in the development of the county circuits of assize and gaol delivery. Groups of commissioners hearing actions concerning landownership and property right (the petty or possessory assizes) and trying prisoners charged with felony held in royal (and privately owned) gaols had been sent into the provinces since Henry III's reign supplementing the responsibility of the eyre for these tasks. The commissions were, however, limited in number and geographical reach. Over the course of the thirteenth century, with the postponement of scheduled eyres and the lengthening time between visits, separate commissions for hearing assizes and delivering gaols became more routine and geographically widespread. Precise circuits were issued for assizes in 1273, 1285 and 1293; gaols were delivered on more localised circuits until 1291–92.[23] The two tasks were not formally united until 1299, though in fact this arrangement only lasted a few years. It was not until 1328 and 1330, under new statutory regulation, that the circuit system was more effectively rationalised.[24] [**4.7**]

Thereafter justices of assize, drawn from the serjeants and judges of the central courts, operated on six circuits, providing an important link between the shires and central government. This was especially so since specific assize justices when visiting a county were allowed (by virtue of a *nisi prius** clause inserted into the writ summoning a jury to appear at Westminster or in king's bench) to take locally the jury trial stage of a case (though not the main pleading in that case) pending in the central courts. This could thus save jurors a journey to the capital if the justices came before the next term set for the appearance of the jury at Westminster. Moreover, a justice's circuit often included a county or counties in which he had personal connections or his own lands were situated. This affiliation was an issue voiced in a parliamentary petition of 1376 on the basis that if the assize justices were too closely associated with the people of their own area, their judgments might accordingly be biased.[25] Although specific complaints were invited, legislation on the matter did not emerge for another nine years. Even after the statue of 1384 the provision was manifestly ignored by chancery and the circuit personnel remained virtually unchanged. The practice suggests that some local knowledge of the area under the justices' jurisdiction was deemed appropriate and the crown was fully aware of the need to temper its 'centralising' tendencies.[26] [**4.8**]

22 Maddern, *Violence*, pp. 22, 31–47.

23 A. Musson, 'The local administration of justice: a reappraisal of the "four knights" system', in *English Government in the Thirteenth Century*, ed. A. Jobson (Woodbridge, Boydell Press, 2004), pp. 97–110.

24 Musson, *Public Order*, pp. 87–122.

25 *RP*, vol. 2, p. 334 (75).

26 A. J. Verduyn, 'The attitude of the parliamentary commons to law and order under

The offences coming before the justices of gaol delivery had previously been presented in lesser courts, by juries at hearings in the hundred courts or in the courts of private jurisdictions, or in the biannual sheriff's tourn.[27] Gaol delivery also provided the forum for appeals of felony recorded in the county court and for the verdicts arising from coroners' inquests if the appellee or accused had been arrested and was being held for trial.[28] Depending upon the scope of their commission the justices tried the whole calendar (list of cases for trial) of prisoners imprisoned in the gaol, individual named prisoners or particular types of felon.[29] In the fourteenth and fifteenth centuries indictments of felony or defendants arrested on suspicion originating from peace sessions frequently came before the gaol delivery justices, some of whom sat as justices of the peace. The close association between the two types of sessions, observable from the considerable overlaps between the personnel involved, not only provided an opportunity for all the relevant local officials to meet together (as can be seen from the list of attendees at Northamptonshire assize sessions in 1416), but also stimulated and facilitated other types of business and social interaction.[30] [**4.9, 4.10**]

Equally important for local justice was the evolution of the office of justice of the peace, which largely took place during the fourteenth century.[31] Developing from the earlier keepers of the peace, who had responsibility for hearing presentments under the statute of Winchester (1285),[32] the justices of the peace, as can be seen from their commission, attracted responsibility not only for hearing and determining felonies and trespasses, but also for enforcing criminal, economic and social legislation contained in the provisions of various statutes including those governing labourers, liveries and Lollards. [**4.11**] Parliamentary complaints about the conduct of sheriffs (and bailiffs of private hundreds) when taking their biannual tourns coupled with the frequency of peace sessions (four times a year) and their general popularity with litigants led to the transfer of the sheriff's criminal jurisdiction to the JPs.[33] [**4.14**]

Edward III', unpublished DPhil thesis, University of Oxford, 1991, pp. 130, 179; Musson and Ormrod, *Evolution*, pp. 15–16, 47–8, 58–60.

27 H. Summerson, 'The structure of law enforcement in thirteenth century England', *AJLH*, 23 (1979), 320–24.

28 For examples of indictments from these officials see Chapter 5.

29 R. B. Pugh, *Imprisonment in Medieval England* (Cambridge, Cambridge University Press, 1968), pp. 255–7, 278; Musson, 'Local administration', p. 100.

30 Musson, 'Local administration', pp. 105–6; Musson, *Public Order*, pp. 100–5, 117–18; Powell, *Kingship*, pp. 56–60, 248–51; Maddern, *Violence*, pp. 48–66.

31 B. H. Putnam, 'The transformation of the keepers of the peace into the justices of the peace, 1327–1380', *TRHS* 4th series, 12 (1929), 19–48; Musson, *Public Order*, pp. 11–82.

32 A. Harding, 'The origins and early history of the keepers of the peace', *TRHS* 5th series, 10 (1960), 85–109; H. Summerson, 'The enforcement of the statute of Winchester, 1285–1327', *JLH*, 13 (1992), 232–50.

33 J. R. Lander, *English Justices of the Peace, 1461–1509* (Gloucester, Alan Sutton, 1989), pp. 6–11.

The statue of 1361 is traditionally regarded as an important landmark in the history of the magistracy. [**4.12**] In many ways, however, the legislation merely consolidated a number of experiments that had been occurring during the early fourteenth century in according determining powers to keepers of the peace.[34] Moreover, the statute is not entirely typical of the later jurisdiction of the JPs since it gave them (albeit only for three years) the determining power they had previously exercised on occasion, unfettered by the supervisory power of the assize justices. From 1344 assize justices were regularly appointed as JPs in all the counties within their circuit and formed the quorum necessary for determining felonies. [**4.13a**] This remained the case (with some exceptions in the 1360s and 1380s) up to the peace commissions issued in 1389. These gave birth to two quorums, one for felonies (comprising the assize justices on their own), the other for all other offences (containing a mixture of assize justices and local men of law). In 1394 this position was altered by statute and a single quorum reinstated, but this time containing local men of law. [**4.13b**] The legislation confirmed the essential make-up of the peace commission for the next two centuries.[35]

The extracts in this chapter provide an idea of the scope of the jurisdiction of these institutions as set out in their articles and commissions. It was in these that the inquisitional and investigative nature of medieval criminal justice can be seen. Articles of inquiry were provided to jurors to which they were required to respond (upon pain of amercement*) and which thus governed the structure of jury presentments and the subject matter of subsequent sessions. The precociousness of the system was in turn responsible for the enormous variety of cases that came before the justices. The system as it developed contained many overlaps both with regard to essential functions and the personnel carrying out judicial and administrative tasks. As a counterpart to the preceding chapter, the extracts here reveal the employment of different types of judicial machinery and something of the policies behind them. While royal programmes of law enforcement were not always fully co-ordinated, nor yet successful, even so they represented a significant attempt to devise suitable methods to combat the problems of law and order posed over nearly three centuries.

---

34 A. Musson, 'Creatures of statute? The earliest justices of the peace', *Archives*, 104 (2001), 21–9; A. Verduyn, 'The politics of law and order during the early years of Edward III', *EHR*, 108 (1993), 842–67; A. Verduyn, 'The selection and appointment of justices of the peace in 1338', *HR*, 68 (1995), 1–25.

35 E. Powell, 'The administration of criminal justice in late-medieval England: peace sessions and assizes', in *The Political Context of Law*, ed. R. Eales and D. Sullivan (London, Hambledon Press, 1987), pp. 49–59.

4.1 The articles of the general eyre

The eyre's jurisdiction over crown pleas was embodied in the 'articles of the eyre', a list of questions put to juries from the various administrative units and jurisdictions within the county (hundreds, boroughs and liberties). The selection of articles below represents those of the old and new chapters (the latter being articles issued after 1254) most closely associated with the functioning of the criminal justice system. There is some duplication between the two. Inquiries were to be made into the activities of different types of lawbreakers and outlaws as well as into how diligently criminal justice was being administered (especially with regard to its proceeds) in the shires. A number of questions are concerned with the behaviour of jurors and officials and reveal a conscious attempt to suppress corruption of the legal process. Several betray a close relationship with the chapters of various statutes (such as Marlborough and Westminster I and II) and Magna Carta. When the juries had been charged with the eyre articles (sworn to tell the truth on each) they were required to make their return. The proceedings of the Kent eyre show how the presentments were entered on the roll in Latin, but the jurors had to present them at the bar of the court in English. Any discrepancy between the two rendered the jurors liable to amercement.*

The Eyre of Kent, 6 & 7 Edward II, ed. F. W. Maitland, L. W. V. Harcourt and W. C. Bolland, SS, 24 (1910), pp. 28–45 [Latin]

Old articles (examples)

Concerning sheriffs and others who have held pleas of the crown, and what pleas.

Concerning counterfeiters and clippers of coins, who they are.

Concerning burglars and evildoers and such as harbour them in time of peace.

Concerning outlaws and fugitives, and those who return following outlawry or flight without warrant.

Concerning delivery of gaols made without the warrant of the lord king or his justices, and similarly concerning those who hold pleas of approvers without warrant.

Concerning the escape of felons.

Concerning bailiffs who take payment for removing jurors from assizes and juries.

Concerning sheriffs and bailiffs who take [gifts] from both parties.

Concerning coroners who have taken a certain amount in money or any kind of reward for exercising their official duty; and whether they have concealed the chattels of felons or fugitives or detained them for their own use and to what extent, and in whose hands etc.

Concerning prisoners and those incarcerated on some suspicion of wrong by the sheriff or bailiffs and by any other bailiffs, how they were released.

Concerning those who by mutual oath bind themselves to give support to actions at law of friends and well-wishers, by which truth and justice are strangled.

New articles (examples)

Concerning franchises granted that have hindered the course of justice and have opposed royal power; and by whom they have been granted and at what time.

Also who, being bailiffs of a lord and any of their sub-bailiffs, or even ministers of the lord king, have not allowed the execution of the commands of our lord the king, but have treated them with contempt, or in some other way have hindered them from taking effect, from the time of the promulgation of the Statute of Marlborough in the fifty-second year of the reign of King Henry, the father of King Edward [1267].

Concerning sheriffs and all others whatsoever taking payment for removing names from the panels of assizes and juries; and from what time.

Concerning sheriffs who hold their tourn more frequently than twice a year and from what time, as in the Great Charter of Liberties etc.

Concerning those responsible for imprisoned felons who for money have permitted them to get away free and unpunished.

Concerning those who have kept approvers imprisoned and have made them appeal trustworthy and innocent people for the sake of gain, and who have hindered them from appealing the guilty; and by whose procurement such things were done and from what time.

Also, who have taken gifts or other profit for carrying out their official duties, or have carried out the orders of the lord king in another way than pertained to their office and at what time.

Concerning those who have not made the effort to pursue and arrest felons both within liberties and outside them when ordered by the sheriff and other bailiffs of the lord king or at the hue and cry of the neighbourhood.

Concerning those who have ravished maidens who are under age, with their will or against it, or any woman of full age against her will.

Concerning sheriffs or other ministers of the king taking reward for carrying out their duties.

Concerning those who by mutual oaths bind themselves deceitfully to support or defend pleas and actions touching their friends or patrons in assizes, juries, or recognitions, to the end that the truth of such pleas or actions may be concealed.

4.2 The Ordinance and articles of Trailbaston (1305)

The countrywide trailbaston commissions of 1305 had precedents in the commissions of oyer and terminer investigating the conduct of officials issued in 1298 and in the exploratory (pre-trailbaston) commissions of inquiry concerning vagabonds and disturbers of the peace sent into individual counties from the beginning of the new century. The 'Ordinance of Trailbaston' was issued in the parliament of April 1305 and intended as follow-up instructions to these inquiries. The justices appointed had a wide brief and were empowered to hear and determine felonies and trespasses coming before them that had been committed in various counties. Since the earlier set of commissioners had not had the power to try offences, the newly appointed justices were to judge and punish the crimes unearthed by the former's inquiries. Although the justices were not allowed to hear writ actions, they were later given separate responsibility for holding assizes (and delivering gaols). Proceedings survive from a number of counties and directly reflect the concerns of the articles. In this they targeted not just those committing serious crimes against people and property, but more specifically those whose concerted actions and threatening behaviour (constituting 'enormous' trespasses) undermined the functioning of the judicial process.[1]

(a) Ordinance of Trailbaston (1305)

RP, vol. 1, p. 178: Ordinance of Trailbaston [Latin]

It is enjoined upon the justices whom the lord king assigned in divers counties to inquire about, hear and determine divers felonies and

---

1 A. Harding, 'Early trailbaston proceedings from the Lincoln roll of 1305', in *Medieval Legal Records*, pp. 144–50. For cases involving conspiracy, laying false claims and the terrorising of jurors see Chapter 8.

trespasses committed, that they proceed in the form written below, namely that in each county where the inquirers have proceeded to make inquiries on felonies and trespasses and failed to inquire into other matters for lack of time or some other reason, they are to hear and determine with respect to such matters committed.

And to judge and punish according to law and custom all those who, having been indicted before them or previously arrested and imprisoned, are found guilty of robberies, arsons, homicides and other felonies committed from the feast of St John the Baptist in the twenty-fifth year of the reign of Edward I to Easter in the thirty-third year of his reign [24 June 1297 to 18 April 1305]. And those whom they find arrested for any felonies committed before the said time, if they are not repleviable* according to law and custom they should commit to gaol until the next visitation of the eyre justices into these parts or until the lord king ordains anything concerning their delivery.

And to judge and punish all those found guilty before them because they have beaten, wounded and maltreated persons of the realm placed on juries, recognitions and assizes for telling the truth and also attacked others in fairs and markets and other common places out of enmity, envy and preconceived malice and all those found guilty before them because they hired the said wrongdoers or received them knowingly after the event or gave or made the command, assent, force and assistance for such beatings and trespasses.

And those whom they find guilty of receiving others into their protection and avowry* for payment by reason of their power or lordship they are to have them stand trial at the king's suit by the indictment made on this, although no one prosecutes against them and if they are convicted thereon, they are to be committed to gaol and then later delivered.

And all those they find indicted, arrested or held in prison for any light and personal trespasses against the king's peace committed within the time aforementioned or before, then those indicted, arrested and imprisoned should be put by simple mainprise* to respond to complainants when they try to sue against them according to common law. In which mainprise it is to be stipulated that they should behave themselves in future in a good and honest and peaceful way against anyone of the realm by not wronging anyone or procuring the wronging of anyone.

And it is ordained that in every enormous trespass in which the party complaining sues or is prosecuted at the king's suit as mentioned before, then if the party defending has not been found and he does not have anything in the county by which he is able to be attached,* the justices shall cause him to be exacted* from county court to county court until, if he has not appeared according to the law and custom of the realm, he is outlawed.[2]

And the lord king wills that in the counties where John de Insula, William Howard and Henry Spigurnel are assigned to deal with matters nothing should be expedited concerning these matters in their absence.

(b) Presentments under the articles of Trailbaston in Kent (1305)

TNA JUST 1/396 m. 15 [Latin]

Jurors of the hundred of Preston … who said on oath that …

Concerning malefactors and disturbers of the peace of the king, homicides, robberies, arsons and other things, nothing, except that a certain John at Cornhill of Sittingborne was indicted by the hundred of Preston before Sir Waresius Valoignes, then sheriff of Kent, in the thirty-second year of the reign of Edward I [1303] for a horse which was stolen of John of Milton in the hundred of Preston and he took it away in theft and the same John at Cornhill afterwards returned to the house of Juliana Draper in the hundred aforesaid after the said felony and the aforesaid John and Juliana were arrested for the said felony and released to the said Waresius Valoignes; and Sir John de Northwode now sheriff released them by mainprise until the next gaol delivery.

They said also that a certain Stephen son of Philip of Preston was indicted for the death of John le Marchal of Canterbury killed at *Syvingwood* in the thirtieth year of the reign of Edward I [1301–2] before Henry de Woghepe coroner of the lord king, was later arrested by officials of the lord king and acquitted before justices of the lord king by the hundred of Dunhamford and still is indicted etc.

Concerning those knowingly receiving and consenting to the same, providing force and help or procuring and ordering the commission of the said trespasses – nothing.

Concerning those who for their reward have made and do make agreement with disturbers of the peace of the king and have hired and do hire them to beat, wound and maltreat etc. they said that whereas a certain Nicholas Potier acquired an acre of land of John son of Philip of Preston and had it in peace there came with force and arms John Noldekyn of

2 See 5.6.

Sandwich and Geoffrey de Arundel of Sandwich and others unknown of Sandwich in the twenty-sixth year of the reign of Edward I [1297–98] through the hiring and procuring of John son of Philip of Preston and ejected the said Nicholas from his land and crops to the grave damage of the same Nicholas etc. and his destruction. And all the said malefactors coerced, threatened and maltreated the same Nicholas against the peace until he satisfied them hurriedly with 12s.

Concerning those who maintain pleas for money and for a share of the thing falsely and maliciously implead others – nothing.

4.3 The revival of the general eyre, Northamptonshire (1329)

Since its suspension in 1294 there had been no general visitations of the eyre, only sessions in individual counties: Cambridgeshire (1299), Cornwall (1302), Kent (1313–14) and London (1321). In 1329 teams of justices sat concurrently in two counties (Northamptonshire and Nottinghamshire) on what was intended to be the start of a countrywide visitation. Chief justice Sir Geoffrey Scrope's speech at the opening of proceedings in Northampton set out his justification for the revival and his agenda for law enforcement. His view of the eyre's effectiveness was somewhat rose-tinted. Originally its visitations had been more frequent than every seven years, but the interval between visits had lengthened because of the sheer amount of business. The eyre's scrutiny was once more visited upon the minutiae of county life in a way that was intrusive to people unused to its style and scope of inquiry. It also reopened the vexed question of landowners having to justify their franchises, which had been a source of discontent during the *quo warranto* inquiries of Edward I's years. The eyre visitations were aborted in the winter of 1330–31 with only four counties visited.

The Eyre of Northamptonshire, 3–4 Edward III, AD 1329–1330, ed. D. W. Sutherland, SS, 97 (1983), vol. 1, pp. 5–6 [French]

Then Sir Geoffrey said, 'My good sirs, some of you who have come here know why it was decided to hold this eyre and many others do not, therefore I will explain. In the last parliament at Northampton complaints were brought to our lord the king from all parts of the kingdom that the people were suffering severely under manifold oppressions of magnates and from the extortions of maintainers, the petty tyranny of bailiffs, and homicides and thefts committed throughout the kingdom, and many from all parts who were troubled asked that measures be taken to deal with these problems. Upon hearing these complaints the king and the magnates assembled in that parliament decided that keepers of the peace should be appointed in every county of the kingdom to redress those wrongs and offences, homicides and felonies. In spite of this measure, even more pressing complaints of the same sort of misdeeds were brought to the king from all parts in his council at Windsor where all the magnates of the land were gathered, the complainants praying that measures be taken to deal with the malefactors. The king therefore asked all who were gathered there to provide means for the better preservation and keeping of the peace of the land and for redressing these offences in some better way. They discussed and debated these matters. The case was set forth there that the peace was not being kept or maintained as before in the times of other kings because in the times of the progenitors of the present king eyres used to be held every seven years throughout the kingdom and served to maintain and keep the peace very well and to do justice to both rich and poor. Therefore the magnates gathered there asked the king to resume this practice in order that the peace of the land might be preserved and kept and the said misdeeds and offences be redressed. The king agreed to what they asked. We therefore charge you leading men of the county in the king's name and ask of you as our lords and friends, that you support no maintainers of false suits and no persons of evil reputation, but that you lend your aid for the keeping of the peace of our lord the king and the punishment of the said malefactors, so that the law may be enforced as it was in times past by means of the eyre.'

4.4 The court of king's bench: the articles of inquiry (1323)

In the aftermath of the civil war and defeat of the supporters of Thomas of Lancaster at the battle of Boroughbridge (1322) the court of king's bench was directed to sit in Lancashire. In addition to articles of inquiry aimed at those intent on undermining the proper functioning of the legal system, there are more general ones touching prises* and economic offences and investigating those who hindered the performance of royal officials. Some specific events are targeted here (the homicides taking place at Chaddock and Worsley) and nquiries were made concerning allegiances, particularly those who were adherents of Thomas of Lancaster and Andrew Harclay. Although Harclay had been rewarded by Edward II for his support in the civil war, he was arrested and executed for treason (adhering to the king's enemies) for attempting to negotiate peace with the Scots. The scope and focus of the articles moves from the general to the specific. The following is a selection of the articles of 1323.[3]

3 For the full version see *South Lancashire in the Reign of Edward II*, ed. G. Tupling, Chetham Society, 3rd series, 1 (1949), pp. 1–7.

TNA KB 27/254 m. 1 [Latin/French]

The king sent to his justices here at Wigan, by notification of Master Robert de Aylestone, keeper of his privy seal, certain articles to be inquired into in the form that follows:

Concerning homicides, robberies and all manner of felonies: by whom committed, of what, and where, and at what time.

Also, concerning conspirators who ally themselves by oath, covenant or by other association that each shall aid and sustain the enterprise of the others, and falsely and maliciously cause people to be indicted or falsely acquitted, or falsely initiate pleas or maintain them or falsely conceal from the indictment those who are indictable.

Also, concerning those who make children under age appeal people of felonies, because of which they are imprisoned and much harmed.

Also, concerning those who retain men of the district in their livery and at their fees in order to maintain their wrongful enterprises and to suppress the truth: both the takers and the givers.

Also, concerning stewards and bailiffs of great lords who by their lordship and excuse of their office or by their authority undertake to maintain or support pleas or quarrels for parties other than those that concern their lords or themselves.

Also, concerning barrators* who threaten and hinder people from coming to assizes and other pleas in the king's court to do what they have to do by order of the king.

Also, concerning those who make confederacies, an oath and association to do wrong and to divide between themselves what men will give them to beat people or spare people or to come to create disorder so that the peace cannot be kept between neighbours, or to defend wrongful seisins or wrongfully to take and maintain pleas or to undertake any other acts of violence against the peace, and who swear that none will fail another in his undertakings, whatever they may be.

Also, concerning sheriffs, constables, bailiffs and other ministers of the king who have taken anything to the detriment of the king's profit.

Also, concerning those who impede sheriffs, coroners or other ministers of the king, whoever they may be, from doing whatever pertains to their office.

Also, concerning those who go armed together through the countryside in terrorisation of the people, making threats and humiliating those who do not wish to meet their demands.

Also, concerning those who have been opposed to our lord the king and have sent some of their men to aid the enemies of our lord the king at Burton Bridge [Burton-on-Trent] or elsewhere.

Also, concerning the fights and homicides that were perpetrated at Chaddock, where they had eighty men on one side and about fifty on the other side, and four men were killed.

Also, concerning the arson and homicide committed at Worsley, which are blamed on the Tyldesley brothers.

Also, concerning those who have taken ransoms from people at their will after the destruction of Sir Adam Banaster.[4]

Also, let inquiry be made concerning which people were at Borough-bridge in the company of the earl of Lancaster.

Also, concerning those who came from Andrew of Harclay, the king's enemy, on a mission to attract the king's people to his side and gave them assurances, some by oath and some in writing.

Also, concerning those who of their own free will switched over to the said Andrew in order to maintain his wickedness contrary to their allegiance.

Also, concerning those who, following the king's prohibition by his writ that no one either ought to be or should go against him under penalty of forfeiture of whatever they possess, have gone against him on the orders of the earl and Sir Robert de Holland.[5]

Also, concerning sheriffs and other ministers of the king who have the peace to maintain: how they have intervened to punish misdeeds and if they are in association and agreement with the same misdoers.

Also, whether they attach* some and allow others to go free through gratitude or for gift or for other reason.

Also, concerning those who threaten the jurors in assizes or on inquests so that they dare not tell the truth.

---

4 Banaster had been a long-serving member of the earl of Lancaster's retinue, but rebelled against him in 1315 and engaged in a series of raids on properties in Wigan, Liverpool, Manchester and Preston (displaying a banner with the king's arms in order to try and justify himself). He was eventually cornered and captured by a Lancastrian force. Banaster and one of his henchmen were executed. See J. R. Maddicott, *Thomas of Lancaster* (Oxford, 1970), pp. 174–7.

5 Although in fact Holland did not back Thomas of Lancaster at Boroughbridge.

4.5 The court of king's bench as a superior eyre

In the early fourteenth century the court travelled extensively around the shires 'trouble-shooting', appearing in areas where its personnel (senior royal judges) and the scope of its jurisdiction could contribute effectively to quelling outbreaks of disorder. Shareshull's declaration at the king's bench sessions at Kingston in 1353 of the superiority of the court and its comparison with the general eyre (made in the course of arguing that the king's bench was entitled to levy fines for escapes which were by statute a matter for the eyre) is further underlined by the instructions for the opening of a provincial session of the king's bench, which were to accord fully with those for the opening of the eyre. Although the king's bench was largely domiciled at Westminster from the end of the fourteenth century, the second extract demonstrates the serious concerns underlying the decision to send the king's bench to restore public order in Shropshire, including the use of a grand jury to obtain information and prosecute offenders.[6]

(a) Declaration of chief justice William Shareshull at Kingston upon Thames (1353)

Liber Assisarum, 27 Edward III, pl. 1 (Le Liver des Assises et Plees del Corone, abridged by Sir Robert Brook (1580), fol. 133) [French]

In Surrey at Kingston in the king's bench before Shareshull fines were levied for the escape of felons notwithstanding the statute that decreed that such things should only be presented in the eyre; the parties were put to respond because Shareshull said that this bench is the eyre and superior to the eyre because if the eyre were sitting in a county and the king's bench arrived in that county the eyre would cease …

(b) The king's bench in Shropshire (1414)

TNA KB 27/613 *Rex* m. 36 (Trinity) [Latin]

A jury of thirty-six jurors from the more honest and prosperous men of the aforesaid county, a grand inquisition which is summoned by Sir Robert Corbet, the sheriff of Shropshire, at the king's command, was returned in this same term before the king at Shrewsbury, Edward duke of York being then present in person by order of the king, and thirty-three of these jurors appeared in person. Whereupon William Hankford, knight, chief justice of England, at once made it known to the said jurors that the community of the realm of England in the last

6 Powell, *Kingship*, pp. 173–94.

parliament of the present king, recently held at Leicester, complained unanimously and in very strong terms to the said king of and about the bad governance of the aforesaid county, which in these days is said to be rife with homicides and rapes far more than the other counties of England. And the present king, deeply concerned about its correction and improvement, has sent his royal court here to inquire into and punish the aforesaid wrongdoings and to do justice thereon to every complainant. Wherefore on the king's behalf they were sworn on God's Holy Gospels and charged to inquire into and make presentments concerning the aforesaid wrongdoings as well as any others whatsoever committed and perpetrated by any persons whatsoever and in whatsoever manner.

4.6 Commissions of oyer and terminer: special and general

(a) Special

Special oyer and terminer commissions usually resulted from petitions to the king from individuals requesting the king's grace to remedy a particular situation in which they found themselves. The abbot of Tewkesbury, who received the following commission as a result of complaining about the driving away of a considerable amount of livestock from his property at Stanway in Gloucestershire, claimed he had no other legal alternative but to sue to chancery for remedy. The fee for obtaining the oyer and terminer commission is noted as being 20s. The surviving proceedings (the commission for which is printed here) demonstrate that the sessions were held within a month of the commission over a period of six days (10–15 August 1340). Three of the justices named in the commission heard the case, Roger Hillary (as specified), William Cheltenham and Robert Dabetot (though the latter was not present on the final day). In spite of awarding in favour of the abbot, the oyer and terminer sessions do not seem to have brought closure to the issue, as he was soon forced to petition the crown again, alleging that although the wrongdoers had been outlawed as a result of the oyer and terminer proceedings, the sheriff of Gloucestershire had refused to seize their lands and chattels; once again they had driven off his livestock and he now feared for his safety.[7]

TNA JUST 1/299/4 m. 1 [Latin]

Edward by the grace of God king of England and France, lord of Ireland, to his beloved and faithful Hugh le Despenser, William Shareshull, Roger Hillary, William Cheltenham and Robert Dabetot, greeting. From the

---

7 See TNA SC 8/76/3790. Probably as a result of this petition the case was called into king's bench in May 1341 (TNA JUST 1/299/4 m. 3).

serious complaint of the abbot of Tewkesbury we have learned that William son of Thomas le Reeve of Kemerton, Richard his brother, Henry Isabele, John Court of Aston upon Carent, Richard le Dyer of Pershore, William Cook of Elmley, William Sterre of Dumbleton, William Roger of Hinton, William Haring of Childs Wickham, Richard de Bosbury of Childs Wickham, John Russel of Childs Wickham and certain other malefactors and disturbers of our peace broke the close of the same abbot at Stanway and took and carried away twenty horses, twenty mares, 100 oxen, 40 bullocks, 100 cows, 40 heifers, 1000 sheep and 150 swine of his worth £300 and inflicted other outrages on him to the grave damage of the same abbot and against our peace. And because we are unwilling that this trespass, if it has been carried out, should remain unpunished, we have assigned you four, three or any two of you, one of whom we desire to be the aforenamed William Shareshull or Roger, our justices to inquire by the oath of worthy and lawful men of the county of Gloucester by whom the truth of the matter can best be known, concerning the names of the aforesaid evildoers who together with the aforesaid William, Richard, Henry, John, Richard, William, William, William, William, Richard and John committed that trespass and concerning the full truth of the aforesaid trespass, and to hear and determine that trespass according to the law and custom of our realm of England. And therefore we command you that at certain days and places which any of you four, three or two, of whom we desire the aforesaid William Shareshull or Roger to be one, shall appoint for this purpose, you make that inquiry and hear and determine the aforesaid trespass in the aforesaid manner, doing therein what pertains to justice according to the law and custom of our realm of England, saving to us amercements* and other matters appertaining to us. We have also commanded our sheriff in the aforesaid county that at certain days and places which any of you four, three or two, of whom we desire the aforesaid William de Shareshull or Roger to be one, shall make known to him, he cause to come before you four, three or two, of whom we desire the aforesaid William Shareshull or Roger to be one, so many and such worthy and lawful men from his bailiwick by whom the truth of the aforesaid matters may best be able to be known and inquired. In witness whereof we will cause to be made these letters patent under the seal of Edward, duke of Cornwall and earl of Chester, our dearest son and keeper of the realm at Westminster on 16 July in the fourteenth year of our reign in England and the first year of our reign in France [1340].

(b) General

This commission (dated 10 December 1340) was directed against a long list of royal officials, some having judicial and administrative responsibilities, others with financial duties within the royal household. It targeted in particular those who committed oppressions and extortions in the course of their employment. Again there is a concern for the corruption of the legal processes through the actions of conspirators and people riding armed without good excuse. These particular commissions were issued for all counties (with personnel appointed for groups of counties) in the wake of Edward III's return from France in 1340 after military disappointment to put his officials on notice that their behaviour would be scrutinised by his 'new inquiries'.

TNA JUST 1/521 m. 1 [Latin]

Commission to Nicholas Cantilupe, John Willoughby, John Kirketon and Roger Baukwell to hear and determine various oppressions, extortions, wrongs and excesses committed in Lincolnshire against the people and the lord king since the lord king assumed governance of the realm by justices, escheators, subescheaters, coroners, sheriffs, undersheriffs and their clerks and ministers, taxers, subtaxers and their clerks, admirals of the fleets and their deputies, keepers and constables of the peace, castles and coasts, collectors and receivers of wool and their deputies, assessors and receivers of the ninth and other royal subsidies, barons of the exchequer, clerks of the chancery and exchequer, clerks of receipt and other royal offices, keepers of forests, verderers, clerks and other ministers of the forests, chases and parks, collectors and controllers of customs, tronagers,* butlers and their deputies, receivers of the king's taxes, keepers of the king's horses and their grooms, stewards and marshals of the king's household, clerks of the market, purveyors of foodstuffs, purveyors for the household of the king, the queen and Edward, duke of Cornwall and earl of Chester, keepers of gaols, electors, triers and arrayers of men at arms, hobelars [light horsemen] and archers, itinerant bailiffs and other bailiffs and royal ministers, and also by conspirators, jurors, usurers, confederates and others who maintain lawsuits in the king's courts, as well as by evildoers who wander about armed at fairs, markets and other public and private places, beating, wounding and maiming people and extorting fines and redemptions, and by archdeacons, officials, rural deans, sequestrators and their commissaries and ministers.

4.7 Assizes and gaol delivery: assize justices to deliver gaols on their circuit

The organisation of gaol deliveries essentially differed from that for the assize circuits until the two tasks were officially joined under the Statute of Fines of 1299. The justices of assize were given responsibility for the gaols within their circuit, which it was intended they should deliver during the central court vacations. Recognising an earlier ruling by the church forbidding clerks in holy orders to be involved in the trial of prisoners (and thus participating in judgments of blood), the assize justices were permitted to share the burden of the commissions with local men. The appointment of local men to try prisoners at gaol delivery was common in the early years of the fourteenth century and their participation became so regularised that during the middle years of Edward II's reign the task was invariably carried out without the presence of central court justices. With the statute of 1330 the link between assizes and gaol delivery was renewed and confirmed. Although some local men of law were reintroduced to panels by the middle of the decade, the practice of appointing them to the assize circuits had disappeared. Under the statute the justices of assize (as justices of gaol delivery) were also required to try the persons indicted before keepers of the peace.

Statute 27 Edward I c. 3 (1299) (SR, vol. 1, pp. 129–30) [French]

For the utility of our realm and for the better maintenance of our peace we have decreed and ordained that the justices assigned to take assizes in each county where they take assizes, as they be appointed, immediately after the assizes have been taken in the same counties shall remain, together if they are lay and if one of them is a clerk then the justice that is a lay man, having associated with himself one of the most discreet knights of the shire, shall deliver the gaols by our writ in those counties both within liberties and outside them of all prisoners according to the form of gaol delivery used previously in those counties.

Statute 4 Edward III c. 2 (1330) (*SR*, vol. 1, pp. 261–2) [French]

Next it is agreed that good men and wise, other than of the places,[8] if they can be found sufficient shall be assigned in all the counties of England to take assizes, juries and certifications and to deliver the gaols; and that the said justices taking assizes, juries and certifications and delivering the gaols shall do so at least three times a year and more frequently if it should be needed; also there shall be assigned good men and loyal in each county to keep the peace; and mention shall be made in the said assignments that those who shall be indicted or taken by

8 It is likely this is referring to the two Benches rather than the counties.

the said keepers, shall not be let to mainprise* by the sheriffs, nor by any other official, if they are not mainpernable* by the law; nor that such indicted persons be delivered except at the common law. And the justices assigned to deliver gaols shall have power to deliver the gaols of those who shall be indicted before the keepers of the peace, and the said keepers shall send their indictments before the said justices; and the said justices shall have power to inquire whether sheriffs, gaolers and others in whose keeping such indicted persons will be make deliverance or let to mainprise any who may have been indicted who are not mainpernable, and to punish the said sheriffs, gaolers and others if they do anything contrary to this ordinance.

4.8 Assizes and gaol delivery: men of law forbidden to act in their own localities (1384)

This statute was an attempt to remove the practice of appointing lawyers as justices of assize and gaol delivery on circuits in which their own private interests lay. The chief justice of the court of king's bench had over the last century sometimes sat on the assize circuits, but intermittently rather than on a regular basis. It was felt, however, that since the court heard appeals against assize judgments it would be anomalous if the chief justice was required to reverse his own decision. The chief justice nevertheless continued to be appointed until the practice was forbidden by statute in 1411.[9]

Statute 8 Richard II c. 2 (*SR*, vol. 2, p. 36) [French]

Also, it is agreed and enacted that no man of law should henceforth be appointed to commissions as a justice of assize or general gaol delivery in his own locality; and that the chief justice of the court of common pleas should be assigned among others to such commissions to take assizes and deliver gaols, but as regards the chief justice of the court of king's bench let it be done according to the custom of the greater part of the last hundred years.

4.9 Assizes and gaol delivery: attendance at the Northampton assizes (1416)

The plea roll from which the following is extracted lists (presumably in order of importance) the leading local officials attending the assizes. There is no corresponding list giving the panels of jurors for respective localities, though such

9 13 Henry IV c.2 (*SR*, vol. 2, pp. 166–7).

lists can be found in the records of the eyre and also survive for general oyer and terminer and peace sessions. The four keepers of the peace mentioned here represent a selection (probably the 'working' members) of the full Northamptonshire peace commission (which at this time was ten strong and included magnates such as Reginald de Grey and central court justices John Cokayne and James Strangways).[10]

TNA JUST 3/56/13 [Latin][11]

DAY OF ASSIZES AT NORTHAMPTON ON MONDAY IN THE FIRST WEEK OF LENT NEXT FOLLOWING [9 March 1416]

Thomas Wake, sheriff [of Northamptonshire]

Names of keepers of the peace in the county of Northamptonshire:

Thomas Woodville
Nicholas Morbury
William Palmer[12]
John Walton

Names of the king's coroners of the said county:

William Lubenham
William Aldewinter
Robert Aleyn
John Harold

Names of bailiffs of liberties as well as of other hundreds in the said county:

Geoffrey Balde and Roger Clerk bailiffs of the liberty of the town of Northampton

John Weldon and John Bamford bailiffs of the liberty of the abbot of Peterborough

John Woodstock, bailiff of the liberty of Joan queen of England in the hundred of Fawsley

Adam Barbour, bailiff of the liberty of the honor of Leicester in the county of Northamptonshire

John Rowley, bailiff of the liberty of the hundred of Higham Ferrers

---

10 TNA C 66/393 m. 32d (see also 4.10b).

11 This is a single loose membrane filed with Nottinghamshire gaol delivery material since the dorse contains relevant Nottinghamshire entries.

12 Palmer was denoted as a member of the quorum (for further discussion of the quorum see 4.13).

Thomas Burdon, bailiff of the liberty of the honor of Gloucester

William Wood, bailiff of the liberty of the honor of Peverell

William Lightfoot, bailiff of the liberty of the honor of Berkhamstead

Thomas Byfeld, bailiff of the liberty of the abbot of Westminster

Thomas Baxter, bailiff of the hundred of Corby and Willybrook

Thomas Carter, bailiff of the hundred of Rothwell

Henry Lodington, bailiff of the hundred of Orlingbury

William Roo, bailiff of the hundred of Hamfordshoe

William Norris, bailiff of the hundred of Spelhoe

William Newman, bailiff of the hundred of Wymersley

William Smith, bailiff of the hundred of Cleley

John Hertwell, bailiff of the hundred of Towcester

William Hervey, bailiff of the liberty and honor of Winchester and bailiff of the hundred of Sutton

John Seaton, bailiff of the hundred of Norton

Thomas Fisher, bailiff of the hundred of Wardon and bailiff of the liberty of the town of Daventry and Binby

John Cranston, bailiff of the hundred of Guilsborough

William Spaunton, bailiff of the hundred of Nobottlegrove

4.10 Assizes and gaol delivery: coincidence of assizes and peace sessions (1420)

The requirement of the quorum and the consequent overlaps in personnel between the assize justices and peace commissioners (see below) meant that it was usually convenient to hold peace sessions at a time when the justices were delivering the county gaol. This was a logical and time-saving move allowing the lawyers of the central courts to rationalise the various aspects of their work in the localities. The coincidence of sessions was not simply an administrative convenience, but also offered an opportunity for the central court justices and interested parties to meet and chat to the local men of law and other dignitaries present at the peace sessions and disseminate to the provinces both formally and informally any royal communications.

(a)

Original Letters Illustrative of English History, ed. H. Ellis, 1st series, 3 vols (London, 1824), vol. 1, pp. 6–7 [English]

Robert Waterton to King Henry the Fifth, A.D. 1420, just before the King's marriage with Katherine of France

Right excellent high and very mighty Prince, and most dread sovereign Lord, I recommend myself to your highness as lowly as any simple true liege man and subject can best think or devise, thanking almighty God of your gracious success and right great conquest with the prosperity of your own person, my lord of Clarence, my lord of Exeter, and all my lords being there in your worshipful service, with all the rest of your right worshipful host. As I have conceived by your right honourable letters written at your City of Rouen the twelfth day of March which I have received very recently since Easter, with other of your letters under your privy seal, charging me to try by all the means that I can to excite and stir such as be able gentlemen within the shire and the country that I dwell in, to come over to you at your wage, armed and arrayed as belongs to their estate to do you service and to certify both to you and to your council of their answer and their will, which high commandment I have begun to labour upon and shall truly continue daily with all my might till I have completed your aforesaid commandment. And upon Wednesday next shall your justices sit at York upon the deliverance of the gaol there and a session of the peace also, at which time I suppose to speak with many of the gentles there and as soon after as I may be answered I shall certify as it has pleased you to command me with all the haste possible. Right excellent, high, and very mighty prince and most dread sovereign Lord I beseech the blessed Trinity to prosper you and keep you and all your worshipful host and send you soon into your realm of England with a joyous marriage and a good peace for his great mercy. Written at your own lodge of Methley the twelfth day of April.

your true liege man and subject
Robert Waterton

(b)

TNA KB 9/224 mm. 164–5 [Latin]

Inquisition held at the lord king's castle of Northampton before John Cokayne and James Strangways justices of the lord king assigned to hold assizes in the county of Northamptonshire and his keepers of the peace and his justices to hear and determine any felonies, trespasses and other wrongdoing in the aforesaid county Tuesday on the feast of St Margaret, virgin, in the sixth year of the reign of King Henry VI [20 July 1428] in full session of the assizes held then and there before the said justices on the oath of … [jury].

Who said on oath that Henry Mulso of Geddington in Northamptonshire, esquire, and Thomas Mulso of Geddington in the same county, esquire, on the Monday before St Margaret in the sixth year of the reign of King Henry VI abovesaid [19 July] at Northampton with many others unknown with force and arms namely drawn swords assaulted Simon Kinsman and his servants and attempted to beat and wound them in great disturbance of the peace and affray of the people of the lord king.

4.11 Justices of the peace: the commission of the peace (1447)

The justices of the peace operated in accordance with the powers (articles) in their commission, which was directed to named justices in a particular county. The commission printed here represents the fullest stage of development in the medieval period, a process that had been occurring over the previous 150 years. The size and composition of the commissions and the powers accorded them fluctuated considerably during the fourteenth century. In the early part of the century the panels comprised two or three members, increasing to six or eight by the mid-fourteenth century. During the 1370s there was a substantial growth in the size of the peace commissions with a number of honorial appointments, sometimes including ecclesiastics. The basic peace-keeping responsibilities were set out in the Statute of Winchester of 1285 and later amplified in the Statute of Northampton (1328) and the Statute of Westminster (1361). Additional powers were received in the various statutes of labourers and those concerning liveries, heresy and counterfeit money. The commissioners were given powers to act as justices and try cases of felony and trespass and any statutory offences coming before them, though cases of extortion were reserved for king's bench justices. They were also authorised to take surety of the peace from those who threatened disorder or assault and had particular responsibility for the arrest and punishment of rioters.

PJP, pp. 3–7 [Latin]

Henry by the grace of God king of England and France and lord of Ireland to his dearest kinsman, Humphrey, duke of Buckingham, Edmund, marquis of Dorset, William, marquis of Suffolk and Thomas, earl of Devon and his beloved and faithful Richard Newton, knight,

Nicholas Ashton, James Ormond, knight, John Chideock, knight, William Stafford, William Carent, John Filliol, John Roger, William Bronnying, John Newburgh, John Stork and Robert Hilary, greetings.

You are to know that we have assigned you jointly and severally to keep and cause to be kept our peace and also the statutes and ordinances promulgated at Winchester, Northampton and Westminster for the keeping of the same peace; and the statutes and ordinances there [Westminster] and at Cambridge concerning huntsmen, labourers, craftsmen, servants, ostlers, mendicants and vagabonds and other mendicants who call themselves travelling men; and similarly the statutes and ordinances at Westminster in the first and second year of the reign of the dearest lord [king] our late grandfather concerning the giving of liveries of signs and companies to knights, esquires or valets and giving other liveries of clothes at least and not using the same liveries in any way; and also a certain statute against Lollards made in the parliament of the dearest lord king our late father held lately at Leicester; and a certain other statute given in the aforesaid parliament of our father held lately at Westminster concerning counterfeiting, clipping, 'sweating' and forging coinage of our kingdom; and also all other ordinances and statutes made for the benefit of our peace and the quiet rule and governance of our people in each and every of their articles in the county of Dorset, both within and outside liberties, according to their force, form and effect. And to castigate and punish all those whom you find offending against the form of the aforesaid statutes and ordinances, as is to be done according to the form of the ordinances and statutes; and to make come before you all those who make threats to any of our people either of physical harm or of burning their houses, to find sufficient surety of the peace and of their good behaviour towards us and our people, and if any of these are unwilling to find surety then let them be sent to our prison until they are willing to find surety thereon.

We also have assigned you, sixteen, fifteen, fourteen, thirteen, twelve, eleven, ten, nine, eight, seven, six, five, four, three and two of you our justices to inquire on the oaths of honest and law-worthy men of the aforesaid county, both within and outside liberties, through whom the truth of things may be better known, concerning all felonies, trespasses, forestalling,* regrating* and extortions in the aforesaid county by whomsoever and howsoever committed or perpetrated, and which might happen to be done there hereafter; and also concerning all those who in gatherings against our peace and in disturbance of our people or with armed force go or ride, or presume to go or ride hereafter; and also all those who lie in ambush to maim or kill our people or presume to lie hereafter; and also concerning those who have worn hoods and other liveries of sole suit[13] by way of confederacy and for the purpose of maintenance against the defence and form of statutes made thereon before this time and others using liveries of this kind in the future; and also concerning ostlers and others who in abuse of weights and measures and in selling foodstuffs and also concerning any workers, craftsmen, servants, ostlers, mendicants and aforesaid vagabonds and others who in the aforesaid county offend or have attempted to offend or who presume to offend or attempt to hereafter against the form of the ordinances and statutes made thereon for the common utility of our kingdom of England and our people of the same kingdom concerning these huntsmen, labourers, craftsmen, servants, ostlers, mendicants and vagabonds and others; and also whatsoever sheriffs, mayors, bailiffs, stewards, constables and keepers of gaols who in carrying out their duties towards these craftsmen, servants, labourers, victuallers, ostlers, mendicants and vagabonds and others aforesaid according to the form of the ordinances and statutes aforesaid have acted wrongly and presume to act wrongly hereafter, or have been tepid, remiss or negligent or happen to be tepid, remiss or negligent hereafter; and to inquire fully into the truth concerning each and every of the articles and each and every of the circumstances mentioned before and other ones against the form of the ordinances and statutes aforesaid by whomsoever and howsoever committed or attempted and what might happen to be done or be attempted hereafter in whatsoever way.

And to inspect all indictments made before you or two of you and others lately assigned our keepers and justices of the peace, by virtue of our various letters to you and the same lately assigned keepers and justices of the peace, to hear and determine felonies, trespasses and misdeeds in the aforesaid county of whatever kind committed in this area and not yet determined and receive at this session all writs and commands made by you and those others lately keepers and justices of the peace by virtue of the aforesaid letters of whatsoever kind returnable at certain future sessions, and hold and adjourn incomplete proceedings thereon and proceedings towards all others of whatsoever kind who have been indicted before you and the same others lately keepers and justices of the peace and who might happen to be indicted before you until they be taken, returned or outlawed …

13 Livery of the same colour or design.

Always providing that if a difficult case on the determination of whatsoever kind of extortion might happen to come before you, then you may
only proceed to render judgment thereon in the presence of at least one
of our justices of one bench or the other or our justices assigned to hold
assizes in the aforesaid county.

And so we command you and each of you that you attentively and
conscientiously keep the peace, ordinances and statutes aforesaid and
on certain days and at places that you sixteen, fifteen, fourteen etc. three
or two of you will provide for this, make inquests on the matters and
hear and determine the aforementioned each and every thing and do
what pertains to justice according to law and custom aforesaid, saving
amercements for us and other things touching us in this respect.

For we have commanded our sheriff of the said county that on the
certain days and at the certain places which you sixteen, fifteen, etc.
three or two of you will make known to him, he should cause to come
before you sixteen, fifteen, etc. three or two of you as many and such
honest and law-worthy men of his bailiwick, both within and outside
liberties, by whom the truth of things in these aforegoing matters will
better be able to be learned and discovered.

4.12 Justices of the peace: the powers of the magistracy (1361)

The Statute of Westminster of 1361 has traditionally been regarded in legal
circles as the Justices of the Peace Act since it set out all the basic powers of
the magistracy. The ideal composition of the peace commission, which had
been put forward over the previous decade and a half, was also enshrined in the
statute: a mixture of magnates, gentry and men of law, providing for a balanced,
workable and sufficiently authoritative judicial body. The form of the commission addressed other issues of concern such as the nomination of justices by the
litigating party (possible when obtaining oyer and terminer commissions) and
the excessive fines sometimes levied by justices of general oyer and terminer
commissions.

Statute 34 Edward III c. 1 (*SR*, vol. 1, pp. 364–5) [French]

That in every shire of England shall be assigned for the keeping of the
peace one lord, and with him three or four of the most worthy in the
shire with some learned in the law and they shall have power to restrain
the offenders, rioters and all other barrators* and to pursue, arrest, take
and chastise them according to their trespass or offence, and to cause
them to be imprisoned and duly punished according to the laws and

customs of the realm and according to what shall seem best to them to do by their discretions and good deliberation; and also to inform themselves and to inquire of all those who have been pillagers and robbers in the regions beyond the sea, and have now returned and go wandering and will not labour as they were accustomed to do in times past; and to take and arrest all those that they may find by indictment or by suspicion and to put them in prison; and to take of those who are not of good reputation, wherever they shall be found, sufficient surety and mainprise* for their good behaviour towards the king and his people; and they are to punish the others duly to the end that the people may not be troubled or injured by such rioters or rebels nor the peace be endangered nor merchants or others passing on the king's highway be disturbed ...

And they are also to hear and determine at the king's suit all manner of felonies and trespass perpetrated in that county according to the laws and customs and that writs of oyer and terminer shall be granted according to the statutes made with regard to them, but the justices who shall be assigned thereto shall be named by the court and not by the party.

And the king wills that all general inquiries granted before this time in any lordship whatsoever shall cease utterly and be repealed on account of the mischiefs and oppressions which have been done to the people by such inquiries. And that fines which are to be made before the justices for trespasses done by any person shall be reasonable and just, having regard to the quantity of the trespass and the cause for which they are made.

4.13 Justices of the peace: the powers of the quorum – men of law to be assigned to deliver gaols

The quorum was a select group of named men within the peace commission whose attendance was required for certain reserved business. It was first enshrined in legislation in 1344 stating specifically that for trying serious offences the keepers of the peace should be joined by 'other men wise and learned in the law', aiming to ensure thereby that trials were only conducted when professional lawyers from the central courts serving on the relevant assize circuits were associated with the local keepers of the peace. From a short-term perspective (1344–50) the provisions were applied in a piecemeal and sporadic manner. Viewed over a longer term (the second half of the fourteenth century) the presence of the quorum assumed increasing importance in the evolution of an acceptable model for determining indictments arising from peace sessions.[14] In 1389 two quorums were initiated: one for felonies, comprising solely assize justices, and another, which included local men of law (usually the 'working' justices), for all other offences. The provisions in the 1394 statute extended the previous arrangement with a single mixed quorum of assize justices and men of law when trying thieves and those caught red-handed. This gave local men of law re-admittance to the inner sanctum when determining certain cases of felony. The working relationship between these two groups therefore continued as a means of avoiding unnecessary delays in the trial of offenders.

(a)

Statute 18 Edward III st. 2, c. 2 (1344) (*SR*, vol. 1, p. 301) [French]

Also, that two or three of the most respected men of the counties shall be assigned as keepers of the peace by the king's commission; and whenever necessary, the same men, with other men wise and learned in the law, shall be assigned by the king's commission to hear and determine felonies and trespasses committed against the peace in the same counties, and set reasonable punishment according to the manner of the deed.

(b)

Statute 17 Richard II c. 10 (1394) (*SR*, vol. 2, p. 90) [French]

Also, whereas notorious thieves and others taken with the mainour,* because of long imprisonment following their arrest, are set at liberty through charters of pardon or favourable juries procured to the great destruction of the people; it is agreed and enacted that there shall be assigned to each commission of the peace throughout the kingdom where there is need, two men of law of the same county as the commission with power to proceed with the delivery of such thieves and felons as often as they deem necessary.

14 Powell, 'Peace sessions', pp. 51–6.

4.14 Justices of the peace: the sheriff's criminal jurisdiction in the tourn (1461)

The sheriff's criminal jurisdiction at the tourn came under scrutiny following numerous complaints that sheriffs and their underlings were arresting and imprisoning innocent people since they were allegedly relying for their presentments on jurors who brought malicious indictments because they lacked conscience and sufficient lands or personal property not to be easily influenced. Under the statute of 1461 the sheriff was obliged to send all the indictments and presentments taken at his tourns to the next peace sessions, thereby delaying the process of arresting offenders. In practice this measure substantially eroded the sheriff's jurisdiction over criminal matters and effectively transferred it to the justices of the peace.

Statute 1 Edward IV c. 2 (*SR*, vol. 2, pp. 389–91) [French]

Our sovereign lord the king, considering the matter by the advice and assent of the lords spiritual and temporal and at the request of the commons assembled in the said parliament and by authority of the same has ordained and established that in all manner of indictments and presentments which shall be taken in future before any of his sheriffs of his counties for the time being, their undersheriffs, clerks, bailiffs or other servants at their tourns or lawdays, they shall not have any power or authority to arrest, attach* or put in prison or levy any fines or amercements* from any person or persons thus indicted or presented – but that the abovesaid sheriffs etc. ... should bring ... all such indictments or presentments taken before them ... in their tourns or lawdays ... and deliver them to the justices of the peace in their next session of the peace which shall be held in the county or counties where such indictments and presentments were taken ... And that the justices of the peace shall have power to award process on all such indictments and presentments as the law requires.

V: THE COURTS IN OPERATION

By comparison with the other kingdoms across Europe, England can be said to have enjoyed an advanced and highly centralised judicial system. By the late fourteenth century the administrative capital was Westminster and the judicial nerve centre itself (housing the courts of king's bench, common pleas, exchequer and chancery) was Westminster Hall. As we saw in the previous chapter, a strong arterial network of regional justice developed over the course of the later medieval period, which nourished and complemented the work of the higher royal courts. It is the wider picture of criminal justice in action, and the interaction of both central and local agencies, that concerns us in this chapter.

The chapter concentrates especially on criminal procedure in the late Middle Ages. Prosecution was begun by appeal or indictment and might reach trial in the royal courts via a number of different channels. The appeal of felony was one of the principal methods of prosecuting an individual for a criminal wrong in the thirteenth century. [**5.1**] The procedure was an involved and lengthy one since it necessitated the appeal being initiated in the county court before being heard by justices of gaol delivery (or by justices in eyre or of king's bench when trying prisoners). The device was essentially a retributive one and allowed the victim or the victim's kin to initiate legal action with the hope of securing the conviction, and thereby the punishment, of the offender. Compensation (settled out of court) for the wrong suffered may also have been a motive (probably evidenced in cases where the appeal was not prosecuted to the bitter end). Although by the fifteenth century fewer prosecutions were initiated by appeal it remained an effective option for criminal prosecutions, especially as a means of harassing opponents.[1] Even if the appellant were non-suited (by failing to appear in court to prosecute) the claim was not necessarily rejected by the court: it could be taken up at the king's suit (prosecuted in the king's name) and the defendant rearraigned accordingly.[2]

A special type of appeal of felony was that made by an approver. Felons could turn king's evidence before the coroner by confessing their own guilt and then implicating their accomplices in crime.[3] [**5.2**] If sufficient of their former associates were convicted (probably at least five, though there was in fact no standard number and an agreement may have been made with the justices in advance) they were pardoned and allowed to go free or abjure the realm.*

---

1 W. A. Morris, *The Early English County Court* (Berkeley, CA, University of California Press, 1926), pp. 114–15; C. Whittick, 'Role of the criminal appeal in the fifteenth century', in *Law and Social Change*, ed. J. A. Guy (London, Royal Historical Society, 1984), pp. 63–5, 68–72.

2 *SCCKB*, vol. 3, pp. lxxii–lxxiv.

3 Hunnisett, *Coroner*, pp. 69–74.

Freedom was not very common, possibly because juries disliked or distrusted approvers, and their accomplices were often only alleged to have been receivers of the offenders or of their stolen goods. The majority of approvers were therefore hanged.[4] The system was open to abuse on both sides: approvers tried to prolong their lives by naming fictitious persons and crimes, while officials and gaolers in turn exploited their positions of responsibility by encouraging felons to turn approver. The approvers' appeal proved advantageous in political terms and was used by the crown to great effect during law-enforcement drives throughout the later medieval period.[5]

Indictment, a sworn statement by jurors, was the other principal method of prosecuting criminal offenders. In response to articles or questions (sometimes known as 'the charge') jurors from hundreds and towns presented to the court the offences on which they had made inquiries or had personal knowledge. Arguably indictment came to be preferred to appeals since the former carried the weight of the community rather than being the accusation of an individual, which could have been brought maliciously.[6] Indictments could, however, mask a personal concern. They could also endorse an appeal by duplicating the private accusation and publicly adopting its content. The manner in which indictments were made, the information from which they derived, and the officials before whom they were heard varied, but over the course of the fourteenth century the indictments produced at trial were increasingly required by the royal justices hearing cases to be precise in form and include full details of the date on which the event occurred, the place, time of day, names of parties, arresting officials, the type and value of stolen goods and other evidential elements.[7] From the thirteenth century indictments might be endorsed by a body known as the 'triers' or grand jury. Comprising jurors of higher status than the normal presenting jury, thereby ensuring weight was attached to a particular accusation, the 'triers' scrutinised the indictments that concerned particularly serious offences made at sessions of the eyre, king's bench, general oyer and terminer or peace sessions.[8]

Indictments normally contain details of the local officials before whom they were made and so provide an insight into the workings of the lower courts, such as when and where they were held and the type of offences being put forward. The sheriff visited biannually the royal hundreds under his jurisdiction in what was known as his tourn or view of frankpledge. [**5.3a**] He reviewed the operation of the tithing system (whereby adult males were organised into groups of ten and held mutually responsible for their behaviour) and received presentments concerning minor offences and more serious crimes occurring

---

4 F. C. Hamil, 'The king's approvers', *Speculum*, 11 (1936), 238–58; Clanchy, 'Highway robbery', pp. 29–32.

5 H. Röhrkasten, 'Some problems of the evidence of fourteenth-century approvers', *JLH*, 5 (1984), 14–22; A. Musson, 'Turning king's evidence: the prosecution of crime in late medieval England', *OJLS*, 19 (1999), 467–79.

6 For problems with indictments from juries see 8.7.

7 Musson, *Public Order*, pp. 176–7.

8 D. Crook, 'Triers and the origin of the grand jury', *JLH*, 12 (1991), 103–16.

since his last visit.[9] The sheriff's jurisdiction over criminal offences was eventually transferred to the justices of the peace in 1461, who already had responsibility for such areas and whose sessions, held four times a year, were twice as frequent.[10] The sessions in hundreds that were in private hands or in liberties (autonomous regions) were held along similar lines to the hundred courts and the sheriff's tourn and known as courts leet. Indictments were heard by the officials responsible for the administration of justice there, the lord's steward or the hundred bailiff. [**5.3e**] At certain times groups of private hundreds came together in what was known as a 'great court' when especially serious offences were presented.[11]

The coroner's prime task, as the name implies, was to uphold royal rights in the shire and this involved him in undertaking both legal and essentially non-legal duties (such as declaring treasure trove, examining shipwrecks and investigating beached whales). In addition to hearing confessions of approvers and those who had taken sanctuary and wished to abjure the realm, the coroner's judicial duties included taking inquests concerning dead bodies. [**5.3b**] The number of coroners per county varied: Yorkshire and Kent both had five, some counties (such as Northamptonshire) had four, while others had fewer (Devon had only two). Private jurisdictions (liberties and towns) generally had two coroners, though Lincoln had as many as four in the fourteenth century. Having been alerted to the death by the person who discovered the body, the coroner was required to view the body, assessing the likely causes of death in the light of any knowledge the members of the jury may have had or been able to glean as to the circumstances surrounding the death. If the circumstances were suspicious and a possible culprit identified an indictment would be made and sent before the gaol delivery justices. In cases of suicide, which were comparatively rare, the coroner had to ascertain the deceased's state of mind and the manner of the death (which may often have been concealed by a verdict of 'misadventure', for instance, in case of drowning) and was responsible for seeing that the body was buried in unconsecrated ground. He also assessed the goods and chattels of homicides and suicides which were forfeit to the crown in perpetuity (the crown holding on to any lands for a year and a day).[12]

The indictments taken at peace sessions provided further scope for criminal prosecution. In the early fourteenth century sessions were held at least twice a year (as the run of Herefordshire indictments from the 1320s evidences). [**5.3c**] The number of sessions per year was formally increased to four and the periods during which they ought to be held determined by statute in 1351 and again in 1362,[13] though the stipulations as to the frequency and timing of sessions were

---

9 W. A. Morris, *The Frankpledge System* (New York, 1910), pp. 112–50; H. M. Jewell, 'Local administrators and administration in Yorkshire, 1258–1348', *Northern History*, 16 (1980), 1–19.

10 See 4.14.

11 Cam, *Hundred Rolls*, pp. 185–7; eadem, *Liberties and Communities in Medieval England* (London, Merlin Press, 1963), pp. 183–204.

12 Hunnisett, *Coroner*, pp. 19–25, 29–34.

13 25 Edward III st. 2, c. 7; 36 Edward III st. 1, c. 12 (*SR*, vol. 1, pp. 313, 374).

not always strictly adhered to.[14] By the late fourteenth century towns and cities had their own justices of the peace, who usually comprised the mayor, bailiffs and leading legal officials (such as the recorder) as well as members of the local gentry. [**5.3d**]

In the early fifteenth century the suppression of riots became a routine part of duties of the justices of the peace. [**5.4**] Under legislation of 1411[15] the justices of the peace had the power to arrest those engaged in an assembly or riot and, making a record in their sessions of whatever occurred, convict the offenders on the basis of that record if their behaviour contravened the statutes of forcible entries issued under Richard II.[16] If the justices were unable to get to the heart of the matter then (along with the sheriff or undersheriff) they were to present a certificate outlining the event and its circumstances to the king's council which would effectively be the equivalent of a jury's presentment. The offenders would then be summoned to appear before the king's council and punished accordingly with further measures taken if they failed to turn up. Another statute introduced in 1414 to secure the effectiveness of the riot legislation enabled individual complainants to invoke it through a special commission of justices of the peace and sheriffs obtainable in chancery.[17] In serious cases, the victims could sue the rioters by bill before the chancellor and if the defendants did not duly appear in chancery they were summoned throughout the county. If they subsequently failed to present themselves in king's bench they were summarily convicted.

Arrest was a specific stage in the pre-trial process and a writ of attachment* by the body (which authorised arrest) would normally be issued following an appeal or indictment by the jury. [**5.5**] In cases of felony the writ of arrest (*capias*)* had to be issued three times before the writ of *exigent** was served. The accused was called to appear at the county court and if he failed to answer the proclamation after four successive county courts he was outlawed before the coroners, who duly made record of it, and any goods and chattels he possessed were forfeit to the crown. The process of summons and arrest appears to modern sensibility to have been a protracted affair, taking between six months and a year to complete, yet it gave due notice and an opportunity to attend court. Sureties were provided for the defendant's appearance and these would be forfeited in the event of his or her failure to attend after the fifth time they had been called. [**5.6**] Moreover, once the exigent was issued and five months were over the process towards outlawry was comparatively swift. Sometimes those exacted* presented themselves before the deadline, having had a legitimate excuse for not being able to attend previously. For those who did not, outlawry befell the men, while the female equivalent was waivery.[18] This meant that the man or woman was technically no longer under the protection of the

---

14 Musson, *Medieval Law*, pp. 147–8.

15 13 Henry IV c. 7 (*SR*, vol. 2, p. 169).

16 15 Richard II st. 2, c. 2; 17 Richard II c. 8 (*SR*, vol. 2, pp. 78, 89).

17 2 Henry V st. 1, cc. 8, 9 (*SR*, vol. 2, pp. 184–6).

18 L. Wilkinson, *Women in Thirteenth Century Lincolnshire* (London, Royal Historical Society, 2007), pp. 153–4, 158.

king's peace and could be apprehended on sight; by the later Middle Ages summary execution was no longer permissible. It will be seen in Chapter 8 [**8.10**] how this state of affairs could deliberately be manufactured by malicious adjustment of the writ.

Most criminal trials were conducted at gaol delivery, but proceedings might also take place, in serious cases of wrongdoing, in the court of king's bench or before parliament or in the king's council.[19] [**5.10**] While little is known regarding the conduct of ordinary criminal trials, as there are no detailed accounts of proceedings (except when something extraordinary occurred), it is possible to use treatises that conveniently set out model interrogations and defences to have some idea of its potential course and of the type of pleadings. [**5.8**] It is also possible to get a picture of the nature of exchanges, the extent to which witnesses and third parties were involved and the disposition of the justices through piecing together the scraps of information that can be gleaned from the plea rolls themselves.[20] [**5.9**]

Trial sessions did not always progress smoothly or without incident. On occasion proceedings could be disrupted by armed force as occurred in Bedford in 1437 and two years later, as a result of rivalries and factionalism among the justices themselves. [**5.10**] The county elite was deeply divided behind the two leading landowners in the region, John, Lord Fanhope and Reginald, Lord Grey of Ruthin. The disagreement arose out of the exercise of lordship and 'honourable administration of law and justice' and in particular the ability to nominate the personnel of the county bench and special commissions of oyer and terminer.[21]

The extracts from gaol deliveries in Norfolk reveal something of the more mundane day-to-day workings of the courts and especially the procedural issues and practical problems that held up the smooth course of trials. [**5.7**] These might include lack of sufficient evidence or an absence of the relevant documentation. Indictments made before the constables of the hundred, for instance, might not be recognised in situations where a man's life was at stake – this appears to have been a matter of debate amongst the judiciary. It is noticeable that defendants arrested purely on suspicion that they had committed a crime (usually theft) were treated differently. Since the formalities of an indictment or appeal had not been entered into, it was generally necessary for someone to come forward and prosecute personally or provide further information to confirm the mere suspicion. If the suspect was not caught red-handed in possession of the stolen goods (otherwise called the 'mainour'*) and was of reputable character, then, providing nobody testified against them, he or she

---

19 There are various examples of cases coming before king's bench in this volume, but generally see also *SCCKB*, vols 1–7. For proceedings in parliament see, for example, *RP*, vol. 4, p. 202 (trial of Sir John Mortimer). For king's council see *PPC* and *Select Cases before the King's Council, 1243–1482*, ed. I. D. Leadham and J. Baldwin, SS, 35 (1918).

20 P. Brand, 'Inside the courtroom: lawyers, litigants and justices in the later Middle Ages', in *The Moral World of the Law*, ed. P. Coss (Cambridge, Cambridge University Press, 2000), pp. 91–112.

21 Maddern, *Violence*, pp. 206–15 (quotation at p. 213).

usually went free without a further date set for trial. Unclaimed property or the chattels of convicted felons went to the king. The sheriff's testimony and that of other officials such as the coroner, hundred bailiff and gaoler, were often necessary for the smooth conduct of the trial. Where an indictment or the stolen goods were not present in court the trial was adjourned and the prisoner remanded until the next session.

Trial at gaol delivery was by the 'twelve good men and true' supposedly from the neighbourhood in which the offence had been committed. Jury membership was not fixed at twelve, however, and an inquest could sometimes be afforced with another six or a further dozen members. In the trial purportedly from the Yorkshire eyre of 1293–94 (reported in the Year Book) it is made a point of principle that the defendant wishes a trial by his peers (those of equal status)[22] when submitting himself to the jury, but in reality exemptions from jury service and difficulties in empanelling jurors having sufficient property meant that that jurors were often drawn from lower social levels and from outside the area where the offence was committed.[23] It was a requirement, however, that jurors should not be closely related to or otherwise connected ('of the affinity') to the defendant. Furthermore, from the mid-fourteenth century jurors could be challenged if the defendant perceived (or alleged) that they had been members of the indicting jury.

In the thirteenth and early fourteenth centuries defendants to homicide could ensure trial by jury at gaol delivery through presentation of a writ *de bono et malo* ('for good and ill"). Initially it was probably sought for cases where the defendant might reasonably have expected to be acquitted, but by the late thirteen century the writ may have become a requirement for trial to proceed.[24] Avoiding putting oneself on the jury incurred the statutory penalty of *prisone forte et dure*, or the later (non-statutory) *peine forte et dure.*[25] [**5.8, 5.9, 5.12**] The pain was intended to discourage the defendant from following this course and either he died as a result of his stubborn refusal or he returned to the courtroom to face the jury. Defendants who died unconvicted escaped the penalty of forfeiture of their goods and chattels.

Trial by battle was traditionally one of the ordeals available to litigants in the twelfth century and earlier. As an option in both civil and criminal trials

---

22 See 1.6.

23 T. A. Green, *Verdict According to Conscience: Perspectives on the English Criminal Trial Jury, 1200–1800* (Chicago, IL, University of Chicago Press, 1985); E. Powell, 'Jury trial at gaol delivery in the late Middle Ages: the Midland circuit, 1400–29', in *Twelve Good Men and True: the English Criminal Trial Jury, 1200–1800*, ed. J. S. Cockburn and T. A. Green (Princeton, NJ, Princeton University Press, 1988), pp. 78–116; A. Musson, 'Twelve good men and true? The character of early fourteenth-century juries', *LHR*, 15 (1997), 115–44; D. Klerman, 'Was the jury ever self-informing', in *Judicial Tribunals in England and Europe, 1200–1700: the Trial in History I*, ed. M. Mulholland and B. Pullan (Manchester, Manchester University Press, 2003), pp. 58–80.

24 R. B. Pugh, 'The writ *de bono et malo*', *LQR*, 92 (1976), 258–67.

25 3 Edward I c. 12 (*SR*, vol. 1, p. 29); H. Summerson, 'The early development of peine forte et dure', in *Law, Litigants and the Legal Profession*, ed. E. W. Ives and A. H. Manchester (London: Royal Historical Society, 1983), pp. 117–25.

battle survived the abolition or phasing out of ordeals in the early thirteenth century following the Fourth Lateran Council of 1215. Although it was never a frequent occurrence thereafter, except in the border regions, it lingered in approvers' appeals in particular.[26] We have included a colourful (almost fantastical) description of one of the last recorded instances of trial by battle (1456). [5.11] Trial by battle was not a complete substitute for jury trial, however, as some fourteenth-century cases illustrate: the jury remained involved and it was they (rather than the justices) who pronounced judgment on the appellee if the approver withdrew from combat at the last moment.[27]

Conviction was comparatively rare and even some of those who were convicted could escape the noose if they could fulfil the necessary requirements to claim benefit of clergy. This concession to clergy was open to abuse and caused justices to be more rigorous in their examination of supposed clerks.[28] [5.12] Punishment, when it came, or was carried out successfully, could be gruesome. Archaic punishments such as marooning on rocks, burying alive or throwing off cliffs remained in some local jurisdictions, but the normal punishment upon conviction for felony was to be publicly hanged by the neck until dead. This method did not always succeed, either because of the hangman's incompetence, bribery or sheer good fortune.[29] [5.13] Burning was adjudged to women found guilty of treason and, from 1401, to persons convicted of heresy. The punishment for men adjudged as traitors – usually, from the late thirteenth century, drawing, hanging and quartering – took the form of a public spectacle (intended to deter others) and was a mixture of symbolic acts, each reflecting elements of the criminous behaviour. Sometimes the offender was beheaded (and his head mounted and displayed on London Bridge) and his innards ceremonially burned. Sending the quartered body parts to the points of the compass (or to specific locations where the king wanted the traitor's destruction to be publicised) was intended to act as a deterrent to others and to prevent adherents from claiming the body.[30] [5.14]

26 P. Hyams, 'Trial by ordeal: the key to proof in the early common law', in *On the Laws and Customs of England: Essays in Honor of Samuel E. Thorne*, ed. M. S. Arnold, T. A. Green, S. A. Scully and S. D. White (Chapel Hill, NC, University of North Carolina Press, 1981), pp. 90–126; Clanchy, 'Highway robbery', pp. 25–61; C. J. Neville, 'Keeping the peace on the northern marches in the later Middle Ages', *EHR*, 109 (1994), 14–15; Musson, 'Turning king's evidence', 473–4.

27 See for example: TNA JUST 3/48 m. 6 (a gaol delivery held at Norwich before William Ormesby and William Inge in October 1309).

28 L. C. Gabel, *Benefit of Clergy in England in the Later Middle Ages* (New York, Octagon Books 1969); J. H. Baker, *The Common Law Tradition: Lawyers, Books and the Law* (London, Hambledon Press, 2000), pp. 177–85; C. J. Neville, 'Common knowledge of the common law', *Canadian Journal of History*, 29 (1994), 462–78; A. K. McHardy, 'Church courts and criminous clerks in the later Middle Ages', in *Medieval Ecclesiastical Studies*, pp. 165–83.

29 Summerson, 'Capital punishment', pp. 124–31.

30 Bellamy, *Treason*, pp. 46–8, 151–2; E. Cohen, 'Symbols of culpability and the universal language of justice: the ritual of public executions in late medieval Europe', *History of European Ideas*, 11 (1989), 407–16; M. B. Merback, *The Thief, the Cross and the Wheel: Pain and the Spectacle of Punishment in Medieval and Renaissance Europe* (London, 1999), pp. 136–46.

Pardoning criminals belonged to the royal prerogative of mercy. Following the pope's example of issuing indulgences to mark the new century (1300) and the jubilee (1350), general pardons were issued by Edward III on the occasion of his fiftieth birthday in 1362 and at his golden jubilee in 1377.[31] The general pardon, as its name suggests, offered an amnesty for all previous wrongdoing (with exceptions only for a few individuals and certain offences) and people could purchase copies to present on arraignment or at trial. [5.15] The political significance of this gesture of national grace was not lost on his successors, who regarded it as a powerful political instrument and it was utilised by subsequent monarchs on various occasions (such as 1382 and 1414) for political purposes irrespective of calendar coincidences.

Individual pardons for criminal wrongdoing were, however, available, and could be purchased either before going to court or at a later date if suitable justification could be given. [5.16] Where the defendant had a valid excuse (such as self-defence or insanity) the matter was normally sent to await a decision at the king's pleasure and usually resulted in a pardon.[32] Purchase of the king's pardon brought the royal coffers a steady but significant income and could be acquired in a variety of contexts with ensuing implications for the ethics of royal government. For example, pardons could be obtained by royal officials in order to cover themselves for offences committed in their line of duty.[33] The issuing of pardons in return for military service, however, was the most contentious exercise of the royal prerogative of mercy. [5.17] On the one hand it provided a ready source of recruits to the king's armies and removed from society undesirable criminal elements, but on the other it appeared to circumvent the traditional judicial processes and enabled the returning veterans (those who had not been eliminated in the fighting) to escape punishment and (in some cases) continue where they had left off. Fears rested on the number of pardons issued as an inducement to recruitment, but that total does not reflect the actual number ever produced in court at a later date, nor does it take into account the opportunity for the community to challenge a pardon when it was produced in court. Nor does it reflect the numbers of criminals who became casualties in the wars. While pardoning in return for military service may have compromised strict judicial process (and its effects are difficult to quantify) it was nevertheless a pragmatic method by which the violent and criminal tendencies of the Folvilles were harnessed (in Edward III's Scottish wars) and in that sense contributed significantly to the maintenance of public order.[34]

---

31 W. M. Ormrod, 'Fifty glorious years: Edward III and the first English royal jubilee', *Medieval History*, new series 1 (2002), 13–20.

32 N. D. Hurnard, *The King's Pardon for Homicide before 1307* (Oxford, Clarendon Press, 1969).

33 See 1.12 and Chapter 7.

34 H. J. Hewitt, *The Organisation of War under Edward III* (Manchester, Manchester University Press, 1966); Powell, *Kingship*, pp. 232–40; H. Lacey, 'The politics of mercy: the use of the royal pardon in fourteenth-century England', unpublished D. Phil thesis, University of York, 2005.

5.1 Appeal of felony: Margaret, wife of William de Chastel (1312)

Appeals of felony could be brought by men or women, though theoretically there were limitations on the scope of women's appeals with regard to the nature of the crime itself (only homicide and rape) and in terms of their relationship to the victim (their husband). An appeal on the death of a husband, as in this example, was therefore a standard recognised claim. In fact the categories were broadened in practice to include other close male relations (sons, brothers, nephews) and female relations (mother, daughter) and other types of crime (such as theft and robbery). By convention, the woman's husband was said to have 'died in her arms', and although it may have happened here, the phrase is more an example of the formulaic approach than a literal requirement.

The effectiveness of the appeal as a method of prosecution relied upon the victim's persistence and her ability to recite the appeal correctly without deviation in both the county court and at trial. It was vital to include all the relevant legal particulars especially words signifying felonious intent (here there is emphasis on premeditation) as well as evidential details (illuminated here by the inclusion of the dimensions of the bridge and the extent of the wound). Also the hue and cry, the local posse, had to be raised and the four neighbouring villages informed. Many appeals did not in fact reach trial as they were settled out of court. The invocation of a breach of 'God's peace' reinforces the extent to which it was perceived divine order had been violated.

TNA JUST 2/106 mm. 5–6 [Latin/French]

At the county court of Northampton held on Thursday next before St Barnabas the Apostle in the fifth year of the reign of Edward II [8 June 1312], Margaret, that was the wife of William de Chastel of Barnwell near Oundle, finds pledges to prosecute her appeal against John Blogwine of Oundle for the death of the said William, who was her husband, namely John Porthors of Polebrook and Robert de Sutton of Barnwell and immediately appeals the said John in these words.

Margaret, that was the wife of William de Chastel of Barnwell near Oundle, who is here, appeals John Blogwine of Oundle for the death of the abovesaid William de Chastel of Barnwell near Oundle, formerly her husband, who was killed in her arms, for that on Monday in the week of Pentecost in May in the fifth year of our lord the king Edward, who now reigns [15 May 1312] (God guard him) while Margaret and the said William de Chastel of Barnwell, near Oundle, who was her husband, were in the peace of God and of our lord king Edward, who now reigns (God guard him), at the hour of vespers in the vill of Oundle in the county of Northampton, on the bridge called in English 'Crowthorpe bridge', which is built of stone and mortar and crosses the river called the Nene from Oundle towards the north and Crowthorpe towards the south (the width of the bridge is twelve feet between the two crosses which stand upon it, and it extends twenty feet from one cross towards the north and forty feet from the other cross towards the south), John Blogwine of Oundle came there the same day, same year, same hour abovesaid, on the same bridge aforenamed, and on an arch towards the west side feloniously and as a felon of our lord the king and against the peace of our lord the king, his crown and dignity, lying in wait in anticipation and with premeditation, assaulted the said William Chastel of Barnwell, near Oundle, who was her husband, feloniously as a felon of our lord the king, and struck the said William Chastel of Barnwell, near Oundle, who was her husband, feloniously and as a felon of our lord the king, with a polished sword of iron and steel. Its length was four and a half feet; its width near the hilt was three and a half inches, in the centre three inches and at the end one inch; the blade was of iron and steel intermixed, the hilt and the pommel were of well-polished iron, and the handle was of iron bound and fretted with iron threads. And with that sword, while she held the said William in her arms, the said John gave him a mortal wound on the left leg five inches from the knee; the wound was eight inches long, four inches wide and four inches deep, extending through the brawn to the bone, so that if there had been no other wound or blow, he would have died of that wound. Thus of that very wound the said William Chastel of Barnwell, near Oundle, who was the husband of the said Margaret, died in her arms at sunset of the said day. This felony the said John Blogwine of Oundle committed feloniously and as a felon of our lord the king against his peace, his crown and his dignity. And after causing the death and committing this felony feloniously and as a felon of our lord the king, he immediately fled. And the said Margaret, who was the wife of the said William Chastel of Barnwell, near Oundle and who is here, at once at the said hour of the said day and year and at the aforesaid place raised the hue and cry against the said John Blogwine of Oundle, as against a felon of our lord the king, and she at once made suit from vill to vill to the four neighbouring vills and so to the bailiffs of our lord the king, and from the bailiffs to the coroners and so to the next county court, which is now being held. And if the said John Blog-wine of Oundle will deny this death and this felony, the said Margaret, formerly the wife of the said William, who is here, is willing to prove it in such a way as the court considers that a woman should.[1]

1 Since it was not considered appropriate for a woman to engage a male opponent in battle (which was an option at trial in appeals of felony), the verdict is arrived at by the jury.

At the county court of Northampton held on Thursday the vigil of the Translation of St Thomas the Martyr at the end of the said regnal year [6 July 1312] Margaret prosecuted her appeal against John Blogwine of Oundle, who was exacted* for the first time but did not appear ... [at the fifth county court a writ was received removing the appeal from the county court: 'for the said appeal cannot be determined according to the law and custom of our realm in any lower court, but only before us or elsewhere before our justices'].

5.2 Approvers' appeals: John Hendon (1400)

Like appeals of felony, approvers' appeals had to conform to strict rules as to the procedure followed, the form of the appeal and its content.[2] The justices were required to confirm that the approver had been treated humanely and that the confession had not been made under harsh conditions or extracted forcibly.[3] A marginal note indicates that Hendon was later hanged and thus unsuccessful in his appeals.

TNA KB 9/185/1 m. 36 [Latin]

John Hendon came before Thomas Cowley coroner of the king's bench at Westminster on Tuesday after St Luke in the second year of the reign of King Henry IV [19 October 1400] and confessed he was a felon of the lord king for the reason that he by night on the Saturday after St Augustine, bishop, in the first year of the reign of King Henry IV [28 August 1400] at Enfield feloniously stole three horses (worth four marks) of the goods and chattels of John Potter of Enfield and turned approver of the lord king and appealed Thomas Swanton staying at Wick in Worcestershire and Thomas Rakton of Ludlow, draper, for the reason that they together with the aforesaid approver on the king's highway in Warwickshire between Warwick and Worcester, which certain highway is less than four leagues distance from Alcester, on the eve of St Mary Magdalene in the first year of the reign of King Henry IV [21 July 1400] feloniously plundered William Newman of Worcester, dyer, of three packs of linen and wool (worth £10) and of three horses (worth 35s) which were all divided three ways between them.

Also the same approver appealed the same men for the reason that they on the Friday next before the Nativity of St John the Baptist in the first year of the reign of King Henry IV [18 June 1400] with the said

2 See also 3.16.
3 *SR*, vol. 1, pp. 141, 165, 284 (c. 10).

approver on the king's highway in Worcestershire between Worcester and Ludlow, which certain highway is less than four leagues distance from Malvern in Worcestershire, plundered certain merchants unknown to them of forty marks of gold in coins and a belt decorated with silver and one dagger decorated with silver (worth 15s) which were all divided three ways between them.

Also the same approver appealed John Wyche of Ludlow, mercer, for the reason that he on the Saturday the following night [19 June] and for a while before and after this date, at various places and times, received the same approver and the aforesaid Thomas Swanton and Thomas Rakton at Ludlow in Shropshire knowing them to be felons of the lord king and to have carried out the aforesaid felonies and various other felonies and robberies ...

Also the same approver appealed John Fythyan[4] for the reason that they together on the feast of St Mary Magdalene in the twenty-third year of King Richard II [22 July 1399] on the highway between Bristol and Worcester in Gloucestershire feloniously plundered a certain man unknown to them of five marks [£3 6s 8d] of gold and silver from which the same approver had for his share five nobles and John Fythyan the other five. And on this the said approver was asked if he wished to appeal further and he said that he did not. So the same approver had three whole days from the aforesaid Tuesday and did not wish to appeal further. So according to the law and custom of the England he ceased his appeal. And similarly the aforesaid approver was asked if he had any goods or chattels, lands or tenements and he said that he did not. And on this the same approver was committed to the prison of the Marshalsea of the lord king in the custody of John Wykes on the aforesaid account.

5.3 Indictment: indictments taken before county and local officials

Indictments were sworn statements made by juries of presentment (either on information resulting from their own inquiries or confirming as true a written bill that had been given to them) before an official authorised to hear them (see below). The jurors were required under the Statute of Westminster of 1285 to put their seals to the indictment in order for it to be valid.[5]

---

4 For a previous appearance by Fythan see 3.8.

5 13 Edward I (*SR*, vol. 1, p. 81).

(a) Sheriff (1363–64)

In one of the few surviving records of this exercise we can glimpse the sheriff of Lancashire at work. These presentments were made in response to articles not unlike those used in the royal courts.[6] The extracts illustrate that presentments focused not simply on felonies, but also encompassed trespasses and breaches of the Statute of Labourers of 1351.[7]

TNA JUST 1/451B m. 1 [Latin]

Inquest held before John de Ipres sheriff of Lancashire in his tourn of Salford held at Belton on the Monday after the quindene of Easter in the thirty-eighth year of the reign of King Edward III [8 April 1364] by [fourteen names] who said on oath that:

William Howereby beat William son of William of Chilton at Belton against the peace on the Monday next after the quindene of Easter in the thirty-eighth year of the reign of King Edward III.[8]

Also they said that Margaret daughter of Adam Spurshaw beat Margery daughter of Richard del Leghe against the peace at Ashton on the Monday next before Palm Sunday in the thirty-eighth year of the reign of King Edward III [11 March 1364].

Also they said that Henry del Gallay took in excess 6s 8d of Adam of [...] at Lever against the form of the statute[9] on the Thursday next after St John the Baptist in the thirty-seventh year of the reign of King Edward III [29 June 1363].

Also they said that Richard Proudmon took in excess against the form of the statute at Manchester of Hugh of Barker 40d on the Thursday next after Purification of the Blessed Virgin Mary in the thirty-seventh year of the reign of King Edward III [9 February 1363].[10]

Inquest held before John Ipres sheriff of Lancashire at his tourn of Amounderness held at Preston on Thursday next after the third week of Easter in the thirty-eighth year of the reign of Edward III [18 April 1364] by [eleven names] who said on oath that:

6 For articles of the sheriff's tourn see 12 Edward I c. 4 (*SR*, vol. 1, p. 55).

7 25 Edward III st. 2, cc. 1–7 (*SR*, vol. 1, pp. 311–13).

8 This appears to be an offence committed on the day of the tourn, but may be a scribal mistake.

9 Statute of Labourers (1351).

10 The plea roll has 'in the abovesaid year' giving this date. Either the offence was not discovered in time for the previous tourn, or it may be a scribal mistake and should rightly be 1364.

Richard Burdens, tailor, beat and wounded Roger le Mercer of Scales at Kirkham against the peace on Easter Sunday in the thirty-eighth year of the reign of King Edward III [24 March 1364].

Inquest held before John Ipres sheriff of Lancashire in his tourn of Leyland held at Leyland on the Tuesday next after the quindene of Easter in the thirty-eighth year of the reign of King Edward III [9 April 1364] by [thirteen names] who said on oath that:

Thomas del Wodes and Thomas del Ireby of Latham came with force of arms to Wrightington to the house of Philip de Perburn and assaulted John Kittoc and beat the said John and imprisoned him against the peace on Monday next after the Nativity of St John the Baptist in the thirty-seventh year of the reign of King Edward III [26 June 1363].

(b) Coroner (1371)

It is apparent from the chronology in the extracts that the coroner viewed the body (undertaking a rudimentary post mortem) and held his inquest remarkably soon after the body had been discovered. If the evidence gleaned from his view and from the jurors pointed towards accidental death or death by misadventure then an appropriate verdict would be reached. Usually the 'first finder', the person who discovered the body, would be arrested as a precaution if he or she did not appear at the inquest, but only for an opportunity to publicly exonerate themselves (and, during the lifetime of the eyre, contribute to the crown's coffers in paying a fine for release). Deaths occurring from natural hazards (such as rivers and wells) and domestic tragedies (resulting from fires and cooking pots) were common.

TNA JUST 2/35 m. 12 [Latin]

Essex: Hundred of Witham – Little Coggeshall

It happened there that on Thursday in Easter week in the forty-fifth year of the reign of King Edward III [10 April 1371] Agnes, wife of John Dryvere of Little Baddow, was found dead at Little Coggeshall and that John Growel first found her dead and notified the four nearest neighbours, namely, Edmund Fuller, Walter Trewe, John Sterre and Richard Hayward, who notified Thomas Peacock, bailiff of the lord king of the hundred aforesaid, which certain bailiff notified John de Gestingthorpe, one of the coroners of the aforesaid county, who came to the aforesaid Coggeshall on the Friday following in the aforesaid week [11 April] to view the body of the aforesaid Agnes. And the aforesaid John Growel, the finder, showed him the body, and he viewed it and felt it, and held an inquest concerning the aforesaid death on the oath of Thomas Lavender, John Mile, Roger Fuller, Adam Sprote, John le Clerk, John Fabyan, John Westwood, John Strogel, John Wheeler, Henry Stork, Richard Draper and John Russell. They say on their oath that John Dryvere, son of Emma of Baddow, husband of the aforesaid Agnes, on Palm Sunday of the abovesaid year [30 March] took the aforesaid Agnes with him to a certain field called Westfield in the aforesaid Coggeshall as far as a certain well abounding in water in the same field and there he hit her close to the head and neck, and so ill-treated her that he almost killed her. And the same John Dryvere, believing the same Agnes to be dead, threw her into the said well, so that the whole body of the same Agnes was in the water apart from her neck and head. Which certain Agnes lay there in the aforesaid water in the aforesaid way until Good Friday [4 April], which was the day the aforesaid John Growel found her lying in the abovesaid manner still alive. And he notified the neigh-bours there, who took her out of the aforesaid well and brought her to the house of Margery Rush in the aforesaid vill, and there she lay alive and weak until the Thursday next in Easter week, at which point she died of the aforesaid injuries. And thus the aforesaid John Dryvere feloniously killed the aforesaid Agnes.

(c) Justices of the peace (1321)

These indictments, a selection from one of a number peace sessions held during the 1320s by Herefordshire keepers of the peace, were appended to the roll of the justices commissioned to determine them in 1326 (one of whom was Richard Baskerville, one of the keepers).[11] The accusations here cover a wide range of offences from homicide, arson, burglary and larceny to trespass against the person.

TNA JUST 1/309 m. 2 [Latin][12]

Indictments before Richard Baskerville and Roger Baskerville, keepers of the peace in Herefordshire at Hereford on the Saturday before the

---

11 A. Musson, 'Creatures of statute? The earliest justices of the peace', *Archives*, 104 (2001), 26–8.

12 The full heading at the start of this membrane reads: Indictments of various persons indicted of various felonies and trespasses before Richard Baskerville and Roger Baskerville, keepers of the peace in the county of Hereford from 18 June in the thir-teenth year of the reign of Edward II [1320] until the Nativity of the Blessed Virgin Mary in the twentieth year of the aforesaid reign [8 September 1326] released to John Inge and his associates under commission of the lord king in the aforesaid county by the aforesaid keepers of the peace as shown in the instructions of the lord king directed to the same keepers of the peace.

feast of St Gregory in the fourteenth year of the reign of King Edward II [7 March 1321].

Walter le Vynor feloniously broke into the house of William le Vynor at the Vineyard of Ledbury and carried off cloth to the value of half a mark.

Roger, brother of Thomas Udeson made hamsoken* on Cecilia wife of the said Thomas and beat, wounded and maltreated her against the peace.

Robert Bollok of Newent and John Muriel of the same feloniously killed William Madour de la Lee at Lea.

Eva, wife of Walter Rose of Walford entered the church of Walford and feloniously took candles worth 2s.

Maurice le Walkare of Wormbridge feloniously and at night set fire to the house of William le Shereman at [left blank].

Juliana wife of Adam Wogan of Upton went off with the goods of her husband valued at 10s through the assent and consent of John son of Hugh le Parker.

John son of Robert Morton beat, wounded and maltreated Roger le Porter of Cotton through assent of Roger Makyns and John his brother and he is a common disturber of the peace.

(d) Borough constables (1467)

The mayor and bailiffs of a town or borough were responsible for law and order within their jurisdiction and the borough constables usually held weekly inquests into misbehaviour. The accusations here cover not just criminal tres- pass, but also highlight the constables' responsibility for curbing unlawful behaviour such as gaming and economic offences such as forestalling.* Some- times jury presentments derived from their personal knowledge or experi- ence of a crime. Interestingly from an ethical point of view, in one case here it appears that Thomas Babington, the recorder, one of the borough officials, is trying the alleged burglary of his property.

Records of the Borough of Nottingham, ed. W. H. Stevenson (2 vols; London and Nottingham, 1882), vol. 2, pp. 260–64. [Latin]

TOWN OF NOTTINGHAM NAMELY BEFORE JOHN HUNT, MAYOR OF THE TOWN AFORESAID, THOMAS BABINGTON, RECORDER, THOMAS THURLAND, THOMAS ALESTRE, JOHN SQUIRE AND OTHERS, KEEPERS OF THE PEACE THERE ON MONDAY NEXT

AFTER THE FEAST OF ST DENIS IN THE SEVENTH YEAR OF THE REIGN OF KING EDWARD IV [5 October 1467]

Inquest of the Western Side

The jurors there present that Richard Fell of Nottingham in the county of the town of Nottingham, husbandman, John Taddon of the same in the county aforesaid, smith, and Thomas Stokes of the same in the county aforesaid, tailor, on Sunday next before the feast of St Bartholomew the Apostle in the seventh year of the reign of King Edward IV [23 August 1467] at Nottingham in the county of Nottingham played at dice and other unlawful games against the form of the statute.[13]

They also say that Elizabeth wife of Richard Fosard of Nottingham in the county of the town of Nottingham, spinster, at the feast of All Hallows in the sixth year of the reign of Edward IV [1 November 1466] at Nottingham in the county of the town of Nottingham took and carried away with force and arms three cheeses of the goods and chattels of Margaret Smith then and there found against the peace of the lord king.

Inquest of the constables

The jurors there present, that William Dawson of Nottingham in the county of the town of Nottingham, litster,* James Dawson of the same in the county aforesaid, baker, and Robert Taylor of the same in the county aforesaid, baker, on the Sunday next after the feast of Saint Denis in the seventh year of the reign of King Edward IV [11 October 1467], at Nottingham, in the county of the town of Nottingham, broke by night the close and house of Thomas Babington, and assaulted Robert Ivenet, against the peace of our lord king.

Also, they say that John Mold of Nottingham in the county of the town of Nottingham, painter, Richard Colman of the same and in the same county, weaver, and Thomas Tall, tailor, otherwise called Thomas Taylor the tenant of Roger Unwin of Nottingham in the county of the town of Nottingham, tailor, on the Sunday next before Michaelmas in the seventh year of the reign of King Edward IV [27 September 1467] at Nottingham, in the county of the town of Nottingham, played at an unlawful and prohibited game called 'quoiting' unlawfully against the form of the statute promulgated thereupon.

13 12 Richard II c. 6 (*SR*, vol. 2, p. 57), confirmed by Henry IV st. 2, c. 4 (*ibid.*, p. 163), whereby the games of tennis, quoits, dice, casting the stone, kails and the like, were forbidden to serving men and labourers, who were enjoined to practise archery instead.

Also, they say that Thomas Marshall of Nottingham in the county of the town of Nottingham, corviser,* on the 10th day of August in the seventh year of the reign of King Edward IV [1467] at Nottingham in the county of the town of Nottingham at a place there called *Sandeclyff* forestalled* four cartloads of sea-coal, not permitting those coals to be taken and carried to the king's market of the said town [to the prejudice and damage of our lord king's people].

(e) Stewards of liberties (1356–64)

The following examples of offences presented at courts leet are drawn from the Suffolk liberties of the earl of Suffolk and the abbey of St Edmunds. The vitality of the court of the liberty of Bury St Edmunds was still apparent during the fifteenth century.[14]

TNA KB 9/157 mm. 3, 4, 5, 39 [Latin]

Inquest taken at the leet held at Carlton Colville [Suffolk] on the Wednesday next after the Close of Easter in the thirtieth year of the reign of King Edward III [4 May 1356] before Adam de Mutford steward of the same leet by [eighteen names] jurors who said on oath that Nicholas Nicole of Barnby on the Friday next after the Close of Easter 25 Edward III [29 April 1351] in theft took and carried off one heifer worth 6s at *Houburgh* of Alicia le Neve* and killed and ate it. And also took in theft of Agnes Hereman at *Houburgh* an ox worth 15s on the Monday next after the feast of Michaelmas in the twenty-seventh year of the reign of King Edward III [30 September 1353] and is a common thief.

Inquest taken at the leet of Orford held on the Wednesday next after St Hilary in the thirty-fourth year of the reign of King Edward III [20 January 1361] before John Lakenheath, steward of the said Robert of Ufford, earl of Suffolk by [twelve names] jurors who said on oath that Roger Gramund at night on the Monday next after St Andrew the Apostle in the regnal year abovesaid [7 December 1360] in theft stole a blanket worth 18d, a featherbed and a fur worth 18d. In testimony to which the said jurors have placed their seals to this indictment.

Inquest taken at the leet of Orford held on the Wednesday next after St Hilary in the thirty-fifth year of the reign of King Edward III [19 January 1362] before John Lakenheath, steward of Sir Robert de Ufford, earl of Suffolk by [twelve names] jurors who said on oath that Roger

14 Maddern, *Violence*, p. 60.

Gramund was indicted at the leet held there [in 1361] that he had stolen cloth, linen and wool to the value of 3s by virtue of which indictment he was arrested and imprisoned in the prison of Orford aforesaid; the same Roger at night on the Monday after the Nativity of St John the Baptist in the regnal year abovesaid [28 June 1361] broke the said prison and escaped until he was recaptured. Also, they say that John le Wright helped the said Roger to break his irons and counselled the same Roger to break the said prison and take flight. In testimony to which they placed their seals to the said indictment.

Inquest taken before William de Rushbroke, steward of the liberty of St Edmund of the great court of St Edmund held there on the Thursday next after St Augustine, bishop, in the thirty-eighth year of the reign of King Edward III [29 August 1364] by [twelve names] jurors who said on oath that William Carmene of Needham on the night of the feast of the Holy Trinity in the thirty-eighth year of the reign of King Edward III [26 May 1364] feloniously entered the house of John Berkelowe in Needham and in the same house took Alicia wife of the said John Berkelowe and ravished and abducted her with goods and chattels of the said John namely charters, muniments and books concerning his tenements and 20s in gold and silver and other goods and chattels namely cloth, linen and wool worth £20. In testimony of which the said jury place their seals.

(f) King's bench justices ('superior eyre') (1323)

In its periodic visitation of various counties the king's bench assumed jurisdiction over all cases pending and delivered gaols of prisoners awaiting trial. It could also hear cases at first instance and the justices could take indictments in criminal matters of the felonies and trespasses presented by jurors.

TNA KB 27/254 m. 2 [Latin]

The jurors of the town of Wigan [Lancs.] present that Stephen son of Richard son of Michael of Wigan feloniously killed Hugh son of Henry of Wigan at Wigan after Low Sunday in the sixteenth year of the reign of [King Edward II] [3 April 1323].

Also that John son of Adam le Taillour of *Pereburn* feloniously killed Hugh del Lone of Ashton at Wigan about the feast of the Assumption of the Blessed Virgin Mary in the seventeenth year of the reign of the present king [c 15 August 1323].

Also that Adam of Bletherhose and Ranulf de Woolley of Cheshire eloniously stole a horse laden with food stuffs and a haketon* belonging to William of Bradshaw worth 40s at Wigan in August of the seventeenth year [1323].

Also that the aforesaid Adam of Bletherhose, John le Reeve of Northley, John son of John le Feure of Pemberton and Adam Oulebil of Hindley feloniously stole a certain other horse of the aforesaid William Bradshaw laden with food stuffs worth 20s at Wigan about Easter in the sixteenth year [c 27 March 1323].

And that Henry of Adburghham, Henry son of Henry le Bowyer of Wigan, Richard son of Henry le Archer, John his brother and Henry of Pleasington feloniously robbed Henry Russel of Wigan of cloth worth £8 and other merchants in his company of goods worth 60s at High Legh on the feast of St Mary Magdalene in the seventeenth year [22 July 1323].

5.4 Indictment: certificate of riot following a student riot in Oxford (1417)

The incident described in this passage is an example of the disturbances occurring in Oxford during the late fourteenth and early fifteenth centuries within the jurisdiction of the chancellor of Oxford University (who is described as a JP),[15] but coming before the county justices. The description of the assembled scholars not only offers a colourful picture of their array, but was clearly necessary to sustain the allegation that it was a dangerous and warlike gathering. The vendetta pursued against lawyer Thomas Cowley (a coroner and attorney in the king's bench) seems to be related to his occupation of certain land in Iffley. Their armed presence may be intended to offer a symbolic challenge to his ownership or seisin of this land, even though such gatherings and displays of violence in the course of establishing an entry on to land had long been prohibited. The episode demonstrates in a medieval setting the overlap of what in modern terms would be called civil and criminal law. The hefty penalties and assurances to the king do not appear to have deterred the students as they are alleged to have reoffended.

TNA KB 9/219 mm. 70–72 [Latin]

Inquest held at Thame on Monday the eve of St Bartholomew in the fifth year of the reign of King Henry V [23 August 1417] before Robert James and Edmund Rede justices of the peace of Oxfordshire both by virtue of their office as justices of the peace and by virtue of the king's

15 See *Oxfordshire Sessions of the Peace in the Reign of Richard II*, ed. E. G. Kimball, Oxford Record Society, 53 (1983), pp. 103–5.

writ and the statute specified in the writ and attached to the present inquest addressed to them and to others.

The jury [named] say on their oath that:

Master Nicholas Danyell of Oxford, in the county of Oxford, scholar, Master John Bathe of the same, scholar, Robert Oppy of the same, chaplain, John Moore of the same, scholar, Richard Moore of the same, chaplain, [...] Moore of the same, scholar, John Repton, infirmarer in Kidlington, Oxfordshire, Nicholas Ryxton of Oxford, scholar, Denis Yonge of the same, scholar, John Cawdray of the same, scholar, Richard Gauge of the same, scholar, Lewis Elys and William Crowell of Sydenham, Oxfordshire, husbandman, on the Thursday after St Peter's Chains in the fifth year of the reign of King Henry V [5 August 1417] with many other evildoers and disturbers of the peace numbering eighty armed men in the style of a 'new insurrection' congregated together at Oxford against the king's peace; and there Nicholas Danyell as their captain and leader left Oxford armed with a breastplate, a pair of plated gloves, vambrace* and rerebrace,* a pricking-pallet* with three ostrich feathers fixed in it, a launcegay* and a Carlisle axe heading to the town of Iffley with the said evildoers there with him armed with hauberks,* doublets of defence, pricking-pallets, launcegays, bows and arrows, to seek out Thomas Cowley, coroner and a king's attorney in the king's bench,[16] in his house at Iffley and kill him if they could find him; notwithstanding that the said Nicholas Danyell and all the said evildoers had been personally forbidden, on behalf of the king, by Master Thomas Chace, chancellor of Oxford University and justice of the peace of the same, from leaving Oxford to take part in any congregation or riot in breach of the king's peace.

And upon this Nicholas Danyell and all the said evildoers advancing towards Iffley assaulted Hugh Eggerley, Richard Hamwell, William Uphull and John Fairchild, Thomas Cowley's servants, who thought nothing amiss, nor had any weapon of defence upon them, and chased them with intent to kill them and chased them for two furlongs shouting continually with a great cry, 'Slay, slay, slay'.

And upon this all the evildoers together came to two acres of land of the said Thomas Cowley, sown with rye the previous year by Thomas Cowley, of which the said Thomas Cowley had been seised* peacefully for a long time with a just title without any disturbance and thus with the aforesaid force embattled in three warlike squadrons took and

16 See 5.2.

carried away then from there the crop in the same two acres of land (worth 5 marks) against Thomas Cowley's will.

And they made such threats against Thomas Cowley and his servants and tenants there and at Oxford to their life and mutilation of their limbs and of burning down their houses and continue so to threaten that the said Thomas Cowley dares not go about the king's business as he ought, nor go about his own business, for fear of death, nor do his servants living with him.

On which show of might and large assembly the said Thomas Cowley sued before the king's council to have a remedy. By which the lord king commanded the chancellor to send a writ ordering that Nicholas Danyell, John Bathe and Robert Oppy and each of them should appear in person before the king undertaking for themselves on pain of £200 that they would find sufficient mainpernors* who were willing to stand surety for them, and compelled each on pain of £40 that they would not cause, nor procure anyone to carry out, any bodily injury or evil to Thomas Cowley, his servants or any of the king's subjects, nor would they make any more riots, congregations or illict conventicles whatsoever. And if they refused to do this before the king then they would be committed instantly to the nearest royal gaol for safe custody until they were willing freely to do this.

Which writ was delivered to Thomas Chace, chancellor of Oxford University at Oxford on the Saturday on the eve of the Assumption of the Blessed Virgin Mary last [14 August 1417] in the presence of several trustworthy persons. On which the chancellor summoned the said Nicholas Danyell and John Bathe into his presence to certify them of the matters which were contained in the said writ and to swear them on behalf of the lord king that in future they would be obedient and compliant in all things contained in the aforesaid writ. And that in the meantime they would keep the king's peace in all things and not hold any clandestine meetings or large assemblies against the peace, each of them on pain of £300 to be forfeited to the king.

And notwithstanding this, the said Nicholas Danyell contemptuously and disdainfully ignoring the command of the king aforesaid and the said chancellor, gathered to him anew several evildoers and peacebreakers, namely the said John Moore, Richard Moore, John Repton, Nicholas Ryxton, Denis Yonge, John Cawdray, Richard Gauge and William Corwell and Lewis Elys, parish clerk of St Aldate's Oxford, and William Sybford of Littlemore, Oxfordshire, husbandman, who all together with other evildoers and disturbers of the peace to the number of sixty armed men, arrayed in the manner of war abovesaid, through the guidance, counsel, help, instigation and favour of the said John Bathe and Robert Oppy on the Tuesday following the said Saturday [17 August 1417] left Oxford making towards Iffley notwithstanding that they had been personally bound by the said chancellor and proctors of the university on behalf of the king not to make any illicit meeting or assembly against the peace.

And the crop of seven and a half acres of the said Thomas Cowley at Iffley sown with barley and peas (worth £10) by Thomas Cowley the previous year, of which Thomas Cowley had been seised for a long time peacefully and without any disturbance, with force and arms they seized and carried off against the will of the said Thomas Cowley and against the peace and against the form of the statutes both of the time of Edward III, Richard II and of the thirteenth year of the reign of Henry IV [1411] recently promulgated forbidding riots, clandestine meetings, or illicit assemblies in any way or entering forcibly any lands or tenements, and in serious commotion and disturbance of the whole county of Oxford and a pernicious example to other evildoers.

5.5 Arrest (1377)

In this case the process of arrest is set out clearly: notification of the indictment is given to the sheriff by the steward (who had heard the allegations at his tourn), who in turn sends a warrant to his bailiffs, the arresting officers, who then take and imprison the named individual. The chain was dependent upon the requisite authority (the jury's seals and the sheriff's orders) being present. The problem highlighted here is how the process could occasionally be vitiated and corrupted at an earlier stage – by the indicting officer's clerk, for instance. Note that the arresting officials were questioned as to whether they were complicit in the situation.

Select Cases of Trespass in the King's Courts, ed. M. Arnold, SS, 100 (1985), pp. 52–3 [Latin]

Roger de Drayton, Thomas Burne, Walter Broune of Chudleigh and Thomas Rygon by Thomas Reymond their attorney come and defend force and wrong when etc. And individually they say that as to coming with force and arms or whatever against the peace etc., that they are not guilty in any way. And concerning this they place themselves on the country;* and the aforesaid Thomas Wenlock similarly. And as to arresting and imprisoning the same Thomas Wenlock, they say indi-

vidually that at the hundred court held at Teignbridge [Devon] on
Monday next before the feast of the Conversion of St Paul in the fiftieth
year of the reign of lord Edward, lately king of England, grandfather of
the present lord king [19 January 1377], the aforesaid Thomas Wenlock
was indicted before John Copplestone of the same hundred on the oath
of twelve etc. concerning this that on Saturday on the feast of St Andrew
the Apostle in the forty-fourth year of the reign of the same grandfather of the king [30 November 1370] a certain goat valued at sixteen
pence was feloniously stolen by him, and also at the same hundred court
held there then the same Thomas Wenlock on the oath of twelve etc.
was indicted for the felonious theft of a cow valued at five shillings, the
which indictments the same John Copplestone sent to John Fitzpayne
then sheriff of Devon; by virtue of which indictment the same sheriff
sent to the aforesaid Roger, Thomas Burne, Walter, and Thomas Rygon
as his bailiffs a warrant for the arrest of the aforesaid Thomas Wenlock
and to bring him with them to the prison of the lord king at Exeter and
incarcerate him there etc. And so they say that by virtue of the aforesaid
warrant they arrested the same Thomas Wenlock and brought him
with them to the prison of the lord king aforesaid and imprisoned him
there, just as it is lawfully permitted them. Whence they do not think
that any wrong can be assigned to them personally in this respect.

And the aforesaid Thomas Wenlock says that he was never indicted
before the aforesaid John Copplestone as he alleged above in pleading.
And he seeks that this be investigated by the country; and the aforesaid
Roger, Thomas Burne, Walter, and Thomas Rygon similarly.

On which day the aforesaid Thomas Wenlock comes in person etc. And
the aforesaid justices before whom etc. sent here their record in these
words:

Afterwards, on the day and at the place within-contained, before the
justices of assize etc., come both the within-named Thomas Wenlock
in person and the within-named Roger, Thomas Burne, Walter, and
Thomas Rygon through their within-named attorney. The jurors similarly come who, having been chosen for this purpose with the consent
of the parties, tried, and sworn, say on their oath that the aforesaid
Thomas Wenlock was not indicted at the hundred court held at Teignbridge on the day and year on which is within just as supposed within
concerning the felony contained within. But they say that a certain John
Petipas a clerk of John Copplestone, steward of John Burdon, lord of
the aforesaid hundred, falsely copied and forged a certain indictment
concerning the aforesaid Thomas Wenlock for the felony contained

within on the day and year on which it is supposed within that the
aforesaid indictment was made, without holding any inquest thereon,
and affixed twelve seals on his own authority at Teignbridge and delivered that indictment to his master, the aforesaid John Copplestone,
the which John Copplestone delivered that indictment to John Fitzpayne then sheriff for carrying out process thereon; the which John
Fitzpayne the sheriff gave an order to the aforesaid Roger, Thomas
Burne, Walter, and Thomas Rygon then his bailiffs to arrest the aforesaid Thomas Wenlock; the which Roger, Thomas Burne, Walter, and
Thomas Rygon by virtue of the aforesaid order directed to them then
arrested the aforesaid Thomas Wenlock and brought him with them to
Exeter Castle and delivered the same Thomas Wenlock to the aforesaid John Fitzpayne then sheriff; the which John Fitzpayne then sheriff
transferred the same Thomas Wenlock to the lord king's gaol there
for the aforesaid cause, to stay there until he be delivered according to
the law etc. The same jurors, being asked whether the aforesaid Roger,
Thomas Burne, Walter, and Thomas Rygon knew anything of the fabri-
cation or forging of the aforesaid indictment, say that they did not.
The same jurors, being questioned what damages the aforesaid John
Wenlock sustained on account of the imprisonment aforesaid, say that
his damages were six marks.

5.6 Summons to court: judicial process

Those who did not answer the summons to court or could not be found and
arrested were given the opportunity to present themselves at the next sessions.
Until they did attend, the process of exaction continued and their names were
read out in the county court each month over the next five months. If they
still had not come forward by the end of this period then they were outlawed.
There were clearly concerns raised in the fifteenth century that if the indictment were false or had arisen through abuse of procedure then innocent people
would be caught up and outlawed as a result of the comparative speed of the
process whereby writs of *exigent** were awarded and outlawry pronounced.[17]
The government appears to have been willing to compromise significantly on
the time periods, allowing the period between the issue of the *capias** and its
return to be 'six weeks at least or longer' at the justices' discretion.

---

17 See 7.12.

(a) The process of exaction and outlawry (1414)

TNA KB 9/219/1 m. 7 [Latin]

Sessions held at Cirencester before Thomas Mille, John Deerhurst and Robert Wytington keepers of the peace of the lord Henry, king of England, father of the present lord king, and justices of the peace of the same lord king, assigned to hear and determine various felonies, trespasses and misdeeds in Gloucestershire on the Tuesday next after the feast of the Holy Trinity in the second year of the reign of King Henry V [5 June 1414]

At which day at the county court of Gloucestershire held [at Gloucester] on Monday 8 January in the first year of the reign of King Henry V [1414] on the sheriff's command the said William Netherton, Thomas Pere and John Stoyle were first exacted* and not found. And at the county court of Gloucestershire held [at Gloucester] on Monday 5 February in the first year of the reign of the lord king abovesaid the said William Netherton, Thomas and John were exacted for a second time and not found. And at the county court of Gloucestershire held [at Gloucester] on Monday 5 March in the first year of the reign of the lord king abovesaid the said William Netherton, Thomas and John were exacted for a third time and not found. And at the county court of Gloucestershire held [at Gloucester] on Monday 2 April in the second year of the reign of the lord king abovesaid [1414] the said William Netherton, Thomas and John were exacted for a fourth time and not found. And at the county court of Gloucestershire held [at Gloucester] on Monday 30 April in the second year of the reign of the lord king abovesaid the said William Netherton, Thomas and John were exacted for a fifth time and not found. And because they were not found at any of these aforesaid county court sessions, so in the presence of Walter Toky and John Solers, coroners of the lord king, they are outlawed.

(b) Complaints of the speed of judicial process (1427)

RP, vol. 4, pp. 327–8 [French]

Also the commons pray that whereas various of the loyal lieges of our lord the king by the false scheming, plotting and conspiracy of certain evildoers are indicted before the king in his Bench[18] of various felonies and treasons by untrustworthy jurors and charged and procured by this through the confederacy and conjecture of the said conspirators;

18 i.e. the court of king's bench

by force of which indictments a writ of *capias*, returnable within two or four days, is awarded to the sheriff of the county where the said king's bench is sitting; on which day if the party indicted does not come an *exigent* is awarded by which the goods and chattels of the said indicted party are forfeit to the king to the ultimate destruction of the various loyal lieges of our lord the king. May it please our sovereign lord the king by the authority of this present parliament to ordain that before any *exigent* is awarded against such indicted persons that a writ of *capias* be issued to the sheriff or sheriffs of the county where the indictment mentioned that the party is or was residing, having a period of three months before the return of the said writ and if any *exigent* is awarded or outlawry pronounced afterwards against any of those indicted before the said writ is so returned, that this *exigent* awarded with outlawry pronounced in it be void and held to have no validity.

Response: Before any *exigent* is awarded against such indicted persons before the king in his Bench, let writs of *capias* be directed both to the sheriff or sheriffs of the county in which they are thus indicted and to the sheriff or sheriffs of the county where they are named in the indictments, having in the same writ of *capias* the space of six weeks at least or longer, if the case requires it, at the discretion of the justices, before return of the same; when the writs have been returned, the justices should proceed in the same manner as they have done before this time; and if any *exigent* is awarded or any outlawry pronounced afterwards against such indicted persons before the return of the said writs, this *exigent* awarded, with the outlawry pronounced in it, shall be void and held to have no validity. And this ordinance will remain in force at the king's pleasure.

5.7 Trial: gaol delivery sessions (early fourteenth century)

The following extracts from gaol delivery trials held in Norfolk in the early fourteenth century show how indictments were scrutinised for inconsistencies and insufficient detail and could fail if they did not match up to the standard required by the justices.

TNA JUST 3/125 mm. 1, 2, 2d, 7, 7d, 8 [Latin]

John le Porter of Worsted and John of Nottingham indicted at Rudham [Norfolk] before Roger Breton and Thomas Milham constables of the hundred of Brothircross that they stole in East Rudham two and a half ells of blue cloth (worth 2s 6d) belonging to William of Ovington, half an ell of green cloth in East Rudham belonging to Richard de Cacton of Brancaster and two haunches from Simon Cordwainer in the same vill (worth 6d). They came and because the sheriff testified that John le Porter and John of Nottingham had not been taken at the suit of anyone with the mainour* and the indictment was not made recently on any robbery or theft committed in the said vill of Rudham it seemed to the court that the said indictment made before the said constables of the hundred is not adequate to bring them to judgment of life and member.

Beatrice wife of John le Porter, Elena wife of John of Nottingham, John son of Hugh le Neve* of Bilney taken on suspicion at Rudham in the company of John of Nottingham and John le Porter with two mazers* worth half a mark came forward and the said Beatrice, Elena and John son of Hugh were asked individually if they claimed any property in the said mazers. They said they claimed nothing. So the said mazers are adjudged to the king and worth 2s for which the sheriff, John de Loudham, is to answer. And because the sheriff testifies that the said Beatrice, Elena and John son of Hugh are not indicted for stealing the said mazers, nor were they taken at the suit of anyone, and also because it was proclaimed that 'if there is anyone who wishes to prosecute them concerning any theft or other misdeeds they should come forward' and no one came to prosecute, so the said Beatrice, Elena and John son of Hugh go without day.*

John le Parker of Ashwell Thorpe and Richard le Palmer indicted at the sheriff's tourn held at Newton Flotman that they feloniously killed John Bonhom of Ashwell Thorpe at night in the vill of Ashwell Thorpe. And the said John le Parker and Richard le Palmer came and were asked individually how they wished to be acquitted of the said death. They denied it and each of them denied all force, felony, death and any breach of the peace and say that they are guilty of nothing and place themselves for good and ill* on the country.* The jury of the hundred of Depwade on oath say that John le Parker and Richard are not guilty of anything concerning the said death nor did they ever withdraw themselves for that reason.[19] So they are acquitted.

Robert of Wychingham, John Portlond of Aylsham and Richard son of the same taken in the vill of Aylsham with the mainour and by the hue and cry with three sheep skins and with a cow stolen by them in the vill of Aylsham came and were asked individually whether they wished

19 A defendant's absence from the neighbourhood prior to arrest could be taken as a sign of guilt.

to be acquitted thereon. They denied all the felonies and placed themselves for good and ill on the country. The jury of South Erpingham say on oath that John Portlond and Richard stole the said skins and the said cow in the said vill of Aylsham with the same Henry[20] recently taken with the mainour, so let the same be hanged. No chattels. The value of the said skins is 7s, for which the vill of Aylsham is to answer. And concerning the said Robert of Wichingham the said jury say that he is not guilty of the theft of the said skins and cow and did not withdraw himself, so he is then acquitted.

John Thirkeal of Shipdham, indicted at the leet of the lord king at Shipdham in the third year of the reign of King Edward III [1329] that he burgled the house of Margerie Herbert of Shipdham in Shipdham and other thefts, came forward. And because the bailiff of the said liberty does not have here on this day the indictment made at the said leet concerning the said John, so the same John is remanded in prison. And the said bailiff is ordered to have the indictment at the next delivery.

Lenota that was the wife of Roger Brun of Wetheringsett was indicted at the leet of Wetheringsett at the same time as Roger her husband, who died in prison, that they received William Attehill, who wickedly and feloniously killed Agnes Colleman of Wetheringsett in the same vill. And the said Lenota came and because William is a fugitive and is not convicted of the said felony so the same Lenota is remanded in prison.

Cecilia, daughter of Thomas le Whyte of Bikerston taken in Norwich at the suit of John Attefield of Kiningham who found pledges, namely William of Thurston and Ralph of Forncett, for prosecuting the same Cecilia concerning 40s in cash stolen from the same John at Kiningham. And the said Cecilia came forward. And the same Cecilia was neither arrested with the mainour, a certain amount of cash belonging to the said John, nor is she indicted before the sheriff or the bailiffs of the town of Norwich, as the sheriff and bailiffs of the town of Norwich testify. So let the said Cecilia go without day. And it is to be known that the said John was not called to prosecute etc. because his suit is considered void as the said Cecilia was not taken with the goods of the same John.

20 This may refer to a thief who had recently turned approver.

5.8 Trial: judge questioning defendant

It is rare to find detailed discussion of criminal trials reported in the Year Books
(the collections of cases that have been reported, often verbatim, by a lawyer
or student present at judicial sessions).[21] This particular trial was ostensibly
held during the eyre of Yorkshire in 1293–94. The underlying case may well be
real and much of what is reported could have occurred. The course of the trial,
however, reads like a model example made for study purposes, ranging through
the various procedural options open to a defendant faced with a serious accusation against him. It is noticeable that counsel is not allowed the defendant
on the grounds that in a criminal trial on indictment the king, rather than the
accuser, is the prosecutor.[22] The didactic elements of this passage are conveyed
by the judge, who sets out the requirements for each option. Bigamy was the
standard rebuttal to a plea of clergy and the evidential details are clarified.[23]
The judge eventually confronts the jury with the substantive accusation of rape
and they answer questions designed to test the elements of the offence. The
different paths taken during the trial come across merely as procedural ploys
invoked by the (seemingly desperate) defendant. It is of course ironic that he
claims he cannot read when he has previously attested to being a clerk. The
letter 'N' (*nomen*) employed in the text suggests either that the reporter wished
to obscure the identity of certain people and places or he did not regard them
as necessary to an understanding of the case. If the text were used for teaching
purposes fictitious names could be inserted as appropriate.

Year Books 30–31 Edward I, ed. A. J. Horwood (RS, 1863), Appendix 2, pp.
529–32 [Latin]

Also, it was presented by the twelve [jurors] of 'Y[oucros]'[24] that
Hugh raped a certain maiden, and he brought her to his manor in the
same vill and knew her carnally against her will.

Hugh was brought up to the bar by Brian and Nicholas de N.

JUDGE: Brian, we are given to understand that you are said to have
told the prisoner that he should not place himself on those who accused
him, and you have done wrong, but because he is related to you, we will
allow you to be near him, but not that you counsel him.

Brian: Sir, he is my relation, but this accusation I wish to be disproved

---

21 A series of reports of early fourteenth-century trials in Newgate survive: Baker, *The
Common Law Tradition*, pp. 165–86.

22 J. B. Post, 'The admissibility of defence counsel in English criminal procedure', *JLH*,
5 (1984), 23–32. Note that defence counsel were allowed in some high-profile cases:
D. Seipp, 'Crime in the Year Books', in *Law Reporting in Britain*, ed. C. Stebbings
(London, Hambledon Press, 1995), pp. 15–34.

23 See also 5.12.

24 Ewcross wapentake.

and wish that it goes fortunately for him, but by me he might be well counselled to refuse the common law;[25] and lest anyone have suspicion of corruption, I will withdraw from his side.

JUDGE: It is presented to us that you have raped etc. as alleged; in what manner do you want to acquit yourself?

Hugh: Sir, I request that I may have counsel so as not to be caught unawares in the king's court for want of advice.

JUDGE: You ought to know that the king is a party in this case and prosecutes by virtue of his office whence in this situation by law it is not allowed that you have counsel against the king, who prosecutes by virtue of his office. If however the woman were bringing a case against you, you would have counsel against her, but not against the king. And so we command on behalf of the king that all pleaders who are of your counsel should leave.

(the pleaders withdrew)

JUDGE: Hugh, reply; see, your possible action and your own action have been put forward against you, to which you are able to respond adequately without counsel whether you have behaved in this manner or not. Also the law ought to be common and equal;[26] and the law is that the king is a party by virtue of office against whom you may not have counsel; and if we were to concede you your counsel against the law and the country* find favourably for you, as it will do God willing, it would be said that you have been delivered through the favour of the justices. And so we do not dare do this, nor ought you to desire this, and so you should respond.

Hugh: Sir, I am a clerk and ought not to respond without my ordinary.*

JUDGE: Are you a clerk?

Hugh: Sir, it is so, because I was rector of the church of N.

Ordinary: We seek him as a clerk.

Hugh: He says it.

JUDGE: We say that you should have lost clerical privilege for the reason that you are bigamous because you have contracted marriage with a widow, and you will answer whether when you contracted with her she was a virgin or not etc. and now it is better to confess the state

25 In other words, the opportunity to place himself on the jury.
26 i.e. applicable to all

rather than to delay; because, mark you, it is possible for it to be verified immediately by the country.

Hugh: Sir, she was a virgin when I married her.

JUDGE: This ought to be verified immediately.

And he charged the twelve jurymen if Hugh etc., who said by virtue of their oath that she was a widow when Sir Hugh contracted with her. But note that etc. were they not sworn anew because the first jury have already been sworn?

JUDGE: And so the court here adjudges that you should respond as a layman and consent to those honest men of the jury, because we know that they are unwilling to lie for us.

Hugh: Sir, I am accused by them; so I will not accept them. Also, sir, I am a knight and ought not to be judged unless by my peers.[27]

JUDGE: Because you are a knight we wish that you are judged by your peers.

And the knights were named. And he was asked if he wished to lay a challenge against any of them.

Hugh: Sir, I do not accept them. You take any inquest you wish as part of your office, but I will not accept it.

JUDGE: Sir Hugh, if you were to be willing to accept them, with God's help, they will find for you if you are willing to accept them. And if you wish to refuse the common law, you will bear the penalty ordained thereon, namely, 'one day you will eat and another day you will drink; and the day you will drink you will not eat and the opposite; and you will eat bread made of barley and not salted, and water etc.', showing to him many reasons why it would not be good to delay thereupon, but better to agree on them.

Hugh: I will accept my peers, but not place myself on the twelve by whom I am accused, so you will hear my challenges towards them.

JUDGE: Freely; let them be read; but if you know any reason why they ought to be removed, name each one orally or in writing.

Hugh: Sir, because I do not know how to read I seek my counsel.

JUDGE: No, because the matter touches the lord king.

Hugh: You have them and you can read them.

JUDGE: No, because they ought to be proposed by your mouth.

27 See 1.6.

Hugh: I do not know how to read them.

JUDGE: How is this, that you wanted to have assistance through clerical privilege and now do not know how to read your challenges?

Hugh remained silent as if confounded.

JUDGE: Do not be dumbfounded, now is the time to speak.

JUDGE (to Sir N. de Leicester): Are you willing to read the challenges of Sir Hugh?

Sir N: Sir, if so, I will need to have his book which he has in front of his hands. (This was admitted) *And the said N*. Sir, it names here challenges against many people, do you wish me to read them publicly?

JUDGE: No, certainly you should read them to the prisoner and privately because they ought to be uttered through his own mouth.

And so it was done. The exceptions having been put forward by his own mouth, because the truth of the challenge was ascertained against them, those against whom the exceptions were put forward were removed from the inquest.

JUDGE: We have challenged Sir Hugh about the rape of a certain woman, he denied it and was asked how he wished to acquit himself thereon; he said by a good jury; whence for good and ill he places himself on you; and so we enjoin you by virtue of your oath, tell us whether Sir Hugh raped the said woman or not.

Jury: We say that she was raped by force by Sir Hugh's men.

JUDGE: Did Sir Hugh consent to the deed or not?

Jury: He did not.

JUDGE: Did they know her carnally?

Jury. Yes.

JUDGE: Against the woman's will or with her consent?

Jury: She consented.

JUDGE: Sir Hugh, because they have acquitted you we acquit you.

5.9 Trial: model interrogation of suspected thief

This thirteenth-century treatise provided the gaol delivery justice with model cases or precedents for his private instruction probably based on composite observation of real sessions. As in the previous example, the progress of the trial was determined by the nature and extent of the judge's questioning of the defendant. It was unlikely that this was normally particularly lengthy since judges would be aware that at most venues there was a long calendar of prisoners to get through.[28] Nevertheless, where the circumstances were unclear or there were evidential details to ascertain concerning the crime, questions were put to the defendant and/or the jury and occasionally to witnesses. Note that this defendant has been arrested on suspicion of theft with the relevant items in his possession (caught with the mainour*). In such cases it helped to have people who could testify positively to the defendant's reputation. The defendant attempts to prove his innocence by battle, but this is refused him since there is no individual accuser. Having refused to place himself on the jury the defendant is ordered on to a starvation diet (as in the previous example). By the fourteenth century it was not so common in practice for the accused to seek to avoid jury trial.

Placita Corone or La Corone Pledee devant Justices, ed. J. M. Kaye, SS, supplementary series, 4 (1966), pp. 17–18 [French]

(Justice to the Sheriff)

'Sheriff, for what is this man arrested?'

'Sir, on suspicion of having taken and stolen cattle, and having hidden them in the district.'

'Did you find anything with him which might give rise to bad suspicion?'

'Yes, sir: two cows which are at hand.'

(Justice to the defendant)

'What is your name, my good friend?'

'Nicholas de C, sir, is my name.'

'Where were you born?'

'In the county of C, sir.'

'In what vill?'

'In the vill of C.'

---

28 R. B. Pugh, 'The duration of criminal trials in medieval England', in *Law, Litigants and the Legal Profession*, ed. Ives and Manchester, 1983), pp. 104–15.

'How did you come by these beasts, which are here now?'

'Honestly and lawfully, sir.'

'Nicholas, the good people of this district gravely complain that their horses, their oxen, their cows, their pigs, their sheep and their lambs are stolen and that you are the seller of many beasts which you never buy: how can it be but that we have a weighty presumption and nasty suspicion that you have not come by these animals lawfully.'

'Sir, if there is any man willing to prosecute me, that I came by these beasts wrongfully, I am ready to defend them as my own bought lawfully in the fair at C, on the day of the fair, etc., by my body or by whatever the king's court awards to prove the entitlement.'

'Nicholas, if as you say you bought them at the fair at C, lawfully with your own money in such fair as an honest dealer, then for what reason have you kept them so concealed for a whole month so that they have not once been seen outside your house, either in the fields or elsewhere where animals go to graze and drink?'

'Sir, I have kept them so enclosed in order to fatten them ready for the time of Martinmas, for fattened beasts are more easily sold than those that are thin.'

'Quite true. Nicholas, so if as you say you bought them lawfully with your own money in such a fair, as an honest trader, I presume that you would be able most surely to place yourself on the country* that you have lawfully come by them.'

'Sir, I have no need to do this, it seems to me, because I am ready to defend them by my body, or by whatever means the king's court may award, as mine, lawfully purchased.'

'Nicholas, you are here arrested and attached in the king's court, because you have these animals and on suspicion of the theft of other types of animal in this district. And in respect of this suspicion nobody's suit lies against you save the king's: and you cannot defend yourself against the king by your body, nor in any way other than by the country; because of which you are bound to pursue this course, if you think it is right.'

'Sir, I am a stranger in this district and less known among these good people than I would need to be. Therefore I dare not place myself on their verdict concerning this suspicion, which is imputed against me without reason.'

'And how do you wish to clear yourself of this presumption and this nasty suspicion?'

'Sir, by my body, if anyone brings suit against me, and in no other way.'

'Gaoler, take this man back to prison. Give him little to eat and less to drink; and on such a day as he eats make sure that he does not drink; and on the day that he drinks see to it that he does not eat. So carry out your duty until our next session.'

'Willingly, sir.'

5.10 Trial: the riots at Bedford peace sessions (1439)

The details of the alleged riot appear as the result of its certification before the king's council in accordance with the riot legislation of Henry IV and Henry V.[29] The examination as recorded was carried out before leading magnates and senior royal officials and proceeded by way of questioning individual justices present at the sessions as to the how events unfolded. The inquisitorial approach was favoured by the king's council.[30] It is interesting to note that there are some discrepancies between the testimonies provided, particularly the number of Fanhope's followers and whether he was holding a dagger or not. Because of these and other discrepancies the council allowed Fanhope to purchase a pardon.

PPC, vol. 5, pp. 35–9 [English]

The 10th day of February the seventeenth year of the king [Henry VI – 1439] at Westminster in the Star Chamber[31] being then present the high and mighty prince, the duke of Gloucester, the bishop of Bath, chancellor, and the bishop of St David's, the earls of Salisbury and Northumberland, the Lord Cromwell, treasurer of England, William Linwood, keeper of the king's privy seal, and Robert Rolleston, wardrober, the king's councillors, examined the people whose names hereon follow upon the riot that occurred at Bedford the 12th day of January in the abovesaid year.

And Thomas Wawton was called first before the said council and sworn upon a book[32] to speak the full truth and not to mix it with any untruth for hate or evil intention, neither for love or favour, but fully report as

---

29 See 5.4.

30 J. F. Baldwin, *The King's Council during the Later Middle Ages* (Oxford, Clarendon Press, 1913), pp. 296–8, 355–6.

31 From about 1343 the king's council usually met in Westminster Palace in a room known as the 'Star Chamber' on account of its painted ceiling.

32 i.e. the Bible or book of Gospels

it was in deed, not sparing for any person or for any thing and he said he would fully speak the truth in such things as should be demanded of him. First he was asked if he had set his seal to the certificate that was given and delivered to the king upon the Lord Fanhope as touching the said matter at Bedford and he answered 'yes'. And at once it was asked if he knew the matter contained in the said certificate and he answered 'yes'. He was asked with what people the Lord Fanhope came to the town of Bedford at that time and in what array. He answered as to the number of persons with 'sixty' and as to their array with 'padded doublets and swords and bucklers and thus arrayed some of them came into the hall and two of them within the bar of the court'. It was asked if the said Lord Fanhope at other sessions before that time was accustomed to come in similar array. He answered 'yes'. He was asked whether he came to the hall before the Lord Fanhope and how many of the justices were there together before the Lord Fanhope came. He answered that he and John Enderby, John Fitz Geoffrey and Harry Etwell came to the hall before the Lord Fanhope. He was asked if they all knew well that the Lord Fanhope was in the town of Bedford and if they talked about him amongst the four of them and to all this he answered 'yes'. He was asked if he sent any word to the Lord Fanhope of their being there together or warned him that they would proceed in the sessions or otherwise that they awaited his arrival. To every one of these he answered 'no', but the four of them sat down and proceeded not to hold the sessions but talked together. He was asked if he and his fellows at such time as the Lord Fanhope came to them showed him any deference or what demeanour they had. He said that his three fellows stood up and he sitting still pulled down his hood.[33] He was asked how the Lord Fanhope behaved towards him after his arrival there and he answered that he sat himself down and called to him John Fitz Geoffrey and William Pek and wanted them to sit down by him. And the said Fitz Geoffrey advised the Lord Fanhope to take with him Wawton and Enderby for they were above the said Fitz Geoffrey in the commission and the said Lord Fanhope answered them 'No, come if you will, the one shall be welcome, the other may choose.' And after this conversation they sat down together. He was asked how the uproar and disturbance occurred amongst them. He answered 'by discourteous language by John Fitz Geoffrey and a servant of the Lord Fanhope, whom the said Lord Fanhope commanded to answer to what was said to him, and the same servant immediately saving the respect of his lord said it was false and so he believed was

33 i.e. bared his head

the said John Fitz Geoffrey'. And Wawton says that immediately he said to the Lord Fanhope 'It is the unruliest session that I have ever seen in Bedford and if it be not otherwise ruled I will complain to the kings council.' To which the Lord Fanhope said, 'Complain as you will, I defy your menacing and all your evil will.' Wawton said he answered 'I set little by your defiance' and with this there was uproar and disturbance in the hall and so there rose up the Lord Fanhope, Wawton, Enderby and all the rest and the Lord Fanhope stood upon the exchequer board, the which board stood before the bench. He was asked if he saw the Lord Fanhope draw any dagger and he said 'truthfully, no'. He was asked if he saw any dagger in his hand and he said 'yes'. Furthermore he was asked in what way he held the dagger in his hand, the point forward, namely thrusting, or else the point towards his elbow, downward, and to this he said he knew not. He was also asked if he saw the Lord Fanhope or any man of his smite any man or behave as if he were going to smite, he said 'no'. He was also asked whether the Lord Fanhope such time as he stood upon the board endeavoured to quell the uproar and argument or alternatively that he stirred up and encouraged the people to cause disturbance and he answered that he endeavoured to stop the uproar and the disturbance that was in the hall. He was asked whether he made an effort to do so adequately or not actively and through pretence of making an effort allowed harm to be done. He answered that to his understanding he worked hard for the keeping of the peace and to stop the uproar and disturbance that was in the hall and as diligently as ever he saw a man do. He was asked what the said Lord Fanhope did such time as the disturbance was quelled. He answered that he went into his inn and caused the said Wawton and others of his fellows to be accompanied by his own servants to their lodgings for their better safety. And the Lord Fanhope desired Wawton to come drinking with him as he had Enderby, saying to Wawton that he should be welcome, for he gave drink to him whom he had less cause to love than some, meaning Enderby.

John Enderby, called before the council in the form rehearsed for Thomas Wawton, similarly swore upon a book to tell the truth in the matter abovesaid, the which he promised to do. Examined upon the first article he said that at the time of making the certificate, the which was sent to the king, his fellows and he were of different opinions and in disagreement nevertheless he set his seal thereto. As to the second, to the third, to the fourth, to the fifth, to the sixth, and to the seventh articles, he accorded in all his disposition and answer with Thomas Wawton. As to the eighth he said that they stood up all such time as the Lord Fanhope came to them. As to the ninth and tenth articles he accorded in substance with the said Wawton confessing also that he himself drew out his own dagger and at the time of the disturbance his man servant brought him a sword, and in what way he parted with his dagger he cannot say. As to the eleventh article he said that he saw not the Lord Fanhope draw any dagger neither that he had any in his hand. Examined upon the twelfth and thirteenth articles he accorded with Thomas Wawton, varying nothing in substance.

John Fitz Geoffrey, sworn upon a book and examined in similar manner to Wawton and Enderby, answered as follows. In the first and second articles he accorded with Wawton. In the third, the fourth, and the fifth, and the sixth articles, he accorded in his deposition with Wawton and Enderby. As to the seventh article he accorded with Enderby and not with Wawton. As to the eighth article he accorded also. As to the ninth article he accords with Wawton. In the tenth article he accords with Enderby, too, that he saw the Lord Fanhope draw no dagger and that he did not have one in his hand. In the eleventh and twelfth articles he accords with Wawton and Enderby and also in the thirteenth article, changing nothing in substance.

Henry Etwell was examined and sworn upon a book to tell the truth. In the first article he accords with his fellows. In the second article he accorded also with his fellows save he varied in number saying that the Lord Fanhope came to Bedford with forty or fifty persons. In the third, the fourth, and the fifth articles he accords with his fellows. In the seventh and eighth articles he accorded with Enderby. In the ninth and tenth articles he accords with Wawton. In the eleventh, twelfth and thirteenth articles he accords with his fellows.

The 24th day of February in the abovesaid year at Westminster Thomas Stratton undersheriff of Bedford, in the presence of the high and mighty prince, the duke of Gloucester, the bishop of Bath, chancellor of England, the earl of Salisbury, the Lord Cromwell, treasurer of England, the Lord Hungerford, William Linwood, keeper of the king's privy seal, the king's councillors, swore upon a book to make true and just answer to that which should be asked him concerning the riot caused at Bedford. First he was asked if he was privy to the certificate that was made to the king by Wawton, Enderby, Fitz Geoffrey, and Etwell and he said 'yes'. Moreover he was asked where he sat at the session time and he answered that he was seated with the Lord Fanhope in as much as he was clerk of the sessions. He was asked how the disturbance began, and he therein accorded with the testimony of Wawton and so he did in all his depositions saving in the eleventh article he varied from all saying that the Lord Fanhope such time as he stood on the exchequer board behaved towards Enderby as though he would have smote him, but he says he smote him not.

5.11 Trial: trial by battle (1456)

This description offers a vivid picture of the etiquette and ritual involved in trial by battle. By the mid fifteenth century it was probably not a common occurrence. Note the clothing and particular choice of weapons as well as the manner of engagement. The commentary is didactic in tone and in revealing the reasons for Whitehorn's continued existence subtly offers a critique on the workings of the legal system. Towards the end the passage takes on elements of a comedy or fantasy. Indeed, the characterisation of the two combatants and the qualities attributed to them naturally leave the reader wondering how reliable the account is and especially whether the defendant (referred to as the 'true labourer' in terms resonant of *Piers Plowman*) really ended his days as a hermit.

Gregory's Chronicle in *The Historical Collections of a Citizen of London*, ed. J. Gaird-ner, Camden Society, 2nd series, 17 (London, 1876), pp. 199–202 [English]

Also that year a thief, one Thomas Whitehorn, was taken in the New Forest beside Beaulieu and put in prison in Winchester. And when the day of deliverance[34] came he appealed many true men, and by this means he kept his life albeit living it in prison. And those men that he appealed were taken and put in strong prison and suffered many great pains, and that was so they should confess and accord unto his false appealing; and some were hanged that had no friends and goods, and those that had goods got their charters of pardon. And that false and untrue appealer had of the king daily 1½d. And this he continued for almost three years and destroyed many men that were some time in his company. And at the last he appealed someone who finally said that he was false in his claims, and said that he would prove it with his hands and expend his life and blood upon his false body. And this matter was very discreetly taken and heard both on the appealer's part and on the defendant's part also. And a notable man and the most sympathetic judge of all this land in sitting upon life and death took this simple man that offered to fight with the appealer and very courteously informed him of all the conditions of the fighting and duel of reproof that should be between a king's appealer,

---

34 Meaning his trial at gaol delivery (though it is given apocalyptic resonance).

false or true, in that one party and between the defendant, true or false, in that other party: that if the appealer prevailed in that fight he should be put in prison again, but he should fare better than he did before the time of fighting, and be allowed 2d by the king every day as long as it pleased the king that he should live; and that in legal proceedings the king may by the law put him to death for being a manslayer because his appealing, false or true, has caused many men's deaths, for a genuinely true man should within twenty-four hours make known publicly all such false hidden things of felony or treason if he is not consenting to the same fellowship, under pain of death. And this appealer is in the same case, wherefore he must needs die by very reason. This is for the appealer's part.

The defendant's part is, as that noble man Master Michael Skilling[35] told and informed the defender, that he and the appealer must be clothed all in white sheep's leather, body, head, legs, feet, face, hands and all. And that they should each have in their hands a stave of green ash, the bark being still upon them, three feet in length, and at one end a club of the same wood extending as far as the extra length gave an advantage. And at the other end a horn of iron, similar to a ram's horn, as sharp at the point as it might be made. And therewith they should make their foul battle upon the most sorry and wretched green that might be found about the town, having neither food nor drink, but both must be fasting. And if their ugly weapon gets broken they must fight with their hands, fists, nails, teeth, feet and legs; it is too shameful to rehearse all the conditions of this foul conflict; and if they need any drink, they must take their own piss. And if the defendant slay that appealer, false or true, the defendant shall be hanged for manslaying, in as much as he has slain the king's approver, for by means of his complaining the king had money of such as were appealed and that money that came from their stuff or goods that they had was put to the king's alms, and his almoner distributed it unto the poor people. But the king may by his grace pardon the defendant if he will, if the defendant is of good repute and of suitable conduct in the town or city where he lives; but this is very seldom seen because of the vile and unmannerly fighting. And by right they should not be buried in any holy sepulchre of Christian man's burying, but cast out as a man that wilfully slays himself.[36] Now be mindful of this foul battle, whether you will undertake it or not. And both parties consented to fight with all the conditions that belong

---

35 A Hampshire justice of the peace.
36 Suicides were not allowed to be buried in consecrated ground.

thereto. And the defendant desired that the judge send to Millbrook, where he dwelled, to inquire of his behaviour and conversation. And all the men in that town said that he was the truest labourer[37] in all that country and the most courteous as well, for he was a fisher and tailor by craft. And the appealer desired the same, but he was not abiding in any place over a month. And in every place where inquisition was made people said, 'Hang up Tom Whitehorn, for he is too strong to fight with James Fisher, the true man with an iron ram's horn.' And this caused the judge to have pity upon the defendant.

The manner of fighting of these two poor wretches near Winchester.

The appealer in his raiment and apparel with his weapon came out of the east side and the defendant out of the south-west side in his apparel with his weapon, weeping very much, and a pair of beads in his hand; and he kneeled down upon the earth toward the east and cried for mercy to God and all the world, and begged every man for forgiveness and every man there being present prayed for him. And the false appealer called and said, 'You false traitor! Why are you so long in false bitter belief?' And then the defendant rose up and said, 'My quarrel is as faithful and also as true as my belief and in that quarrel I will fight' and with the same words so hit out at the appealer that his weapon broke: and then the appealer smote a stroke to the defendant, but the officers were ready so that he should smite no more and they took away his weapon from him. And then they fought together with their fists for a long time and rested themselves, and fought again, and then rested again; and then they went together head to head. And then they both bit with their teeth so that the leather of their clothing and their flesh was all torn in many places of their bodies. And then the false appealer threw that meek innocent down to the ground and bit him in the testicles so that the simple innocent cried out. And by chance more than strength that innocent recovered upon his knees and took that false appealer by the nose with his teeth and put his thumb in his eye, so that the appealer cried out and begged him for mercy, for he was false to God and to him. And then the judge commanded them to cease and heard both their tales; and the appealer admitted that he had accused him and eighteen men wrongfully and besought God for mercy and forgiveness. And then he was confessed and hanged, on whose soul God have mercy. Amen.

As for the defendant, he was pardoned of his life, limb and goods, and went home; and he became a hermit and within a short time died.

37 Best or most honest worker.

5.12 Benefit of clergy

Benefit of clergy could be claimed before or after the jury verdict by those who were ostensibly clerks. A successful plea meant the defendant would no longer be tried or punished in the secular court, but would be transferred to ecclesiastical jurisdiction instead. A display of literacy as might befit a clerk was the main criterion. Although those with a smattering of letters might think themselves able to escape secular punishment there were in fact strict tests and procedures for claiming benefit of clergy. Not only was there a requirement to be able to recite the Latin 'neck verse' (as it was known), which was verses from Psalm 51 ('Miserere mei, Deus'), but the claimant had to be tonsured, dressed in clerical garb rather than lay clothes and actually be claimed as a clerk by a representative of the ordinary.* While a number of those who claimed benefit of clergy were able to fulfil the requirements, the secular justices were often suspicious and usually ensured that the tests were rigorously conducted. Nevertheless they were careful not to tread on the church's jurisdiction and in this example it is noticeable that consultations take place before a decision is made.

TNA KB 27/265 *Rex* m. 18 [Latin]

And as regards the aforesaid Henry Lamberd:[38] because he is indicted before the king at Warwick that he feloniously robbed Thomas Murney of Coventry at Combe Wood of ten pounds of silver around the feast of Michaelmas in the seventeenth year of the present king's reign [Edward II – c 29 September 1323], and that he is a common thief due to various thefts, and because the same Henry feloniously robbed a certain merchant at *le Wythegelone* near Alspath of a horse worth 13s 4d and of six pounds of silver, the same Henry was brought in again by the marshal and having been asked as to how he wishes to acquit himself of the aforesaid robberies and felonies, he says in the English language that he is a clerk without making any other response. And he is asked whether he wishes or knows how to speak in the Latin or the French language. He says that he is English and born in England, and perfectly able to speak his mother tongue and unwilling to reply using another language. And the archdeacon of Westminster, the ordinary of that place appointed to claim clerks, comes here and says that, if the same Henry should be a clerk, he would freely claim him as a clerk, otherwise he would not. And because the aforesaid Henry is dressed in rayed cloth cut on the cross, has neither tonsure nor clerical dress, and the aforesaid ordinary does not claim him as a clerk, except that he says that he would freely claim him if he were a clerk, the penalty inflicted on those felons who reject the common law of the realm having

38 The previous entry referring to Henry Lamberd has been erased.

been read out to him, it is put to the same Henry whether he wishes to say anything else instead of the reply he had given previously. He says definitely that he does not. As a result, with deliberation upon the matters, the advice and opinion of the justices having been canvassed, it is considered that the aforesaid Henry, as one rejecting the common law of the realm, is to be committed to the Marshalsea prison in the custody of the marshal to suffer the penalty[39] etc., remaining there according to the law and custom of the realm concerning felons of this kind used up to this time etc. until etc.[40]

5.13 Punishment: the hanging of felons (1285)

Hanging was the normal punishment for felons. In the medieval period hanging involved slow strangulation as there was no drop. The neck was not broken as occurred during judicial hangings (with a drop) in a later age. Surviving a hanging was usually reckoned to be miraculous and the body taken to sanctuary, whereupon the king was petitioned by well-wishers for a pardon. In this case Walter owed his survival to being cut down too soon rather than divine intervention. Remaining for fifteen days in the sanctuary of a church he then escaped to another place of sanctuary before eventually obtaining a pardon. Following this particular occurrence the king initiated an investigation into how the officials in Norwich had failed to execute Walter and supposedly for this failure briefly took the liberty of the city into his own hands.

TNA JUST 1/579 m. 71 [Latin]

The jury presented that Walter Eghe on Monday in the first week of Lent in the thirteenth year of the reign of the present king [Edward I] [12 February 1285] in the time of Roger of Wyleby, Adam le Clerk, James Jade and William of Burwode, bailiffs of the lord king, was taken on indictment at the court leet of the city of Norwich for cloth stolen at the house of Richard de la Ho and other things stolen and later on the Wednesday next following [14 February] was brought before the same bailiffs and all the community of the whole city in the toll booth and appeared before them without prosecution by any others. And asked whether he wished to acquit himself of the theft imputed to him he placed himself for good and ill on the country.* And the aforesaid bailiffs together with the community aforesaid held an inquest to see if he was guilty or not, by which inquest it was held that the said Walter was

39 The *peine forte et dure* (see 5.9).
40 There is a marginal note indicating starvation diet.

guilty because of which it was adjudged that the same Walter should be hanged; and they hanged him and when he had been cut down from the gallows and taken to the church of St George for burial he was found to be still alive. And asked by whom the said Walter had been cut down from the aforesaid gallows the jury replied that it was by William son of Thomas Stanhard, who came and acknowledged this as well. So he is committed to gaol. Questioned as to the chattels of the said Walter, the sheriff responded that they amounted to 4 marks.

And it was testified by the twelve of the jury that the said Walter remained in the said church for fifteen days and there was kept by the parishes of St Peter Hungate, St Mary the Less, St Simon and St Jude, and St George before the gate of the cathedral church of Holy Trinity [St George Tombland] and that after the fortnight following he escaped from the custody of these parishes; and so to judgment concerning the escape on the said four parishes. And the same Walter after he had escaped placed himself in the cathedral church of Holy Trinity, Norwich and stayed there until the king pardoned suit of his peace.

[Walter came and offered a charter of pardon from the king witnessed by him at Burgh on 24 March 1285.]

5.14 Punishment: the execution of traitors, Gilbert Middleton (1317)

The chronicler's account indicates that Gilbert de Middleton had already suffered at the hands of the northerners before he even arrived for 'trial' in London. During Edward I's reign the punishment for traitors had become increasingly brutal. The spectacle of Middleton's death pre-dated more frequent use of drawing, hanging and quartering as a form of punishment for traitors during the last five years of Edward II's reign.

Johannis de Trockelowe Annales, ed. H. T. Riley (RS, 1866), p. 101 [Latin]

The said Gilbert indeed with his natural brother [John] was led bound to Newcastle, where he was admitted by the inhabitants according to his deserts and after a few days put on a certain ship which was awaiting a favourable wind in the port of Newcastle upon Tyne. He unwillingly asked pardon for the damages and injuries frequently inflicted by him on Saint Oswin[41] and his men. At length, there being a strong north wind, and the sea swelling terribly, he was brought scarcely alive to Grimsby

41 Patron saint of Tynemouth Priory.

where he was taken to London with his feet tied together beneath a horse, to receive the reward of his merits. And judgment being brought against him he was led to the gallows bound with ropes tied to horse tails and all the right with lordship which he or his brothers insisted that they had in the county of Northumberland was terminated by their hanging.

5.15 Pardon: general royal pardon (1377)

The king's pardon was a tangible sign of the royal prerogative of mercy. The general royal pardon of 1377 marked Edward III's golden jubilee as monarch, and was intended as a show of goodwill to his subjects. The precedent of his fiftieth birthday is mentioned and his subjects are encouraged to behave themselves better in the future. The general pardon covers all offences except treason, murder and rape and includes release from fines, amercements,* forfeitures and debts (though qualified as being only up to the fortieth year of the reign). The standard fee in chancery for a copy of a general pardon was 18s 4d.

RP, vol. 2, p. 365 [French]

Our lord the king, having consideration for the very great charges and losses, which his said people have had and borne in times past, both as a result of the wars and otherwise through the plague of people, the murrain of beasts and the frequent failure of the fruits of the land in the bad years before this time, concerning which our lord the king has great compassion, and is therefore willing now in this present fiftieth year of his aforesaid reign of England to give them greater grace than ever he gave them before, because this year is rightly the year of jubilee, or the completion of the year of grace of his reign aforesaid, by which his said commons may be the better comforted and then have the greater courage to prosper in the future. And also our said lord the king, remembering how in the thirty-sixth year of his said reign of England, which was the fiftieth year of his birth [1362] he gave great grace and pardon to his said commons of England, pardoning them then all escapes of felons, and chattels of felons and fugitives, trespasses, negligences, misprisions,* ignorances and all other articles of the eyre, and many other things that occurred and happened within the kingdom of England, of which the punishment was incurred in fine or in ransom, or in other financial penalties, or alternatively in imprisonment, or in amercement of the community of vills or of individuals, or in charge of free tenement* of those that never trespassed, such as heirs, or the tenants of escheators,* sheriffs and coroners, at the king's suit, wishing and granting then that his same commonalty should be totally discharged until the thirteenth day of October, the said thirty-sixth year of his reign, at which day the same pardon was given, as is more fully contained in the same; he wishes and grants to the honour of God, who for so long has allowed him to reign over his same people in such prosperity, that his commons of England and each individual person of the same of whatever estate or condition they may be, both small and great, should have now and enjoy similar graces and pardons of all things contained within the pardon aforesaid, which have occurred or happened from the said thirteenth day of October until the beginning of this aforesaid fiftieth year. And moreover, our said lord the king has also pardoned and released to his aforesaid commons all types of gifts, alienations* and purchases made by them, or any of them, without licence from the king, of lands and tenements held of him in chief and all manner of entries, if any have been made into their inheritances after the death of their ancestors without suing them out of the king's hands by due process until the beginning of the same fiftieth year; with the exception of those tenements which are alienated in mortmain,* and also those tenements which are now seised* into the hands of our lord the king by reason of such alienations and entries. And also he has pardoned entirely and released all fines,* amercements, issues, forfeitures, reliefs and scutages* that were made, occurred or happened within the same realm of England, and with this all manner of debts and accounts accrued until the fortieth year of the reign of England of our said lord the king [1366] and also all types of actions and demands, which he has or may have, either by himself alone or alternatively jointly with other persons, against any of his said commons; both by reason of the same accounts and debts and otherwise by reason of the export of wools, leather, wool fells or other merchandise overseas, against the prohibitions and ordinances made thereon, both under cover of and in the name of merchants, or through the excuse of letters patent granted at Dordrecht or elsewhere overseas or through any other way whatever for these reasons, and both during the time of Walter of Charlton and his associates, formerly farmers of the subsidies and customs, and in other times up to the fortieth year of his said reign in England; with the exception of those debts which are adjudged by seisin of lands or tenements or determined in some other way, and with the exception of those debts that are due him at present from any that have been sheriffs, escheators, collectors of customs and subsidies, and of tenths or fifteenths, farmers of manors, victuallers and others that have held high office with the king before this time, and who are still living. And also our said lord the king generally pardons the suit of his peace[42] for all types of felonies committed or perpetrated before the beginning of the said fiftieth year, with the outlawries, if any were pronounced on the same for such reasons; excepting absolutely treasons, murders, common thefts and rapes of women. But in any event, it is not the king's intention that William Wykeham, bishop of Winchester, shall be included within the abovesaid pardon and grace, nor enjoy anything of the same;[43] nor that any other person enjoy anything of the said grace or pardon of felonies if he does not specially sue for his charter between this day and the Nativity of St John the Baptist next coming [24 June].

5.16 Pardon: personal pardon (1318)

Here Ellis Martel has purchased a pardon to clear himself of the death of Thomas le Leure. The unusual circumstances surrounding the crime are described in 7.15c. A royal pardon could in fact be obtained at any time during the prosecution process, not only following conviction. By buying a pardon and presenting it upon arraignment a defendant could avoid undergoing trial.

TNA KB 27/235 m. 98 (Hilary) [Latin]

Edward, by the grace of God king of England, lord of Ireland and duke of Aquitaine, to all bailiffs and lieges to whom these letters present may come, greeting. Know you that in our present parliament convoked at York we have by our special grace and with the agreement of the prelates, earls and community of our realm there assembled pardoned Ellis Martel, a retainer of our beloved and trusty cousin, Thomas, earl of Lancaster, the suit of our peace and whatever by reason of our suit pertains to us with respect to all manner of felonies and trespasses committed in whatsoever way in breach of our peace by Ellis within our realm up to the seventh day of August last, and also outlawry, if any has been pronounced up until now against Ellis on account of these things, and we grant him our firm peace therein, being unwilling that Ellis, on account of what pertains to us by reason of our suit in respect of the aforesaid felonies and trespasses, should be interfered with, molested in any way or harmed by us or our heirs, our justices, sheriffs or any other

---

42 i.e. the need to answer in the king's court

43 Wykeham was specifically excluded from the scope of the pardon following his recent disgrace for his part in the Good Parliament of 1376.

of our bailiffs and servants. In witness thereof we have made these our
letters patent. Witness myself at York the first day of November in the
twelfth year of our reign [1318].

5.17 Pardon: recruitment for war

The first extract illustrates pardons granted by Edward I to those serving in
his Scottish and Gascon campaigns in the last decade of the thirteenth century.
In the second example, following the inquisitions of the 1414 'superior eyre' in
Shropshire, a temporary surety* of the peace was obtained by a number of the
indicted, several of whom were later chosen to be in Thomas, earl of Arundel's
retinue for service at Agincourt in 1415.

(a)

Calendar of London Trailbaston Trials under Commissions of 1305 and 1306, ed. R.
B. Pugh (London, 1975), pp. 90, 100 [Latin]

Simon le Seler is indicted in the king's bench for slaying Walter of
Winchester, cobbler, at Ivylane. Having been arrested, he says he ought
not to answer to the king's suit because the king has pardoned him suit
of his peace by letters patent dated Portsmouth 7 July 22 Edward I
[1294] provided he would go on his service to Gascony. And he shows a
certificate [in French] dated 19 March 26 Edward I [1298] at Bourg sur
Mer [France] from Roger la Warre, captain of the garrison at Bourg,
and Gilbert de Briddessale, marshal of that garrison, that he had served
therein as an unmounted serjeant of crossbowmen. So he is aquitted.

John de Bradequer is indicted in the king's bench for slaying Hervey,
sometime cook to John Wade, in the parish of St James, Garlickhythe
[London]. Brought before the court he pleads pardon for the death of
Hervey le Keu issued to John de Shropham by letters patent dated 10
November 31 Edward I [1303] at Dunfermline for service undertaken
for the king in Scotland. The jury of twelve say the two Johns are one
and the same. So he is aquitted.

(b)

TNA KB 27/613 *Rex* m. 36 (Trinity) [Latin]

At the quindene of St John the Baptist [7 August 1414] ... John Werle
of Oswestry, esquire, Roger Corbet of Colehurst in the county of Shrop-

shire, esquire, Richard Lacon of Lacon in the county of Shropshire, esquire, and John Burley of Broomcroft the younger in the county of Shropshire, esquire, Ralph Brereton, esquire, Robert Corbet of Moreton [Moreton Corbet] in the county of Shropshire, esquire, and John Winsbury of Winsbury in the county of Shropshire, esquire, came in their own persons before the king at Westminster and surrendered themselves to the prison of the lord king's marshalsea of the king's bench for various treasons, felonies, rebellions, trespasses, contempts, extortions and oppressions, previously presented against them before the king by the aforesaid inquisitions and other inquisitions of various hundreds of the county of Shropshire, and they are committed to Thomas Warde, the marshal etc. And they were questioned separately about the aforegoing matters. And on the aforesaid arraignment the same John Werle, Roger Corbet, Richard Lacon, John Burley, Ralph Brereton, Robert Corbet and John Winsbury have a day assigned by the court for a jury to be returned thereon on their behalf by the sheriff and taken on the aforesaid matters on the day after All Souls next following [3 November]. Whereupon as advised by the court the aforesaid John Werle, Roger Corbet, Richard Lacon, John Burley, Ralph Brereton, Robert Corbet and John Winsbury were told to find security that they would keep the lord king's peace as regards the said king and his people, and especially as regards the said jurors on the aforesaid inquisitions in accordance with their aforesaid petition. And on this there came Thomas, earl of Arundel, Sir John Wiltshire, John Winsbury, esquire, and Robert Corbet of Moreton, esquire, and they undertook on behalf of the aforesaid John Wele, Roger Corbet, Richard Lacon, John Burley and Ralph Brereton that they and each one of them would behave themselves properly as regards the lord king and all his people and especially as regards the said jurors of the aforesaid inquisitions etc. until the said day after All Souls.[44] And each of the aforesaid John Wele, Roger Corbet, Richard Lacon, John Burley and Ralph then undertook by himself on his own behalf that each of them for ever afterwards would properly behave and conduct himself as regards the lord king and all his people.

44 In the event Robert Corbet was replaced in the military retinue by John Hammond, Bereton by Robert Lathbury, Burley by Meredith Vaughan and Winsbury by John Covert (TNA E 101/47/1).

VI: ARBITRATION

The network of royal and local courts offered a convenient forum for litigation and the punishment of criminal activity, but should not be regarded as the sole means of dispute resolution. It is now recognised that formal adjudication (resort to the courts) was but one method by which legal disputes were settled and that resort to violence and apparently criminal activities were often symptoms or a reflection of wider confrontations, often inter- and intra-familial feuds.[1] Indeed, the methods available for resolving conflict should be viewed across a spectrum ranging from violent self-help at one end, through mediation, negotiation and arbitration to adjudication in the courts at the other end. We have seen in Chapters 2 and 3 the paths that violent self-help could take and in Chapters 4 and 5 how the courts developed and operated in response to violence and lawlessness. By examining the extra-judicial forms employed in the later Middle Ages, namely negotiation, mediation and arbitration, this chapter acts as a corrective to the traditional preoccupation with formal legal proceedings.[2]

The difference between these various methods of dispute settlement lay in the degree and nature of third-party involvement. Negotiation implies that the parties tried to come to terms of their own accord, while mediation introduced a neutral party to aid settlement. Arbitration involved the surrender of negotiating and adjudicating powers to a panel of arbiters and/or an impartial umpire. These methods might be adopted singly in a comparatively simple dispute, but in complex ones several alternatives could be combined to offer a more flexible and sophisticated strategy.[3] Issues concerning property ownership usually lay at the heart of disputes, so cases did not necessarily directly involve criminality. Acts of felony and trespass were nevertheless part and parcel of disputes and frequently gave rise to negotiation or arbitration, as in the Erdswick–Ferrers dispute [**6.5**], where both parties had engaged in periodical skirmishing and

---

1 S. Roberts, 'The study of disputes: anthropological perspectives', in *Disputes and Settlements: Law and Human Relations in the West*, ed. J. Bossy (Cambridge, Cambridge University Press, 1983), pp. 1–19; J. W. Bennett, 'The medieval loveday', *Speculum*, 33 (1958), 351–70; M. T. Clanchy, 'Law and love in the Middle Ages', in *Disputes and Settlements*, ed. Bossy, pp. 47–67; J. L. Rosenthal, 'Feuds and peace-making: a fifteenth century example', *NMS*, 14 (1970), 84–90; P. R. Hyams, *Rancor and Reconciliation in Medieval England* (Ithaca and London, Cornell University Press, 2003).

2 E. Powell, 'Arbitration and the law in England in the later Middle Ages', *TRHS* 5th series, 33 (1983), 49–67; *idem*, 'Settlement of disputes by arbitration in fifteenth century England', *LHR*, 2 (1984), 21–43.

3 Powell, *Kingship*, pp. 93–5, 101–2.

carried out armed raids on the other.[4] As with the overlap between civil and criminal law, we should not regard the formal judicial apparatus and extra-legal methods as incompatible or mutually exclusive. Litigants recognised the benefit of utilising both law courts and arbitrament.[5] Initiating litigation, for instance, could be regarded as a preliminary stage in the arbitration process; and could be threatened or continued if the parties were unable or unwilling to agree to terms.[6] Furthermore, if the terms of an award were breached then bonds to pay large sums of money were enforceable at common law (and later in chancery).[7]

The documents relating to the dispute in the early fifteenth century between William Paston and Walter Aslake demonstrate a number of these features and highlight the interplay of litigation, out-of-court manoeuvring, mediation and negotiation in the parties' efforts to reach a lasting settlement. [6.1] Indeed, the sheer diversity of options and range of resorts, both legal and extra-judicial, is brought home: Paston initiated a trespass suit in the Norwich city court, Aslake petitioned parliament, Paston presented a bill against the sheriff when accounting at the exchequer, Aslake obtained a writ from chancery. Aside from the use of litigation, the intervention of (or submission of cases to) third parties is apparent. In 1424 Sir Thomas Erpingham, a Norfolk JP, arranged for the dispute to go to arbitration (supposedly at Paston's request), but upon the failure of the negotiations, in spring 1425 he invited the duke of Gloucester to oversee another attempt. This arbitration was duly completed in the summer of that year and initially seemed successful. When this latest attempt collapsed the duke of Norfolk intervened (this time at the instigation of Aslake, who had fought in his retinue in 1417). Norfolk eventually managed to broker a settlement, though not until 1428 and not before Aslake had further prompted Paston to come to terms by initiating a suit in king's bench in 1427 claiming that Paston had bribed the jurors in the Norwich city case.[8]

Magnates had a special interest in settling quarrels within their own territorial regions or spheres of influence. In particular the maintenance of harmony within an affinity was one of the obligations of lordship.[9] As Dr Castor points

---

4 Powell, 'Settlement of disputes', 28–9.

5 J. B. Post, 'Courts, councils and arbitrators in the Ladbroke Manor dispute, 1382–1400', in *Medieval Legal Records*, pp. 289–339.

6 Powell, 'Arbitration', 57–9; S. J. Payling, 'Law and arbitration in Nottinghamshire, 1399–1461', in *People, Politics and Community in Later Medieval England*, ed. J. Rosenthal and C. Richmond (Gloucester, Alan Sutton, 1987), pp. 147–8.

7 Powell, 'Arbitration', 63–6; D. J. Clayton, 'Peace bonds and the maintenance of law and order in late medieval England', *BIHR*, 108 (1985), 133–48; C. Rawcliffe, '"That kindliness should be cherished more, and discord driven out": the settlement of commercial disputes by arbitration in later medieval England', in *Enterprise and Individuals in Fifteenth Century England*, ed. J. Kermode (Stroud, Alan Sutton, 1991), pp. 109–10.

8 Maddern, *Violence*, p. 47.

9 S. M. Wright, *The Derbyshire Gentry in the Fifteenth Century*, Derbyshire Record Society, 8 (1983), p. 125; R. Horrox, *Richard III: A Study in Service* (Cambridge, Cambridge University Press, 1989), p. 66.

out, contacts and relationships within a network, such as the crown-duchy of Lancaster affinity, could be an important factor in successfully resolving disputes.[10] Aslake's approach to the duke of Norfolk and the pressure to conform placed by the duke on Paston (whom he had retained in his service) highlights the interplay of personal connections against a background of fluctuating power structures in the region.[11] Given their political and social standing and the pre-existing practical machinery of their councils and households, great lords or bishops were in great demand to settle disputes.[12] Indeed, in several of the examples chosen here it is possible to observe great lords acting as impartial umpires: Richard Beauchamp, earl of Warwick, William, Lord Roos, and Humphrey, duke of Buckingham. [**6.3**]

As the ultimate arbiter and peacemaker, the monarch too had an important role to play in mediating the disputes of those of high status. Much depended upon the force of the king's personality and his ability to persuade unruly magnates and gentry that conciliation rather than violence and recrimination were the way forward. There is evidence to show that Edward III and Edward IV, in particular, were quite prepared to act in this capacity.[13] Henry IV was concerned to act impartially in the dispute between Robert Tirwhit and Lord Roos and 'bring the case to a satisfactory conclusion' when they came before him in parliament. [**6.6**] Henry V compelled the representatives of two rival factions to settle their differences while he consumed a dish of oysters at Windsor Castle. [**6.2**]

Arbitration itself did not occur in isolation from the legal world. Its procedures bear the imprint of legal practice, while legal thought frequently influenced deliberations. Indeed, judges and lawyers often advised on the terms of awards or had the negotiations referred to them either as consultants or as actual arbiters, especially if the matters involved complex problems of legal title.[14] [**6.4**] While their contents had to be legally watertight, arbitration awards were also imbued with religious and moral overtones. As can be observed from the Paston–Aslake dispute and the letter from justice Bingham, agreements were sometimes solemnized in a church and the process might include swearing an oath on the Gospels.[15] Thereafter concord was often communicated visually and symbolically through a kiss of peace and the act of the parties coming

---

10 Castor, *Duchy*, pp. 77–8.

11 *Ibid.*, p. 107.

12 C. Rawcliffe, 'The great lord as peacekeeper: arbitration by English noblemen and their councils in the later Middle Ages', in *Law and Social Change in British History*, ed. J. A. Guy and H. G. Beale (London, Royal Historical Society, 1984), pp. 34–55.

13 W. M. Ormrod, *The Reign of Edward III* (New Haven and London, Yale University Press, 1990), pp. 55–6; Rawcliffe, 'Great lord as peacekeeper', p. 52.

14 Payling, 'Law and arbitration', 150–51; S. J. Payling, 'Arbitration, perpetual entails and collateral warranties in late medieval England: a case study', *JLH*, 13 (1992), 32–62.

15 Rawcliffe, 'Commercial disputes', p. 110; M. J. Bennett, 'A county community: social cohesion amongst the Cheshire gentry, 1400–25', *Northern History*, 8 (1973), 25–8; Clanchy, 'Law and love', p. 58.

together socially for a special feast or even just a drink in the tavern.[16]

The importance of extra-judicial forms is further demonstrated by their employment in areas where the common law could not provide remedy for disputes, for example, where family settlements employed feoffments to use.* Arbitration and the court of chancery's equitable jurisdiction made up for the deficiency. Moreover, arbitration not only offered a peaceful outcome, but something for each party, rather than humiliation or punishment for one side. In achieving settlement the different methods balanced flexibility with economy and speed.[17]

Negotiation and private treaties were actively encouraged among the gentry and members of the nobility. The records provided in this section tend to reflect the importance which the upper strata of society gave to these options and the complex nature of the problems leading to their recourse to them.[18] Since they naturally occurred outside the normal legal forum and as such do not figure in the court records, the survival of the documentation for awards or the mention of arbitration proceedings in court says a lot about the respect for the procedure and recourse to them.[19] It should also be remembered that arbitration was widely used by merchants as means of achieving compromise in trade and commercial disputes[20] and behind the closed doors of gilds, misteries, religious confraternities and the private household.[21] On a smaller scale, 'lovedays' were equally favoured by the less affluent parts of society.[22]

Undoubtedly a key resource employed by all levels of society, mediation and arbitration constituted a significant response to the breakdown in social relations in potentially providing for amicable and non-confrontational approaches. The formal meeting of the disputants to settle competing claims occurred at

16 Clanchy, 'Law and love', p. 59; B. A. Hanawalt, *'Of Good and Ill Repute': Gender and Social Control in Medieval England* (New York and Oxford, Oxford University Press, 1998), pp. 40, 49.

17 Powell, 'Arbitration', 64–6; S. J. Payling, *Political Society in Lancastrian England* (Oxford, Clarendon Press, 1991), pp. 207–13.

18 I. Rowney, 'Arbitration in gentry disputes in the later Middle Ages', *History*, 67 (1982), 367–76.

19 Clanchy, 'Law and love', pp. 57–61. It is significant that some of these are preserved in the rolls of parliament. See C. Rawcliffe, 'Parliament and the settlement of disputes by arbitration in the later Middle Ages', *Parliamentary History*, 9 (1990), 316–42.

20 Rawcliffe, 'Commercial disputes', pp. 99–117; L. Attreed, 'Arbitration and the growth of urban liberties in late medieval England', *JBS*, 31 (1992), 205–35; Maddern, *Violence*, pp. 175–205.

21 B. R. McRee, 'Religious gilds and regulation of behaviour in medieval towns', in *People, Politics and Community*, ed. Rosenthal and Richmond, pp. 108–22; C. Barron, 'Lay solidarities: the wards of medieval London', in *Law, Laity and Solidarities: Essays in Honour of Susan Reynolds*, ed. P. Stafford, J. L. Nelson and J. Martindale (Manchester and New York, Manchester University Press, 2001), pp. 218–33.

22 Clanchy, 'Law and love', pp. 59–60, 66–7; M. K. McIntosh, *Autonomy and Community: The Royal Manor of Havering, 1200–1500* (Cambridge, Cambridge University Press, 1986), p. 198.

the appointed loveday. It was expected that both parties would be accompanied by a retinue of friends, servants, advisers (often lawyers) and other supporters. There was, however, a danger that the size of the retinue, especially if the number of supporters on one side outweighed those on the other, could be employed to overawe proceedings and become a display of potential armed force. A balance had to be preserved between the necessary show of support and standing that a retinue could provide and the need to ensure proceedings were conducted peacefully and fairly. Where one of the parties stepped outside these bounds and breached social conventions, such as arriving with an outsize entourage, as occurred on the occasion of the loveday between Lord Roos and Robert Tirwhit, the offending party was required to apologise publicly, provide redress and correct the offence caused. [**6.6**]

We should bear in mind, however, that arbitration was not a total panacea and that it had its limitations: attempts at settlement could fail.[23] In Staffordshire in the early years of Henry V's reign its effectiveness was severely tested and it is clear from [**6.5**] (a demand to recover mutual bonds taken out to ensure the conditions of the arbitration award were observed and the peace maintained) that negotiations collapsed after the initial stages. The parties came to arbitration as a means of settling a feud between Hugh Erdswick of Sandon and Edmund Ferrers of Chartley. The feud probably arose over a territorial dispute, since the two men were near neighbours in the central part of the county, but the conflict escalated and broadened to become a struggle for power and influence within the local community. Where mediation, negotiation and arbitration were successful, agreement and reconciliation naturally allowed for reintegration within the value systems, network of relations and power structures that formed the basis of everyday life and work.

---

23 B. McRee, 'Peace-making and its limits in late medieval Norwich', *EHR*, 109 (1994), 831–66; M. D. Myers, 'The failure of conflict resolution and the limits of arbitration in King's Lynn', in *Traditions and Transformations in Late Medieval England*, ed. D. Biggs, S. D. Michalove and A. Compton Reeves (Leiden, Brill, 2002), pp. 81–107.

6.1 The disputing process: the Paston–Aslake dispute (1426)

This example, drawn from the Paston Letters, demonstrates how complex and intricate the disputing process could be. The first extract comprises a written submission to the arbiters by William Paston, who sets out (perhaps less than impartially) the background for their benefit and as an answer to the complaints of his opponent. It apparently survives from a fifth inconclusive attempt at arbitration in 1426. The passage shows the previous intervention of third parties as intermediaries and gives details of the failed arbitration process. William Paston somewhat disingenuously suggests that Sir Thomas Erpingham (whom he in fact engaged to arrange the initial arbitration) was predisposed towards his opponent, Walter Aslake. This may reflect Paston's own disappointment because Erpingham was unwilling to accept his apparently 'unreasonable' demands. Note also how Paston appears to be offended at Aslake's alleged lack of prior connection with the duke of Norfolk, underlining (in interlineations – denoted here by square brackets) his own association and credentials. The second extract represents Aslake's petition to the Leicester parliament of 1426 (addressed to the duke of Bedford in effusive terms) and rehearses events from Aslake's point of view.[1] Not surprisingly it differs from Paston's account of the course of the lawsuit, especially in alleging corruption on the part of Paston and shire officials. The bad relations seem to have stemmed from Paston acting as defence counsel for the prior of Norwich in a lawsuit waged against Aslake. The Paston–Aslake dispute also highlights the closeness of relations between lawyers and major landowners and the ability of one or other of the parties to manipulate the legal process, which will be discussed further in Chapter 8.

PL, vol. 1, pp. 7–12; vol. 2, pp. 505–7 [English]

(a) Memorandum to arbitrators

Be it remembered that where, on the night before the feast of the Circumcision of our Lord Jesus in the second year of the reign of King Henry VI [31 December 1423], certain unknown malefactors, felons and breakers of the king's peace, to the number of eighty and more by estimation, with plotting and malice aforethought feloniously broke into the dwelling place of John Grys of Wighton in Wighton in the shire of Norfolk, and hewed with carpenters' axes the gates and doors of the said place and took the said John, and his son and a man servant of his bodily and led them from the said dwelling place the space of a mile to a pair of gallows to have hanged them there; and for want of ropes convenient to their felonious purpose they slew and murdered there

---

1 The petition from Aslake can also be found in TNA SC 8/135/6715.

the said John Grys, his son and his man servant in the most horrible manner that ever was heard spoken of in that country.

Whereupon Walter Aslake, intending and planning to put William Paston in dread and intolerable fear of being slain and murdered in the abovesaid form with force and against the king's peace, on the shire day of Norfolk[2] held at Norwich on the twenty-eighth day of August in the said second year of the reign [1424] being there at that time a great congregation of people because of the said shire day, made to the said William Paston personally and by Richard Killingworth, at that time his servant, numerous threats of death and dismembering conveyed through certain English bills rhymed in part and set by the said Walter and Richard upon the gates of the priory church of the Holy Trinity, Norwich and on the gates of the church of the Friars Minor of Norwich and the gates of the same city called the Needham gates and the West-wick gates and in other places within the said city, making mention and conveying the intent that the said William and his clerks and servants should be slain and murdered in similar form to the said form in which the said John Grys was slain and murdered; containing also these two words in Latin, 'et cetera', by which words it was commonly understood that the framers and makers of the said bills intended more malice and harm to the said William, his clerks and servants than was expressed in the said bills; wherefore the said William, his said clerks and servants for a long time after were put in great and intolerable dread and fear of being slain and murdered by the said malefactors and felons, wherefore the said William, his said clerks and servants dared not go out or ride freely.

Whereupon the said William personally affirmed a plaint of trespass against the said Walter and Richard. Process continued thereupon until the said Walter and Richard were found guilty of the said trespass by an inquisition[3] thereon taken in due and lawful form, by which inquisition the damages of the said William for the said trespass were assessed at £120. After this plaint had been affirmed and before any plea upon the said plaint had been pleaded, the said Walter and William were induced to treat in the same matter by Thomas Erpingham, knight, a mighty and great supporter of the said Walter against the said William in all these matters and in the circumstances thereof, in the form that follows, that is to say that the said William should sue forth the said plaint and

2 Day when the county court was held.
3 Investigation carried out by a jury and so sometimes used synonymously with 'jury'.

the execution thereof at his own will, and the said Walter should defend himself in the said plaint at his own will, except that he should not take any benefit either by protection or writ of *corpus cum causa** or through any lord's letters upon the said suit. And whatsoever the outcome in the said plaint, the process, execution, or the suit thereof, the said Walter and William should abide by and obey the ordinance of certain persons named at that time by the said William and Walter as arbitrators, if they could agree; or otherwise the decision of an umpire also named that same time concerning all the said trespass, plaint, suit and all the circumstances thereof, providing that the said arbitrament and ordinance of the said arbitrators, or else the decision of the said umpire, were made within forty days of the judgment given in the said plaint.

And afterwards on the Thursday next before Pentecost in the third year of the reign of the said king [24 May 1425] at London in the presence of the right excellent high and mighty prince the duke of Gloucester, and by his commandment and at the suit and request of the said Thomas Erpingham, it was agreed between the said William and Walter that they should abide by and obey the ordinance and award concerning all the said matters of two of these four persons: William Phelip, knight, Henry Inglose, knight, Oliver Groos and Thomas Derham chosen on the side of the said William Paston; and two of these four persons: Simon Felbrigg, knight, Brian Stapleton, knight, Robert Clifton, knight and John Berney of Reedham chosen on the side of the said Walter; or else the decree and judgment of an umpire to be chosen by the same arbiters. The which William Phelip, Brian Stapleton, Robert Clifton, Oliver Groos, John Berney and Thomas Derham taking upon them the charge of the formulation of the said award and ordinance by the assent of the said Thomas Erpingham, on the Friday next after the feast of the Assumption of Our Lady in the said third year of the reign [17 August 1425] at Norwich took sureties of the said William and Walter by their faith and their promise to hold to their ordinance of all the said matters; and the same day before noon made their full ordinance and arbitrament of all the same matters in the church of the Grey Friars at Norwich, and afterwards had a conversation with the said Thomas Erpingham upon the same award and ordinance made, and after the same conversation, the same day after noon, the same ordinance and written award was read before the said arbiters and the said Walter and William and examined, agreed and assented, and was affirmed and sealed by the seals of the same six arbiters and the said Walter and William and left in the hands of the said Sir Brian to be kept safely in full remembrance of the said award and ordinance, the which award and ordinance the said William was at all times ready to obey and perform up to the said feast of Michaelmas [29 September], when the said Walter utterly refused to keep or perform the said award.

And where the said Walter, by judgment of the chancellor of England on the sixteenth day of July in the said third year of the reign, was remitted to the king's prison at Norwich because of the said suit, the said Walter went free from custody from the said sixteenth day of July to the said day of the making of the said arbitrament and award, and from that day up to Michaelmas then next following, the said William in the mean time evermore supposing that the said Walter would have kept and performed the said ordinance, arbitrament and award. And at the coming of the right high and mighty prince, the duke of Norfolk, from his castle at Framlingham to the city of Norwich after the said day of the making of this arbitrament and ordinance and before the feast of Michaelmas then next following, the said Walter by his cunning and misleading information caused the said duke to be heavy lord[4] to the said William, where the said William at the time of the said information was, with Sir John Jenny, knight, and others of the counsel of the said duke of Norfolk in his lordships in Norfolk and Suffolk then fallen to him by the death of the right worthy and noble lady his mother,[5] occupied about the due service of writs of *diem clausit extremum** after the death of the said lady, and whereas the said William Paston, by assignment and commandment of the said duke of Norfolk at his first passage over the sea into Normandy in the time of King Henry V, was the steward of the said duke of Norfolk for all his lordships in Norfolk and Suffolk from his said passage upto the said feast of Michaelmas. [And in addition to that as serjeant at law, though he be unworthy, was retained by the said duke of Norfolk all the time that he was serjeant before the same feast of Michaelmas. And albeit that the fees and the wages that the said William is owed for his said service represent a great sum to his lowly degree, if the said duke of Norfolk from his noble and bountiful grace is pleased to grant to the said William in right any part of the favour of his good lordship, the said William would ever be his poor and true bedesman* and ever in his heart think that all his said service and all the service that he ever did to the said duke of Norfolk was bountifully and sufficiently rewarded.]

---

4 Norfolk's behaviour towards Paston is severe in manner, negating the mutual expectations associated with good lordship that should have flowed from being in the duke's service.

5 Elizabeth FitzAlan, duchess of Norfolk (d. 1425).

And where the said Walter, neither before the time of the said trespass and making of the said bills nor before the said coming of the said duke of Norfolk to Norwich ever after, nor at any time while the said suit was pending, nor at the time of the making of the said arbitrament and ordinance, was ever the servant of the said duke of Norfolk either at fees or at wages, nor retained in his service, nor sued to him to be supported by his high lordship in this said matter, to the knowledge of the said William or to any common knowledge in the shires of Norfolk, Suffolk, or in Norwich. The suit that the said Walter made for support in this said matter was through the mediation of the said Thomas Erpingham to the said duke of Gloucester by whose rule and commandment the said arbitrament and award was made in the form aforesaid.

And notwithstanding the said trespass and grievance done to the said William by the said Walter, or that the said William is not satisfied of the said £120 or any penny thereof, and has held back from all manner of execution, suing of goods and chattels that by force of the said process or any other he might have had against the said Walter or his sureties,* or that the said William has suffered the said Walter to go free for a long time when he might have had his body in custody in lawful form, the said Walter by petitions in the last two parliaments held at Westminster and at Leicester, and at various times in various other manners has bad-mouthed and slandered the said William badly and in ways other than courtesy or truth require, and moreover caused the said William to be threatened horribly with death, beating and the dismembering of his person by certain servants of the Lord FitzWalter and other persons and by fearful and dreadful letters and messages, wherefore neither the said William, nor his friends nor his servants in his company sitting in the said parliament at Leicester durst not, and still dare not, ride or go freely about such occupation as they are accustomed and disposed to do, to their great and importable dread and vexation in their spirits and to the great harm and damage and loss of their poor goods.

[Moreover, the said Walter has sued and still rigorously sues a writ of *decies tantum** against ten persons of the said inquisition and two of the servants of the said William and four other persons, supposing them by his said suit to have corruptly taken £62 and more in money from the said William in his said suit; the which suit of *decies tantum* the said Walter between God and himself honestly knows is untrue. And also the said Walter has sued and still sues Adam Aubre, one of the said inquisition, in the court of the said duke of Norfolk in his manor of

Forncett by cause and occasion of the said matters, in which suit in the said court it is proceeded against the said Adam in a manner other than law, conscience or good faith requires.]

Moreover, the said William, at the commandment of the duke of Norfolk, has submitted himself to abide by the ordinance of divers persons in all the said matters: once at Leicester on the Wednesday next before Palm Sunday in the fourth year of the reign of the said king [20 March 1426], another time at Red Cliff in April of the same fourth year of the reign, made after the form of certain indentures made for that purpose; the which submission with all the circumstances thereof the said William has been at all times ready to obey.

The reason why the said Walter by the said English bills and in other form put and set the said William and his said clerks and servants in dread and intolerable fear of being slain and murdered and wronged them in the form aforesaid, was only for as much as the said William counselled the prior of Norwich in his true defence against the intent of the said Walter in a suit that he made against the said prior concerning an advowson* of the church of Sprowston in the county of Norfolk whereto the said Walter has neither sufficient title nor right in any way whatsoever by any grounds declared by him before this time.

This scroll is made only for the information of the worthy and worshipful lords the arbiters, reserving always to the maker the privilege reasonably to add and diminish, etc., with sympathetic consideration for his ignorance in such occupation and lack of leisure.

(b) Petition to the duke of Bedford by Walter Aslake against William Paston (1426)

To my high excellent and mighty prince duke of Bedford, protector and defender of the realm of England and regent of France.

Please it to your high and gracious lordship to consider the great damage from wrong and injury that William Paston, serjeant of law, has done to Walter Aslake of the county of Norfolk, who is beseecher of this bill.

The said Paston accused the said Walter of consenting to the indicting of a bill which one Richard Killingworth set up in slander of the name of the said Paston and of his clerks, as he says; of which bill the said Walter was never guilty and so he is ready to acquit himself by worthy and true men of his country, and also as manhood requires, if the law will give him leave. For which scheming the said Paston came into the presence of Sir Thomas Erpingham, justice of the peace of the shire of Norfolk, and required him to have surety of the peace of the said Walter; and so he had. And while the said Walter went to fetch surety, the said Paston entered a plaint of trespass in the court of Norwich against the said Walter in the custody of the said Sir Thomas; so the said Walter might not pass until the said Sir Thomas sent for him and delivered him, because of his prior arrest. And afterwards the said Walter brought in surety of the peace a great sum, so that the said Paston was content. Then Sir Thomas Erpingham said to the said Paston, 'Provided you are agreed with this surety and you cannot show any bodily harm but only defamation of your name, of which the said Walter is ready to acquit himself, as he says, it seems to me by my discretion there applies no more to [...]⁶ thereto in temporal⁷ law as I have heard but the surety that I have taken therefore at your request.' 'Yes, sir', said the said Paston, 'he must answer to the plaint of trespass.' The said Sir Thomas said, 'It will not be necessary. You shall choose four persons and entrust all things to them, and if the said Walter has done you any trespass it shall be redressed as the four will award, or otherwise an umpire.' And thus we chose on each side in the presence of the said Sir Thomas.

The said Paston besought the said Sir Thomas to consider his estate of serjeant, that he might not enter a plaint of trespass and withdraw it like any other man with his reputation; that he would not be displeased that the said Walter should answer to his plaint and bind himself by his troth that he should not sue any writs of *supersedeas** of the peace, nor *corpus cum causa*, nor protection, nor writ of error, nor yet take any benefits of lords' letters or of ladies' pertaining to this plea of trespass. And the said Sir Thomas thought that this was a remarkable asking and unreasonable, and asked the said Paston what he meant if Walter should obey this. And the said Paston swore on the hand of the said Sir Thomas by the faith of his troth, that the said Walter should not be damaged in his body or his goods, whatsoever the inquest said, but as the four men would award that were chosen before.

And under this pretence the said Walter was deceived for the same night at nine of the bell the sheriffs of Norwich, William Grey and Piers Brasyer, and Paston, by assent empanelled an inquest at nine of the bell at night. And the twenty-four appeared at nine on the following

6 Some words are lost here.

7 Temporal (civil) as opposed to spiritual (ecclesiastical or canon) law.

morning and they were so sure of their verdict that the said Walter was newly arrested before the court began. And at the bar they declared not against him but that the aforesaid Richard Killingworth made the bill and wrote it and set it up, and said that Walter helped to compose it; for which composition the inquest condemned the said Walter in £120, and judgment was given forthwith. Then the said Paston, seeing his advantage in scheming of law, broke his faith and his troth that he had made to the said Sir Thomas, as it is heretofore rehearsed, and has put the body of the said Walter in the prison of Norwich for half a year, and he is still a prisoner to this day. And they released Richard Killingworth, that did the deed, and was condemned as seriously as the said Walter, from his imprisonment and his debt and let him pass, seeing their intention was fulfilled as far as he was concerned.

The said Walter, seeing his harm, sued a *corpus cum causa* to appear before the chancellor to have remedy for these mischiefs so completely fabricated. The sheriffs aforesaid made the said Walter and three sureties to be bound in an obligation of 200 marks and each one of us in the whole, with a condition written on the back that the said Walter should keep his day* before the chancellor specified in the writ, and to return in the custody of their officer to the prison of Norwich in case he were sent back; and so he was. And so he did, as the rolls of record of the chancery make mention and all the court knows. Paston by collusion and by assent of the aforesaid sheriffs himself put a bill upon the sheriffs in the exchequer at their account, that they should have let Walter Aslake go out of custody, when he was his prisoner for £120, and the said sheriffs confessed that his bill was true in every word without any opposition, as the collusion was made as it appears in the process in the exchequer to the utter destruction of the said Walter, and his sureties for ever more, unless remedy be imposed through your high and gracious discretion that these judgments thus given by malicious plotting without any ground of truth, might be annulled and thrown out and rejected for ever more in this present parliament.

Wherefore, gracious lord, at the reverence of God, give credence to this humble bill in honour of the Holy Trinity and in the way of charity.

6.2 Peacemaking and negotiation: Henry V settles a dispute while eating a dish of oysters

The spirit and resoluteness of Henry V is nicely captured here by the chronicler in what is probably an apocryphal story. Henry's threat of coercion, the spur to compromise, should be seen as an important political tool in settling disputes and maintaining public order.[8]

The Brut, ed. F. W. D. Blie, EETS 131, 136 (1906–8), vol. 2, pp. 595–6 [English]

In the first year of his reign there were two knights at great debate: one was a Lancastrian, the other, a Yorkshireman and they each built up as strong a force as they could and skirmished together; and men were killed and injured on both sides. And when the king heard about it, he sent for them: and they came to see the king at Windsor just as he was going to dinner; and once he was informed that they had arrived, he commanded them to come before him. And then he asked them whose men they were. His liegemen, they replied. 'And whose men are they that you have raised to fight for your quarrel?' His men, they answered. 'And what authority or mandate had you to raise up my men or my people to fight and kill each other as part of your quarrel? In doing this you deserve to die.' And they could not excuse themselves, but besought the king for his grace. And then the king said by the faith that is owed to God and to St George, unless they agreed and accorded by the time he had eaten his oysters they would both be hanged before he supped. And then they went away and agreed between themselves and returned when the king had eaten his oysters. And then the king said, 'Sirs, how do things stand with you?' And then they knelt down and said, 'If it please your good grace we are agreed and accorded.' And then the king said by the faith that is owed to God and to Saint George, that if ever they were responsible for any further insurrection or the death of his subjects, without his mandate, they, or any other lords within his realm, whatever they were, would be put to death in accordance with the law. And after that no lord dared to make neither party nor strife: and thus they began to keep his laws and justice and therefore he was loved and feared.

8 Powell, *Kingship*, pp. 230–31.

6.3 Peacemaking and negotiation: the great lord as peacemaker (1455)

The following extract is the arbitration award of Humphrey, duke of Buckingham in the dispute between Sir John Gresley and Sir William Vernon in 1455. It is noteworthy first for the expression of 'good lordship' inherent in the duke of Buckingham's role as impartial arbiter and peacemaker; secondly, for its emphasis on harmony between the parties (with provision to notify the duke or his son if there are any grievances) and, thirdly, for the mutual provision of monetary compensation for those wronged or physically injured. Payment is to be made for the benefit of the widow and maintenance of her children following the killing of the husband/father by one of the parties, while servants of the other party are to receive compensation on a sliding scale according to the gravity of their injuries. This may indicate that, informally at least, the notions of compensation for victims of violent crime (obvious to historians of the Anglo-Saxon period in the *wergild* payments) persisted into the later Middle Ages.[9]

Descriptive Catalogue of the Charters and Muniments of the Gresley Family, ed. I. H. Jeayes (London, 1895), no. 437 [English]

Award by Humphrey, duke of Buckingham 12 September 1455 (signed H. Buckingham)

Settlement of divers controversies, strifes, debates … [which were pursued] for a long time between Sir William Vernon, knight, Roger Vernon, his brother, their men servants and tenants on one side and Sir John Gresley, knight, Nicholas, his brother and their men servants and tenants on the other.

First we award that the said Sir William and Sir John shall be complete friends and of friendly dealing and pardon and each put aside all grudges against the other and any rancour of the heart. And neither of them shall vex, trouble or pick a quarrel with any cousin, friend, servant, tenant or wellwisher of the other concerning past matters or quarrels that the same Sir William and Sir John had. And if any reason for grudging occurs between them in the future the party that finds himself aggrieved shall notify us of the cause of his grudge if we are in the country or else our son Stafford in our absence without any resort to violence and we or our said son in our absence arrange for redress in the matter.

---

9 See R. R. Davis, 'The survival of the bloodfeud in medieval Wales', *History*, 54 (1969), 338–57.

Also for as much as it was previously awarded that the said Sir William should pay to Anne, formerly the wife of John Herte, who was killed at Burton by the servants of the said Sir William, 20 marks to be given for the soul of the said John and for the relief of the said Anne and her children, of which 17 marks still remain unpaid, we award that the said Sir William pay the said Anne 17 marks to be paid in even amounts at the feasts of Christmas and Lammas [1 August] next coming.

Also we award that the said Sir John shall pay for the benefit of Thomas Webbe of Shelley, tenant of the said Sir William, who was maimed and injured by the servants of the said Sir John, 13s 4d for a severe wound to the head and for another serious wound to the face 13s 4d and 6s 8d each for six other wounds and for an injury to the thumb on his left hand 100s, amounting to 12 marks 6s 8d [£8 6s 8d].

6.4 Peacemaking and negotiation: the judge as mediator (1462)

This example shows how a judge (of king's bench) could be involved as a mediator and how the chief justice himself could help settle matters out of court when necessary, even though presidents of the court were under no legal obligation to do so. The proposal outlined in the letter followed a failed attempt by six arbiters and an umpire (John, Lord Beaumont) to resolve the differences between the parties, Sir William Plumpton and Henry Pierrepont (arising from an affray which resulted in the death of Pierrepont's father, Henry, killed by one of Plumpton's relatives, Robert Green, and the homicide of a certain John Green by John Pierrepont). An appeal of homicide was later brought in the court of king's bench by Pierrepont's widow. Bingham's entreaties were successful in that the parties eventually submitted to his arbitration in May 1462.[10] The restriction on the number of persons attending and the manner of their array is significant. The venue, St Peter's church, is also significant: the sacred space of a church was frequently used for solemnising arbitration awards.

The Plumpton Correspondence, ed. T. Stapleton, Camden Society, original series, 4 (1839), pp. 3–4.

To my right honourable and reverent cousin, Sir William Plumpton, knight.

Right worshipful and reverent cousin, after due and hearty recommendations, by the advice of my master, Sir John Markham, chief justice, I had discussions with Henry Pierrepont, esquire concerning the dispute that is between you and him, and he is agreed, if it please you, to put

10 Powell, 'Arbitration', 59.

everything that is in dispute between you and him in the hands of the said Sir John and me, and if you will do the same, we for the ease of you both and the peace of the country will take the matter upon us and we will appoint you both to be at Nottingham upon the Monday next after Low Sunday next coming [2 April 1462] at evening, you to be lodged there upon the Long Row in the Saturday market, at your pleasure, and the said Henry against St Mary's church; and each of you, not to exceed twelve persons and you and each of your persons to be unaccompanied, and in no other form, and the place of meeting for you and us to be at St Peter's church; and if this please you, I trust to God the matter in dispute between you and him shall reach a good conclusion; and therefore I pray you to send word in writing to my son Richard Bingham as to how you will agree in this matter that he may let my master, Sir John Markham, Henry Pierpoint and me have knowledge of your disposition in the said matter. The day of your treaty shall be at Nottingham early upon the Tuesday next after Low Sunday [27 April 1462], and my said master and I shall so act between you, that if you will both be ruled by reason, by the grace of God which may ever keep you, you shall both be satisfied. Written at Middleton the eighth day of January.

Your humble cousin,
Richard Bingham, knight.

6.5 Arbitration procedure: arrangements for arbitration between Edmund Ferrers and Hugh Erdswick, Staffordshire (1413)

The arrangements made in an attempt to end the dispute between Edmund Ferrers and Hugh Erdswick are notable for what they reveal about the procedure of arbitration itself. From the passage it can be seen that mediators were used for the preliminary negotiations and that the arbitrators themselves were prominent members of local society. A figure of considerable stature, the earl of Warwick, was appointed as an umpire in case of any disagreement. A date and meeting place were fixed and a time limit also set for the completion of negotiations. The peaceful resolution of the conflict was paramount. The size of the retinue accompanying both sides to the loveday was carefully regulated and both parties were obliged to offer bonds for maintaining the peace towards each other between the selection of arbitrators and the making of the award. In the event neither side observed their undertakings and the attempts to settle the dispute dissolved.

Collections for a History of Staffordshire, William Salt Archaeological Society, 17 (1896), pp. 51–2 [Latin]

In the suit of Edmund, Lord Ferrers of Chartley against Walter Bullock, clerk, to deliver up to him two bonds by which he and Hugh Erdswick were mutually bound in a sum of 500 marks. Hugh Erdswick appeared and pleaded that the bonds should not be given up to Edmund; and he stated that discord and strife having arisen between him and Robert Sampson and Roger his brothers on one side and the said Edmund and Thomas and Edward his brothers and Richard Peshale, esquire, on the other; and similarly between the said Edmund on one side and Thomas de Tommenhorn, knight, and Thomas Giffard, esquire, on the other, by the mediation of friends who had intervened to appease the strife, each of them, namely the said Edmund and Hugh had been mutually bound over in a sum of 500 marks and the bonds had been given to Walter Bullock for safe custody upon certain conditions, namely that the said Edmund and Hugh on Monday after the Translation of St Edward the Confessor following in the first year of the reign of King Henry V [16 October 1413] should come to a certain meadow between Amerton and Gayton [Staffs.] each with fifty persons, no more of whom four should be knights, twenty gentlemen and the rest yeomen and that there should be appointed arbiters for each party, namely Humphrey Stafford, John Bagot knights and John Savage, esquire, on the side of Edmund; and on the side of Hugh, Thomas Gresley and John Cokayne, knights, and William Venables, esquire, or others of similar status and rank in the place of the said arbiters, in case any was unable to attend; provided that the number of arbiters should always remain the same; and in case the arbiters could not agree, Richard earl of Warwick had been chosen by Edmund and Hugh as umpire;[11] and that the arbitration should be completed before the feast of All Saints [1 November] and that the said Edmund and his brothers and Richard Peshale and all of their kinsmen or persons of their affinity, friends and servants and the said Hugh, his brothers, Thomas de Tommenhorn and Thomas Giffard and all of their kinsmen, affinity, friends and servants should in the meantime keep the peace and do nothing, nor procure anybody to perform anything, which would tend to break the peace: and if one side was willing to fulfil the above conditions and the other side would not do so, the bonds should be given up to the party which was willing to perform them. And likewise the said Robert Sampson and Roger his brothers, Thomas de Tommenhorn and Thomas Giffard and all of their kinsmen and affinity, friends and servants should faithfully observe the same conditions.

11 Literally as a 'non equal' (*in nonparem*).

And Hugh stated further that Nicholas Peshale, the brother of the said Richard Peshale, on the Sunday after the feast of All Saints [5 November 1413] at Newport, Salop, had assaulted, beaten and ill-treated John Swetnam, chaplain, the servant of Thomas Giffard and therefore as the said Richard Peshale and his kinsmen had not kept the peace according to the conditions the bond should be delivered up to him.

Edmund denied that Nicholas Peshale had beaten and ill-treated the said John Swetnam or that he was a servant of Thomas Giffard and he stated that he and his brothers and Richard Peshale had always been ready to fulfil the conditions of the bonds as stated above by Hugh, but that neither the arbitrators nor the umpire had made any award and nevertheless Robert the brother of Hugh and one John Holborne, servant of Robert, on Thursday after the Translation of Edward the Confessor in the first year of the reign of King Henry V [19 October 1413] had assaulted his servant John Grey at Tyxdale [Tixall] and would have beaten and killed him and had chased him beyond the heath called Tyxdale Heath and that the said John was so exhausted and over-come by the chase that he nearly died and his life was despaired of and therefore as the kinsmen and servants of Hugh had not fulfilled the condition of the bonds they ought to be given up to him.

Hugh denied that the said John Grey was a servant of Edmund and repeated his plea as above and appealed to a jury, to be summoned for the octave of St Hilary [20 January].

6.6 Arbitration: dispute between Lord Roos and Robert Tirwhit (1411)

The dispute between William, Lord Roos and Robert Tirwhit, a judge of king's bench, attracted the attention of king and parliament when Tirwhit reneged on the terms of the loveday brokered by the chief justice of king's bench, William Gascoigne, by coming to the arbitration flanked by a large body of armed supporters, obviously considerably more than his opponent. The resubmis-sion to negotiation and the display of reconciliation and humility forced upon Tirwhit is significant.

RP, vol. 3, pp. 649–50 [French]

Between Lord Roos and Robert Tirwhit. Be it remembered that on Wednesday 4 November [1411], after parliament had been opened, Lord Roos delivered a petition against Robert Tirwhit, one of the justices of king's bench, to our lord the king in parliament, as follows:

To our most sovereign lord the king and the lords spiritual and temporal in this present parliament, William de Roos of Helmsley, knight, declares and complains both on behalf of our lord the king and himself that since Robert Tirwhit one of the justices of your bench, most dread lord, recently sued in your said bench a writ of trespass against John Rate, steward of the said William's courts of his manor of Melton Ross, Richard Robinet, the said William's bailiff of his said manor, John Bernard, John Tottenay, Thomas Gurnall, John Hammon, Stephen Doye, William Bocher, John Kedy, John his son, John Moys, Robert Andrew and William Richardson, some of whom are tenants at will and some villeins of the said William de Roos, alleging that they had dug in the private turbary* of the said Robert Tirwhit at Wragby [Lincs.] and cut down his trees and shrubs formerly growing there and cut his grass and ferns once growing there and took and carried off the said grass and ferns and the said trees and shrubs, together with the turves from the said turbary, estimated to be worth £40; in which place both the said William de Roos and his aforesaid tenants claim right of common pasture to dig for turves and estovers.*

Whereupon the said William de Roos, on behalf of himself and his said tenants, and the said Robert, submitted themselves with the said suit and all its corollaries to the arbitration and ordinance of William Gascoigne, chief justice. Whereupon the said William Gascoigne, with the agreement of the aforesaid parties, ordered them to be before him on Saturday after the feast of Michaelmas last [3 October] at Wragby in the county of Lincoln, with their documents, in order to explain their titles and rights in this matter. And the said William Gascoigne decided that the said William de Roos should come there with two of his kinsmen or other friends in a peaceful manner, with as many men as customarily rode with them. And that the said Robert should come peacefully with two of his kinsmen or friends, with as many men as is fitting for their estate and position. At which time and place, in the presence of the said William Gascoigne, the same William de Roos in accordance with the aforesaid ordinance and agreement was ready to explain his title and right and abide by the aforesaid ordinance.

Yet the said Robert Tirwhit did not abide by the said submission to arbitration, ordinance and agreement even though he was a justice of assize and keeper of the peace in the said county of Lincoln nor did he respect in any way the status of the said William de Roos, who was one of the justices of the peace in the same county, but in order to override the ordinance and judgment of the said William Gascoigne plotted by

scheming and malice aforethought to raise and assemble at the aforesaid place and time a large number of men, numbering about 500 armed
and equipped for war, against your peace and in contempt of you, most
dread lord, contrary to the statutes ordained and provided in this case
to the great disturbance of all the surrounding lands; and they lay in
wait there in several groups in a warlike manner close to the said place
specified by the said William Gascoigne to ambush the said William de
Roos, Henry, Lord Beaumont and Thomas, Lord Warre kinsmen to the
said William de Roos who had gathered together for the same matter
according to the same agreement, in order to forcibly overcome and
dishonour the aforesaid agreement to the great shame, disgrace and
dishonour of the said William de Roos and the other two lords who
were present there with him, who were unaware of this wrong and
ambush.

May it please you, most dread lord, with the advice of your most wise
lords in this present parliament, to ordain and provide whatever remedy,
punishment and redress for this evil trespass and offence against both
you, most dread lord, and the said William de Roos as seems most
necessary to you so that such assemblies and lawlessness can be avoided
in future.

Which petition having been read and heard and the many arguments
put by both parties as well as the answers and responses made to them
on various days assigned to them by the lord our king in parliament
had been heard, finally, that is to say on Friday 27 November, both the
said Lord Roos with his counsel and the said Robert Tirwhit with his
counsel came before the king and the lords in the same parliament, And
there the said Lord Roos explained to our said lord the king how he had
sued his said petition and touching the same petition he was prepared
to submit himself to whatever it might please our same lord the king
to ordain or decide in this matter, to which our same lord the king
replied that he did not want to command him to do this. Then the said
Robert explained to our same lord the king how through foolishness
and ignorance he had acted in this matter otherwise than he ought, to
his displeasure, and that for this crime against our same lord the king
he put himself on the mercy of our said lord the king, and requested
his mercy and pardon. Then the king asked the same Robert if he put
himself in his mercy for his ignorance, or for his deed. And the said
Robert replied for the deed specified in the said petition. Moreover,
touching the trespasses and wrongs done by the said Robert to the said
Lord Roos as alleged in his said petition the same Robert submitted

himself to the ordinance and judgment of two lords who were related to the said Lord Roos, anyone it pleased him to name. Whereupon the said Lord Roos said that he truly wished it.

Then before the king and the aforesaid lords he nominated the archbishop of Canterbury and Lord Grey, the king's chamberlain, assuming that they were willing to take it upon themselves. And the said Robert asked the said archbishop and chamberlain if they would take it upon themselves. To which our same lord the king said that it did indeed please him that the said Robert had submitted himself thus and he certainly was willing to accept his submission: and he accepted it, because, he said, that if he [Tirwhit] sought to justify his said deed, he [the king] would have had to act as judge between the said Lord Roos and him. But because he had submitted himself in this way, our same lord the king wanted to act impartially between them to help them to bring the case to a satisfactory conclusion. And on account of the good behaviour of the said Robert towards the said Lord Roos in this matter and the good behaviour and conduct of this same Robert towards our said lord the king, he [the king] afterwards said that his mercy would not be entirely lacking in this affair; and thereupon the same archbishop and chamberlain were charged to take it upon themselves. And the same archbishop and chamberlain by order of the king and at the request of the parties there took it upon themselves to accomplish it with God's help. Which archbishop and Lord Grey having deliberated fully and taken advice on these aforesaid matters made their ordinance and judgment on this matter as follows:

This is the ordinance that Thomas, archbishop of Canterbury and Richard, Lord Grey, chamberlain of our liege lord the king, have made between William, Lord Roos on the one side and Robert Tirwhit, justice of king's bench, on the other. First, where the aforesaid Lord Roos at the last parliament of our said liege lord held at Westminster complained by a petition alleging against the same Robert that he, the Saturday night after the feast of Michaelmas last [3 October 1411] at Wragby in Lincolnshire assembled a great number of men armed and arrayed against the peace, to lie in wait for the same Lord Roos and to harm him and dishonour him there, against the form of the loveday arranged between the same parties by William Gascoigne, chief justice of the aforesaid king's bench, to whose ordinance the aforesaid Lord Roos and Robert had submitted themselves, touching certain common pasture and turf-digging that the said Lord Roos claims for himself and his tenants of Melton Ross in the village of Wragby – as in the supplication – as it is alleged by the same petition; to which loveday the two parties should have come, each one with a certain number of followers according to his degree and as it was previously ordained by the aforesaid William Gascoigne. To whom at the same loveday the said Robert would not admit that he had submitted himself in that matter, but he said that it was his intention that the said William Gascoigne should treat between the aforesaid Lord Roos and him.

And in the same parliament, when the same petition had been read and understood, the aforesaid Robert said to our aforesaid liege lord the king that he knew well that in the matter submitted against him in the said petition he had not behaved himself as he should have done, whereupon he besought the king for grace and said that he would promise to encourage the Lord Roos to choose two lords of his kin and then the said Robert would submit himself to their ordinance in the aforesaid matter and all the circumstances thereof. And there, at the desire of our said liege lord, the said Lord Roos chose the aforesaid archbishop of Canterbury and chamberlain who, by virtue of the submission that the said Robert made in this, have ordained in the manner and form that follows: that is to say that touching the aforesaid matter of common pasture and turf-digging the aforesaid Lord Roos and Robert shall fully abide by the ordinance and arbitrament of the aforesaid William Gascoigne, who at the expense of both parties shall come to the aforesaid common place at such reasonable time as the aforesaid Lord Roos likes to assign. Also, at such reasonable time as it shall please the same Lord Roos to assign, the same Robert Tirwhit shall deliver two tuns of Gascon wine to Melton Ross; and at such a day as is reasonable thereafter as it shall please the Lord Roos, the said Robert shall bring to the same place two fattened oxen and twelve fattened sheep to be eaten at a dinner by those who shall be there.

On which day the said Robert shall cause to come all the knights, esquires and yeoman who had led the men on his side at the aforesaid loveday; and in the presence of the said Lord Roos and all the others there, the aforesaid Robert shall recite the words that he said to our aforesaid liege lord in the parliament aforesaid and in particular he shall say to the aforesaid Lord Roos: 'My Lord Roos, I know well that you are of such birth, estate and might that if you had wished you could have come to the aforesaid loveday with such an array that I would have been unable to challenge it; but yet it pleased you to come in a less well-attended manner, considering your status. And, through unreliable information, I was afraid of bodily harm, so with the intention of protecting myself I assembled these persons that are here and numerous others, not to cause harm or offence to you my Lord Roos; and I will here apologise in any way you will devise. Moreover, for as much as I am a justice, I should have behaved myself more discreetly and peacefully than any other common man. I know well that I have failed and offended you, my Lord Roos, whereof I beseech you for your grace and mercy and offer you five hundred marks to be paid at your will.'

Also it is ordained that once this offer has been made the aforesaid Lord Roos shall say that in reverence for the king, who in this case has showed him good and righteous lordship, he will not take anything from the said Robert except the aforesaid wine, oxen and sheep, for the dinner of those present there. And furthermore the said Lord Roos in the presence of those who are there shall openly forgive the said Robert and all the others in the abovesaid array who were assembled at the loveday and came with the same Robert all their offence and trespass with the exception of four persons, namely Richard Haunsard knight, William Kelk, Roger Berneston and Roger Kelk son of William, which same four persons we ordain that the same Robert shall bring at the assignment of the said Lord Roos to his own castle, Belvoir, into his presence; so that they too can acknowledge their offence and submit themselves to the same Lord Roos, beseeching him for grace and mercy. And when they made this submission, the same Lord Roos shall act towards them in such a way that they shall feel themselves treated well with favour and grace.

VII: THE PERSONNEL OF JUSTICE

The task of law enforcement and the staffing of the legal system required a large number of full-time and part-time officials, ranging from the royal judges of the central courts down to village constables. Appointments did not take place in a vacuum, and depending upon the status of the office-holder and their position within the hierarchy may have been subject to various national or local considerations and to prevailing political or social pressures.[1] At every level within the system the problem of bribery and corruption was evident, and was the source of much controversy during the period.

The dismissal of the higher judiciary from office en masse and the instigation of inquiries into their conduct (as well as the state of local justice) occurred in 1289–90 and again under Edward III in 1340–41.[2] On both occasions the action was politically motivated and provided a public shock to the judicial system, but did not uncover the scale of incompetence or corruption that might have been envisaged. Edward I made an example of chief justices Ralph Hengham and Thomas Weyland,[3] [**7.3**] while Edward III's chief justice, Richard Willoughby, accused of selling laws 'as if they had been oxen or cows', was paraded around various counties to face the charges of local jurors.[4] To restore public confidence in justice prior to the king's departure for a new campaign in France a broad ordinance concerning judicial conduct was issued in 1346.[5] A restyled oath of office formed a central part of this ordinance. [**7.1**] Royal justices had sworn oaths before taking office since at least the thirteenth century (from when the earliest recorded example derives).[6] The ordinance also introduced harsh penalties for those whose behaviour did not match up

---

1 For example: R. Virgoe, 'The crown and local government: East Anglia under Richard II', in *The Reign of Richard II*, ed. F. R. H. du Boulay and C. Barron (London, Athlone Press, 1971), pp. 218–41; D. Biggs, 'Henry IV and his JPs: the Lancastrianization of justice, 1399–1413', in *Traditions and Transformations in Late Medieval England*, ed. D. Biggs, S. D. Michalove and A. C. Reeves (Leiden and Boston, Brill, 2002), pp. 59–79.

2 P. Brand, 'Edward I and the judges: the state trials of 1289–93', in *Thirteenth Century England I*, ed. P. R. Coss and S. D. Lloyd (Woodbridge, Boydell Press, 1986), pp. 31–40; N. M. Fryde, 'Edward III's removal of his ministers and judges, 1340–1', *BIHR*, 48 (1975), 159–61.

3 P. Brand, *The Making of the Common Law* (London, Hambledon Press, 1992), pp. 113–33, 152–5; A. L. Spitzer, 'The legal career of Thomas Weyland and Gilbert Thornton', *JLH*, 6 (1985), pp. 65–7, 74–6.

4 *Year Books of Edward III: 14 and 15 Edward III*, ed. L. O. Pike (London, RS, 1889), pp. 258–63; Musson, *Medieval Law*, pp. 57–9.

5 Maddicott, *Law and Lordship*, pp. 40–48.

6 Brand, *Common Law*, pp. 149–51.

to the ideal. Chief justice William Thorp was the first to feel its full rigour when only four years after the ordinance he was accused of wrongdoing and duly prosecuted by Edward III, keen to enforce new ethical standards. Having suffered the ordeals of trial, Thorp was lucky upon conviction to receive from the king a last-minute reprieve on the strength of his previous royal service.[7]
[**7.4**]

There was a general impression (prevalent in literary works) that judges and lawyers made considerable sums from their professional activities.[8] This perception may have elements of truth, but masks some of the realities of royal judicial service: there was a profound shift during the thirteenth and fourteenth centuries from clerical to lay justices, which altered the way in which their service could be rewarded. Benefices could no longer be awarded, and even though salaries were supposed to be paid, the king was often in arrears with wages. In order to survive (economically and socially) judges in particular were forced to supplement their official salaries with what they could secure from private work. Indeed, judges' salaries in the mid-fourteenth century had remained frozen at the same level for at least the last eighty years.[9] The retaining of judges and legal counsel by magnates and monastic houses (similar to the body of legal advisers attached to large corporations today) was a convention of the age and, although it attracted much criticism, it did not necessarily imply or involve corruption.[10] [**7.2**] The fee paid was usually a retainer or a courtesy gift – in case the litigant had need of specialised advice, or in recognition of general service. It should not be (though it inevitably was) construed simply as a bribe to show especial favour or bend the rules.[11]

Yet the targeting of royal justices during the Peasants' Revolt revealed a lack of public esteem for their general conduct and vaunted ethical stance. The 'popular' view on retaining is encapsulated in the macabre puppet show enacted with the heads of chief justice John Cavendish and the prior of Bury St Edmunds during the Revolt in Suffolk. In the wake of the Peasants' Revolt the commons in parliament were equally vociferous in calls for reform, particularly with regard to liveried retainers. [**7.5**] Further legislative action followed under Richard II when the Ordinance of Justices was confirmed as a statute in 1378 and general provisions aimed at retaining were passed in the Statute of Liveries in 1390. The issue of retaining nevertheless remained a contentious one into the fifteenth century.[12]

---

7 Maddicott, *Law and Lordship*, pp. 48–51, 84–5.

8 Musson, *Medieval Law*, pp. 69–75.

9 *SCCKB*, vol. 4, pp. xxii–xxv; Maddicott, *Law and Lordship*, pp. 17–18.

10 N. Ramsey, 'Retained legal counsel, c.1275–1475', *TRHS* 5th series, 35 (1985), 95–112; Maddicott, *Law and Lordship*, pp. 5–10.

11 R. Horrox, 'Service', in *Fifteenth-Century Attitudes*, ed. Horrox, pp. 70–71.

12 R. Storey, 'Liveries and commissions of the peace, 1388–90', in *Reign of Richard II*, ed. du Boulay and Barron, pp. 131–52; N. Saul, 'The commons and the abolition of badges', *Parliamentary History*, 9 (1990), 302–15; Maddicott, *Law and Lordship*, pp. 72–81.

Sir John Fortescue's picture of the incorruptibility of royal judges and their strong sense of ethical values jars considerably with the complaints of maintenance and corruption against fellow royal justice William Paston, and, indeed, Fortescue's own conduct in this regard. [**7.6, 7.7**] For it is known that he himself was in receipt in 1457 of 'a robe of gold cloth with crimson velvet' from Sir John Fastolf, 'so that the said judge would be more favourable in his judgment' towards an associate of Fastolf imprisoned in king's bench.[13] The contemplative life which Fortescue claims the judges enjoyed, in a peaceful world centred around the royal courts at Westminster Hall and the Inns of Court, offers another idealised picture. On occasion, the tranquillity (if it ever existed) would have been shattered by the clerks of the courts, whose conduct was not always what one would expect of civil servants. [**7.8**]

From the personnel of central justice the chapter moves to the stalwarts of local justice. At county level, the two most important offices were those of sheriff and justice of the peace. JPs, in common with all royal justices, were required to swear an oath on assuming office. [**7.9**] This did not necessarily prevent wrongdoing on their part, but did at least set a standard by which their professional conduct could be judged. As the case of John Whittlebury demonstrates, disruption to peace sessions, death threats and even murder could befall the incumbents. [**7.10**] During the 1350s and again in 1376 there were petitions in parliament calling for the exclusion of sheriffs, coroners, undersheriffs and gaolers from the office of JP on the grounds of an alleged propensity of these officials to issue false indictments and recoup for themselves the heavy fines extorted for suit of prison* and mainprise.* It does not appear, however, that the measures taken in response to these claims were adequately enforced.[14]

The sheriff was the lynchpin of local government and the king's representative in the county. His duties were multifarious, encompassing both executive and judicial functions and requiring close liaison with the exchequer, chancery and the various courts. By the later fourteenth and fifteenth centuries sheriffs were changed annually, though reappointment in subsequent years (after a suitable interval) was common.[15] [**7.11**] The sheriff often bore the brunt of complaints of injustice on the one hand and inefficiency or incompetence on the other. As we have seen in previous chapters, both royal inquiries and the 'outlaw literature' especially targeted the sheriff. Because he was responsible for serving legal process and summoning juries, it was the sheriff and his staff who were most susceptible to bribery and misconduct. The actions of John Thornton, undersheriff of Northamptonshire, suggest that in some cases the

---

13 See Oxford, Magdalen College, Fastolf Papers 42; J. Rose, 'Litigation and political conflict in fifteenth-century East Anglia: conspiracy, and attaint actions and Sir John Fastolf', *JLH*, 27 (2006), pp. 58–9, 80.

14 A. J. Verduyn, 'The attitude of the parliamentary commons to law and order under Edward III', unpublished DPhil thesis, University of Oxford, 1991, pp. 131, 175.

15 W. A. Morris, *The Medieval English Sheriff to 1300* (Manchester, Manchester University Press, 1927); R. Gorski, *The Fourteenth Century Sheriff: English Local Administration in the Late Middle Ages* (Woodbridge, Boydell, 2003).

administration of justice could be hindered by royal officials whose motivation stemmed from the loyalty they felt towards their lords rather than arising from any concept of disinterested public service. [7.12] Recognition of the sheriff's potential influence and the need to have him 'on-side' is equally apparent in the letter from John Gresham to John Paston. [7.13]

The office of coroner was another vital cog in the administration of criminal justice in the county. Unlike the single sheriff (whose duties could span two counties) there were usually four coroners per county and two in a liberty. As we observed in Chapter 5, not only did the coroner hold inquests concerning homicide and suicide, but he was also responsible for all abjurations, appeals and outlawries as well as a host of miscellaneous duties arising from his receipt of special writs and attendance at the county court. His rolls, therefore, contained a wealth of important details and provided key documentation of the crown's rights. Their loss or destruction would amount to a significant gap in the administrative record. Coroners also acted as a watchdog on the sheriff and could be called upon to assume the latter's duties in default.[16] Their work could be seriously hindered by the actions of those who were unwilling to co-operate.[17] [7.14]

Much of the day-to-day lesser work in the field of criminal justice was carried out by lower-ranking officials working in the hundreds and townships.[18] The various officials operating below shire level were indispensable to the functioning of the lower courts, especially in pursuing and arresting suspects, and generally in helping to maintain the peace. They were also given responsibilities under the Statute of Labourers. Increasingly they became the target of threats and physical assaults and found themselves squeezed between the wishes of the community on the one hand and the demands of the crown on the other.[19] [7.15] The gaolers staffing prisons were also caught in a difficult situation because they were responsible for escapes from their custody, which were not infrequent given the incentive provided by the pitiful conditions in many medieval gaols and their poor state of repair.[20] Their responsibility made them a target for legal action by litigants seeking compensation for the losses resulting from their negligence. Liability could be incurred in trespass and debt for creditors who escaped from their custody and also in covenant and (by the fifteenth century) assumpsit,* where the gaoler had undertaken (*assumpsisset*) the

---

16 Note the concern demonstrated by the coroners and the attempt to minimise their interference.

17 Hunnisett, *Coroner*.

18 H. M. Cam, 'Shire officials: coroners, constables and bailiffs', in *The English Government at Work, 1327–1336*, ed. F. Willard, W. A. Morris and W. H. Dunham, 3 vols (Cambridge, MA, Medieval Academy of America, 1945–50), vol. 3, pp. 165–7.

19 A. Musson, 'Sub-keepers and constables: the role of local officials in keeping the peace in fourteenth-century England', *EHR*, 117 (2002), 1–24.

20 R. B. Pugh, *Imprisonment in Medieval England* (Cambridge, Cambridge University Press, 1968), pp. 196–8, 232–54.

duty of guarding the prisoners, but had breached his obligations.[21] In spite of regulations governing the keeping of gaols issued in 1356 and 1393, not surprisingly gaolers were susceptible to allegations of cruelty and torture. They were clearly open to bribery in addition to legitimately charging for 'hospitality'.[22] At this level the 'privatised' character of medieval justice is apparent: the official in charge of the Marshalsea prison of the king's bench contracted out his duties to a deputy. [**7.16**]

---

21 R. C. Palmer, *English Law in the Age of the Black Death, 1348–1381: A Transformation of Governance and Law* (Chapel Hill, NC and London, University of North Carolina Press, 1993), pp. 260–67.

22 Pugh, *Imprisonment*, pp. 165–91.

7.1 Judges of the central courts: the judges' oath of office (1346)

The insistence upon standards of judicial conduct could be effective only if there was widespread recognition of the level of ethical behaviour that was expected. The requirement that the Ordinance of Justices be read out and exhibited in public places within the county would have been significant for raising public consciousness in this respect. The inclusion of the text of the ordinance in the chronicle of Adam Murimuth is not only an indication of how chronicles can be repositories of legislation, but also may be taken as symbolising the ordinance's perceived importance to contemporaries. The crux of the judge's oath does not represent anything new. To do right to all subjects equally irrespective of position or wealth had been an important element in earlier versions as had the prohibition of reward. The essential difference between this and earlier versions of the oath was the onus placed on a judge when holding office to accept neither payment nor robes from anyone but the crown. Hospitality in the form of sustenance was acceptable provided the entertaining was not lavish. To ameliorate the restriction on earnings the king agreed to increase judges' salaries and provide robes for summer and winter. The severity of the penalties for violation of the oath was also increased. It was not only his judicial position and wages that would be forfeit. Upon conviction the offender's lands, goods and even his life were placed at the king's mercy.[1]

Adae Murimuth Continuatio Chronicarum. Robertus de Avesbury de Gestis Mirabilibus Regis Edwardi Tertii, ed. E. M. Thompson (RS, 1889), pp. 193–4: the Ordinance of Justices (1346) [French]

Edward by the grace of God king of England and France and lord of Ireland to the sheriff of Devonshire, greeting. Because by various complaints made to us we have understood that the law of our land, which we are bound by oath to maintain, is less well kept and its execution disturbed many times by maintenance and procurement in many ways both in court and in the regions; we, greatly moved by conscience in this matter, and for this reason desiring both for the pleasure of God and for the comfort and quiet of our subjects and to salve our conscience and to save and keep our aforesaid oath, with the assent of the great and other wise men of our council, have ordained and expressly give orders to all our justices that they shall from now on exercise fairness in law and provide right to all our subjects, rich and poor, without having regard to anyone, without omitting to do right as a result of any letters or commands that may come to them from us or from any other person or for any other reasons whatsoever; and if any letters, writs, or commands should come to the justices or others deputed to do law and right according to the custom of the realm in disturbance of the

1 See 7.4.

law or of the execution of the same or of doing right to the parties, we command that the said justices should proceed and hold their course and their processes in the pleas and business pending before them just as if no such letter, writs or mandates had come to them; and they should certify to us in council as to any such orders which are contrary to the law, as is said above. And to the end that our said justices should do equal right to all people in the manner abovesaid without showing more favour to one than to another, so we have ordained and have caused our said justices to swear that from henceforth as long as they shall hold office they shall not take either fees or robes from any man except from ourself and that they shall take neither gift nor reward, by themselves or by others, in secret or publicly, from any man that shall have any business before them, unless it is food or drink and that of negligible value; and that they shall not give counsel either to great or small in cases where we are party or which touch us or could touch us in any way, upon pain of being at our will in body and possessions and lands and at our pleasure if they act contrary to their oath. And for this reason we have caused their fees to be increased in such a manner as ought reasonably to suffice.

7.2 Judges of the central courts: pensions paid to judges (1338)

The extract indicates that the Knights Hospitallers paid what appears to have been a standard fee of 40s to all judges and clerks in the exchequer, common and king's benches and in chancery. Although the sum of £10 to the chief justice of common pleas appears out of step with the payment to the chief justice of king's bench, in fact Geoffrey le Scrope (chief justice king's bench) had received from the Hospitallers life grants of a manor in Yorkshire and a small holding in Northamptonshire, which probably brought his total up to £10 and on a par with his opposite number.[2] Two payments to puisne[*] judges appear anomalous and may imply closer connections: the 100s (£5) to William Shareshull and Richard Willoughby's payment of 5 marks (the recording of which in marks rather than in pounds or shillings obscures the fact that he was paid considerably more than most other judges).

The Knights Hospitallers in England: Being the Report of Prior Philip de Tame to the Grand Master Elyan de Villanova for AD 1338, ed. L. B. Larking, Camden Society, original series, 65 (1857), pp. 203–4 [Latin]

Also … various pensions paid from the treasury per year to various persons both in the court of the lord king and justices, clerks, officers

2 *Knights Hospitallers*, ed. Larking, pp. 112, 134; Maddicott, *Law and Lordship*, p. 26.

and other ministers in his various courts and also other associates of magnates – both for lands, tenements, rents and liberties of the Hospital and of the Templars and especially to maintain the lands of the Templars, namely:

Barons in the exchequer of the lord king

Sir Robert de Sadington, knight, chief baron of the exchequer   ... 40s
Sir William de Everden, baron of the exchequer 40s
Sir Robert de Scorburgh, per year 40s
Sir William de Stowe, engrosser of the aforesaid exchequer
    per year 40s
Sir Gervase de Wilford, one of the remembrancers of the
    exchequer 40s
Sir William de Brocklesby, the other remembrancer.................. 40s
Sir Roger Gildesburgh, apposer of the aforesaid exchequer 40s

Also in the common bench that is the king's court concerning pleas of lands and tenements pleaded and determined according to the laws of England, namely:

Sir William de Herle,[3] knight, chief justice in the same court,
    per year £10
Sir William de Shareshull, justice in the same court.............. 100s
Sir Richard de Aldeburgh, justice in the same court 40s
Sir John Shardelowe, justice in the same court 40s
Sir Thomas de Maughan, clerk in the same court..................... 40s
Sir John Asheby, another clerk in the same court 40s

And a robe with Bougie fur[4] of the livery of the clerks of the prior

And in the king's bench and it is the principal court of England in which all pleas of trespasses, felonies and conspiracies are pleaded, namely:

Sir Geoffrey le Scrope, chief justice in the same court 40s
Sir Richard de Willoughby, justice in the same court .... 5 marks
                                                            [£3 6s 8d]
And Thomas de Thorp, the prior's attorney in the same court
    for prosecuting and defending the business of the house 40s

Also in the other court of the lord king which is called the chancery, namely:

3 This should rightly be Sir John Stonor, who took over on Herle's retirement in 1335.

4 Highgrade lambskin.

Sir John de St Paul, clerk, per year.. 40s
Sir Henry de Ednestowe, clerk of the same court 40s
Sir Michael de Wath, clerk there 40s
Sir Thomas de Bamburgh 40s

7.3 Judges of the central courts: chief justice Thomas Weyland (1289)

The downfall of Thomas Weyland, chief justice of common pleas, came not so much through abuse of his judicial office as masterminding a murder or at least receiving the killers after the event.[5] Weyland's position among the minor clergy and his connection with the Friars Minor are highlighted by the fact that he sought sanctuary in Babwell Priory. He was eventually 'starved out' and forced to confront this allegation against him. The archbishop of Canterbury provided a personal recommendation as to his fate and testimony of his standing in the church's eyes following allegations of bigamy. Weyland did not in fact stand trial, but was allowed to abjure the realm* and go into exile abroad. He was finally pardoned and returned to England, probably not long before his death in around 1298.

(a)

Annals of Dunstable, ed. H. R. Luard (RS, 1866), pp. 355–7 [Latin]

Meanwhile the clamour of the poor came to the king that the justices and other ministers whom he had put in charge of his kingdom had been subverted, corrupted by gifts for judgments; [...] also that they had agreed to homicides and they had received killers knowingly. The lord king carried out diligent inquiries upon these articles and twelve jurors said on their oath that Thomas Weyland, chief justice of the lord king in the [common] bench, had engineered a certain homicide through his esquires and afterwards received the same killers. Having been arrested and detained by ministers of the king on account of that homicide, he escaped secretly from their hands and sought the place of the Friars Minor at Bury St Edmunds and there was admitted to their order. And since he remained there for forty days and then was unwilling to leave, all type of food stuffs were withdrawn by the laity. The brothers, however, afflicted by hunger and thirst, left the monastery of the said place and were unable to return; and, as it is said, only

5 P. Brand, 'Chief justice and felon: the career of Thomas Weyland', in *The Political Context of Law*, ed. R. Eales and D. Sullivan (London, Hambledon Press, 1987), pp. 27–47.

three or four veterans remained with the said Thomas. And the lord king sent for the minister of the Friars Minor asking why he had dared to admit as a friar a felon of his kingdom? And when the king was given to understand that this event occurred without the knowledge of the same minister he ceased his indignation against the friars. Later the said Thomas, realising that he could not be protected by the church, or by this order, and that he did not have much in the way of food provisions, put on his lay garb again and under the escort of Sir Robert Malet, who had custody of him at this time, was placed in the Tower of London. At length arraigned before the king's council on the aforesaid charges of felonies and other treasons committed against the king and his kingdom he was given three options: namely, either to stand trial by the judgment of his peers, or to have life imprisonment, or perpetually to abjure the kingdom of England and the lands of the king. And he, constrained on all fronts, abjured the realm of the lord king. And he was assigned the port of Dover; and thus walking barefoot and with his head uncovered bearing a crucifix in his hand, coming to the port, he crossed the sea. And all his goods moveable and immoveable were confiscated.

(b)

Registrum Epistolarum Fratris Johannis Peckham, Archiepiscopi Cantuariensis, ed. C. T. Martin (RS, 1882–86), vol. 3, pp. 968–9: letter from Archbishop Pecham to Robert Malet (22 November 1289) [French]

Brother John, by the permission of God priest of Canterbury, to his very dear friend and spiritual son, Sir Robert Malet, greeting, grace and blessing. Sir, I received your letter the day of Lady Saint Cecilia, and I understood well from your letter that you have no desire to vex the friars and you tell me that you wish to hear good news of the king to whom I have sent my messengers. And know, sir, that I have sent Sir Nicholas de Knoville and Master Reynold de Wraudon, and a foot messenger with letters, and I have as yet had no reply. Wherefore I think for sure that the king is deliberating and that he will do some kindness, which I desire more to hear for the honour of the king and yourself than I do for Thomas Weyland. For know that the said Thomas, as I have heard, since I wrote to you previously, is a subdeacon, and he is not a bigamist, although since he became a subdeacon he kept two gentlewomen one after the other, but wife he never married, and cannot suffer death by judgment, and whoever will do the contrary, let him know that he will incur such a sentence that he must go to Rome to be absolved. Sir, again I pray you to have pity on the friars, for they were never so ill treated in Christendom as they are under your hands, albeit it is against your will, I believe. Besides this, sir, I do not believe that they have ever done anything against the king's crown. For to the crown belongs not only cruelty and rigour of justice, but even more, pity and mercy, through which Holy Church, by the king's will, saves evildoers, by sanctuary of the church, by orders, and by religious habit, as appears in the north country, where murderers after their crime take themselves off to the great abbeys of the Cistercians as lay brothers and are safe. Sir, God have you in his keeping.

7.4 Justices of the central courts: chief justice William Thorp (1350)

William Thorp's disgrace, coming only four years after the Ordinance of Justices, demonstrates Edward III's concern to stamp out corruption at the highest levels and his willingness to make an example of someone as exalted as his chief justice. The correspondence shows that the king placed great emphasis on the fact that Thorp had reneged on this oath. The appointment of magnates and representatives of the royal household to the commission together with confirmation of the judgment against Thorp made in the parliament of February–March 1351 further suggest that such a misdemeanour was viewed with extreme seriousness.[6] During the trial held in early November 1350, a week after his dismissal from office, Thorp confessed his guilt in the matter of receiving bribes amounting to £100 at king's bench sessions in Lincoln, but it is interesting that the king ordered the search of all the rolls relating to Thorp's activity as chief justice and his activity in other judicial capacities. Thorp deserves some credit for pleading guilty rather than raising technicalities or objections. Although he faced death at one point, he was eventually pardoned by the king 'in gratitude for his previous services'. Thorp was readmitted to the ranks of the judiciary a year later, though in a different department and (as second baron of the exchequer) in a less exalted position.[7]

(a)

Foedera, Conventiones, Literae et Cuiuscunque Generis Acta Publica, ed. T. Rymer, 4 vols in 7 (London, 1816–30), vol. 3, part 1, pp. 209–10 [Latin]

It is commanded to John Beauchamp that he have the body of William Thorp before the aforementioned justices [Richard, earl of Arundel,

---

6 Maddicott, *Law and Lordship*, pp. 48–51.

7 For full biography see R. W. Kaeuper, 'Thorp, Sir William (d. 1361)', *ODNB*.

Thomas Beauchamp, earl of Warwick, William Clinton, earl of Huntingdon, John Grey of Rotherfield, steward of the household and Bartholomew Burghersh, chamberlain] on the Thursday after All Saints [4 November 1350] at Westminster to answer the lord king concerning matters confessed earlier by him; at which day, before the aforementioned justices there, the said John Beauchamp led in the said William Thorp and in the presence of William the said writ and oath were read etc. The form of the oath follows in these words: [recital of 1346 judges' oath].[8]

And on this the same William having been charged on behalf of the lord king on the aforegoing matters, namely for the reason that he, against the aforesaid oath, by his authority, while he occupied the office of justice as it is said earlier, took £10 from Richard de Saltby, £20 from Hildebrand Bereswerd, £40 of Gilbert Haliland, £20 from Thomas Derby of St Bartholomew and £10 from Robert de Dalderby, who had been indicted for various felonies, deceits and trespasses before him in his sessions at Lincoln in 24 Edward III [1350]; and by process thereon carried out against them the royal writ of *exigent** etc. was adjudged and in hindrance of the suit and right of the lord king and against the form of his aforesaid oath, for the aforesaid money taken by the same William from the said Richard de Saltby and others separately as said above, he had that writ respited. And he said that he was not able to deny the matters imputed to him, rather he confessed and placed himself for this at the mercy of the lord king etc. So it is considered that the same William be committed to the prison of the Tower of London and that all his lands, tenements, goods and chattels be taken and seized into the hands of the lord king until the said king of his royal will and power has expressly made known his wishes on this.

Letters patent sent to the above commissioners (19 November 1350)

[1346 oath recited] And recently from a trustworthy report we have learned that William Thorp, knight, lately our chief justice, who took the said oath before us, the prelates, nobles and said magnates on the cross belonging to lord John, of happy memory, lately archbishop of Canterbury, and in the oath imposed such penalty that if he, against the form of the aforesaid oath, were delinquent in any way he would receive the judgment of drawing and be adjudged to be hanged and that whatsoever lands, tenements, goods and chattels he had would be forfeited to our possession; the said oath not carrying weight, nor the punishment

8 See 7.1.

it imposed on him, nor the great sum of money, nor the three robes, which were above and beyond his accustomed fee in the said office, after he took his said oath of us in this part, considering how many great sums of money he took in his aforesaid office, from various of our subjects, against the form of his said oath, for which we have caused the same William to be arrested and his body committed to our prison. And immediately afterwards, having taken considered counsel with you and with the many other magnates and leading men of our kingdom who are with us, it was agreed that if the same William were duly convicted of this malfeasance, he would suffer the aforesaid penalty.

William Thorp was summoned before the justices at Westminster on Friday before St Edmund, king [19 November 1350].

At which day the said William Thorp came before the aforesaid justices led by John Sawtry, deputy to John Darcy, keeper of the said Tower, and when the said letter patent had been read in the presence of the same William, and by virtue of the same royal writ, reciting and declaring the power and will of the king, it was decided by the said justices assigned to make judgment according to the will of the lord king and according to his royal power that because the said William Thorp, who, maliciously, falsely and rebelliously broke the oath of the lord king, which he is bound to keep to his people, as much as he could, and for the reasons abovesaid expressly acknowledged by the same William, as is said above, let him be hanged and that all his lands and tenements, goods and chattels remain forfeit to the lord king.

[Edward III pardoned William Thorp by letters patent warranted by the privy seal on 19 November 1350.]

(b)

RP, vol. 2, p. 227: confirmation of the judgment in parliament (1351) [French]

And let it be remembered that our lord the king summoned in full parliament the record and process of the judgment rendered against Sir William Thorp, his former chief justice, and caused them to be read publicly before the great men of parliament in order to know their advice. And after examining this each in turn, thus it seemed to them all that the record and process were lawfully and properly made and that the judgment rendered on this was reasonable since William had bound himself by oath to such a penalty if he acted contrary to it and he confessed that he had received gifts against his said oath. And on this it was agreed thereon by the great men of the same parliament that if any such case should occur henceforth concerning any such matter, our lord the king should summon before him those great men as may please him and by their good advice act on the same as pleases his royal lordship.

7.5 Judges of the central courts: demonstrations of public hostility

Grievances about justice stood at the heart of the rebels' aims in 1381.[9] The macabre and carnivalesque enactment described below in the first extract offers a very physical expression of attitudes towards the law. It shows an appreciation of the close relationship perceived to exist between landowners and royal judges and the playing out in reality of themes in the outlaw ballads.[10] Cavendish had long been retained by the abbey of Bury St Edmunds and both he and the prior had probably made enemies among the local inhabitants. His presence in the provinces rather than with the court of king's bench at the time can be accounted for by the fact that the Revolt occurred during the legal vacation when he was fulfilling his duties as a justice of assize in Suffolk.

The petition in the second extract is symptomatic of the debate on royal justice and retaining arising during these years[11] and a manifestation of the public concern and criticism of the way justice was administered. To allay doubts over judicial impartiality and to underline Richard II's commitment to justice the 1346 Ordinance of Justices was confirmed and issued as a statute in 1384.[12] By the 1390s the furore against the retaining of judges had died down and largely ceased to be a parliamentary issue, although the giving of badges of livery in general remained contentious into Henry IV's reign and beyond.

(a)

Memorials of Bury St Edmunds, ed. T. Arnold (RS, 1896), vol. 3, pp. 128–9 : murder of chief justice John Cavendish during the Peasants' Revolt (1381) [Latin]

On this pillory had been fixed on a lance the head of the chief justice of England, who had been beheaded the preceding night in the vill of Lakenheath, and who had been the most faithful friend of the aforesaid prior and abbey of St Edmund, and because of this, as was plausibly conjectured, he suffered the punishment of death. Therefore, playing with the heads they put the head of the prior to the head of the justice,

9 See Chapter 2.
10 See 2.5, 8.1 and 8.4.
11 See 4.8.
12 8 Richard II c. 3 (*SR*, vol. 2, p. 37).

now to the ear as if giving advice, now to his mouth as if showing friendship wishing through this charade to make mockery of the friendship and counsel which they had mutually between them in life. Afterwards, however, when they had grown tired of the peculiar sport they left the head of the prior on the pillory.

(b)

RP, vol. 3, p. 200: parliamentary calls for reform (1384) [French]

Also the commons pray that whereas there is great rumour and complaint that the common law has not been able to run its course as it ought to have for the reason that the judges of the one bench and the other and the barons of the exchequer are of the retinue of and receive fees from lords and others and as it is said take large gifts from parties bringing cases before them, both in their benches and other places where they are called for advice both between the king and a party and between party and party; may it please our lord the king to ordain by statute in this present parliament that none of his said justices nor barons, either by their own actions or through another in secret or publicly shall take robes, fees or pension, gift, or favour from anyone except solely from the king, unless it be food or drink and that of negligible value, on pain of such serious penalty to be set in this parliament that each of their estate shall be in fear of acting against or contravening it in the future.

The king wills it on pain of loss of office and also to pay fine and ransom to the king. And let this be done by statute.

7.6 Judges of the central courts: complaints against William Paston, justice, for maintenance and corruption

The complaints here made to the king in parliament indicate that judges were still being retained and the relationship between landowners and judges remained close. The allegations here are that Paston acted outside the accepted and legitimate bounds of professional behaviour contained in the justices' oath. It appears also that the special legal clothing denoting a serjeant-at-law, the coif (similar to a white skull-cap, but tied beneath the chin), was perceived to have symbolic significance: the wearer was a just and truthful man. William Paston's desire for land may have caused him to commit 'great mischief',[13]

---

13 For the implications of this phrase in legal terms see N. Doe, *Fundamental Authority in Later Medieval England* (Cambridge, Cambridge University Press, 1990), pp. 108–31, 155–74.

though he maintained somewhat self-righteously in a letter of 1426 (to certain monks of Bromholm) that he had not trespassed against Juliana Herbard. While it is unlikely that Herbard's allegations are entirely true given that the value of the land amounted to 30s, her relentless pursuit of Paston over the next forty years suggests that he had committed some indiscretion in his youth.[14] The reference to 'conscience and good faith' is an invocation of notions of equity and fairness. The edge of the original copy of the petition from Herbard is damaged and unreadable as denoted by square brackets.

PL, vol. 2, pp. 508–11 (nos 869 and 870) [English]

(a) Petition to parliament by William Dallying (c 1433)

May it please the commons of the present parliament to know that William Paston, one of the justices of our sovereign lord king, takes various fees and rewards from numerous people within the shires of Norfolk and Suffolk and is retained for every matter in the said counties, that is for to say, by the town of Yarmouth 50s yearly; by the abbot of St Benets [Holme] 26s 8d; by the prior of St Faiths 20s [and of my Lady Rothenhale 20s][15] and of the prior of Norwich 40s; and of the prior of Pentney 20s; and by the town of Lynn 40s; and by the prior of Walsingham 20s; and by Katherine Shelton 10 marks against the king to be of her counsel to destroy the right of the king and of his ward, that is to say Ralph, son and heir of John Shelton.

(b) Petition to Henry VI by Juliana Herbard (c 1426)[16]

To our very sovereign lord king and to his very gracious council

Your humble bedeswoman* Juliana Herbard, widow, of Norwich, daughter and heir to Henry Herbard and to Margaret his wife, sometime daughter of William Palmer of Little Plumstead, shows and beseeches meekly that whereas William Paston of Paston in the shire of Norfolk, a serjeant of law, and other certain persons of his affinity and consent have grievously and wrongfully disinherited and put out the same Juliana from her rightful inher[itance against] reason and law, good faith, and conscience; that is to say from a messuage* with nineteen acres of arable land, seven acres of heath, with the appurtenances, in Little Plumstead

---

14 C. Richmond, *The Paston Family in the Fifteenth Century: The First Phase* (Cambridge, Cambridge University Press, 1990), pp. 35–7.

15 Crossed out.

16 See TNA SC 8/169/8449, /169/8450.

in the shire of Norfolk aforesaid, and upon the same messuage and land and to the undoing of the same Juliana the damages to the same Juliana during the said years amount to £57 without her harms of strip and waste* and her costs for the value of the messuage and land yearly 30s and more, the which is withheld wrongfully from the same Juliana, as is shown by various evidences entailed to the same Juliana that the aforesaid William Paston wrongfully and untruly, against good faith and conscience, withholds from the same Juliana and as all the cont[…] it is more fully known by the schedule annexed to this bill of the said great wrongs done to the same beseecher. The which wrongfully withholding of her land amounts to the sum of £57 beforesaid, for the which sum and right of the land and messuage William Paston proffered to the foresaid Juliana 6 marks and the same Juliana judged by reason and conscience that it was too little and denied him his desire. And thereupon the same William Paston plotted and spoke ill against the same Juliana for to [...] and by false conspiracy suddenly sent the same Juliana to prison to one of the Counters* of London, and there kept her in prison fourteen nights or more, fettered by both feet, and threatened the same Juliana to keep her there all the days of her life [...] grant to receive the foresaid 6 marks for the sum and land with the messuage aforesaid, and thereto to make him a general release of the aforesaid land and messuage and acquittance general of all manner of actions.

And for fear of remaining in prison and [...] Juliana granted in prison to the same William Paston all his desire for the same sum, and after her said grant the same William Paston suddenly sent after the same Juliana between 9 and 10 of the clock in the night by a servant of the sheriff's ho[use ...] night constrained the same Juliana to enseal him a blank charter upon the which the same William Paston wrote with his own hands a general release of the sum and land beforesaid and an acquittance general of all manner of actions in excluding [...] was sealed in the night by the foresaid Juliana. Then the said William Paston suddenly the same night by the same servant sent her again to prison into the same Counter of London, and paid her not a penny nor parcel of money, nor money's worth of the sum [...] answer by eight weeks in the last parliament time, to her great hindering and everlasting undoing against God's law and the law of the land and against good faith and conscience without any rightful title, she being the king's true liege [...] king's liege man and a man sworn to do right and law as well to the poor as to the rich and in this he is untrue and truly renounced the oath he made to the king and his wise council, for the which oath the judges delivered him [...] a coif of truth with the appurtenances of clothing for a sign to be known for a just man before any other, the which coif with the appurtenances he has forfeited and is worthy to perjure himself in the court by your wise discretions [...] eschewing of more mischiefs coming by him and other maintainers of the same science now in the king's tender age, having consideration gracious lords, of the good governance and justice done and used in the king's ch[ancery ...] and made to be a judge and a governor of the said city and thereto sworn to do right to the king's liege people as well to the poor as to the rich, and thereupon as old usage and custom [...]furred at the cost of the king's chamber to be known before any other as for a judge of the city. And if by chance it happens that an alderman is found guilty and convicted before the mayor and his fellow judges of the said city in any [...]according thereto, that then the aforesaid mayor, by the advice of his fellows and of the recorder, shall judicially strip him of his dignity and take away his cloak and discharge him of his freedom in buying and selling within [...]to his great reproof and everlasting shame in example to all others.

Wherefore may it please your high regality and wise discretions to consider the mischiefs before rehearsed and to ordain due [...] extortioners that thus oppress, cause mischief to, and overburden the king's liege people in all shires throughout the realm. And also that it pleases your highness, in reverence of Our Lady, to grant to this said [...]Paston to appear before your noble presence and to examine him of these matters and causes before rehearsed, and also charging him to show the evidences whereby the mother of the said beseecher or any other [...]any other of the said messuage and land the which is entailed to the same Juliana; and so to ordain that the said beseecher may receive her evidences and to be admitted for to receive her said land [...] as reason, law, good faith and conscience asks, for the love of God and by way of charity.

7.7 Judges of the central courts: incorruptibility of royal judges

The picture afforded by Sir John Fortescue, chief justice of king's bench under Henry VI, confirms the ethical stance expected of royal judges, but his portrayal of a day in the life of a judge and their incorruptibility is an idealised one. It is unlikely that judges had quite the opportunity for contemplation and that their lives were so carefree. While it may act as a corrective to some of the views of royal judges, this should more realistically be read as a programme for reform.

Sir John Fortescue, *De Laudibus Leges Anglie*, ed. S. B. Chrimes (Cambridge, Cambridge University Press, 1942), ch. 51, p. 126 [Latin]

You must know, however, prince, that the justice among other things will swear that he will administer justice without favour to all men pleading before him, whether enemies or friends, and will not delay to do so even if the king should command him to the contrary by his letters or by word of mouth. Also he will swear that he will not receive from anyone besides the king any fee or pension or livery, nor take a gift from anyone having a plea before him apart from food and drink which are of no great price … I also wish you to know that the justices of England do not sit in the king's courts except for three hours a day, that is, from eight o'clock in the morning till eleven, because those courts are not held in the afternoon … Hence the justices after they have refreshed themselves, pass the whole of the rest of the day in studying laws, reading holy scripture, and otherwise in contemplation at their pleasure, so that their life seems more contemplative than active. Thus they lead a quiet life, free of all worry and worldly cares. Nor was it ever found that any of them was corrupted by gifts or bribes.

7.8 Court officials: the clerks of king's bench (1415)

The account of this scuffle in Westminster Hall in 1415 brings an air of human realism to the otherwise dry bureaucratic world of the central courts. The event presumably occurred while the king's bench was in recess and the clerks were copying up documents rather than during an actual session.

TNA KB 9/188 mm. 3, 3d [Latin]

Memorandum that Thomas Cowley, Hugh Holgot, William Waldeby, Thomas Beston, Thomas Crowe, John Winchecombe, John Solos, John Dabernon, Robert Hore, Thomas Whatton, John Corve, Henry Chorley, Thomas Waldeby, Thomas Greswold, Simon Welles, clerks of king's bench, having been charged and sworn by the justices of the same bench to inform them of the truth concerning a dispute and uprising between Thomas Thwaytes of Holborn in the suburbs of London, one of the clerks of the said bench and William Felton of Holborn one of the clerks of Thomas Cowley said on their oath that as the said Thomas and William were sitting and writing in the said bench at Westminster on the Saturday next before the feast of St Martin in the third year of the reign of Henry V [9 November 1415] the same William spoke to the same Thomas asking him to hand over a certain document to a certain third party outside the bar behind the back of the same Thomas which certain document he handed to the same Thomas, who refused to do this, upon which the same William threw the document towards the said third party and in throwing that document it landed under the table of the same bench near to where the said Thomas was sitting. And the said William got up from the seat he was occupying and went to the place where the document lay and tried to pick up the same and as he was not able to reach it with his hand he took from John Snellard, usher of the same bench, the shaft of a certain arrow which he was accustomed to carry for estimating length and then went with it to the said place bending down to retrieve the document. And as he was bending down there Thomas placed his hands on the neck of the same William reaching below him pushing him down further. And when the same William got up from the same place he struck Thomas on his bare head with the arrow shaft. And the same Thomas angered by this said, 'Why, I ask you, have you behaved in this way?' And on this the same William said that if he was angry when he had done this, then he was more so and immediately struck the same Thomas on the bare head again with the said shaft with force and arms against the peace. At which Thomas snatching the shaft from the hands of the same William broke it and threw it outside the bar. And the same William having witnessed this said that if he could meet the said Thomas outside the aforesaid bench he would fight him over this. And the same Thomas replied to him that he would meet him in whatever place he wished.

7.9 Justices of the peace: the oath of the justices (1390)

The oath set out below bears a striking similarity to the one contained in the Ordinance of Justices of 1346 and was presumably modelled on this. Indeed there was a specific request made to parliament in 1346 that the oath of the justices of the peace be the same as that recently ordained. The example below was appended to the returns made to chancery for administering the oath and is the form as used in 1390, which itself bears a similarity to the earliest recorded form of the oath (employed in 1351).

PJP, p. 8 [French]

You will swear that you will serve the king and his people well and loyally as a justice of the peace according to the effect and form of the commission issued to you and your other colleagues;[17] and conceal the counsel of the king; and will do right as far as you are able to all, both to the poor and to the rich; and that you will take no gift from anyone to do wrong or delay justice; and that neither for the great nor for the rich,

17 See 4.11.

nor for hatred, nor for the estate of any person, nor for benefit, gift or
promise of anyone made to you or that could be made to you, either by
art or by design, interfere with or postpone justice contrary to reason
and contrary to the laws of the land; but without regard for anyone's
estate or person you will loyally do right and justice to all according to
the aforesaid laws. So help you God and his saints.

7.10 Justices of the peace: the hazards of office (1336)

Whittlebury was a justice of the peace and an MP for Rutland. Whatever
the circumstances of this dispute with Harington or the nature of the threats
made to him, he clearly believed that a just outcome could be achieved and had
faith enough in the legal system or at least its power to achieve settlement by
threat of proceedings. Unfortunately help arrived too late: Whittlebury had
already been stabbed and clubbed to death by Richard de Harington and Robert
Crowe, the very people he feared.[18] While it should be remembered that the
text of the petition forming the basis of or justifying a commission of oyer and
terminer contained merely the allegations of one party and should not necessarily be taken at face value, Whittlebury's death before he could achieve justice
equally indicates that not all the claims made in petitions were exaggerated
and formulaic.[19]

TNA SC 8/205/10202 [French]

To our lord the king and to his council here John de Whittlebury,
keeper of the peace in the county of Rutland, shows and complains
that whereas Sir John de Harington, Richard, William and Walter his
brothers, John le Warner, brother of the vicar of Whissendine, Baldwin
de Harington, Roger Ibbe, Roger Whiteknave, William his son, Thomas
Toppe Leyne, Robert Crowe, William, servant of John de Harington,
Andrew Godesson and Walter de Ashwell of Whissendine together
with other malefactors unknown through the maintenance of Sir John
de Harington and his brothers are accustomed to beat, trample and
wrong the people of Whissendine daily. And nightly are at the tavern
and then go with all their unruly crowd around the vill of Whissendine
and break the doors and windows of the good people of the vill and beat
the good men and women in their own dwellings against the peace so
that no man of the vill is so bold as to carry out the watches in order
to maintain the peace as is commanded by our lord the king under the
Statute of Winchester [1285].

18 *Calendar of Inquisitions Miscellaneous, 1307–49*, p. 370.
19 See 4.6.

So my colleague and I have twice been to Whissendine and Oakham in order to maintain the peace to inquire upon the complaints that we have heard committed against the peace; the said Sir John de Harington and Richard his brother have come with force and arms with all their unruly crowd against the peace before us, and have so threatened to beat and trample the juries that no man either dares to appear before us or indict them, and us they have openly threatened of life and limb.

And because before now my colleague and I have sued complaints by petition in parliament concerning these same matters and others and no remedy has been made, so are we in great danger because Sir John de Harington came to Whissendine by force and arms against the peace with these above named people and other evildoers unknown of his unruly crowd and to the manor of the said John de Whittlebury the Tuesday next before the feast of the Holy Trinity last past [21 May 1336] when the said John de Whittlebury was asleep and in front of his gates assaulted and beat Thomas de Whittlebury his son, William Dyot and John de Sherington servants of the said John de Whittlebury so they were in peril of death and threatened to kill the said John de Whittlebury and ever since they have expected it daily. So he prays remedy to our lord the king and his good council that they will send by commission two serjeants at arms of the king's household to arrest the said Sir John de Harington and the others named in this petition wherever they may be found for no man of Rutland dare either to indict or arrest them and to send them to the Tower of London because the sheriff of Rutland dares not hold them.

7.11 Legal officials: the form of the sheriff's oath (1460)

The oath of office here (as administered to John Scott, sheriff of Kent, 8 September 1460) includes clauses relating to treating rich and poor equally and not accepting bribes, which had been at the heart of the oath since the ordinance of sheriffs of 1258.[20] It also restrains the holder from interfering with a person's right. It was in the area of administering writs and empanelling juries that there was the most scope for confusion and corruption. The employment of good and proper subordinates was essential to the operation of the bailiwick and the onus was on the holder to ensure they were appropriate people for the job and duly sworn. In common with JPs and other local officials the sheriff was required to aid the ecclesiastical courts in the investigation and suppression of heresies.

20 *Documents of the Baronial Movement for Reform, 1258–1267*, ed. R. F. Treharne and I. J. Sanders (Oxford, Clarendon Press, 1973), pp. 120–21.

Literae Cantuarienses, ed. J. B. Sheppard, 3 vols (RS, 1887–89), vol. 3, pp. 235–7
[English]

You shall serve the king well and truly in the office of the sheriff of
Kent and to the king's profit in everything that your office requires you
to do as completely as you can or may. You shall truly keep the king's
rights and all that pertains to the crown. You shall not assent to the
decrease, lessening or concealment of the king's rights or of his franchises and wherever you shall have information that the king's rights or
the rights of the crown are concealed or withdrawn, be it in lands, rents,
franchises, or suits or any other things, you shall do your best to restore
them to the king; and if you cannot do it, you shall certify the king or
someone of his council concerning the matter, such persons as you trust
will pass it on to the king. You shall not respite the king's debts for
any gift or favour wherever you may raise them without great grievance to the debtors. You shall truly and justly treat the people of your
shrievalty and do right equally to the poor as to the rich in that which
your office requires. You shall not wrong a man in return for any gift
or bribe or promise of wealth, nor for favour, nor out of hate. You shall
not disturb any man's right. You shall truly acquit at the exchequer all
those from whom you receive anything in the way of the king's debts.
You shall take nothing through which the king may lose or on account
of which right may be disturbed, hindered, or the king's debts delayed.
You shall truly return and truly serve all the king's writs as completely
as you can. You shall not have as your undersheriff or as any of your
sheriff's clerks those who have served as such during the previous year.
You shall not take any bailiff into your service except those that you
are prepared to answer for. You shall make each one of your bailiffs take
an oath such as the one you take yourself in everything that pertains to
their employment. You shall not accept any writ for you or for any of
your staff unsealed under the seal of any justice except for justices in
eyre, or assize justices in the same shire that you are sheriff or justices
of Newgate. You shall appoint your bailiffs from the true and sufficient
men of the county. Also you shall take great pains and diligence to
destroy and cause to cease all manner of heresies and errors commonly
called heresies within your bailiwick from time to time, or whenever
you are required to by the said ordinaries and commissaries, to the
extent of your power and assist and aid all ordinaries and commissaries of holy church and favour and maintain them. You shall dwell
in your own right proper person within your bailiwick during your
period of office. You shall not let out your shrievalty or any bailiwick
for any man to farm. You shall truly set and return reasonable and

due issues from those that are within your bailiwick according to their estate or behaviour and appoint your jury panels yourself. And above all in eschewing and restraint of manslaughters, robberies and other many serious offences that are committed daily, namely by such as call themselves soldiers and by other vagrants, which continually increase in number and multitude so the king's true subjects may not safely ride or go to do such things as they have to do to their intolerable hurt and hindrance. You shall truly and adequately with all possible diligence execute the statutes which you know of. All these things you shall truly keep as God help you and his saints.

7.12 Legal officials: abuse of the office of sheriff (1418)

John Thornton's position as undersheriff gave him easy access to the juries empanelled for indictments and trial proceedings. His chicanery was exposed when after interrogation he eventually confessed in the court of king's bench in 1418 that he had secured the outlawry of Thomas Clare through a forged indictment on behalf of his master, Sir Thomas Green, who was sheriff of Northamptonshire in 1416–17 and engaged at that time in a dispute with Clare over estates in Oxfordshire. The account offers a valuable insight into the process by which indictments could be procured and show how verbal assurances and the social and official status of both accuser and accused could be crucial. Here there seems to have been a reluctance on the part of the jurors to indict a 'gentleman' for theft, but no hesitation when as a result of a deception the same man was incorrectly styled as a 'husbandman'. The passage also indicates that influence and access as opposed to objective reporting could play a part in criminal prosecution.[21]

TNA KB 27/629 m. 9d [Latin]

This is the confession of John Thornton, sometime servant of Sir Thomas Green, sworn and examined before the justices of the king's bench upon an indictment and outlawry of felony wrought against Thomas Clare of Lillingstone Dansy in the county of Oxford, gentleman. First the aforesaid John acknowledges that the aforesaid Thomas Clare arraigned an assize of novel disseisin* against Sir Thomas Green and others for lands and tenements in the abovesaid Lillingstone, the which action was put in the arbitrament of Ralph Green and John Barton the younger chosen for Sir Thomas Green and others, and of John Wilcotes and John Langston chosen for Thomas Clare, the loveday to be held at Buckingham. And there these arbitrators could not accord and in riding homewards there came a yeoman called John Wadupp to the aforesaid Sir Thomas Green and said: 'Sir, we may only be in rest,[22] for this Clare I shall prove him a thief, for I found two oxen in the forest and he took them out by night.' And Sir Thomas said again he should be indicted of felony therefore, and sent for the abovesaid John Thornton and charged him to labour this indictment to delay Clare from action. And the aforesaid John made his clerk fashion a bill against a session that was held at Rothwell in the following form: 'Be it inquired for the king if Thomas Clare of Lillingstone Dansy in the county of Oxford, gentleman, day and year and place, feloniously stole two oxen belonging to John Wadupp', the which day, year and place is contained in the process of this indictment sent in before the justices abovesaid. And because he was called 'gentleman' the inquest would not affirm it, and so there was nothing to do there at that day.[23]

And the aforesaid John acknowledges that on another day there was a session arranged at Wellingborough and there he made his clerk draw up another bill with the name of Thomas Clare 'husbandman' and took it to the inquest saying: 'Sirs affirm this for I know it is true and my master will give good thanks to you to affirm it and he will say to you that it is true when he speaks next with you.' And so at his instance they indicted Thomas Clare 'husbandman' and delivered the bill to the justices of the peace, and they took it to their clerk and the aforesaid John acknowledges that he sat by the clerk of the peace, he at that time being undersheriff, and took the bill and made his clerk remove 'husbandman' and put in 'gentleman'. And thus came out two writs of *capias** and an *exigent** against Thomas Clare 'gentleman', the which *exigent* was announced at three shires[24] and at the fourth shire many people were expected to come to choose knights of the shire for the parliament. And so he caused his clerk to call that *exigent* much earlier and to his knowledge there was only one coroner if there were even any, for he says by his oath that he is well advised that he entered with two coroners while the clerk was calling the *exigents* and one of the coroners that he came in with blamed the clerk for calling the *exigents* before any of those that should record the court had come in. And the aforesaid John said by his oath that neither the justices of the peace nor the coroners nor the inquest nor any of them knew that this matter was brought about out of malice, nor to his knowledge that it was carried through in deceit.

22 i.e. temporarily adjourned
23 Hearing or session.
24 County courts; see 5.6.

7.13 Legal officials: the sheriff's influence (1449)

This letter of October 1449 to John Paston from James Gresham, written in haste and so not elaborating fully, offers tantalising glimpses of the sheriff's world and the influence he could wield through exercise of his position.

PL, vol. 2, pp. 33–4 (no. 447) [English]

After all due recommendation it may please you to know that the king is now in the marches of Wales, so it is said, with the intention that he may be near the area if my lord of Buckingham, who is commissioner now in Wales for various offences done there to the crown, would sue to have his commission enlarged if he were discontented etc. And men cannot say what time the king shall return to London again, save men judge that he will be here at the beginning of the parliament.

I have your writs of error* already sealed, but I cannot acknowledge any error therein; but still they shall serve for a preliminary draft.

Thomas Denys asked me why you did not observe the scheme that he urged on you for removing the strength at Gresham etc.; he would it should yet be done.

It seems that Francis Costard is not yet in support, for his *venire facias** between William Prentys and Francis Costard, complainants, and Henry Halman comes in now served a fortnight from St Michael [13 October] in the worst possible way, as you shall learn when you look on the panel which I send you with this.

It seems it were well you should hurry here to lobby the sheriff that shall be this next year, for as you know well, much of a man's desire that is in trouble lies in the sheriff's favour and especially in our shire; for I myself fear that all others that are your adversaries will be before you, which God defend.

I sent you a little bill which was written at Babraham [Cambs.]. Whether you have it or not I know not; nevertheless it is not of any great substance.

No more, but Almighty God send you all the good speed as you would desire, amen. Written in haste at London the sixteenth day of October.

Your humble servant James Gresham.

7.14 Legal officials: the coroner

As keeper of the crown pleas, the coroner's records were vital to his function. They were rolls 'of record' and hundred jurors making presentments could be amerced* if the justices found differences between their statement and the rolls. Moreover, if the roll did not support an event it was assumed or deemed not to have occurred. Thus the roll itself and the details it contained could be prized enough for unscrupulous men to wish to alter or destroy the record. The behaviour in the first example clearly obstructed the work of such busy officials. The deliberate hindering of the coroner's duties by preventing the holding of an inquest (as in 1336) was another nuisance and one that occurs with some regularity in the legal records, particularly in relation to the behaviour of lords of liberties and officials.[25]

(a)

The Records of the City of Norwich, ed. W. Hudson and J. C. Tingey (2 vols; Norwich, 1906–10), vol. 1, pp. 205–6 [Latin]

Memorandum that Henry Turnecurt and Stephen de Balsham were killed in Norwich in the parish of St George before the gate of the cathedral church of the Holy Trinity on the feast day of the apostles St Philip and St James [1 May 1264]. The coroners and bailiffs came forward and made an inquest. Once the inquest had been held and written up on the schedule there came Master Mark de Brunhale, clerk and Ralph Knight with many others threatening the said coroners that they would cut them into little pieces unless they handed over the said schedule. And afterwards they took Roger the coroner and led him to his house nearby by force with swords and staves until the same Roger took the schedule out of his chest. And they took the said Roger with the aforementioned schedule to the church of St Peter Mancroft and there the said Ralph took and carried off the said schedule by force from the hands of the said Roger and before his companions a number of foolish people cut it into small pieces. And the same Roger with great fear and trembling scarcely escaped from their hands.

(b)

TNA JUST 1/390 m. 3 [Latin]

The grand jury of the county of Kent present that … when Thomas son of John at Boure was killed by John Kest of Powenden at Newenden

25 See also 3.3.

in a place called Losenham in the hundred of Selbrittenden a certain William Colet, then borsholder* in the same hundred, when John Priket, coroner, had come there to view the body to exercise his office, the said borsholder maliciously hid the body of the said Thomas, who had been killed in a certain house, so that the coroner was not able to view the body until neighbours of the borsholder then broke into the said house, and thus he impeded the office of coroner in contempt of the king.

7.15 Legal officials: local peacekeeping

Much of the routine work of peacekeeping devolved upon lesser officials at the level of the hundred and the town or village. Their peacekeeping duties are sometimes explicitly mentioned in the records as exemplified in two of the extracts below. Although the local posse in pursuit of a suspected offender sometimes dispatched him themselves, by the fourteenth century the exercise of summary justice even on outlaws and thieves caught in the act was frowned upon by the courts and required the perpetrators to explain and exonerate themselves. In the example from Lincolnshire, the local constables refused to behead a supposed thief as they maintained it was not the usual custom to behead anyone restrained or under arrest without first taking him before the sheriff. They also clearly undertook elementary detection. It is significant that Ellis Martel and his servants carried the body to the 'gallows tree pits' as part of their attempt to justify the murder. The additional responsibilities arising under the Statute of Labourers of 1351, namely the taking of oaths of recalcitrant labourers and reporting offenders to the justices, caused problems for the local officials deputed to carry out these tasks.[26]

(a) Commissions to keepers of the peace for hundreds in Essex (1321)

TNA C 66/155 m. 7d [French]

The king to his faithful and loyal James Lambourne and Edmund Baddow greeting. As many malefactors and disturbers of our peace come, stay and go daily in the hundred of Chelmsford also ambushing, lying in wait and committing divers homicides, arsons of houses, robberies, felonies and false undertakings and alliances against us and the estate of our crown, maltreating people and doing other wrongs in which our peace is greatly infringed and troubled in many ways and our people in serious disorder and danger, we are much vexed. We to ensure our peace and the safety of you and of the commonalty of the said hundred wishing to give aid and suitable remedy in this region aforesaid assign you and each

26 L. Poos, 'The social context of the Statute of Labourers enforcement', *LHR*, 1 (1983), 27–52.

of you to guard and keep the aforesaid hundred and to arrest and, by the power and strength of the men of the said hundred who are chosen by you for this, take all those who by reason of the alliances and suspicious companies are to be found in your parts coming, going or staying, armed or unarmed, on foot and by horse, secretly or publicly, by day or night, and also all felons, robbers, murderers, fomenters of false disputes and maintainers of men and all other malefactors and disturbers of our peace; such men shall have power to arrest notorious suspects and bring them to our prison of Colchester Castle and deliver them to our sheriff of Essex or through his deputy and keep them in our said prison until we have given further command on this matter ...

And we desire that for this guarding and so as to do it more securely you cause to take for your expenses, and the expenses of those who have been chosen by you to do this, a levy from all those who have lands and tenements in the town of the said hundred, including those within the liberty [of Colchester], in the most suitable and least onerous manner that you can ...

And we commend to you those we have assigned chief keepers of our peace throughout the said county of Essex.

(b) The duties of village constables (1295)

TNA JUST 3/95 m. 6 [Latin]

The tithing-men of the vill and the constables of the peace of the king, rightly and by authority of their office and according to the law and custom of the realm ... have jurisdiction and power to attach malefactors and disturbers of the peace and those who are pursued by the hue and cry for felony and homicide.

(c) The exercise of summary justice in Lincolnshire (1319)

TNA KB 27/235 m. 98 (Hilary) [Latin]

The jurors of the vills of Canwick, Bracebridge, Washingborough, Branston and Mere [Lincs.] present before Thomas Makerel, coroner of the lord king, that on the Monday next before the feast of St Margaret the Virgin in the twelfth year of the reign of King Edward II [10 July 1318] at Canwick in the house of Ellis Martel a dispute arose between the said Ellis and a certain Thomas Leure of Kirby of Leicestershire, his servant, after sunset on this matter: when the same Thomas demanded his wages from the said Ellis for the time he remained with him in his service, the same Ellis refused to pay him any wages, saying that the same Thomas had not yet completed his time or his contract. And so, after insulting words of this sort had continued between them right into the night in the same house, with a candle burning there and the doors shut, the same Ellis, assembling before him Walter of Blankney, his carter, and William of Kelby of Leicestershire, his groom, drew out a certain falchion* and said that he would pay him everything owed. And so in a premeditated assault he feloniously struck the aforesaid Thomas in the chest near the right nipple with the said falchion. When the said Ellis ordered Walter and William to do the same to him, Walter feloniously struck him on the head with a certain pole-axe. And the said William feloniously struck him in the back with a long knife. And the aforesaid Ellis, Walter and William gave him no fewer than nine mortal wounds. After committing these acts, the aforesaid Ellis and the others in the aforesaid house tied the aforesaid Thomas' hands with a certain rope. And immediately the same Ellis, fearing the scandal arising from the deed, instructed a certain William the Carpenter of Canwick and Adam son of Richard del Hill, the constables of the aforesaid vill, and Martin Swayneson of the same vill to come to him. They came and finding the said Thomas in this state bound, wounded and with blood gushing out, the same Ellis and the others, to justify their deed, maliciously asserted that Thomas had wanted to steal a certain white mare of theirs and on that account they had apprehended him and tied him up.

And after that the said Ellis directed the aforesaid constables and Martin to take Thomas, thus bound, outside the vill and there behead him. They responded that in no way could they do this, saying that it was not the custom in the county of Lincoln to behead anyone restrained or for whatever reason arrested, 'rather it is the custom to take a prisoner of this kind to Lincoln and to present him to the sheriff with the stolen goods, from which it follows that, if restrained in this way he were handed over with the mare, assuming he had been arrested while stealing it, we would willingly receive him and tomorrow morning at Lincoln would hand him over to the sheriff of Lincoln with the said mare as his stolen goods, so that he could deal with him according to the usual custom here'.

The same Ellis absolutely refused to do this, saying that he did not want to lose or abandon his mare. The aforesaid constables and Martin went away together. And immediately afterwards, around midnight the aforesaid Ellis, Walter and William, seeing that the aforesaid Thomas was seemingly dying from the aforesaid wounds and almost dead, took him and carried him in turn as far as a field in Bracebridge in a certain place called *Galgtrepittes*,[27] their journey from the said Ellis' house, both on the road and on the growing grass, brought to light by the blood gushing profusely from the body's aforesaid wounds. And they conveyed him to the aforesaid place. Then, dead already and his hands still tied, Ellis there beheaded him with the aforesaid falchion. This severed head they carried with them to the vill of Canwick and when morning came handed it to the aforesaid constables with threats and intimidation so it could be taken to Lincoln. Through fear of the aforesaid Ellis, they took the head and, carrying it to Lincoln, presented it to the sheriff. And once they had been examined thereupon, the aforesaid constables fully admitted the aforesaid deed before the said sheriff and that they did not know where the body of this decapitated man was and how it had happened at night without their knowledge and without the hue and cry being raised and how the head was handed to them by the said Ellis and the others, who had beheaded him when tied up. It seemed to the sheriff according to their report that in this case these men had no cause to behead him, especially as they kept him tied up and he had not taken flight on account of theft or felony. He did not accept the presentment of this beheading. The aforesaid constables immediately went away and carried the aforesaid head back to Ellis' house where they had previously received it and left it there. Afterwards the aforesaid head was restored to the body in the aforesaid place by the said Ellis and the others. As to this the jurors say that no others are under suspicion thereupon.

(d) The duty to enforce the Statute of Labourers (1378)

Essex Sessions of the Peace, 1351, 1377–79, ed. E. C. Furber, Essex Archaeological Society, 3 (1953), pp. 169–71 [Latin]

Presentments of the hundred of Dunmowe taken there the day and year abovesaid [2 August 1378] on the oath of John Richmond of Thaxted, Nicholas Richmond, John Bieng, John Seerle, John Hert, William Michel, William Davy, John Lacy, William atte Fanne, Henry Folville and Richard Arnold who said on their oath that no constable of the hundred of Dunmowe has done his duty of making labourers swear to serve and take wages according to the statute.

Also, they present that Henry Duthe of Pleshey is a common fighter and rebel against constables.

27 Probably 'gallows tree pits'.

Also, they present that John son of Laurence Whelere of Shelewe [Shellow Bowells], wheelwright takes 7s for a pair of wheels against the statute and also they are substandard.

Also, they present that John Love of High Easter is a common[28] reaper and moves from place to place to obtain excessive wages and encourages others to do the same against the statute.

Also, they present that William servant of Stephen Pousin labourer refused to serve for 40s per annum.

Also, they present that John Cole of High Roding cobbler sells for excess payment and moreover is a rebel.

7.16 Legal officials: gaolers

The responsibility of the gaoler for the prisoners within his purview was an unenviable one given the dilapidated state of many medieval gaols. Inmates escaped from prison on what seems to have been a fairly regular basis judging by the inquiries launched at gaol delivery sessions or indictments for the felony of prison breach. If they reached 'sanctuary' (which might mean the high altar of a church or within the jurisdictional boundaries of designated religious foundations) they could not be harmed and had a period of forty days' respite during which time they could confess to the coroner and abjure the realm.* The descriptions of escapes offer an insight not just into the daring exploits of prisoners, but also an indication of their disposition, the methods of restraining them, how gaols were laid out and how they were run. In spite of legislation gaolers probably received money from the prisoners in their charge and, as in the case of William Fynborough, the marshal of the king's bench Marshalsea, were even willing to contract out their duties to a deputy.

(a) An attempted rescue from the court of king's bench (1413)

TNA KB 27/609 *Rex* m. 16 (Trinity) [Latin]

John Swan, deputy of John Preston, marshal of the Marshalsea of the lord king before the same king presents that, whereas Henry Buckley of Blankney, who was appealed at the suit of Juliana, that was the wife of Nicholas Letters of Boothby, for the death of the same Nicholas, formerly husband of the same Juliana, by writ of the lord king in the county of Lincoln, and for that reason on the Tuesday next after the octave of St John the Baptist in the first year of the reign of King Henry V [4 July 1413], by command of the lord king in open court in the great

---

28 i.e. 'self-employed'

hall of pleas of the lord king then held at Westminster was entrusted to the custody of the same deputy to be guarded safely. And the same Henry being thus in custody at that time at the lower bar where there are prisoners chained up, John Shaw of the county of Lincoln came threateningly with nine men armed with swords and bucklers and daggers, saying to the same deputy, 'You sir, who made you so bold as to have this prisoner away from the upper bar', and with that he struck him on his chest. And Swan immediately replied to the same John Shaw that he acted by order of the court. And Shaw next said to the same deputy that he wanted to have the said Henry from him 'in spite of his teeth',[29] threatening the same deputy then and there of life and limb. And immediately he dragged the same Henry from the hands and possession of the same deputy the distance of the same lower bar, and he would have led the same Henry all the way to the sanctuary of Westminster if he had not been quickly obstructed by the bystanders, and this as a result of the hue and cry raised then and there by officials and servants etc. of the said marshal. And by order of William Hankford, knight, chief justice of the lord king hearing this, immediately the said John Shaw was taken hold of and arrested and brought to the bar in front of the lord king.[30]

(b) A mass breakout from the Marshalsea prison of king's bench (1422)

Year Books of Henry VI: 1 Henry VI AD 1422, ed. C. H Williams, SS, 50 (London, 1933), p. 73 [Latin]

A jury of divers hundreds ... presented that whereas a certain John Payntor and Thomas of Exeter and other felons of the lord king had been indicted for various felonies and seditions and were placed for safe keeping in the prison of the Marshalsea of the bench of the late king at Southwark before the same king, to be kept in safe custody in the same, however, a certain William Taillour of *Sureston*[31] in the county of Buckingham, tailor, scheming to release the aforesaid felons from the aforesaid prison, on the eighteenth day of March in the ninth year of the reign of King Henry V [1422], at the vill of Westminster feloniously caused to be made and caused to be delivered to the aforesaid felons certain instruments, namely knives, files, hatchets and various

---

29 An idiomatic expression Sayles translates as 'whether he liked it or not' (*SCCKB*, vol. 7, p. 216).

30 i.e. before the justices of the king's bench

31 This may be a misreading for Turweston.

other instruments for breaking the stocks, chains and other bonds in which the aforesaid felons were detained and restrained. And with these same instruments the aforesaid felons released themselves and later broke the aforesaid prison and absconded from there on the said day and year. And the said William Taillour at midnight then next following received the aforesaid felons at the Stews, knowing them to have broken the aforesaid prison in the form aforesaid and he feloniously brought them across from there to Bridewell, London, in boats and from there feloniously led them to sanctuary at Westminster.

(c) Receipt of money for prisoners (1330)

Statute 4 Edward III c. 10 (SR, vol. 1, p. 264) [French]

Also, whereas in times past sheriffs and keepers of gaols would not receive thieves, persons appealed, indicted or found with the mainour,* taken and attached by the constables and vills without taking from them grievous fines and ransoms for their reception, by which the said constables and vills have been less inclined to take thieves and felons because of such outrageous charges, and the thieves and the felons are the more encouraged to offend; it is agreed that from henceforth the sheriffs and gaolers shall receive and keep safely in prison such thieves and felons handed over by the said constables and vills without taking anything for their reception; and that the justices assigned to deliver gaols shall have power to hear those who wish to complain about the sheriff and gaolers in such cases, and also to punish sheriffs and gaolers if they are found culpable.

(d) Contracting out the gaoler's duties (1409)

TNA KB 27/614 m. 34d [Latin]

William Kingsmill lately of London, scrivener, was attached to respond to William Fynborough lately marshal of the Marshalsea of the bench of lord Henry lately king of England, father of lord Henry V, the present king of England, concerning a plea of trespass by bill ... And the same William Fynborough in person before the present king complains that since the same William Kingsmill on Saturday on the eve of Pentecost in the tenth year of the reign of the said late king [25 May 1409] had undertaken to guard all prisoners of the aforesaid Marshalsea prison who at that time were under the safe custody of the same William Fynborough and entrusted to the same William Kingsmill by the aforesaid William Fynborough and had undertaken to keep them safe and secure at the vill of Westminster from the said eve of Pentecost for a full two years then following and whereas the same William Fynborough when various prisoners had been entrusted to his custody had among them a certain prisoner to be guarded securely by consideration of the court of the bench of the said late king, the same William Fynborough the said day and year there delivered and entrusted to the aforesaid William Kingsmill, then his deputy of the said Marshalsea prison, a certain prisoner to be guarded safely, namely John Scult of Germany, concerning £40, which Thomas Stindle lately attorney of the said late king before the same late king at Westminster recovered against the same John through a certain bill of debt, and £35 6s 8d, which Henry Pountfreyt a citizen of London recovered against the same John, under the name of John Scult, Easterling,* through a plea of debt before Geoffrey Brook lately one of the sheriffs of the city of London in the court of the said late king in the same city, and £7, which Thomas Mortimer citizen and alderman of London recovered against the same John, under the name of John Scult merchant of Germany, in a plea of debt in the said court of the late king before the said Geoffrey lately one of the sheriffs of London, and £7 3s 4d, which Richard Taillour citizen and esquire of London recovered against the same John, under the name of John Anneys Scult, Easterling of Germany, in the court aforesaid of the said late king before the aforesaid Geoffrey lately one of the sheriffs of London, and £41, which William Lowe citizen and fishmonger of London recovered against the same John, under the name of John Scult, Easterling of Germany, in a plea of debt in the said court aforesaid of the said late king before the same Geoffrey lately one of the sheriffs of London, and also £13 5s which Thomas Cowley of Oxford recovered against the same John in a plea of debt in the said court aforesaid of the said late king before the aforesaid Geoffrey lately one of the sheriffs of London. The said William Kingsmill on the twelfth day of July in the tenth year of the reign of the said late king [1409] permitted the said John Scult to go at large outside the aforesaid Marshalsea prison and escape to the vill of Westminster as a result of which the same William Fynborough said that he has suffered loss and has damages to the value of £200.

VIII: CORRUPTION AND ABUSE

The smooth and successful operation of the judicial system was challenged and sometimes hindered by the existence of corrupt practices and abuse of its procedures. Concerns about the inadequacies of the law and problems in the workings of justice are surprisingly well articulated in examples of the imaginative literature of the period and appear to offer an indictment of the whole system.[1] We should, however, distinguish between that which was merely satirising the law and those pieces actually challenging, rather than rejoicing in, the status quo.[2] Of the texts included here the early fourteenth-century *An Outlaw's Song of Trailbaston* and the early fifteenth-century *A London Lickpenny* offer a satirical picture of the law in operation, while other works such as Langland's *Piers Plowman* (from the second half of the fourteenth century) express worries about the legal system in a more far-reaching, polemical fashion.[3]

As with all texts, official or unofficial, we must be careful not to take them literally or entirely at face value and be alive to the rhetoric and conventions of the genre. We should also be conscious of the social and literary context in which they arose and the interpretative structures affecting their production.[4] That there is more than a grain of truth, however, in the attitudes displayed in some of the portraits is borne out by the evidence of cases of corruption, conspiracy and abuse of process coming before the courts. Moreover, some of the literary sketches are rooted in a distinct historical and cultural context.[5] The prime focus and apparent motivation for writing *An Outlaw's Song* is the Ordinance of Trailbaston of 1305 and the set of general oyer and terminer commissions issued in its wake.[6] The poem has therefore a specific historical location, and

---

1 A. P. Baldwin, *The Theme of Government in Piers Plowman* (Cambridge, D. S. Brewer, 1981); R. W. Kaeuper, 'An historian's reading of *The tale of Gamelyn*', *Medium Aevum*, 52 (1983), 51–62; J. R. Maddicott, 'Poems of social protest in early fourteenth-century England', in *England in the Fourteenth Century*, ed. W. M. Ormrod (Woodbridge, Boydell, 1986), pp. 130–44; A. J. Pollard, 'Idealising criminality: Robin Hood in the fifteenth century', in *Pragmatic Utopias: Ideals and Communities, 1200–1630*, ed. R. Horrox and S. Rees Jones (Cambridge, Cambridge University Press, 2001), pp. 156–73.

2 P. Coss, 'Aspects of cultural diffusion in medieval England', *P&P*, 108 (1985), 35–79; Musson and Ormrod, *Evolution*, pp. 166–75.

3 See also the examples from literary texts in Chapter 2 (at 2.5).

4 S. Rigby, *Chaucer in Context* (Manchester, Manchester University Press, 1996); P. Strohm, *Hochon's Arrow: The Social Imagination of Fourteenth Century Texts* (Princeton, NJ, Princeton University Press, 1992).

5 J. Coleman, *English Literature in History* (London, Hutchinson, 1981); J. Taylor, *English Literature in the Fourteenth Century* (Oxford, Clarendon Press, 1987).

6 See Chapter 4 (at 4.2, 4.6).

indeed the justices mentioned, Martin, Knoville, Spigurnel and Belflour, were assigned to the circuit covering the south-western counties. Interestingly the contrast in temperament alleged between the local men on the commission and the central court justices suggests that those who understood local conditions were the preferred judicial option. Ironically, the Ordinance of Trailbaston and the Ordinance of Conspirators of the same year were designed to tackle the very forms of corruption and abuse of the judicial system that the anonymous author is complaining about.[7] [**8.1**]

In several of the following extracts the law's overriding concern with rationality is considered to be a hollow boast. In *An Outlaw's Song*, for example, criticism is levelled at the substantive law in terms of its recent ordinance ('there is little reason in several of its points'), while in *A Song on the Venality of the Judges* it appears to be the legal profession who 'depart from reason': on one level it could be taken that the judges have gone mad, on another, that their decisions have strayed from the guiding principles underpinning law and justice we encountered in Chapter 1. [**8.2**]

The main theme in the extracts, however, is venality. Although it was a charge contemporaries first levelled against the church (with allegations of the canonical offence of simony), it is a mark of the precociousness of royal justice in England and the success of the emerging legal profession that from the late thirteenth century the theme of venality increasingly came to be used in connection with the functioning of the courts.[8] Expressed in terms of the corruptibility of judges, lawyers, officials and jurors, venality is perceived as omnipresent in the exercise of justice: money is found oiling the wheels of justice and regarded as a prerequisite for securing the services of a lawyer, a hearing in court and, eventually, redress. The euphemistic 'labour' and 'speed' frequently recur in this context and gain their own resonances. 'Speed' implies a case has been 'fast-tracked' not only with undue haste, but also advantageously. 'Labour' used in connection with the legal process (and juries in particular) has connotations of manipulation or of working hard to persuade. When a poor man labours in vain, it carries the ironic suggestion that a poor man can work hard to gain money to pursue a suit, but even then it will not be sufficient to satisfy greed or achieve his ends.[9]

The intimacy of the relationship between money and the legal system is portrayed in terms of their marriage. In *A Song on the Venality of the Judges* money is considered to be wedded to the courts, while in the passage from *Piers Plowman* Lady Meed, a personification of the power of money, is married to False, whose brothers, Simony and Civil Law, are her close friends. Meed's

---

7 Musson, *Medieval Law*, pp. 150–51.

8 J. A. Yunck, *The Lineage of Lady Meed: The Development of Medieval Venality Satire* (Notre Dame, IN, University of Notre Dame Press, 1963).

9 Discussions of 'labour' in the medieval period do not seem to have expanded their conceptual framework to include this euphemistic use: see for example the Introduction to *The Middle Ages at Work*, ed. K. Robertson and M. Uebel (New York and Basingstoke, Palgrave Macmillan, 2004).

character and actions display a distinct lack of morality. Such immoral behaviour and lack of charity is felt to carry implications for the soul as highlighted by the phrase 'for God', an invocation of charity, which is denied by the Westminster courts (in *A London Lickpenny*) and by the chief justice himself (in the *Gest of Robin Hood*). [**8.3, 8.4**]

Corrupting the proper functioning of the legal system and abusing judicial procedure had technical definitions. Conspiracy and maintenance were the prime focus of royal concern.[10] Conspiracy involved agreements to pervert the course of justice by making malicious accusations or bringing in false verdicts. It also stretched to those who retained persons to carry out their schemes. [**8.5**] Although frequently employed as a generic term for abuse of the judicial system, maintenance in its more specific forms included the harbouring of criminals, the packing and intimidating of juries as well as the bribing of lawyers and judges. Two other offences of particular royal concern were champerty and ambidextry. The former involved the receiving of a portion of the proceeds in return for assistance in a suit. The latter represented the taking of gifts from both parties to a suit.[11] Embracery was the term for intimidating or otherwise corrupting jurors. The cases included here demonstrate that such behaviour was not condoned and prosecutions were brought against people who could be identified and captured.[12]

The literary sources make the point that it is not just the judges and lawyers that required payment: all those involved with the court at whatever level had to be paid or rewarded in some fashion. Whilst this may appear to modern eyes as straightforward bribery, this was not necessarily the case.[13] In an age when officials and bureaucrats did not receive salaries, payment by the public in the form of donations (in cash or goods) was the norm. Whether it was a reward or a bribe was essentially ambiguous without other evidence as to the donor's intentions.

Aside from the demands of the legal profession and its susceptibility to bribery (or at least to criticism for it), the shortcomings identified in the sources derived from the reality of the legal system itself: its reliance upon the jury system and the integrity of unpaid local officials. The case of Knapp underscores this as he played the system to ensure he was placed upon juries in his own county. [**8.6**]

10 A. Harding, 'The origins of the crime of conspiracy', *TRHS* 5th series, 33 (1983), 89–108.

11 J. Rose, 'Of ambidexters and daffidowndillies: defamation of lawyers, legal ethics and professional reputation', *Roundtable*, 8 (2001), 423–67.

12 In 1345 a man who threatened a jury as it was giving the verdict in the presence of the justices at the bar of the court of king's bench and then pursued them to the gate of Westminster Palace was given a sentence of life imprisonment and it was ordered that his right hand be cut off (though the order was not executed immediately): *SCCKB*, vol. 6, pp. 41–2.

13 The practice of 'tipping' in a restaurant or hotel is a relic of this system. The amount, timing and intentions behind the action are significant. While the payment can be a reward for good, attentive service (or in expectation of it) it can also indicate a desire to receive favourable treatment (either generally or in specific stated terms).

This potentially enabled Knapp to influence the opinion of his fellow jurors and thus ensure decisions regarding persons and property that may have been to his advantage. Thomas Coteroun attempted to obtain a favourable verdict by paying large sums to the petty jury, while Hugh Pipard tried strong-arm tactics to nobble a juror empanelled in an assize case between him and another landowner. [8.8] In other instances jurors were forced on to assizes against their will, presumably either those who had succeeded in gaining respite or an exemption from sitting, or those who were not expecting to serve because they were not properly qualified to do so (thus diluting the strict property qualifications intended to keep the system free from abuse).[14] The practicalities of the administration of justice and trying to empanel juries meant that compromises had to be made.[15]

As the principal agent involved in the day-to-day administration of justice in the shire and the person responsible for the instigation of criminal process, ensuring the arrest of suspects and empanelling jurors, the sheriff was the figure to influence and consequently one of the main targets for criticism. Langland graphically portrays this relationship in *Piers Plowman* by depicting Lady Meed riding piggyback on the sheriff, an image given visual representation in one of the manuscripts of the poem.[16] Although in another passage we are advised that 'sheriffs of shires' would be ruined without Meed, the relationship is ambiguous since in reality her actions would ruin sheriffs because they would have to account for all the mayhem (such as freeing prisoners) she causes. The message appears to be that bribery produces only superficial gains and leaves the system in chaos.

If venality and straightforward bribery are seen as one evil, the relationships developed between judges/lawyers and their clients and their deliberate abuse of legal procedure are regarded as equally serious shortcomings of the system. Part of the problem lies in modern and contemporary perceptions of what constitutes ethical behaviour. Perceptions of corruption within the law derived to a large extent from the close relationship between lawyers and landowners. This emerged in part from the retaining of lawyers for advice and assistance as legal counsel (a relationship which often continued after promotion to the bench) and in part also from their natural affinity of interest as property owners and members of county society.[17]

Influencing judicial proceedings was traditionally a reflection of complex social

---

14 S. L. Waugh, 'Reluctant knights and jurors: respites, exemptions and public obligation in the reign of Henry III', *Speculum*, 85 (1983), 937–88.

15 J. B. Post, 'Jury lists and juries in the late fourteenth century', in *Twelve Good Men and True: the English Criminal Trial Jury, 1200–1800*, ed. J. S. Cockburn and T. A. Green (Princeton, NJ, Princeton University Press, 1988), pp. 65–77.

16 Oxford University, Bodleian Library MS Douce 104.

17 N. Ramsay, 'Retained legal counsel, c.1275–c.1475', *TRHS* 5th series, 35 (1985), 102; Maddicott, *Law and Lordship*, pp. 19, 21, 24; N. Fryde, 'A medieval robber baron: Sir John Molyns of Stoke Poges, Buckinghamshire', in *Medieval Legal Records*, pp. 197–222.

relationships and especially the elaborate networks of patronage, clientage and friendship that existed in medieval society. While the obligations of the patron/client relationship themselves were not explicitly defined, the loyalty and support encouraged and expected extended to litigation.[18] In the *Paston Letters* it is noticeable that 'honour and worship', what would be understood today as prestige, standing, dignity and respect, are key motivational factors underlying the characters' actions. These were the intangible benefits for both parties that derived from 'service' and 'good lordship'.[19] [8.7]

It is of course difficult from the historian's perspective to discern what was legitimate and acceptable and what was frowned upon and intended to influence proceedings unduly. Distinctions should be made between legal chicanery, forgery and clear manipulation of the system at one end of the spectrum, and subtle exercise of favour, use of legal knowledge and the strengthening of existing symbiotic relationships, at the other. [8.7, 8.9, 8.10] In a society where gifts and favours were an expected and accepted feature of social transactions, the receiving of gifts, for instance, may simply have been regarded as one of the entitlements of office with little attention paid to the motives of the giver. Moreover, there can be less of a clear demarcation of official conduct when the lines of appropriate behaviour were hazy even to contemporaries. There was nevertheless a perceived difference between oiling the wheels and setting them upon a different track.

To an extent therefore what we in modern times would regard as corruption and abuse was in fact embedded in the nature of medieval society itself. Society was in turn subject to the relationships created through or developed within 'bastard feudalism', the malign effects of which were supposedly manifested in perversion of justice, the parading of retainers and co-operation in disputes.[20] Evaluations of the forces operating within this form of feudal order have been mixed.[21] Much of the blame for such undue influence has been placed on the devolution of powers within the judicial system and the role played by the gentry in administering it.[22] Inevitably it is not a black and white matter, and more nuanced interpretations point towards the importance of judging by contemporary standards, looking closely at the expectations and attitudes

18 A. R. Smith, 'Litigation and politics: Sir John Fastolf's defence of his English property', in *Property and Politics*, ed. A. J. Pollard (Gloucester, Alan Sutton, 1984), pp. 59–75; J. Rose, 'Litigation and political conflict in fifteenth century East Anglia: conspiracy and attaint actions and Sir John Fastolf', *JLH*, 26 (2006), 53–80.

19 R. Horrox, 'Service', in *Fifteenth-Century Attitudes*, ed. Horrox, pp. 61–78.

20 K. B. McFarlane, 'Bastard feudalism', in *idem, England in the Fifteenth Century*, ed. G. L. Harriss (London, Hambledon Press, 1981), pp. 23–43; C. Carpenter, 'The Beauchamp affinity: a study of bastard feudalism at work', *EHR*, 95 (1980), 514–32; J. G. Bellamy, *Bastard Feudalism and the Law* (London, Routledge, 1989).

21 P. R. Coss, 'Bastard feudalism revised', *P&P*, 125 (1989), 27–64 and the debate between D. Crouch, D. A. Carpenter and P. R. Coss in *P&P*, 131 (1991), 165–203. See also S. Walker, *The Lancastrian Affinity, 1369–1399* (Oxford, Clarendon Press, 1990), pp. 235–61.

22 See Chapter 4.

of consumers, and recognising the paradoxes and ambiguities inherent in the system.[23]

Indeed, we should not underestimate contemporaries' concern at the extent of corruption and abuse, nor their efforts to expose and eradicate perceived problems. Again, consideration should be given to the intrinsic dynamic of medieval society, to the strength of a man's word, to the nature of relationships and notions of service (ties that could be seen as honourable and respectable).[24] The established nature and continued existence of these factors did not preclude or inhibit a growing appreciation of weaknesses within the system and recognition that it could be reformed to operate more efficiently and successfully. Nor was it felt necessary to reconcile the paradoxical desire to articulate the system's failings whilst remaining firmly embedded within it. For all their biting satire and clear social messages the poems identifying legal shortcomings do not offer suggestions as to how the system might be altered or made more accommodating to litigants who were not so affluent or lacked influential friends and support. The failure to provide a panacea suggests a profound limitation on perspectives, but also emphasises the reality of medieval society both for contemporaries and for historians: bastard feudalism *was* society and it was impossible to stand outside it.[25]

23 M. Hicks, *English Political Culture in the Fifteenth Century* (London and New York, Routledge, 2002), pp. 1–8; Horrox, 'Service', p. 78.

24 J. M. W. Bean, *From Lord to Patron: Lordship in Late Medieval England* (Manchester, Manchester University Press, 1989); C. Given Wilson, *The Royal Household and the King's Affinity: Service, Politics and Finance in England, 1360–1413* (New Haven, Yale University Press, 1986).

25 Horrox, 'Service', pp. 77–8; P. Hyams, *Rancor and Reconciliation in Medieval England* (Ithaca, NY, Cornell University Press, 2003).

8.1 Corruption: the evils of the legal system

In this poem the author is standing outside the legal system commenting on what he fears are its shortcomings: deceit, bad law, uncertainty, malicious prosecution and the harsh treatment of prisoners. The natural world inhabited by the outlaw is extolled and the atmosphere is charged with the imagery of the greenwood. The anonymous author purports to be one of the returning soldiers who has been fighting in the Gascon wars (in a stanza omitted here), but he has an insider's knowledge of the legal system and may well have been a royal clerk. His use of language, such as 'indict' and 'deliverance' (signifying gaol delivery) and the French word 'ateindre' (implying the process of attaint of jurors) and frequent mentions of the paucity of 'reason' indicate an awareness of judicial procedure and legal concepts. He is cynical about the litigious nature of people of the day and underlines the suspicion with which even a little knowledge of the law is viewed. It is claimed the poem is written on parchment, the material favoured for legal records because of its endurance, and was cast on to the highway to be picked up and read. This literary conceit not only suggests it is to be regarded as an open letter (letter patent), but also assumes the audience would recognise the method of dissemination, a way of hiding the identity (and location) of the political voice behind it.[1] The 'game of Trailbaston' and the pronouncement 'I shall make their heads fly off' conjure up images of a form of 'rough' or summary justice similar to that expressed in some of the examples in Chapter 2. Cutting out the tongue was a highly emblematic punishment and signalled the removing of falsity and deceit.

'An Outlaw's Song of Trailbaston', in *Anglo-Norman Political Songs*, ed. I. S. T. Aspin, Anglo-Norman Texts, 11 (1953), pp. 73–6 [French]

The desire comes over me to rhyme and compose a story about an ordinance provided in the land. It would have been better if the thing had still to be enacted; if God does not prevent it, I believe war will flare up.

These are the articles of Trailbaston. Saving the king himself, may he have God's curse who first granted such a commission! For there is little reason in several of its points.

Sir, if I want to chastise my servant with a cuff or two to correct him, he will take out a bill against me and cause me to be arrested, and made to pay a big ransom before I get out of prison.

Forty shillings they take for my ransom, and the sheriff comes for his

---

1 W. Scase, 'Strange and wonderful bills: bill casting and political discourse in late medieval England', in *New Medieval Literatures*, ed. R. Copeland, D. Lawton and W. Scase, 6 vols (Oxford, Clarendon Press, 1998), vol. 2, pp. 243–4.

reward for not putting me in a deep dungeon. Now consider, sirs, is this reasonable?

Because of this I will keep myself in the woods in the beautiful shade; there is no deceit nor any bad law in the forest of Belregard, where the jay flies and the nightingale sings always without ceasing.

But the bad jurors, on whom may God have no pity, out of their deceitful mouths they have indicted me for wicked robberies and other misdeeds, so that I dare not be received by my friends.

...

If these wicked jurors will not reform, so that I may ride and go to my country, if I can reach them I shall make their heads fly off. I would not give a penny for all their threats.

Martyn and Knoville are pious men, and pray for the poor, that they may live in safety. Spigurnel and Belflour are cruel men; if they were in my keep[2] they would not be returned.

I will teach them the game of Trailbaston and will break their backs and their rumps, their arms and their legs, it would be reasonable; I will cut out their tongues and their lips as well.

Whoever first initiated these things will never be reformed in his lifetime; I will tell you truly, there is too much sin in it, because through fear of prison many a man will become a thief.

There are those who will become thieves that never were so, that for fear of prison dare not come into peace ...

...

You who are indicted, I advise you, come to me, at the green forest of Belregard where there is no annoyance, only wild beasts and beautiful shade; for the common law is too uncertain.

If you know your letters and are tonsured, you will be called[3] before the justices; again you may be returned to prison in the custody of the bishop until you have been purged; ... and suffer privation and very hard penance[4] and perhaps you will never have deliverance.

...

Formerly I knew little that was worthwhile, now I am less wise; this is

---

2 This may be read as both 'custody' and 'castle'.

3 There may be a suggestion of the technical term 'appealed' (see 5.1).

4 This may be a reference to the *peine forte et dure* (see 5.8) or to the penances meted out under canon law.

what the bad laws do to me by their great outrage, that I dare not come into peace among my family. The rich are taken for ransom, the poor dwindle away.

...

Yet I shall await grace and hear people speak. Some speak bad of me that do not dare to approach me and would willingly see my body ill-treated. But God can save a man in the middle of a thousand devils.

He who is the son of Mary can save me; for I am not guilty, I am indicted out of spite.[5] God curse whoever put me in this place! The world is so fickle, he is mad that trusts it.

...

If I know the law better than they do they will say, 'That conspirator begins to be untrustworthy.' And I will not come within ten leagues of them. Of all neighbourhoods cursed be those.

I beg all good people that they will pray for me that I may be able to go and ride into my country. I never killed a man, certainly not of my own free will, nor was I a wicked robber to do people harm.

This rhyme was made in the wood beneath a laurel tree, there sings the blackbird and the nightingale and the hawk ranges. It was written on parchment to be better remembered and thrown on the highway so that people might find it.

8.2 Corruption: venality in the courtroom

The poem begins by echoing the Beatitudes (Christ's Sermon on the Mount). Its main concern is the partiality exhibited in the courtroom (especially to the rich over the poor – in spite of the judge's oath to treat all persons equally) and the bribery seen as all-pervading. In this respect some of the imagery is imaginative: judges licking up honours, while their clerks appear starved, their mouths agape for gifts. The unfair treatment of the indigent is said to be enshrined in the conventions of the court which are in turn elevated to the status of law. As in An Outlaw's Song the sheriff also comes under scrutiny. Press-ganging the poor to serve on juries and intimidating them into saying what is required is a common complaint. The driving off of cattle describes the process of distraint* of goods which was a legitimate option for the sheriff. While it may have been abused as suggested, it may also have been misinterpreted or misunderstood by owners.

---

5 Writs *de odio et atia* were available if a defendant felt he had been the victim of a malicious appeal or indicted out of hate and spite: N. Hurnard, *The King's Pardon for Homicide before A.D. 1307* (Oxford, Clarendon Press, 1969), pp. 79–82.

'A Song on the Venality of the Judges', in *Thomas Wright's Political Songs*, ed. P.
Coss (Cambridge, Cambridge University Press, 1996), pp. 224–9 [Latin]

Blessed are they who hunger
And thirst and do justice,
And hate and avoid
The wickedness of injustice;
Whom neither abundance of gold
Nor the jewels of the rich
Draw from their inflexibility,
Nor from the cry of the poor;
They judge what is just
And do not shy away from right
Through favour of the rich.
But now in a wonderful manner
The age deceives many,
And draws them into danger,
For love of the world,
That they may lick up honours.
The cause of this is money,
Which almost every court
Has now taken in wedlock.

There are judges
Whom partiality and bribes
Seduce from justice;
These are they I remember well,
That render account to the devil
And serve him solely.
For the law of nature commands,
That a judge in giving judgment
Should not be a favourer of anyone
For either prayer or price;
What therefore good Jesus,
Will become of the judges,
Who for prayer or gifts
Depart from reason?
In reality such judges
Have numerous messengers;
Listen for what purpose.
If you wish to claim,
A messenger will approach you,

And speaks in confidence,
Saying, 'Dear friend,
Do you wish to plead?
I am one who can help you
In various ways;
If you wish to obtain anything
By his aid,
Give me half
And I will help you.'

At his feet sit clerks,
Who are as if they are starved,
Gaping for gifts;
And proclaiming it as law
That those who give nothing,
Although they come early,
Will have to wait.

But if some noble lady,
Beautiful or charming,
With horned head,[6]
Encircled with gold,
Comes for judgment,
Such a one expedites her business
Without uttering a word.

If it be a poor weak woman,
Not having any little gifts,
Beauty or good family,
Whom Venus does not trouble,
She goes straight home,
Her business unaccomplished,
With sorrow reaching to her heart.

There are some at this court
Who express judgment
And are called pleaders;[7]
Worse than the others.
They take with both hands,[8]

6 The fashionable horned headdress.
7 The Latin word used here 'relatores' suggests 'narratores' (pleaders).
8 The technical term is 'ambidexters' – they take money from both sides.

And so deceive those,
Whose defenders they are.
And what about the ushers?
Who say to the poor
Following the court,
'Poor man, why do you bother?
Why do you wait here?
Unless you give money
To everybody at this court,
You labour in vain.
Why then, wretch, do you weep?
If you have brought nothing
You will remain entirely outside.'

Concerning the sheriffs,
Who can fully relate
How hard they are to the poor?
He who has nothing to give
Is dragged here and there
And is placed on assizes
And forced to swear,
Without daring to murmur.
But if he should murmur,
Unless he make satisfaction immediately,
He is cast adrift.

The same people have this vice,
When they enter the house
Of some countryman,
Or well-known abbey,
Where drink and food,
And all necessaries,
Are given to them devotedly.
Such things are no benefit,
Unless by and by the jewels
Follow after the meal,
And are distributed to all,
Beadles and servants
And all who are with them.
Nor yet are they pacified,
Unless they be given

Robes of various colours
For their wives.
If these are not sent secretly
Then later they proceed as follows;
How ever many cattle they find
Are driven off violently
To their manors,
And the owners themselves are confined
Until they make satisfaction,
So that they give double;
Then and not till then they are released.

8.3 Corruption: bribery and the law courts at Westminster

Bribery and the power of money is personified in Langland's *Piers Plowman* by Lady Meed, who is seen to have seduced all in her path, officials and jurors, both of the ecclesiastical and of the royal courts. Her lack of moderation gives her a low reputation, but she accomplishes much legal business even causing cases to be settled, though her motives and her 'love' are by implication questionable. Conscience, who is responsible for morality and applying the rules of reason (natural law), comments on Meed's activities and the chaos she brings. The symbiotic relationship between money and the legal process is further highlighted in *The London Lickpenny*'s satirical portrait of a litigant trying to obtain justice in the Westminster courts. The would-be litigant treats the serjeants of the law deferentially and notices their special form of dress. Certain words or notions crop up in each stanza, such as 'speed' (translated as 'succeed' or 'prosper', but has connotations of 'jumping the queue' or 'achieving the desired outcome' as well as harking back to the motto 'speak, spend, speed' current in the protest literature of 1381).[9] He repeatedly asks for charity, but receives none. Aside from its criticism of venality, this poem also offers a realistic feel of the bustle and chaos that undoubtedly characterised the Westminster courts, housed as they were in the same building alongside each other.[10] Justice was literally competing (in the market place) with pickpockets and tradesmen touting their wares.

9 S. Justice, *Writing and Rebellion: England in 1381* (Berkeley and Los Angeles, CA, and London, University of California Press, 1994), pp. 13, 133–4.

10 J. H. Baker, 'Westminster Hall', in *idem, The Common Law Tradition: Lawyers, Books and the Law* (London, Hambledon, 2000), pp. 248–52.

(a)

William Langland, *The Vision of Piers Plowman*, ed. A. V. C. Schmidt, 2nd edn (London, J. M. Dent, 1995), pp. 29–30, 43–4 (B text II, ll. 57–77, III, ll. 131–46, 154–62) [English]

At the marriage of this maid were many men assembled,
Knights and clerics and other common people,
Such as assizors and summonors, sheriffs and their clerks,
Beadles and bailiffs and brokers of trade,
Purveyors and providers of food and advocates of the court of Arches;*
I cannot number the throng that ran about Meed.
But Simony and Civil Law and assizors of courts
Were the most intimate with Meed of any men, it seemed to me.
And Flattery was the first that fetched her out of her chamber
And as a broker brought her to be united with False.
When Simony and Civil Law saw the will of both of them,
They assented for silver to say as both wished.
Then Liar ran forward and said 'Look! Here is a charter
That Guile with his great oaths gave them together,'
And requested Civil Law to see and Simony to read it.
Then Simony and Civil Law both stand forth
And unfold the deed of enfeoffment* that False has made,
And thus begin these men to cry out aloud,
'Be it known to all present and to come, etc'.[11]
Know and bear witness you who live upon the earth,
That Meed is married more for her goods
Than for any virtue or fairness or any noble lineage.
. . .
[Conscience speaks] 'For she is loose with her sex, garrulous of
    tongue,
As common as the cartway to servants and to all,
To monks, to minstrels, to lepers in hedges.
Assizors and summonors, such men praise her,
Sheriffs of shires would be ruined if she were not,
For she makes men lose both their land and their life.
She lets prisoners go free and often pays for them,
And gives the gaolers gold and groats[12] together
To unfetter the false – to flee where he wishes;
And takes the true by the hair and ties him firmly,

11 A standard formula for charters and proclamations. See Chapter 2.
12 A silver coin worth 4d.

And hangs him that never did harm out of hatred.
To be condemned in consistory[13] she counts as nothing,
For she provides copes for the bishop's officer and coats for his clerks.
She is absolved as soon as it pleases her;
She may do nearly as much in a single month
As your privy seal in six score days![14]
...
For she is favourable to False and injures Fidelity often.
By Jesus! with her jewels she corrupts your justice
And lies against the law and blocks his way,
That faith may not have his course, her florins[15] go so thickly.
She leads the law as she likes and makes "lovedays".[16]
And makes men lose through love of her that which legal proceedings
    might win –
The confusion for a mean man though he litigate for ever.
Law is so haughty and reluctant to make end:
Without presents or pence he satisfies very few.'

(b)

'The London Lickpenny', in *Historical Poems of the Fourteenth and Fifteenth Centuries*, ed. R. H. Robbins (New York, Columbia University Press, 1959), pp. 130–34. [English]

> To London once my steps I bent,
> Where truth in no manner should be cowardly,
> Toward Westminster without delay I went,
> To a man of law to make complaint,
> I said, 'for Mary's love, that holy saint,
> Pity the poor that would proceed.'
> But for lack of money, I could not succeed.
>
> And as I thrust the crowd among
> By perverse chance my hood was gone,
> Yet for all that I stayed not long
> 'Til at the king's bench I was come.

13 In the bishop's (consistory) court.
14 i.e. 120 days or four months.
15 A gold coin worth 6s 8d.
16 Here there is a play on words. See Chapter 6 (p. 190) for their technical meaning and
    context.

Before the judge I kneeled immediately,
And prayed him for God's sake to take heed
But for lack of money, I might not succeed.

Beneath them sat clerks a great throng,
Which earnestly did write in agreement.
There stood up one and cried about
'Richard, Robert and John of Kent!'
I knew not well what this man meant,
He cried so thickly there indeed.
But he that lacked money might not succeed.

Unto the common place[17] I went then
Where sat one with a silken hood[18]
I did him reverence for I ought to do so
And told my case as well as I could
How my goods were defrauded me by falsehood.
I got not even a murmer of his mouth for my meed!
And for lack of money I might not succeed.

Unto the Rolls I took me from thence,
Before the clerks of the Chancery
Where many I found earning of pence
But none at all once looked at me.
I gave my plaint upon my knee,
They liked it well when they had it read
But lacking money I could not proceed.

In Westminster Hall I found out one,
Which went in a long gown of ray[19]
I crouched and knelt before him at once,
For Mary's love of help I him pray.
'I know not what you mean,' did he say;
To get me thence he did me bid
For lack of money I could not succeed.

Within this hall neither rich nor yet poor
Would do any bit for me, although I should die,

17 Common bench or court of common pleas.
18 This may in fact be 'houve' (coif).
19 A striped cloth.

Which seeing I took me out of the door,
Where Flemings[20] began on me for to cry:
'Master, what will you long for or buy?
Fine felt hats or spectacles to read?
Lay down your silver and here you may succeed.'
...
Then I travelled into Kent
For of the law would I meddle no more,
Because no man to me took intent,
I prepared me to do as I did before
Now Jesus that in Bethlem was born
Save London, and send true lawyers their meed!
For whoso lacks money, with them shall not succeed.

8.4 Corruption: the close relationship between landowners and the law

The Robin Hood ballads play upon the theme of close relations between lawyers and landowners and illustrate the retaining practices of the great monastic institutions.[21] The justice states that he gets both robes (possibly in the abbey's distinctive livery) and a retainer fee. Although the *Gest* itself may have been composed as early as the 1330s, the Robin Hood ballads were extremely popular in the second half of the fourteenth century, a time when antipathy to retaining lawyers was high. In this extract the unreasonableness of the abbot and the justice (who act in accord) comes through in their not allowing the knight a time extension in which to pay his debts. There is a sense here in which money overcomes notions of equity and fairness. At the end of the story, however, the knight succeeds in raising the necessary money to retain his lands. The abbot asks the justice for his fee back, but the latter keeps it.

A Gest of Robyn Hode, in *Rymes of Robin Hood: An Introduction to the English Outlaw*, ed. R. B. Dobson and J. Taylor, revised edn (Stroud, Sutton, 1997), pp. 85–6 (excerpts) [English]

The abbot and the chief cellarer,
Started forth very boldly,
The justice of England
The abbot there did retain.

---

20 Flemish merchants.
21 For direct evidence of payments see 7.2.

The chief justice and many more
Had taken into their hands
Wholly all the knight's debt
To put that knight to wrong
…
Lords at dinner were sat
In that abbot's hall;
The knight went forth and kneeled down
And greeted them great and small.

'Good day sir abbot,' said the knight,
'I am come to keep my day.'*
The first word the abbot spoke,
'Have you brought my payment?'

'Not a penny,' said the knight,
'By God that made me;'
'You are a cursed debtor,' said the abbot,
'Sir justice, drink to me.'

'What do you here,' said the abbot,
'If you haven't brought your payment?'
'For God,' then said the knight,
'To pray for a longer day.'

'Your day has come,' said the justice,
'Land get you none.'
'Now good sir justice be my friend,
And defend me from my foes.'

'I am retained by the abbot,' said the justice,
'Both by robes and fee':
'Now, good sir sheriff, be my friend.'
'More than that, by God,' said he.

8.5 Abuse of judicial procedure: conspiracy and champerty

Concern about judicial abuse had been present in the articles of the eyre, but was given a higher profile through the ordinances defining conspiracy more closely issued in 1293 and 1305. Indeed, conspiracy became classed as a criminal trespass when the second ordinance was promulgated and added to the brief of the trailbaston commissions.[22] Allegations of conspiracy frequently appeared in judicial inquiries, but the historian should be wary about the extent of wrongdoing as the evidence was not always clear-cut or the situation could be misinterpreted. Legitimate groups and alliances were sometimes portrayed as conspiratorial, while the advice and assistance in litigation given by lawyers could equally be confused with corrupt conduct.[23]

Ordinance of Conspirators (1305) (*SR*, vol. 1, p. 145) [French]

Conspirators are those who make alliances among themselves by oath, covenant or some other alliance that each of them will aid and support the undertaking falsely and maliciously to indict or cause to be indicted or falsely to acquit people or falsely to initiate or maintain pleas and also those who cause children under age to appeal people of felonies through which they are imprisoned and greatly harmed; and those who retain men of the country by their robes or by their fees to maintain their evil undertakings and suppress the truth, both the takers and the givers, and stewards and bailiffs of great lords who through lordship, office or power undertake to maintain or support pleas or quarrels for parties other than those touching the estate of their lords or themselves ...

This ordinance and final definition of conspirators was made and finally agreed by the king and his council in this parliament [1305] etc. And it was ordained that the justices assigned to hear and determine various felonies and trespasses in every county of England should have a transcript thereof.

Champerters are those that initiate pleas and suits and cause them to be initiated either by their own procurement or by another's, and sue them at their own cost, to have part of the disputed land or a share of the gains.

22 A. Harding, 'The origins of the crime of conspiracy', *TRHS* 5th series, 33 (1983), 89–108.

23 P. Brand, *The Origins of the English Legal Profession* (London, Blackwell, 1992), pp. 140–41.

8.6 Abuse of judicial procedure: maintenance – the case of Richard Knap (1400)

The activities of Richard Knap and his accomplice here highlight the covert and sinister side of maintenance and show the extent to which 'rotten apples' could exist apparently unchecked within the judicial system. His systematic targeting of parties and unashamed dealings are exemplified by the allegation that he deliberately purchased property so as to be empanelled on juries at Westminster. The accusatory couplet towards the end of this passage was recorded in English.

TNA KB 9/184/1 mm. 9, 9d [Latin]

Also it is presented that where it is ordained by the statute of the lord king etc. that no minister of the lord king or any other person [...] is to seek anything on behalf of the parties to the case or take other profits from there by maintaining pleas, complaints or matters that are in the royal courts as contained more fully in the same [...] statute,[24] however, the said Richard Knap, tailor, and Roger, usher of the exchequer, mutually confederate and bound to maintain [...] and sustain false complaints within the county of Middlesex both between the lord king and a private party and between two private parties to destroy and oppress [...] on the grounds that other lieges of the lord king sued complaints and always undertook business there for them on the side of whichever false complaint they maintained [...] within the said county for certain profits derived from there and often subverted the laws and customs of the realm of England through their false malice, high plotting and cunning and by unjust governance people were defamed and were outlawed from regular judicial process and [they] also sold anyone as if selling a bull or a cow; and the said Richard and Roger on the Wednesday three weeks after Easter in the first year of the reign of King Henry IV [12 May 1400] and other times in various places such as the vill of Westminster, Westminster Hall and Knightsbridge and other places within the said county maintained and supported a certain complaint between John Sadler complainant and William Parker concerning a plea of trespass that is in king's bench before the same king to such an extent that the said Richard and Roger on the aforesaid day and year and at other times rode to the said vill of Knightsbridge and Hendon to the various jurors who had been empanelled between the said parties namely Robert Orchard and others and procured them on the side of the said William promising them divers

24 13 Richard II st. 3 (*SR*, vol. 2, pp. 74–5).

sums of money. And that the same are common maintainers of all false complaints within the county of Middlesex against the form of the aforesaid ordinance.

Also it is presented that Richard Knap bought and acquired for himself a building in the vill of Westminster holding in fee-farm so that he might be placed and empanelled on assizes, juries and other inquests to oppress and destroy his neighbours within the vill of Westminster ... and he is such a common procurer and defamer of parties through falseness that he is not ashamed thereof nor has fear there. And were he to have been lawfully indicted he said that he would be granted an acquittal by paying a fine there. And also they said that the said Richard is a common maintainer of all false complaints in the county of Middlesex and that this false maintenance is the largest part of his whole livelihood and that he is the root of all deceit committed within the aforesaid county. And also the same jurors say that he is the contriver 'of many false wiles and of all Middlesex chief caster of guiles'.

On account of this the said jury humbly implore your respectful discretion that the said Richard because of the falsities and aforesaid maintenance be discharged from all oaths before you or any other justices so as to improve and strengthen the whole law.

8.7 Abuse of judicial procedure: maintenance in East Anglia during the 1450s

Sir John Fastolf had suffered considerably (to the tune of at least 5000 marks (£3333) or so he claimed in a draft petition) as a result of the machinations of William de la Pole, duke of Suffolk and his servants and was keen to lay charges against them for acquiring his property illegally. Fastolf and John Paston were allied in a struggle to remove Thomas Tuddenham and John Heydon, the most prominent members of Suffolk's affinity, from the political and administrative scene in East Anglia and endeavoured to gather enough information about their activities to achieve their indictment at oyer and terminer sessions. Lord Scales gained custody of a proportion of de la Pole's lands after his death in 1450 and assumed leadership of his former servants in the region.[25] These letters date from after de la Pole's death, which provided an opportunity for his opponents to take action. It is clear from the passage that whilst Paston and Fastolf complained about the supposed conspiracy and abuse of Heydon and Tuddenham, they were not adverse to making the most of relationships and information and employing similar underhand tactics themselves.

PL, vol. 2, pp. 44, 62–3 [English]

25 Castor, *Duchy*, pp. 144–52, 156–71.

(a) Letter from Sir John Fastolf to John Paston and others (14 September 1450)

To my right trusty cousin and friends John Berney JP and Sir Thomas Howes parson of Castle Combe [Wilts.]

Right trusty and well beloved cousin and friends, I greet you well. And for as much as I understand that the oyer and terminer shall be held at Norwich upon Thursday next coming, and since it is so that I have matters broached there against Appleyard and others that have put me to great wrong and damage, as you know best, which matters I desire to reach a good conclusion to my worldly honour and standing, wherefore I send to you my right trusty servant John Bocking, to wait upon my learned counsel and other trusty friends of mine, there to help, solicit and labour my burdensome matters as you shall best advise him; and praying you to spare for no reasonable cost to lay out and do at this time wherever it shall be thought expedient so that my matter may reach a good conclusion for my worship. And especially you should labour sufficiently the bill of maintenance against Appleyard, for as I understand he was the greatest cause that the inquest passed against me so untruly, whereas I gave him no cause; giving credence to the said Bocking in that which may concern this matter or any other to my worship and profit. I give very great weight to this matter because it tends more to my worship and heart's well-being than only my profit.

Our Lord have you in his keeping. Written at London the fourteenth day of September the twenty-ninth year of King Henry VI [1450].

J. FASTOLF

(b) Letter to John Paston from William Wayte (9 January 1451)

To my right reverend and right worshipful master, my Master Paston, in all haste possible.

Sir, it may please you to know that my Lord Scales sent these pursuant to my master on the twelfth day[26] that my master should meet with him at Winch before my lord of Oxford[27] on the Thursday next following. And when my master[28] came thither he delivered to my master a letter

26 Twelfth Day of Christmas, 6 January.
27 John de Vere, 12th earl of Oxford.
28 William Yelverton, king's bench justice.

from my lord chancellor, which my master will show you at Lynn. I should send you a copy thereof, but it is so long that I had no leisure to write it.

My master rode to Walsingham on the Friday following, and there he met with the sheriff and the sheriff delivered to my master a letter from my lord Norfolk,[29] which I send you a copy of. And at Walsingham my master received a letter from Osborn your man. And there Heydon's man made his boast that he was a justice of the peace on Cawston Heath, and so it seems by their behaviour that they trust of a good year.

And, sir, when my master came on Saturday there was delivered to my master a letter from Sir John Fastolf and another letter came to me from John Bocking, which I send you a copy of. Sir, God send us a fair day at Lynn, and that there may be people enough to cry upon the Lord Scales that he maintain not Sir T.T. and H. in their wrongs, as the copy of B.'s letter makes mention.

And, sir, in the reverence of God, labour your matters wisely and secretly, for Wyndham slandered you greatly before my lord of Oxford and my Lord Scales that you should raise so many people with great array out of Norwich; and therefore, sir, let the people be wisely and forthrightly guided in their speaking and ordering. Also my Lord Scales sent for the parson of Swaffham and various men of the same town to meet with him before my lord of Oxford the said Thursday, for to treat with them for Sir Thomas Tuddenham, and there was the bailiff of Swaffham and Sir Thomas Tuddenham's priest. And so my Lord Scales gave the parson of S. strong words and equally to men of the same town. And the parson answered my Lord Scales forthrightly in the best way, and there were strong words between Blake the bailiff and Tuddenham's priest, that my lords and my master were overcome by them. And so it is likely that my Lord Scales shall make no loveday, and so all of Swaffham will be there in their best array.

Also, sir, Brigg was at Walsingham, and there he bragged great words and said to many different men that all those that laboured against them should be thanked. And he said that it were but eight persons, and if men be men now he should be thanked and told at Lynn in the best manner. He is now with the Lord Scales. The Lord Scales blamed Thomas Denys, John Lister and me for all those indictments, and the Lord Scales says that I made all the bills and the panel; and so he is a severe lord to me and to Thomas Denys. Prentys is at home with the

29 John Mowbray, 3rd duke of Norfolk.

Lord Scales.

The sheriff told me that he will do as much as he may for the city of Norwich. Sir, I would there were a thousand of good courageous men to cry out on Tuddenham, Heydon, Prentys and Brigg for their false extortions. Also, sir, at the reverence of God make an end between Sexeford and men of Salle; it lies in your power.

I shall make ready your forcible entries against Lynn with the grace of God, which have you in his keeping. Written at Rougham on Saturday night in haste.

Sir, I sent you a foolish letter by Richard Yemmis. I beseech you beware to whom you show your letters. Let them be burnt.

By your servant W. Wayte.

8.8 Abuse of judicial procedure: embracery

In the first extract (a case reviewed by the king's bench in 1354) the defendant gets his comeuppance for trying to influence proceedings as the agent double-crosses him. The adviser took the money offered (which amounted to 100s for himself and 8s 4d for each juror) and then persuaded the jury to convict (paying them only 3s 4d, a fraction of what he was initially given). It seems strange that Thomas should go to such lengths unless he were guilty or believed he would be found so, but equally strange that Richard betrayed him. Thomas made no challenge of the jurors because he believed them to be in his pocket and suffered the consequences. In the second extract (from peace sessions in Hampshire) it is alleged that one of the parties tried to influence the outcome of an assize by ensuring the appointment of one of the jurors and later assaulted him since at the appropriate moment he apparently did not say what he had been instructed to say.

(a)

TNA KB 27/374 m. 35 (Hilary) [Latin]

The jurors [of various hundreds in Surrey] present that in the twenty-second year of the reign of the present king of England [Edward III],[30] a certain Thomas Coteroun was indicted for the death of Robert le Modere, feloniously killed at Milford by which indictment he was arrested and committed to Guildford gaol. And afterwards the same

---

30 The twenty-second year of his reign spanned from 25 January 1348 to 24 January 1349.

Thomas sent for Richard Prudet to be of his council in procuring his delivery. And the same Richard undertook to get his delivery for a hundred shillings for his labour and for a hundred shillings to be distributed among the jury, which money the same Richard was paid at Guildford at three weeks after Easter in the same year [c 11 May 1348] by the hands of Emma Coteroun, the said Thomas' mother, through which the same Richard, against the delivery of the said gaol which was in the week of Pentecost then next following [c 8 June 1348], procured John of Salford and John of *Muxenbrook* to say that the same Thomas was guilty, and for this purpose he gave each of them twenty shillings for themselves and their fellows. And he came back to the same Thomas Coteroun and said to him that he could most certainly be confident of being acquitted and delivered if the aforesaid John and John were sworn in. And thereupon, when the same Thomas was arraigned before the justices, the same John and John were sworn in without any challenge from the said Thomas, and the same Thomas was condemned by them and their fellows through the deceit of Richard himself.

(b)

TNA JUST 1/796 m. 2 [Latin/French][31]

The jurors of the county aforesaid [Hampshire] namely Edward Gorges, John Rutherfield, John Craft, John Chanyn, John Kybbelwyk, Richard Young, William Clevere, Thomas at Berton, John Heyne, John Adam, John Wiseman and Robert at Hall present that whereas John atte Dean was returned and empanelled on an inquest of an assize of mort d'ancestor* between Hugh Pipard and a certain Hubert Cordray and the said Hugh, it is supposed, assailed the said John for the words that he was unwilling to say for him on the said assize, the said Hugh came the Thursday on the feast of the Ascension of our Lord God in the fourteenth year of the present king [Richard II – 4 May 1391] on the highway of West Farnham with force and arms, that is to say, bucklers and other types of arms, and assaulted the said John beating, wounding and maltreating him so that the said John was in despair of his life against the peace of our lord the king; and they also present that the said Hugh is a common disturber of the peace, maintainer of quarrels and embracer of juries.

31 The use of two languages in the indictment is unusual, but can be accounted for by the interpolation of the text of a private bill (in French) that had presumably previously been endorsed by the jury.

8.9 Perversion of judicial process: forging the great seal and writs (1325)

This case came to light as a result of the delivery of Winchester gaol by the court of king's bench. It demonstrates how the king's writs and formal legal procedures were susceptible to alteration and falsification by anyone possessing a little administrative know-how.

TNA KB 27/260 *Rex* m. 25 (Easter) [Latin]

Philip Burdon, chaplain, arrested by the sheriff of Hampshire with two forged original writs, fashioned by him for his own use and sealed in the shape of the king's great seal and found with him, came led by the same sheriff. And questioned as to how he personally came to have the aforesaid forged and suspect writs, he says that at another time he purchased in the lord king's chancery a writ close of novel disseisin* together with another writ patent in accordance with it under his own name; and he says that on a certain day when he was on the Isle of Wight pondering how he could get revenge upon certain enemies of his who had committed various trespasses against him, he caused the aforesaid two forged writs to be written out under his name against certain enemies of his who were named in those two forged writs. And he says that later he alone, without anyone else knowing, opened up the wax of the aforesaid writ close of novel disseisin and also of the writ patent cautiously with a certain knife belonging to him and took out the aforesaid writ of novel disseisin and likewise the patent version from the same wax and underneath the wax from the aforesaid writ close placed one of his forged writs and underneath the wax of the writ patent he placed the other of his forged writs and closed them up. And concerning this forgery and deceit he puts himself at the king's pleasure etc. And because the court is given to understand by several trustworthy men that Philip and certain others of his company have among them a counterfeit impression of the king's seal in metal for sealing writs, with which certain seal they sealed the aforesaid two forged writs found with the same Philip as well as numerous other writs, the sheriff is directed to summon to come before the king at Southampton on Monday next before the feast of Pentecost [20 May 1325] twenty-four, both knights and others etc., from the Isle of Wight where it is said the aforesaid writs were sealed, to carry out an inquiry etc. concerning the counterfeiting of the aforesaid seal and those who seditiously counterfeited it and used it for sealing forged writs of this kind. And meanwhile Philip is committed to gaol in the custody of the same sheriff etc.

8.10 Perversion of judicial process: the theft of legal records from the treasury (1403)

This case demonstrates an awareness of how legal records could provide vital evidence in disputes. It also highlights the way in which the ties of lordship and clientage could smother the ideals of justice. Freeman was a servant of John, Lord Lovell, a member of the king's council. Lovell was embroiled in a dispute with William Doyle and clearly instructed Freeman to steal the bundle of records thus weakening his oppenent's case. In the indictment the theft is framed as treason, but Lovell was able to intervene on behalf of his servant, ensuring he was granted bail by providing security for him when the latter appeared before the king's council. Freeman eventually obtained a pardon, no doubt through the intercession of his master.

TNA KB 9/192 m. 8 [Latin]

The jurors present that John Freeman, falsely, feloniously and treasonably planning to destroy and disinherit both our lord the king and the prelates and magnates of the realm and the greater part of the king's subjects, and to subvert and bring to nothing the laws and judgments made in the courts of the king's predecessors, did on Wednesday before All Saints in the fourth year of the reign of King Henry IV [25 October 1402] falsely, feloniously and treasonably break into and enter the royal treasury at Westminster, in which the fines,* records and other documents touching the king and his people are kept. From there he stole and took away all the fines, from every county of England, for the fifteenth to the twentieth years of the reign of Edward III, grandfather of the present king [1341–47], which were filed in a certain bundle in the custody of the king's Treasurer and chamberlain. He did so mainly with the intention falsely and maliciously to disinherit William Doyle from the manor of Hinton [Northants], because a certain fine touching the said manor and of great value in showing the said William's title was contained in the said bundle. The manor of Hinton is still in dispute between the said William and John, Lord Lovell. The offence was committed to the manifest disinheritance of the king and the prelates and magnates of the realm of England and the greater part of the king's subjects and to the final and perpetual destruction of the law of England.

INDEX

This index covers the introductions to chapters, headnotes and the original documents, but does not comprehensively list all persons and places mentioned in the text. For certain subject matter cross-references, the thematically arranged sections in the Contents should be used as a supplementary aid. Note: 'n.' after a page reference indicates the number of a note on that page.